Mike Holt's Illustrated Guide to

UNDERSTANDING NEC® REQUIREMENTS FOR
BONDING AND GROUNDING

Based on the 2017 NEC®

NOTICE TO THE READER

The text and commentary in this book is the author's interpretation of the 2017 Edition of NFPA 70, the *National Electrical Code®*. It shall not be considered an endorsement of or the official position of the NFPA® or any of its committees, nor relied upon as a formal interpretation of the meaning or intent of any specific provision or provisions of the 2017 edition of NFPA 70, *National Electrical Code*.

The publisher does not warrant or guarantee any of the products described herein or perform any independent analysis in connection with any of the product information contained herein. The publisher does not assume, and expressly disclaims, any obligation to obtain and include information other than that provided to it by the manufacturer.

The reader is expressly warned to consider and adopt all safety precautions and applicable federal, state, and local laws and regulations. By following the instructions contained herein, the reader willingly assumes all risks in connection with such instructions.

Mike Holt Enterprises disclaims liability for any personal injury, property or other damages of any nature whatsoever, whether special, indirect, consequential or compensatory, directly or indirectly resulting from the use of this material. The reader is responsible for relying on his or her personal independent judgment in determining safety and appropriate actions in all circumstances.

The publisher makes no representation or warranties of any kind, including but not limited to, the warranties of fitness for particular purpose or merchantability, nor are any such representations implied with respect to the material set forth herein, and the publisher takes no responsibility with respect to such material. The publisher shall not be liable for any special, consequential, or exemplary damages resulting, in whole or part, from the reader's use of, or reliance upon, this material.

Mike Holt's Illustrated Guide to Understanding NEC® Requirements for Bonding and Grounding, Based on the 2017 NEC®

Second Printing: September 2018

Author: Mike Holt
Technical Illustrator: Mike Culbreath
Cover Design: Bryan Burch
Layout Design and Typesetting: Cathleen Kwas

COPYRIGHT © 2017 Charles Michael Holt
ISBN 978-0-9863534-3-7

Produced and Printed in the USA

All rights reserved. No part of this work covered by the copyright hereon may be reproduced or used in any form or by any means graphic, electronic, or mechanical, including photocopying, recording, taping, or information storage and retrieval systems without the written permission of the publisher. You can request permission to use material from this text by e-mailing Info@MikeHolt.com.

For more information, call 888.NEC.CODE (632.2633), or e-mail Info@MikeHolt.com.

NEC®, NFPA 70®, NFPA 70E® and National Electrical Code® are registered trademarks of the National Fire Protection Association.

This logo is a registered trademark of Mike Holt Enterprises, Inc.

If you are an instructor and would like to request an examination copy of this or other Mike Holt Publications:

Call: 888.NEC.CODE (632.2633) • Fax: 352.360.0983
E-mail: Info@MikeHolt.com • Visit: www.MikeHolt.com/Instructors

You can download a sample PDF of all our publications by visiting www.MikeHolt.com.

I dedicate this book to the
Lord Jesus Christ, *my mentor and teacher.*
Proverbs 16:3

"For All Your Electrical Training Needs"

Mike Holt
ENTERPRISES, INC.
888.NEC.CODE (632.2633)

www.MikeHolt.com

We Care...

Since the day we started our business over 40 years ago, we have been working hard to produce products that get results, and to help individuals in their pursuit of learning more about this exciting industry. I have built my business on the idea that customers come first, and that everyone on my team will do everything they possibly can to take care of you. I want you to know that we value you, and are honored that you have chosen us to be your partner in electrical training.

I believe that you are the future of this industry and that it is you who will make the difference in years to come. My goal is to share with you everything that I know and to encourage you to pursue your education on a continuous basis. That not only will you learn theory, code, calculations or how to pass an exam, but that in the process you will become the expert in the field and the person who others know to trust.

We are dedicated to providing quality electrical training that will help you take your skills to the next level and we genuinely care about you. Thanks for choosing Mike Holt Enterprises for your electrical training needs.

God bless and much success,

Mike Holt

Exam Preparation | Continuing Education | Apprenticeship Products | In-House Training

"...as for me and my house, we will serve the Lord." [Joshua 24:15]

TABLE OF CONTENTS

About This Textbook xi

How to Use the *National Electrical Code* 1

Article 90—Introduction to the *National Electrical Code* 7
- 90.1 Purpose of the *NEC* 7
- 90.2 Scope of the *NEC* 9
- 90.3 *Code* Arrangement 11
- 90.4 Enforcement 12
- 90.5 Mandatory Requirements and Explanatory Material 14
- 90.6 Formal Interpretations 14
- 90.7 Examination of Equipment for Product Safety 14
- 90.9 Units of Measurement 15

Article 90—Practice Questions 16

CHAPTER 1—GENERAL RULES 19

Article 100—Definitions 21
Part I. General 21
- 100 Definitions 21

Article 110—Requirements for Electrical Installations 39
Part I. General Requirements 39
- 110.1 Scope 39
- 110.2 Approval of Conductors and Equipment 39
- 110.3 Examination, Identification, Installation, Use, and Product Listing (Certification) of Equipment 40
- 110.5 Conductor Material 40
- 110.6 Conductor Sizes 40
- 110.7 Wiring Integrity 41
- 110.8 Suitable Wiring Methods 41
- 110.11 Deteriorating Agents 41
- 110.12 Mechanical Execution of Work 42
- 110.14 Conductor Termination and Splicing 42

Chapter 1—Practice Questions 47

CHAPTER 2—WIRING AND PROTECTION 53

Article 250—Grounding and Bonding 55
Part I. General 55
- 250.1 Scope 55
- 250.2 Definition 55
- 250.4 Performance Requirements for Grounding and Bonding ... 56

Earth Shells 60
- 250.6 Objectionable Current 62

Objectionable Current 63

Dangers of Objectionable Current 65
- 250.8 Termination of Grounding and Bonding Conductors 66
- 250.10 Protection of Fittings 67
- 250.12 Clean Surfaces 67

Part II. System Grounding and Bonding 67
- 250.20 Systems Required to be Grounded 67
- 250.21 Ungrounded Systems 68
- 250.24 Service Equipment—Grounding and Bonding 69
- 250.28 Main Bonding Jumper and System Bonding Jumper 73
- 250.30 Separately Derived Systems—Grounding and Bonding ... 74

Special Section 250.30 Separately Derived Systems 80

Outdoor Installations 80

Indoor Installations 81
- 250.32 Buildings Supplied by a Feeder 83
- 250.34 Generators—Portable and Vehicle-Mounted 85
- 250.35 Permanently Installed Generators 85
- 250.36 High-Impedance Grounded Systems 86

Part III. Grounding Electrode System and Grounding Electrode Conductor 86
- 250.50 Grounding Electrode System 86
- 250.52 Grounding Electrode Types 87
- 250.53 Grounding Electrode Installation Requirements 90

Measuring the Ground Resistance 94

Soil Resistivity 95
- 250.54 Auxiliary Grounding Electrodes 95
- 250.58 Common Grounding Electrode 96
- 250.60 Lightning Protection Electrode 96
- 250.62 Grounding Electrode Conductor 97

Table of Contents

250.64	Grounding Electrode Conductor Installation	98
250.66	Sizing Grounding Electrode Conductor	102
250.68	Termination to the Grounding Electrode	103
250.70	Grounding Electrode Conductor Termination Fittings	105

Part IV. Grounding Enclosure, Raceway, and Service Cable Connections 106

250.80	Service Raceways and Enclosures	106
250.86	Other Enclosures	106

Part V. Bonding 106

250.90	General	106
250.92	Bonding Equipment for Services	107
250.94	Bonding Communications Systems	110
250.96	Bonding Other Enclosures	111
250.97	Bonding Metal Parts Containing 277V and 480V Circuits	112
250.98	Bonding Loosely Jointed Metal Raceways	113
250.102	Grounded Conductor, Bonding Conductors, and Jumpers	113
250.104	Bonding of Piping Systems and Exposed Structural Metal	115
250.106	Lightning Protection System	119

Part VI. Equipment Grounding and Equipment Grounding Conductors 120

250.110	Fixed Equipment Connected by Permanent Wiring Methods—General	120
250.112	Specific Equipment Fastened in Place or Connected by Permanent Wiring Methods	120
250.114	Cord-and-Plug-Connected Equipment	120
250.118	Types of Equipment Grounding Conductors	121
250.119	Identification of Equipment Grounding Conductors	125
250.120	Equipment Grounding Conductor Installation	126
250.121	Use of Equipment Grounding Conductors	127
250.122	Sizing Equipment Grounding Conductor	127

Part VII. Methods of Equipment Grounding 131

250.130	Equipment Grounding Conductor Connections	131
250.134	Equipment Connected by Permanent Wiring Methods	131
250.136	Equipment Considered Grounded	132
250.138	Cord-and-Plug-Connected	132
250.140	Ranges, Ovens, and Clothes Dryers	132
250.142	Use of Neutral Conductor for Equipment Grounding (Bonding)	133
250.146	Connecting Receptacle Grounding Terminal to Metal Enclosure	134
250.148	Continuity and Attachment of Equipment Grounding Conductors in Metal Boxes	137

Chapter 2—Practice Questions 139

CHAPTER 3—WIRING METHODS AND MATERIALS 157

Article 300—General Requirements for Wiring Methods and Materials 161

Part I. General		161
300.1	Scope	161
300.3	Conductors	162
300.10	Electrical Continuity	164

Article 314—Outlet, Device, Pull, and Junction Boxes; Conduit Bodies; and Handhole Enclosures 165

Part I. Scope and General		165
314.1	Scope	165
314.3	Nonmetallic Boxes	165
314.4	Metal Boxes	165
Part II. Installation		166
314.25	Covers and Canopies	166
314.28	Sizing Conductors 4 AWG and Larger	167
314.30	Handhole Enclosures	167

Article 320—Armored Cable (Type AC) 169

320.1	Scope	169
320.2	Definition	169
320.108	Equipment Grounding Conductor	170

Article 330—Metal-Clad Cable (Type MC) 171

330.1	Scope	171
330.2	Definition	171
330.108	Equipment Grounding Conductor	172

Article 334—Nonmetallic-Sheathed Cable (Types NM and NMC) 173

334.1	Scope	173
334.2	Definition	173
334.108	Equipment Grounding Conductor	174

Article 348—Flexible Metal Conduit (Type FMC) 175

348.1	Scope	175
348.2	Definition	175
348.60	Grounding and Bonding	175

Article 350—Liquidtight Flexible Metal Conduit (Type LFMC) 177

350.1	Scope	177

350.2	Definition	177
350.60	Grounding and Bonding	178

Article 352—Rigid Polyvinyl Chloride Conduit (Type PVC) 179
352.1	Scope	179
352.2	Definition	179
352.60	Equipment Grounding Conductor	179

Article 356—Liquidtight Flexible Nonmetallic Conduit (Type LFNC) 181
356.1	Scope	181
356.2	Definition	181
356.60	Equipment Grounding Conductor	182

Article 358—Electrical Metallic Tubing (Type EMT) 183
358.1	Scope	183
358.2	Definition	183
358.60	Grounding	184

Article 362—Electrical Nonmetallic Tubing (Type ENT) 185
362.1	Scope	185
362.2	Definition	185
362.60	Equipment Grounding Conductor	186

Article 386—Surface Metal Raceways 187
386.1	Scope	187
386.2	Definition	187
386.60	Equipment Grounding Conductor	187
386.70	Separate Compartments	188

Article 392—Cable Trays 189
392.1	Scope	189
392.2	Definition	189
392.60	Equipment Grounding Conductor	190

Chapter 3—Practice Questions 191

CHAPTER 4—EQUIPMENT FOR GENERAL USE 195

Article 404—Switches 197
404.1	Scope	197
404.9	Switch Faceplates	197
404.12	Grounding of Enclosures	198

Article 406—Receptacles, Cord Connectors, and Attachment Plugs (Caps) 199
406.1	Scope	199
406.3	Receptacle Rating and Type	199
406.4	General Installation Requirements	200
406.6	Receptacle Faceplates	202
406.11	Connecting Receptacle Grounding Terminal to Equipment Grounding Conductor	202

Article 408—Switchboards, Switchgear, and Panelboards 203
408.1	Scope	203
408.40	Equipment Grounding Conductor	203

Article 410—Luminaires, Lampholders, and Lamps 205
410.1	Scope	205
410.30	Supports	206
410.44	Methods of Grounding	207

Article 440—Air-Conditioning and Refrigeration Equipment 209
440.1	Scope	209
440.2	Definitions	209
440.9	Grounding and Bonding	210

Article 450—Transformers 211
450.1	Scope	211
450.10	Grounding and Bonding	211

Chapter 4—Practice Questions 213

CHAPTER 5—SPECIAL OCCUPANCIES 217

Article 501—Class I Hazardous (Classified) Locations 219
501.1	Scope	219
501.30	Grounding and Bonding	219

Article 502—Class II Hazardous (Classified) Locations 221
502.1	Scope	221
502.30	Grounding and Bonding	221

Table of Contents

Article 503—Class III Hazardous (Classified) Locations 223
- 503.1 Scope 223
- 503.30 Grounding and Bonding 223

Article 517—Health Care Facilities 225
- 517.1 Scope 226
- 517.2 Definitions 226
- 517.12 Wiring Methods 227
- 517.13 Grounding of Equipment in Patient Care Spaces 227
- 517.16 Isolated Ground Receptacles 230

Article 525—Carnivals, Circuses, Fairs, and Similar Events 233
- 525.1 Scope 233
- 525.30 Equipment Bonding 233
- 525.31 Equipment Grounding 234
- 525.32 Portable Equipment Grounding Conductor Continuity 234

Article 547—Agricultural Buildings 235
- 547.1 Scope 235
- 547.2 Definitions 236
- 547.5 Wiring Methods 236
- 547.10 Equipotential Planes 236

Article 555—Marinas, Boatyards, and Commercial and Noncommercial Docking Facilities 239
- 555.1 Scope 239
- 555.15 Grounding 239

Chapter 5—Practice Questions 241

CHAPTER 6—SPECIAL EQUIPMENT 245

Article 600—Electric Signs and Outline Lighting 247
- 600.1 Scope 247
- 600.7 Grounding and Bonding 248

Article 640—Audio Signal Processing, Amplification, and Reproduction Equipment 251
- 640.1 Scope 251
- 640.7 Grounding and Bonding 252

Article 645—Information Technology Equipment 253
- 645.1 Scope 253
- 645.14 System Grounding and Bonding 253
- 645.15 Equipment Grounding and Bonding 254

Article 680—Swimming Pools, Spas, Hot Tubs, Fountains, and Similar Installations 255
Part I. General Requirements for Pools, Spas, Hot Tubs, and Fountains 256
- 680.1 Scope 256
- 680.2 Definitions 256
- 680.7 Grounding and Bonding Terminals 258
- 680.8 Cord-and-Plug-Connected Equipment 258

Part II. Permanently Installed Pools, Outdoor Spas, and Outdoor Hot Tubs 258
- 680.20 General 258
- 680.21 Motors 258
- 680.23 Underwater Luminaires 259
- 680.24 Junction Box, Transformer, or GFCI Enclosure 261
- 680.25 Feeders 261
- 680.26 Equipotential Bonding 262

Part IV. Spas and Hot Tubs 265
- 680.40 General 265
- 680.42 Outdoor Installations 265
- 680.43 Indoor Installations 266

Part V. Fountains 267
- 680.50 General 267
- 680.53 Bonding 267
- 680.55 Methods of Equipment Grounding 267

Part VII. Hydromassage Bathtubs 267
- 680.70 General 267
- 680.74 Equipotential Bonding 267

Part VIII. Electrically Powered Pool Lifts 268
- 680.80 General 268
- 680.83 Bonding 268

Article 690—Solar Photovoltaic (PV) Systems 269
Part I. General 269
- 690.1 Scope 269
- 690.2 Definitions 269

Part IV. Wiring Methods 270
690.31	Wiring Methods	270
690.33	Connectors	271

Part V. Grounding and Bonding 271
690.41	System Grounding	271
690.42	Point of Grounding Connection	272
690.43	Equipment Grounding and Bonding	272
690.45	Size of Equipment Grounding Conductors	273
690.46	Array Equipment Grounding Conductors	274
690.47	Grounding Electrode System	274

Chapter 6—Practice Questions 276

CHAPTER 8—COMMUNICATIONS SYSTEMS 281

Article 800—Communications Circuits 283

Part I. General 283
800.1 Scope 283

Part III. Protection 284
800.90 Primary Protection 284

Part IV. Grounding Methods 284
800.100 Cable and Primary Protector Bonding and Grounding 284

Article 810—Radio and Television Satellite Equipment 289

Part I. General 289
810.1	Scope	289
810.7	Grounding Devices	290

Part II. Receiving Equipment—Antenna Systems 290
810.15	Metal Antenna Supports—Grounding	290
810.20	Antenna Discharge Unit	290
810.21	Bonding Conductor and Grounding Electrode Conductors	290

Part III. Amateur and Citizen Band Transmitting and Receiving Antenna Systems 293
810.57	Antenna Discharge Units	293
810.58	Bonding Conductor or Grounding Electrode Conductors	293

Article 820—Community Antenna Television (CATV) and Radio Distribution Systems (Coaxial Cable) 295

Part I. General 295
820.1 Scope 295

Part III. Protection 296
820.93 Grounding of the Outer Conductive Shield of Coaxial Cables 296

Part IV. Grounding Methods 296
820.100 Bonding and Grounding Methods 296

Chapter 8—Practice Questions 300

FINAL EXAM A—STRAIGHT ORDER 303

FINAL EXAM B—RANDOM ORDER 313

APPENDIX A— ANALYSIS OF 2017 *NEC* CHANGES RELATING TO BONDING AND GROUNDING 323

INDEX 345

About The Author 347
About the Illustrator 348
About the Mike Holt Team 349

Notes

ABOUT THIS TEXTBOOK

Mike Holt's Illustrated Guide to Understanding NEC® Requirements for Bonding and Grounding, Based on the 2017 NEC®

This textbook covers Article 250 Grounding and Bonding, as well as the *Code* rules contained in the *National Electrical Code®* that relate to bonding and grounding. Grounding and Bonding is the most important and least understood article in the *NEC®*. Surveys have repeatedly shown that the majority of electrical shocks and power quality problems are due to improper bonding or grounding.

We've included an Appendix in this textbook for additional information. It contains the summary and analysis of the changes to the *NEC* for 2017 as they relate to the bonding and grounding *Code* rules covered in this textbook. If the  icon appears next to the *NEC* rule heading, it indicates that the analysis of the change for this rule can be found in Appendix A.

This textbook is easy to use because of Mike's informative and practical writing style. Just like all of Mike Holt's textbooks, this one is built around hundreds of full-color illustrations that show the requirements of the *National Electrical Code* in practical use, helping you visualize *Code* rules as they're applied to electrical installations. This illustrated textbook also contains cautions regarding possible conflicts or confusing *NEC* requirements, tips on proper electrical installations, and warnings of dangers related to improper electrical installations.

Sometimes a requirement seems confusing and it might be hard to understand its actual application. When this occurs, this textbook will point the situation out in an upfront and straightforward manner. We apologize in advance if that ever seems disrespectful, but our intention is to help the industry understand the current *NEC* as best as possible, point out areas that need refinement, and encourage *Code* users to be a part of the change process that creates a better *NEC* for the future.

Keeping up with requirements of the *Code* should be the goal of everyone involved in electrical safety—whether you're an installer, contractor, inspector, engineer, or instructor. This textbook is the perfect tool to help you do that.

The Scope of this Textbook

This textbook, *Mike Holt's Illustrated Guide to NEC Requirements for Bonding and Grounding, Based on the 2017 NEC*, covers the general installation requirements contained in the *NEC* from Article 90 through 820, that Mike considers to be of critical importance, as relates to bonding and grounding.

This program is based on solidly grounded ac systems, 600V or less, using 90°C insulated copper conductors sized to 60°C rated terminals for 100A and less rated circuits, and 75°C rated terminals for over 100A rated circuits, unless indicated otherwise.

How to Use this Textbook

This textbook is to be used along with the *NEC* and not as a replacement for it. Be sure to have a copy of the 2017 *National Electrical Code* handy. You'll notice that we've paraphrased a great deal of the *NEC* wording, and some of the article and section titles appear different from the text in the actual *Code* book. We believe doing so makes it easier to understand the content of the rule, so keep this in mind when comparing this textbook to the actual *NEC*.

Always compare what's being explained in this textbook to what the *Code* book says. Get with others who are knowledgeable about the *NEC* to discuss any topics that you find difficult to understand, or join our free Code Forum www.MikeHolt.com/forum to post your question.

This textbook follows the *Code* format, but it doesn't cover every change or requirement. For example, it doesn't include every article, section, subsection, exception, or Informational Note. So don't be concerned if you see that the textbook contains Exception 1 and Exception 3, but not Exception 2.

Cross-References. *NEC* cross-references to other related *Code* requirements are included to help you develop a better understanding of how the *NEC* rules relate to one another. These cross-references are indicated by *Code* section numbers in brackets, an example of which is "[90.4]."

Informational Notes. Informational Notes contained in the *NEC* will be identified in this textbook as "Note."

About This Textbook

Exceptions. Exceptions contained in this textbook will be identified as "Ex" and not spelled out.

Allow yourself sufficient time to work through the text along with the outstanding graphics and examples, to give yourself the opportunity for a deeper understanding of the *Code*.

Technical Questions

As you progress through this textbook, you might find that you don't understand every explanation, example, calculation, or comment. Don't become frustrated, and don't get down on yourself. Remember, this is the *National Electrical Code*, and sometimes the best attempt to explain a concept isn't enough to make it perfectly clear. If you're still confused, visit www.MikeHolt.com/forum, and post your question on our free Code Forum. The forum is a moderated community of electrical professionals.

Textbook Corrections

We're committed to providing you with the finest product with the fewest errors, and take great care to ensure our textbooks are correct. But we're realistic and know that errors might be found after printing. The last thing we want is for you to have problems finding, communicating, or accessing this information, so we list it on our website.

If you believe that there's an error of any kind (typographical, grammatical, technical, etc.) in this textbook or in the Answer Key, and it's not listed on the website, send an e-mail and be sure to include the textbook title, page number, and any other pertinent information.

To check for known errors, visit www.MikeHolt.com/corrections.
To report an error, email corrections@MikeHolt.com.

Key Features

The layout and design of this textbook incorporate special features and symbols designed to help you navigate easily through the material, and to enhance your understanding.

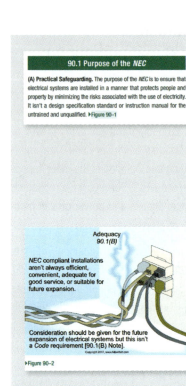

Code Rule Headers

The *Code* rule being taught is identified with a chapter color bar and white text.

Full-Color, Detailed Educational Graphics

Industry-leading graphics help you visualize the sometimes complex language of the *NEC*, and illustrate the rule in real-world application(s). This is a great aid to reinforce learning.

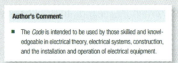

Author's Comments

The author provides additional information to clarify the rule, and help you understand the background and context of the information.

About This Textbook

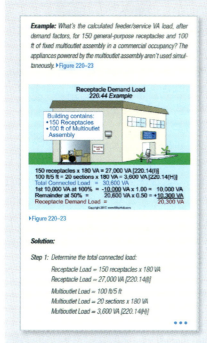

Examples

Practical application questions and solutions are contained in framed yellow boxes. These support the rules and help you understand how to do the calculations. If you see a blue ellipsis (● ● ●) at the bottom of the example, it's continued on the following page.

Underlined *Code* Changes

All changes to the text in the *Code* for the 2017 *NEC* are identified by underlining in the chapter color.

Additional Background Information Boxes

Where the author believes that information unrelated to the specific rule will help you understand the concept being taught, he includes these topics, easily identified in boxes outlined in the chapter color.

Modular Color-Coded Page Layout

Chapters are color-coded and modular to make it easy to navigate through each section of the textbook.

Danger, Caution, and Warning Icons

These icons highlight areas of concern.

 Caution—Possible damage to property or equipment.

 Warning—Severe property damage or personal injury.

 Danger—Severe injury or death.

QR Codes

 A few **QR Codes** are found throughout the textbook, and can be scanned with a smartphone app to take you to a sample video clip to watch Mike and the DVD panel discuss this rule.

Formulas

 Formulas are easily identifiable in green text on a gray bar.

2017 Code Change Icon

 This icon appears next to the *Code* rule heading to indicate that the analysis of the change for this rule can be found in Appendix A.

About This Textbook

Additional Products to Help You Learn

Bonding and Grounding DVDs, Based on the 2017 NEC

One of the best ways to get the most out of this textbook is to use it in conjunction with the corresponding DVDs. Mike Holt's DVDs provide a 360° view of each topic with specialized commentary from Mike Holt and his panel of industry experts. Whether you're a visual or an auditory learner, watching the DVDs will enhance your knowledge and understanding.

To order a copy of the DVDs at a discounted price, call our office at 888.632.2633.

Understanding the NEC Complete Training Library

When you really need to understand the NEC, there's no better way to learn it than with Mike's NEC Complete Training Library. It takes you step-by-step through the NEC, in Code order with detailed illustrations, great practice questions, and in-depth DVD analysis. This library is perfect for engineers, electricians, contractors, and electrical inspectors.

- **Understanding the National Electrical Code—Volume 1** textbook
- **Understanding the National Electrical Code—Volume 2** textbook
- **NEC Exam Practice Questions** workbook
- *General Requirements DVD*
- *Bonding and Grounding DVDs* (3)
- *Wiring and Protection DVD*
- *Wiring Methods* and *Materials DVDs* (2)
- *Equipment for General Use DVD*
- *Special Occupancies and Special Equipment DVDs* (3)
- *Limited Energy and Communications Systems DVD*

2017 NEC Changes— DVD Training Program

Don't let the scale of the changes to the *Code* intimidate you. This package will get you up to speed on the most essential 2017 *NEC* changes. The book is well-organized, easy to follow, and the full-color illustrations bring the material to life. The DVDs bring together a group of experts from the field to discuss the changes and how they apply in the real world.

- **Changes to the NEC 2017** textbook
- *Changes to the NEC 2017 DVDs* (3)

Theory DVD Training Program

Understanding electrical theory is critical for anyone who works with electricity. This textbook teaches the fundamentals that you need in order to understand and comply with *NEC* rules that govern installations—starting from basic scientific principles, to electrical formulas, to practical applications of electricity. This library includes:

- **Basic Electrical Theory** textbook
- *Electrical Fundamentals and Basic Electricity DVD*
- *Electrical Circuits, Systems, and Protection DVD*
- *Alternating Current, Motors, Generators, and Transformers DVD*

2017 Code Book and Tabs

The ideal way to use your *Code* book is to tab it for quick reference—Mike's best-selling tabs make organizing the *NEC* easy. In addition, the newest version of the tabs are color-coded to match the chapters of this textbook— a feature that'll allow you easily to cross-reference this textbook with the *NEC*. If you're using your *Code* book for an exam, please confirm with your testing authority that a tabbed *Code* book is allowed into the exam room.

To order a *Code* product visit www.MikeHolt.com/products or call 1.888.632.2633

HOW TO USE THE *NATIONAL ELECTRICAL CODE*

The original *NEC* document was developed in 1897 as a result of the united efforts of various insurance, electrical, architectural, and other allied interests. The National Fire Protection Association (NFPA) has sponsored the *National Electrical Code* since 1911.

The purpose of the *Code* is the practical safeguarding of persons and property from hazards arising from the use of electricity. It isn't intended as a design specification or an instruction manual for untrained persons. It is, in fact, a standard that contains the minimum requirements for electrical installations. Learning to understand and use the *Code* is critical to you working safely, whether you're training to become an electrician, or are already an electrician, electrical contractor, inspector, engineer, designer, or instructor.

The *NEC* was written for those who understand electrical terms, theory, safety procedures, and electrical trade practices. Learning to use the *Code* is a lengthy process and can be frustrating if you don't approach it the right way. First of all, you'll need to understand electrical theory and if you don't have theory as a background when you get into the *NEC*, you're going to be struggling—so take one step back if you need to, and learn electrical theory. You must also understand the concepts and terms, and know grammar and punctuation in order to understand the complex structure of the rules and their intended purpose(s). Our goal for the next few pages is to give you some guidelines and suggestions on using your *Code* book to help you understand what you're trying to accomplish, and how to get there.

Language Considerations for the *NEC*

Terms and Concepts

The *NEC* contains many technical terms, so it's crucial for *Code* users to understand their meanings and applications. If you don't understand a term used in a rule, it will be impossible to properly apply the *NEC* requirement. Article 100 defines the terms that are used in two or more *Code* articles; for example, the term "Dwelling Unit" is found in many articles. If you don't know the *NEC* definition for a "dwelling unit" you can't properly identify the *Code* requirements for it.

Many articles have terms unique to that specific article, and the definitions of those terms are only applicable to that given article. These definitions are usually found in the beginning of the article. For example, Section 250.2 contains the definitions of terms that only apply to Article 250—Grounding and Bonding.

Small Words, Grammar, and Punctuation

It's not only the technical words that require close attention since simple words can make a big difference to the application of a rule. Was there a comma; was it "or," "and," "other than," "greater than," or "smaller than"? The word "or" can imply alternate choices for wiring methods. A word like "or" gives us choices while the word "and" can mean an additional requirement must be met.

An example of these words being used in the *NEC* is found in 110.26(C)(2), where it says equipment containing overcurrent, switching, "or" control devices that are 1,200A or more "and" over 6 ft wide that require a means of egress at each end of the working space. In this section, the word "or" clarifies that equipment containing any of the three types of devices listed must follow this rule. The word "and" clarifies that 110.26(C)(2) only applies if the equipment is both 1,200A or more and over 6 ft wide.

Mike Holt Enterprises • www.MikeHolt.com • 888.NEC.CODE (632.2633)

How to Use the *National Electrical Code*

Grammar and punctuation play an important role in establishing the meaning of a rule. The location of a comma can dramatically change the requirement of a rule such as in 250.28(A), where it says a main bonding jumper must be a wire, bus, screw, or similar suitable conductor. If the comma between "bus" and "screw" was removed, only a "bus screw" could be used. That comma makes a big change in the requirements of the rule.

Slang Terms or Technical Jargon

Trade-related professionals in different areas of the country often use local "slang" terms that aren't shared by all. This can make it difficult to communicate if it isn't clear what the meaning of those slang terms are. Use the proper terms by finding out what their definitions and applications are before you use them. For example, the term "pigtail" is often used to describe the short piece of conductor used to connect a device to a splice, but a "pigtail" is also a term used for a rubberized light socket with pre-terminated conductors. Although the term is the same, the meaning is very different and could cause confusion.

NEC Style and Layout

It's important to understand the structure and writing style of the *Code* if you want to use it effectively. The *National Electrical Code* is organized using eleven major components.

1. Table of Contents
2. Chapters—Chapters 1 through 9 (major categories)
3. Articles—Chapter subdivisions that cover specific subjects
4. Parts—Divisions used to organize article subject matter
5. Sections—Divisions used to further organize article subject matter
6. Tables and Figures—Represent the mandatory requirements of a rule
7. Exceptions—Alternatives to the main *Code* rule
8. Informational Notes—explanatory material for a specific rule (not a requirement)
9. Tables—Applicable as referenced in the *NEC*
10. Annexes—Additional explanatory information such as tables and references (not a requirement)
11. Index

1. Table of Contents. The Table of Contents displays the layout of the chapters, articles, and parts as well as the page numbers. It's an excellent resource and should be referred to periodically to observe the interrelationship of the various *NEC* components. When attempting to locate the rules for a particular situation, knowledgeable *Code* users often go first to the Table of Contents to quickly find the specific *NEC* rule that applies.

2. Chapters. There are nine chapters, each of which is divided into articles. The articles fall into one of four groupings: General Requirements (Chapters 1 through 4), Specific Requirements (Chapters 5 through 7), Communications Systems (Chapter 8), and Tables (Chapter 9).

- Chapter 1—General
- Chapter 2—Wiring and Protection
- Chapter 3—Wiring Methods and Materials
- Chapter 4—Equipment for General Use
- Chapter 5—Special Occupancies
- Chapter 6—Special Equipment
- Chapter 7—Special Conditions
- Chapter 8—Communications Systems (Telephone, Data, Satellite, Cable TV, and Broadband)
- Chapter 9—Tables–Conductor and Raceway Specifications

3. Articles. The *NEC* contains approximately 140 articles, each of which covers a specific subject. It begins with Article 90, the introduction to the *Code*, and contains the purpose of the *NEC*, what's covered and what isn't covered, along with how the *Code* is arranged. It also gives information on enforcement and how mandatory and permissive rules are written and how explanatory material is included. Article 90 also includes information on formal interpretations, examination of equipment for safety, wiring planning, and information about formatting units of measurement. Here are some other examples of articles you'll find in the *NEC*:

- Article 110—Requirements for Electrical Installations
- Article 250—Grounding and Bonding
- Article 300—General Requirements for Wiring Methods and Materials
- Article 430—Motors and Motor Controllers
- Article 500—Hazardous (Classified) Locations
- Article 680—Swimming Pools, Fountains, and Similar Installations
- Article 725—Remote-Control, Signaling, and Power-Limited Circuits
- Article 800—Communications Circuits

4. Parts. Larger articles are subdivided into parts. Because the parts of a *Code* article aren't included in the section numbers, we have a tendency to forget what "part" an *NEC* rule is relating to. For example, Table 110.34(A) contains working space clearances for electrical equipment. If we aren't careful, we might think this table applies to all electrical installations, but Table 110.34(A) is located in Part III, which only contains requirements for "Over 1,000 Volts, Nominal" installations. The rules for working clearances for electrical equipment for systems 1,000V, nominal, or less are contained in Table 110.26(A)(1), which is located in Part II—1,000 Volts, Nominal, or Less.

5. Sections. Each *NEC* rule is called a "*Code* Section." A *Code* section may be broken down into subsections by letters in parentheses like (A), numbers in parentheses like (1), and lowercase letters like (a), (b), and so on, to further break the rule down to the second and third level. For example, the rule requiring all receptacles in a dwelling unit bathroom to be GFCI protected is contained in Section 210.8(A)(1) which is located in Chapter 2, Article 210, Section 8, Subsection (A), Sub-subsection (1).

Many in the industry incorrectly use the term "Article" when referring to a *Code* section. For example, they say "Article 210.8," when they should say "Section 210.8." Section numbers in this textbook are shown without the word "Section," unless they begin a sentence. For example, Section 210.8(A) is shown as simply 210.8(A).

6. Tables and Figures. Many *NEC* requirements are contained within tables, which are lists of *Code* rules placed in a systematic arrangement. The titles of the tables are extremely important; you must read them carefully in order to understand the contents, applications and limitations of each table. Many times notes are provided in or below a table; be sure to read them as well since they're also part of the requirement. For example, Note 1 for Table 300.5 explains how to measure the cover when burying cables and raceways, and Note 5 explains what to do if solid rock is encountered.

7. Exceptions. Exceptions are *Code* requirements or permissions that provide an alternative method to a specific rule. There are two types of exceptions—mandatory and permissive. When a rule has several exceptions, those exceptions with mandatory requirements are listed before the permissive exceptions.

Mandatory Exceptions. A mandatory exception uses the words "shall" or "shall not." The word "shall" in an exception means that if you're using the exception, you're required to do it in a particular way. The phrase "shall not" means it isn't permitted.

Permissive Exceptions. A permissive exception uses words such as "shall be permitted," which means it's acceptable (but not mandatory) to do it in this way.

8. Informational Notes. An Informational Note contains explanatory material intended to clarify a rule or give assistance, but it isn't a *Code* requirement.

9. Tables. Chapter 9 consists of tables applicable as referenced in the *NEC*. The tables are used to calculate raceway sizing, conductor fill, the radius of raceway bends, and conductor voltage drop.

10. Annexes. Annexes aren't a part of the *NEC* requirements, and are included in the *Code* for informational purposes only.

- Annex A. Product Safety Standards
- Annex B. Application Information for Ampacity Calculation
- Annex C. Raceway Fill Tables for Conductors and Fixture Wires of the Same Size
- Annex D. Examples
- Annex E. Types of Construction
- Annex F. Critical Operations Power Systems (COPS)
- Annex G. Supervisory Control and Data Acquisition (SCADA)
- Annex H. Administration and Enforcement
- Annex I. Recommended Tightening Torques
- Annex J. ADA Standards for Accessible Design

11. Index. The Index at the back of the *Code* book is helpful in locating a specific rule.

Author's Comment:

- Changes in the 2017 *Code* book are indicated as follows:
    - Changed rules are identified by shading the text that was changed since the previous edition.
    - New rules aren't shaded like a change, instead they have a shaded "N" in the margin to the left of the section number.
    - Relocated rules are treated like new rules with a shaded "N" in the left margin by the section number.
    - Deleted rules are indicated by a bullet symbol "•" located in the left margin where the rule was in the previous edition.

How to Locate a Specific Requirement

How to go about finding what you're looking for in the *Code* book depends, to some degree, on your experience with the *NEC*. Experts typically know the requirements so well that they just go to the correct rule. Very experienced people might only need the Table of Contents to locate the requirement they're looking for. On the other hand, average users should use all of the tools at their disposal, including the Table of Contents, the Index, and the search feature on electronic versions of the *Code* book.

Let's work through a simple example: What *NEC* rule specifies the maximum number of disconnects permitted for a service?

Table of Contents. If you're an experienced *Code* user, you might use the Table of Contents. You'll know Article 230 applies to "Services," and because this article is so large, it's divided up into multiple parts (actually eight parts). With this knowledge, you can quickly go to the Table of Contents and see it lists the Service Equipment Disconnecting Means requirements in Part VI.

> **Author's Comment:**
>
> - The number 70 precedes all page numbers because the *NEC* is NFPA Standard Number 70.

Index. If you use the Index, which lists subjects in alphabetical order, to look up the term "service disconnect," you'll see there's no listing. If you try "disconnecting means," then "services," you'll find that the Index indicates the rule is located in Article 230, Part VI. Because the *NEC* doesn't give a page number in the Index, you'll need to use the Table of Contents to find it, or flip through the *Code* book to Article 230, then continue to flip through pages until you find Part VI.

Many people complain that the *NEC* only confuses them by taking them in circles. Once you gain experience in using the *Code* and deepen your understanding of words, terms, principles, and practices, you'll find the *NEC* much easier to understand and use than you originally thought.

Customizing Your *Code* Book

One way to increase your comfort level with the *Code* book is to customize it to meet your needs. You can do this by highlighting and underlining important *NEC* requirements. Preprinted adhesive tabs are also an excellent aid to quickly find important articles and sections that are regularly referenced. Be aware that if you're using your *Code* book to prepare to take an exam, some exam centers don't allow markings of any type. Visit www.MikeHolt.com/tabs for more information.

Highlighting. As you read through textbooks or find answers to your questions, be sure you highlight those requirements in the *NEC* that are the most important or relevant to you. Use one color, like yellow, for general interest and a different one for important requirements you want to find quickly. Be sure to highlight terms in the Index and the Table of Contents as you use them.

Underlining. Underline or circle key words and phrases in the *Code* with a red or blue pen (not a lead pencil) using a short ruler or other straightedge to keep lines straight and neat. This is a very handy way to make important requirements stand out. A short ruler or other straightedge also comes in handy for locating the correct information in a table.

Different Interpretations

Industry professionals often enjoy the challenge of discussing the *NEC* requirements. This discussion is important to the process of better understanding the *Code* requirements and application(s). If you decide you're going to participate in one of these discussions, don't spout out what you think without having the actual *NEC* book in your hand. The professional way of discussing a *Code* requirement is by referring to a specific section, rather than talking in vague generalities. This will help everyone involved clearly understand the point and become better educated.

Become Involved in the *NEC* Process

The actual process of changing the *Code* takes about two years and involves hundreds of individuals making an effort to have the *NEC* as current and accurate as possible. As you study and learn how to use it, you'll find it very interesting, enjoy it more, and realize that you can also be a part of the process. Rather than sitting back and just reading it and learning it, you can participate by making proposals and being a part of its development. For the 2017 *Code*, there were 4,000 public inputs and 1,500 comments. Hundreds of updates and five new articles were added to keep the *NEC* up to date with new technologies, and pave the way to a safer and more efficient electrical future.

Let's review how this process works:

STEP 1—Public Input Stage

Public Input. The revision cycle begins with the acceptance of Public Input (PI): the public notice asking for anyone interested to submit input on an existing standard or a committee-approved new draft standard. Following the closing date, the Committee conducts a First Draft Meeting to respond to all public inputs.

First Draft Meeting. At the First Draft (FD) Meeting, the Technical Committee considers and provides a response to all Public Input. The Technical Committee may use the input to develop First Revisions to the standard. The First Draft documents consist of the initial meeting consensus of the committee by simple majority. However, the final position of the Technical Committee must be established by a ballot which follows.

Committee Ballot on First Draft. The First Draft developed at the First Draft Meeting is balloted: to appear in the First Draft, a revision must be approved by at least two-thirds of the Technical Committee.

First Draft Report Posted. First revisions which pass ballot are ultimately compiled and published as the First Draft Report on the document's NFPA web page. This report serves as documentation for the Input Stage and is published for review and comment. The public may review the First Draft Report to determine whether to submit Public Comments on the First Draft.

STEP 2—Public Comment Stage

Public Comment. Once the First Draft Report becomes available, there's a public comment period during which anyone can submit a Public Comment on the First Draft. After the Public Comment closing date, the Technical Committee conducts/holds their Second Draft Meeting.

Second Draft Meeting. After the Public Comment closing date, if Public Comments are received or the committee has additional proposed revisions, a Second Draft Meeting is held. At the Second Draft Meeting, the Technical Committee reviews the First Draft and may make additional revisions to the draft Standard. All Public Comments are considered, and the Technical Committee provides an action and response to each Public Comment. These actions result in the Second Draft.

Committee Ballot on Second Draft. The Second Revisions developed at the Second Draft Meeting are balloted. To appear in the Second Draft, a revision must be approved by at least two-thirds of the Technical Committee.

Second Draft Report Posted. Second Revisions which pass ballot are ultimately compiled and published as the Second Draft Report on the document's NFPA website. This report serves as documentation of the Comment Stage and is published for public review.

Once published, the public can review the Second Draft Report to decide whether to submit a Notice of Intent to Make a Motion (NITMAM) for further consideration.

STEP 3—NFPA Technical Meeting (Tech Session)

Following completion of the Public Input and Public Comment stages, there's further opportunity for debate and discussion of issues through the NFPA Technical Meeting that takes place at the NFPA Conference & Expo®. These motions are attempts to change the resulting final Standard from the committee's recommendations published as the Second Draft.

STEP 4—Council Appeals and Issuance of Standard

Issuance of Standards. When the Standards Council convenes to issue an NFPA standard, it also hears any related appeals. Appeals are an important part of assuring that all NFPA rules have been followed and that due process and fairness have continued throughout the standards development process. The Standards Council considers appeals based on the written record and by conducting live hearings during which all interested parties can participate. Appeals are decided on the entire record of the process, as well as all submissions and statements presented.

After deciding all appeals related to a standard, the Standards Council, if appropriate, proceeds to issue the Standard as an official NFPA Standard. The decision of the Standards Council is final subject only to limited review by the NFPA Board of Directors. The new NFPA standard becomes effective twenty days following the Standards Council's action of issuance.

Author's Comment:

- Proposals and comments can be submitted online at the NFPA website at www.nfpa.org/doc# (for NFPA 70, go to www.nfpa.org/70 for example). From the homepage, look for "Codes & Standards," then find "How the Process Works." If you'd like to see something changed in the *Code*, you're encouraged to participate in the process.

Notes

ARTICLE 90
INTRODUCTION TO THE *NATIONAL ELECTRICAL CODE*

Introduction to Article 90—Introduction to the *National Electrical Code*

Many *NEC* violations and misunderstandings wouldn't occur if people doing the work simply understood Article 90. For example, many people see *Code* requirements as performance standards. In fact, the *NEC* requirements are bare minimums for safety. This is exactly the stance electrical inspectors, insurance companies, and courts take when making a decision regarding electrical design or installation.

Article 90 opens by saying the *NEC* isn't intended as a design specification or instruction manual. The *National Electrical Code* has one purpose only, and that's the "practical safeguarding of persons and property from hazards arising from the use of electricity." The necessity of carefully studying the *NEC* rules can't be overemphasized, and the role of textbooks such as this one are to help in that undertaking. Understanding where to find the rules in the *Code* that apply to the installation is invaluable. Rules in several different articles often apply to even a simple installation.

Article 90 then describes the scope and arrangement of the *NEC*. The balance of this article provides the reader with information essential to understanding the *Code* rules.

Typically, electrical work requires you to understand the first four chapters of the *NEC* which apply generally, plus have a working knowledge of the Chapter 9 tables. That understanding begins with Article 90. Chapters 5, 6, and 7 make up a large portion of the *Code*, but they apply to special occupancies, special equipment, or other special conditions. They build on, modify, or amend the rules in the first four chapters. Chapter 8 contains the requirements for communications systems, such as twisted pair conductors for telephone and data systems, satellite receivers, antenna systems, and coaxial cable wiring. Communications systems (twisted wire, antennas, and coaxial cable) aren't subject to the general requirements of Chapters 1 through 4, or the special requirements of Chapters 5 through 7, unless there's a specific reference in Chapter 8 to a rule in Chapters 1 through 7.

90.1 Purpose of the *NEC*

(A) Practical Safeguarding. The purpose of the *NEC* is to ensure that electrical systems are installed in a manner that protects people and property by minimizing the risks associated with the use of electricity. It isn't a design specification standard or instruction manual for the untrained and unqualified. ▶Figure 90–1

Author's Comment:

- The *Code* is intended to be used by those skilled and knowledgeable in electrical theory, electrical systems, construction, and the installation and operation of electrical equipment.

(B) Adequacy. The *Code* contains requirements considered necessary for a safe electrical installation. If an electrical system is installed in compliance with the *NEC*, it will be essentially free from electrical hazards. The *Code* is a safety standard, not a design guide.

90.1 | Introduction to the *National Electrical Code*

▶Figure 90–1

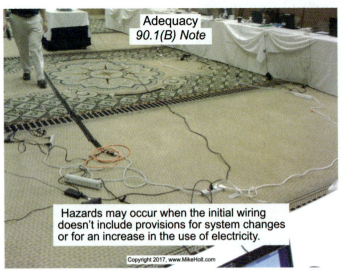
▶Figure 90–3

NEC requirements aren't intended to ensure the electrical installation will be efficient, convenient, adequate for good service, or suitable for future expansion. Specific items of concern, such as electrical energy management, maintenance, and power quality issues aren't within the scope of the *Code*. ▶Figure 90–2

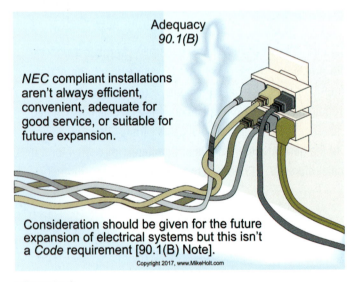
▶Figure 90–2

Note: Hazards in electrical systems often occur because circuits are overloaded or not properly installed in accordance with the *NEC*. These often occur if the initial wiring didn't provide reasonable provisions for system changes or for the increase in the use of electricity. ▶Figure 90–3

Author's Comment:

- See the definition of "Overload" in Article 100.
- The *NEC* doesn't require electrical systems to be designed or installed to accommodate future loads. However, the electrical designer (typically an electrical engineer) is concerned with not only ensuring electrical safety (*Code* compliance), but also with ensuring the system meets the customers' needs, both of today and in the near future. To satisfy customers' needs, electrical systems are often designed and installed above the minimum requirements contained in the *NEC*. But just remember, if you're taking an exam, licensing exams are based on your understanding of the minimum *Code* requirements.

(C) Relation to International Standards. The requirements of the *NEC* address the fundamental safety principles contained in the International Electrotechnical Commission (IEC) Standard, including protection against electric shock, adverse thermal effects, overcurrent, fault currents, and overvoltage. ▶Figure 90–4

Author's Comment:

- The *NEC* is used in Chile, Ecuador, Peru, and the Philippines. It's also the *Electrical Code* for Colombia, Costa Rica, Mexico, Panama, Puerto Rico, and Venezuela. Because of these adoptions, it's available in Spanish from the National Fire Protection Association, 617.770.3000, or www.NFPA.org.

Introduction to the *National Electrical Code* | 90.2

▶Figure 90–4

90.2 Scope of the *NEC*

(A) What Is Covered by the *NEC*. The *NEC* contains requirements necessary for the proper installation and removal of electrical conductors, equipment, cables, and raceways for power, signaling, fire alarm, optical cable, and communications systems (twisted wire, antennas, and coaxial cable) for: ▶Figure 90–5

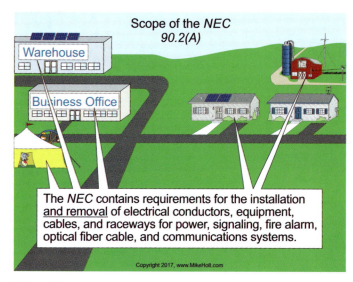

▶Figure 90–5

Author's Comment:

- The *NEC* contains the following requirements on the removal of equipment and cables; temporary wiring 590.3 and abandoned cables for Audio [640.6(B)], Signaling [725.25], Fire Alarm [760.25], Optical Fiber [770.25], Twisted Pair [800.25], and Coaxial [820.25].

(1) Public and private premises, including buildings, mobile homes, recreational vehicles, and floating buildings. ▶Figure 90–6

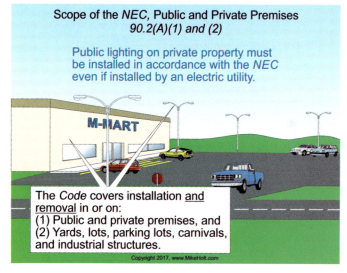

▶Figure 90–6

(2) Yards, lots, parking lots, carnivals, and industrial substations.

(3) Conductors and equipment connected to the electric utility supply.

(4) Installations used by an electric utility, such as office buildings, warehouses, garages, machine shops, recreational buildings, and other electric utility buildings that aren't an integral part of a utility's generating plant, substation, or control center. ▶Figure 90–7

(B) What Isn't Covered by the *NEC*. The *NEC* doesn't apply to the installation of electrical or communications systems (twisted wire, antennas, and coaxial cable) for:

(1) Transportation Vehicles. The *NEC* doesn't apply to installations in cars, trucks, boats, ships and watercraft, planes, or electric trains.

(2) Mining Equipment. The *NEC* doesn't apply to installations underground in mines and self-propelled mobile surface mining machinery and its attendant electrical trailing cables.

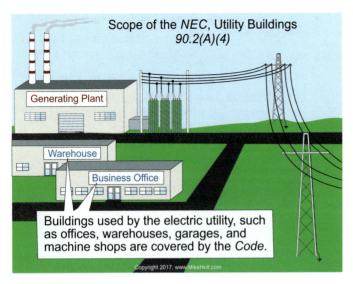
▶Figure 90–7

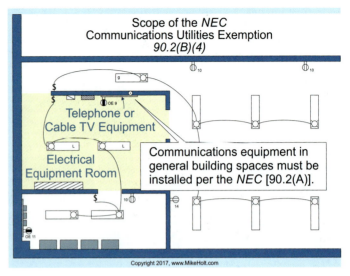
▶Figure 90–9

(3) Railways. The *NEC* doesn't apply to railway power, signaling, energy storage, and communications wiring.

(4) Communications Utilities. If the installation is under the exclusive control of the communications utility, the installation requirements of the *NEC* don't apply to the communications (telephone) or network-powered broadband utility equipment located in building spaces used exclusively for these purposes, or located outdoors if the installation is under the exclusive control of the communications utility. ▶Figure 90–8 and ▶Figure 90–9

(5) Electric Utilities. The *NEC* doesn't apply to electrical installations under the exclusive control of an electric utility, where such installations:

a. Consist of electric utility installed service drops or service laterals under their exclusive control. ▶Figure 90–10

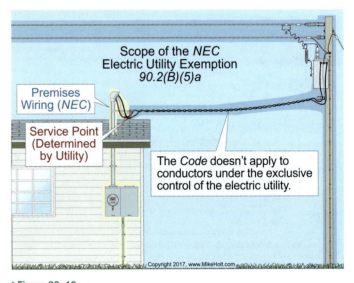
▶Figure 90–10

b. Are on property owned or leased by the electric utility for the purpose of generation, transformation, transmission, energy storage, distribution, or metering of electric energy. ▶Figure 90–11

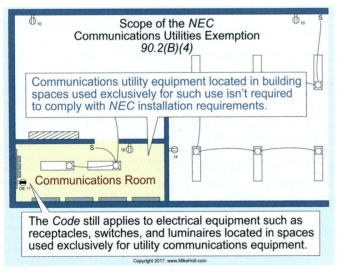
▶Figure 90–8

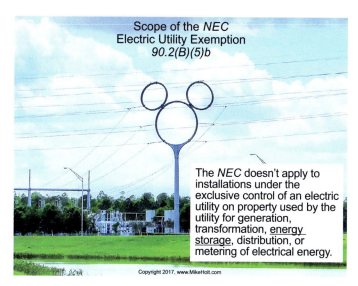

▶Figure 90–11

Author's Comment:

- Luminaires located in legally established easements, or rights-of-way, such as at poles supporting transmission or distribution lines, are exempt from the *NEC*. However, if the electric utility provides site and public lighting on private property, then the installation must comply with the *Code* [90.2(A)(4)].

c. Are located on legally established easements or rights-of-way. ▶Figure 90–12

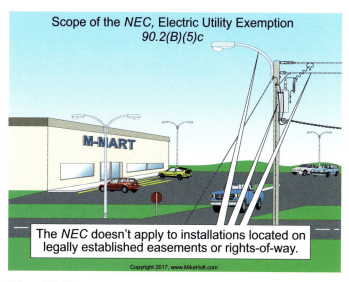

▶Figure 90–12

d. Are located by other written agreements either designated by or recognized by public service commissions, electric utility commissions, or other regulatory agencies having jurisdiction for such installations; limited to installations for the purpose of communications, metering, generation, control, transformation, transmission, energy storage, or distribution of electric energy where legally established easements or rights-of-way can't be obtained. These installations are limited to federal lands, Native American reservations through the U.S. Department of the Interior Bureau of Indian Affairs, military bases, lands controlled by port authorities and state agencies and departments, and lands owned by railroads.

Note to 90.2(B)(4) and (5): Utilities include entities that install, operate, and maintain communications systems (twisted wire, antennas, and coaxial cable) or electric supply (generation, transmission, or distribution systems) and are designated or recognized by governmental law or regulation by public service/utility commissions. Utilities may be subject to compliance with codes and standards covering their regulated activities as adopted under governmental law or regulation.

90.3 *Code* Arrangement

General Requirements. The *Code* is divided into an introduction and nine chapters followed by informational annexes. Chapters 1, 2, 3, and 4 are general conditions. ▶Figure 90–13

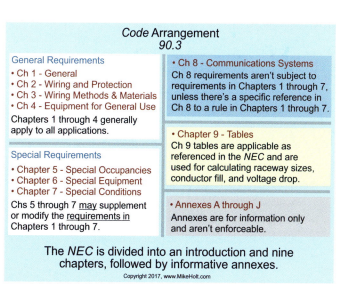

▶Figure 90–13

90.4 | Introduction to the *National Electrical Code*

Author's Comment:

- These first four chapters may be thought of as the foundation for the rest of the *Code*.

Special Requirements. The requirements contained in Chapters 5, 6, and 7 apply to special occupancies, special equipment, or other special conditions, which may supplement or modify the requirements contained in Chapters 1 through 7, but not Chapter 8.

Communications Systems. Chapter 8 contains the requirements for communications systems (twisted wire, antennas, and coaxial cable) which aren't subject to the general requirements of Chapters 1 through 4, or the special requirements of Chapters 5 through 7, unless there's a specific reference in Chapter 8 to a rule in Chapters 1 through 7.

Author's Comment:

- An example of how Chapter 8 works is in the rules for working space about equipment. The typical 3-ft working space isn't required in front of communications equipment, because Table 110.26(A)(1) isn't referenced in Chapter 8.

Tables. Chapter 9 consists of tables applicable as referenced in the *NEC*. The tables are used to calculate raceway sizing, conductor fill, the radius of raceway bends, and conductor voltage drop.

Annexes. Annexes aren't part of the *Code*, but are included for informational purposes. There are ten annexes:

- Annex A. Product Safety Standards
- Annex B. Application Information for Ampacity Calculation
- Annex C. Raceway Fill Tables for Conductors and Fixture Wires of the Same Size
- Annex D. Examples
- Annex E. Types of Construction
- Annex F. Critical Operations Power Systems (COPS)
- Annex G. Supervisory Control and Data Acquisition (SCADA)
- Annex H. Administration and Enforcement
- Annex I. Recommended Tightening Torques
- Annex J. ADA Standards for Accessible Design

90.4 Enforcement

The *Code* is intended to be suitable for enforcement by governmental bodies that exercise legal jurisdiction over electrical installations for power, lighting, signaling circuits, and communications systems, such as: ▶Figure 90–14

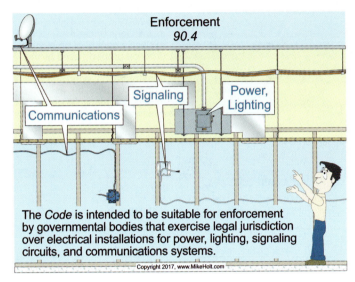

▶Figure 90–14

Signaling circuits which include:

- Article 725 Class 1, Class 2, and Class 3 Remote-Control, Signaling, and Power-Limited Circuits
- Article 760 Fire Alarm Systems
- Article 770 Optical Fiber Cables and Raceways

Communications systems which include:

- Article 810 Radio and Television Equipment (satellite dish and antenna)
- Article 820 Community Antenna Television and Radio Distribution Systems (coaxial cable)

Author's Comment:

- The installation requirements for signaling circuits and communications circuits are covered in Mike Holt's *Understanding the National Electrical Code, Volume 2* textbook.

The enforcement of the *NEC* is the responsibility of the authority having jurisdiction (AHJ), who is responsible for interpreting requirements, approving equipment and materials, waiving *Code* requirements, and ensuring equipment is installed in accordance with listing instructions.

Author's Comment:

- See the definition of "Authority Having Jurisdiction" in Article 100.

Interpretation of the Requirements. The authority having jurisdiction is responsible for interpreting the *NEC*.

Author's Comment:

- The AHJ's decisions must be based on a specific *Code* requirement. If an installation is rejected, the authority having jurisdiction is legally responsible for informing the installer of the specific *NEC* rule that was violated. ▶ Figure 90–15

▶ Figure 90–15

Author's Comment:

- The art of getting along with the authority having jurisdiction consists of doing good work and knowing what the *Code* actually says (as opposed to what you only think it says). It's also useful to know how to choose your battles when the inevitable disagreement does occur.

Approval of Equipment and Materials. Only the authority having jurisdiction has authority to approve the installation of equipment and materials. Typically, the authority having jurisdiction will approve equipment listed by a product testing organization, such as Underwriters Laboratories, Inc. (UL). The *NEC* doesn't require all equipment to be listed, but many state and local AHJs do. See 90.7, 110.2, 110.3, and the definitions for "Approved," "Identified," "Labeled," and "Listed" in Article 100. ▶ Figure 90–16

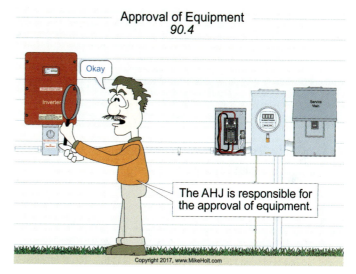

▶ Figure 90–16

Author's Comment:

- According to the *NEC*, the authority having jurisdiction determines the approval of equipment. This means he or she can reject an installation of listed equipment and can approve the use of unlisted equipment. Given our highly litigious society, approval of unlisted equipment is becoming increasingly difficult to obtain.

Approval of Alternate Means. By special permission, the authority having jurisdiction may approve alternate methods where it's assured equivalent safety can be achieved and maintained.

Author's Comment:

- Special permission is defined in Article 100 as the written consent of the authority having jurisdiction.

Waiver of New Product Requirements. If the current *NEC* requires products that aren't yet available at the time the *Code* is adopted, the authority having jurisdiction can allow products that were acceptable in the previous *Code* to continue to be used.

Author's Comment:

- Sometimes it takes years before testing laboratories establish product standards for new *NEC* requirements, and then it takes time before manufacturers can design, manufacture, and distribute those products to the marketplace.

90.5 Mandatory Requirements and Explanatory Material

(A) Mandatory Requirements. In the *NEC* the words "shall" or "shall not," indicate a mandatory requirement.

Author's Comment:

- For the ease of reading this textbook, the word "shall" has been replaced with the word "must," and the words "shall not" have been replaced with "must not." Remember that in many places, we'll paraphrase the *Code* instead of providing exact quotes, to make it easier to read and understand.

(B) Permissive Requirements. When the *Code* uses "shall be permitted" it means the identified actions are permitted but not required, and the authority having jurisdiction isn't permitted to restrict an installation from being completed in that manner. A permissive rule is often an exception to the general requirement.

Author's Comment:

- For ease of reading, the phrase "shall be permitted," as used in the *Code*, has been replaced in this textbook with the phrase "is permitted" or "are permitted."

(C) Explanatory Material. References to other standards or sections of the *NEC*, or information related to a *Code* rule, are included in the form of Informational Notes. Such notes are for information only and aren't enforceable as requirements of the *NEC*.

For example, Informational Note 4 in 210.19(A)(1) recommends that the voltage drop of a circuit not exceed 3 percent. This isn't a requirement; it's just a recommendation.

Author's Comment:

- For convenience and ease of reading in this textbook, Informational Notes will simply be identified as "Note."
- Informational Notes aren't enforceable, but Table Notes are. This textbook will call notes found in a table "Table Notes."

(D) Informative Annexes. Nonmandatory information annexes contained in the back of the *Code* book are for information only and aren't enforceable as requirements of the *NEC*.

90.6 Formal Interpretations

To promote uniformity of interpretation and application of the provisions of the *NEC*, formal interpretation procedures have been established and are found in the NFPA Regulations Governing Committee Projects.

Author's Comment:

- This is rarely done because it's a very time-consuming process, and formal interpretations from the NFPA aren't binding on the authority having jurisdiction.

90.7 Examination of Equipment for Product Safety

Product evaluation for safety is typically performed by a nationally recognized testing laboratory that's approved by the authority having jurisdiction. The suitability of equipment use is determined by the application of product safety listing standards that are compatible with the *NEC*.

Author's Comment:

- See Article 100 for the definition of "Approved."

Except to detect alterations or damage, listed factory-installed internal wiring and construction of equipment need not be inspected at the time of installation [300.1(B)]. ▶Figure 90–17

Introduction to the *National Electrical Code* | 90.9

▶Figure 90–17

Note 1: See 110.3 on the required use of listed products.

Note 2: "Listed" is defined in Article 100.

Note 3: Annex A contains a list of product safety standards that comply with the *NEC*.

90.9 Units of Measurement

(B) Dual Systems of Units. Both the metric and inch-pound measurement systems are shown in the *NEC*, with the metric units appearing first and the inch-pound system immediately following in parentheses.

Author's Comment:

- This is the standard practice in all NFPA standards, even though the U.S. construction industry uses inch-pound units of measurement. You'll need to be cautious when using the tables in the *Code* because the additional units can make the tables more complex and more difficult to read.

(D) Compliance. Installing electrical systems in accordance with the metric system or the inch-pound system is considered to comply with the *Code*.

Author's Comment:

- Since the use of either the metric or the inch-pound system of measurement constitutes compliance with the *NEC*, this textbook uses only inch-pound units.

ARTICLE 90 PRACTICE QUESTIONS

Please use the 2017 *Code* book to answer the following questions.

Article 90. Introduction to the *National Electrical Code*

1. The *Code* isn't intended as a design specification standard or instruction manual for untrained persons.

   (a) True
   (b) False

2. Compliance with the provisions of the *NEC* will result in _____.

   (a) good electrical service
   (b) an efficient electrical system
   (c) an electrical system essentially free from hazard
   (d) all of these

3. The *Code* contains provisions considered necessary for safety, which will not necessarily result in _____.

   (a) efficient use
   (b) convenience
   (c) good service or future expansion of electrical use
   (d) all of these

4. Hazards often occur because of _____.

   (a) overloading of wiring systems by methods or usage not in conformity with the *NEC*
   (b) initial wiring not providing for increases in the use of electricity
   (c) a and b
   (d) none of these

5. The *NEC* applies to the installation of _____.

   (a) electrical conductors and equipment within or on public and private buildings
   (b) outside conductors and equipment on the premises
   (c) optical fiber cables and raceways
   (d) all of these

6. This *Code* covers the installation of _____ for public and private premises, including buildings, structures, mobile homes, recreational vehicles, and floating buildings.

   (a) optical fiber cables
   (b) electrical equipment
   (c) raceways
   (d) all of these

7. The *NEC* does not cover electrical installations in ships, watercraft, railway rolling stock, aircraft, or automotive vehicles.

   (a) True
   (b) False

8. The *Code* covers underground mine installations and self-propelled mobile surface mining machinery and its attendant electrical trailing cable.

   (a) True
   (b) False

9. Electric utilities may include entities that install, operate, and maintain _____.

    (a) communications systems (telephone, CATV, Internet, satellite, or data services)
    (b) electric supply systems (generation, transmission, or distribution systems)
    (c) local area network wiring on the premises
    (d) a or b

10. Utilities may be subject to compliance with codes and standards covering their regulated activities as adopted under governmental law or regulation.

    (a) True
    (b) False

11. The *NEC* does not apply to electric utility-owned wiring and equipment _____.

    (a) installed by an electrical contractor
    (b) installed on public property
    (c) consisting of service drops or service laterals
    (d) in a utility office building

12. Utilities may include entities that are designated or recognized by governmental law or regulation by public service/utility commissions.

    (a) True
    (b) False

13. Chapters 5, 6, and 7 apply to special occupancies, special equipment, or other special conditions and may supplement or modify the requirements in Chapters 1 through 7.

    (a) True
    (b) False

14. Communications wiring such as telephone, antenna, and CATV wiring within a building shall not be required to comply with the installation requirements of Chapters 1 through 7, except where specifically referenced in Chapter 8.

    (a) True
    (b) False

15. Installations shall comply with the material located in the *NEC* Annexes because they are part of the requirements of the *Code*.

    (a) True
    (b) False

16. The authority having jurisdiction shall not be allowed to enforce any requirements of Chapter 7 (Special Conditions) or Chapter 8 (Communications Systems).

    (a) True
    (b) False

17. By special permission, the authority having jurisdiction may waive specific requirements in this *Code* where it is assured that equivalent objectives can be achieved by establishing and maintaining effective safety.

    (a) True
    (b) False

18. The authority having jurisdiction has the responsibility for _____.

    (a) making interpretations of rules
    (b) deciding upon the approval of equipment and materials
    (c) waiving specific requirements in the *Code* and permitting alternate methods and material if safety is maintained
    (d) all of these

19. If the *NEC* requires new products that are not yet available at the time a new edition is adopted, the _____ may permit the use of the products that comply with the most recent previous edition of the *Code* adopted by that jurisdiction.

    (a) electrical engineer
    (b) master electrician
    (c) authority having jurisdiction
    (d) permit holder

20. In the *NEC*, the word(s) "_____" indicate a mandatory requirement.

    (a) shall
    (b) shall not
    (c) shall be permitted
    (d) a or b

21. Explanatory material, such as references to other standards, references to related sections of the *NEC*, or information related to a *Code* rule, are included in the form of Informational Notes.

    (a) True
    (b) False

22. Nonmandatory Informative Annexes contained in the back of the *Code* book are _____.

    (a) for information only
    (b) not enforceable as a requirement of the *Code*
    (c) enforceable as a requirement of the *Code*
    (d) a and b

23. Factory-installed _____ wiring of listed equipment need not be inspected at the time of installation of the equipment, except to detect alterations or damage.

    (a) external
    (b) associated
    (c) internal
    (d) all of these

24. Compliance with either the SI or the inch-pound unit of measurement system shall be permitted.

    (a) True
    (b) False

CHAPTER 1

GENERAL RULES

Introduction to Chapter 1—General Rules

Before you can make sense of the *Code*, you must become familiar with a few basic rules, concepts, definitions, and requirements. As you study the *NEC*, you'll see that these are the foundation for a proper understanding of the *Code*.

Chapter 1 consists of two topics. Article 100 provides definitions so people can understand one another when trying to communicate about *Code*-related matters and Article 110 provides the general requirements needed to correctly apply the rest of the *NEC*.

Time spent learning this general material is a great investment. After understanding Chapter 1, some of the *Code* requirements that seem confusing to other people will become increasingly clear to you. The requirements will begin to make sense because you'll have the foundation from which to understand and apply them. When you read the *NEC* requirements in later chapters, you'll understand the principles upon which many of them are based, and not be surprised at all. You'll read them and feel like you already know them.

- **Article 100—Definitions.** Part I of Article 100 contains the definitions of terms used throughout the *Code* for systems that operate at 1,000V, nominal, or less. The definitions of terms in Part II apply to systems that operate at over 1,000V, nominal.

  Definitions of standard terms, such as volt, voltage drop, ampere, impedance, and resistance, aren't listed in Article 100. If the *NEC* doesn't define a term, then a dictionary suitable to the authority having jurisdiction should be consulted. A building code glossary might provide better definitions than a dictionary found at your home or school.

  Definitions located at the beginning of an article apply only to that specific article. For example, the definition of a "Pool" is contained in 680.2, because this term applies only to the requirements contained in Article 680—Swimming Pools, Fountains, and Similar Installations. As soon as a defined term is used in two or more articles, its definition should be included in Article 100.

- **Article 110—Requirements for Electrical Installations.** This article contains general requirements for electrical installations for the following:
  - Part I. General
  - Part II. 1,000V, Nominal, or Less

Notes

ARTICLE 100 DEFINITIONS

Introduction to Article 100—Definitions

Have you ever had a conversation with someone, only to discover that what you said and what he or she heard were completely different? This often happens when people in a conversation have different definitions for the words being used, and that's why the definitions of key terms are located right at the beginning of the *NEC* (Article 100), or at the beginning of each article. If we can all agree on important definitions, then we speak the same language and avoid misunderstandings. Because the *Code* exists to protect people and property, it's very important to know the definitions presented in Article 100.

Here are a few tips for learning the many definitions in the *NEC*:

- **Break the task down.** Study a few words at a time, rather than trying to learn them all at one sitting.
- **Review the graphics in the textbook.** These will help you see how terms are applied.
- **Relate the definitions to your work.** As you read a word, think about how it applies to the work you're doing. This will provide a natural reinforcement to the learning process.

Part I. General

100 Definitions

Scope. This article contains definitions essential to the application of this *Code*; it doesn't include general terms or technical terms from other codes and standards. In general, only those terms that are used in two or more articles are defined in Article 100.

Accessible (as it applies to wiring methods). Not permanently closed in by the building structure or finish and capable of being removed or exposed without damaging the building structure or finish. ▶Figure 100–1

Approved. Acceptable to the authority having jurisdiction, usually the electrical inspector. ▶Figure 100–2

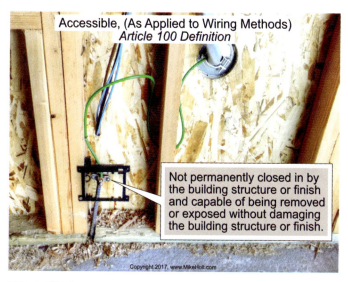

▶Figure 100–1

100 | Definitions

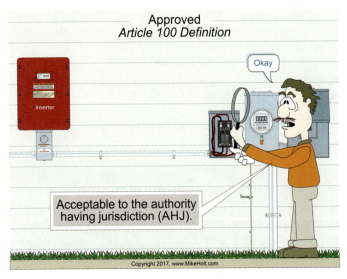

▶Figure 100–2

Author's Comment:

- Product listing doesn't mean the product is approved, but it can be a basis for approval. See 90.4, 90.7, 110.2, and the definitions in this article for "Authority Having Jurisdiction," "Identified," "Labeled," and "Listed."

Authority Having Jurisdiction (AHJ). The organization, office, or individual responsible for approving equipment, materials, an installation, or a procedure. See 90.4 and 90.7 for more information.

Note: The authority having jurisdiction may be a federal, state, or local government department or an individual, such as a fire chief, fire marshal, chief of a fire prevention bureau or labor department or health department, a building official or electrical inspector, or others having statutory authority. In some circumstances, the property owner or his/her agent assumes the role, and at government installations, the commanding officer, or departmental official may be the authority having jurisdiction.

Author's Comment:

- Typically, the authority having jurisdiction is the electrical inspector who has legal statutory authority. In the absence of federal, state, or local regulations, the operator of the facility or his or her agent, such as an architect or engineer of the facility, can assume the role.

- Some believe the authority having jurisdiction should have a strong background in the electrical field, such as having studied electrical engineering or having obtained an electrical contractor's license, and in a few states this is a legal requirement. Memberships, certifications, and active participation in electrical organizations, such as the International Association of Electrical Inspectors (IAEI), speak to an individual's qualifications. Visit www.IAEI.org for more information about that organization.

Bonded (Bonding). Connected to establish electrical continuity and conductivity. ▶Figure 100–3

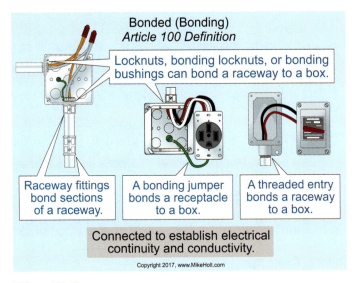

▶Figure 100–3

Author's Comment:

- The purpose of bonding is to connect two or more conductive objects together to ensure the electrical continuity of the ground-fault current path, provide the capacity and ability to conduct safely any fault current likely to be imposed, and to minimize voltage between conductive components. ▶Figure 100–4 and ▶Figure 100–5

Bonding Conductor or Jumper. A conductor that ensures electrical conductivity between metal parts of the electrical installation. ▶Figure 100–6

Definitions | 100

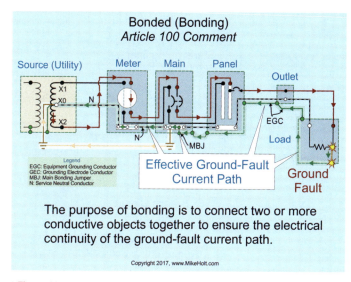

▶Figure 100–4

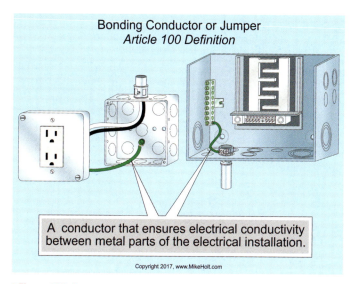

▶Figure 100–6

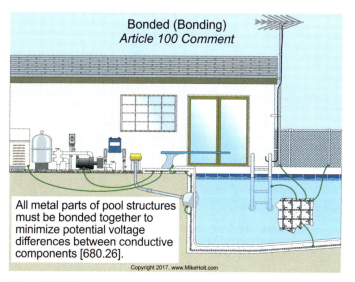

▶Figure 100–5

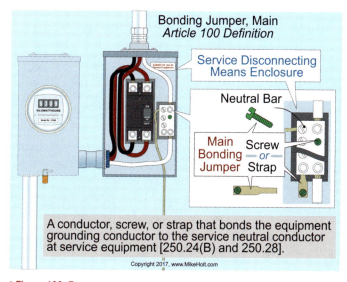

▶Figure 100–7

Bonding Jumper, Main. A conductor, screw, or strap that connects the circuit equipment grounding conductor to the neutral conductor at service equipment in accordance with 250.24(B) [250.24(A)(4), 250.28, and 408.3(C)]. ▶Figure 100–7

Bonding Jumper, System. The connection between the neutral conductor and the supply-side bonding jumper or equipment grounding conductor, or both, at a separately derived system transformer or separately derived system generator. ▶Figure 100–8 and ▶Figure 100–9

100 | Definitions

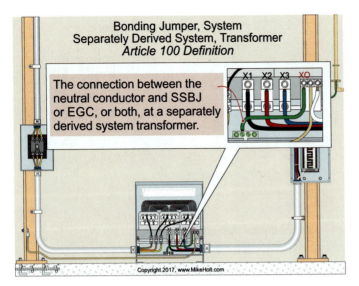
▶Figure 100–8

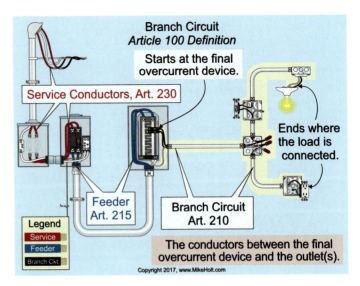
▶Figure 100–10

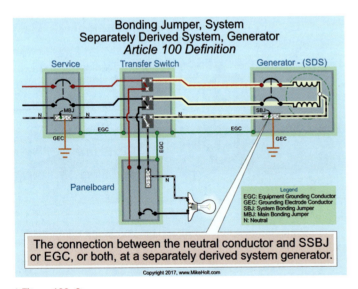
▶Figure 100–9

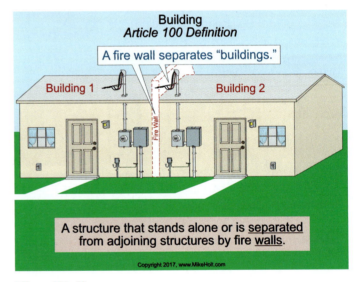
▶Figure 100–11

Branch Circuit [Article 210]. The conductors between the final overcurrent protection device and the receptacle outlets, lighting outlets, or other outlets as defined in this article. ▶Figure 100–10

Building. A structure that stands alone or is separated from adjoining structures by fire walls. ▶Figure 100–11

Cabinet [Article 312]. An enclosure for either surface mounting or flush mounting provided with a frame in which a door can be hung. ▶Figure 100–12

Author's Comment:

- Cabinets are used to enclose panelboards. See the definition of "Panelboard" in this article.

Connector, Pressure (Solderless). A device that establishes a conductive connection between conductors or between a conductor and a terminal by the means of mechanical pressure. ▶Figure 100–13

Definitions | 100

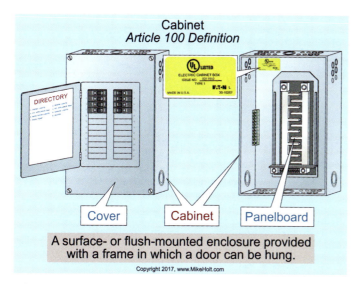
▶Figure 100–12

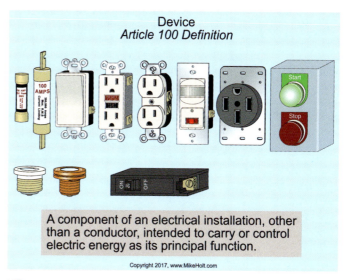
▶Figure 100–14

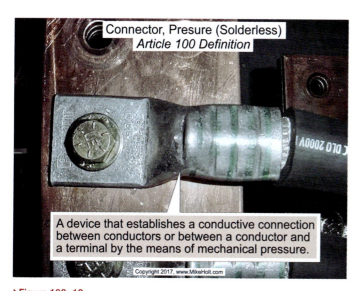
▶Figure 100–13

Device. A component of an electrical installation, other than a conductor, intended to carry or control electric energy as its principal function.
▶Figure 100–14

Author's Comment:

- Devices include receptacles, switches, illuminated switches, circuit breakers, fuses, time clocks, controllers, and so forth, but not locknuts or other mechanical fittings. A device may consume very small amounts of energy, such as an illuminated switch, but still be classified as a device based on its principal function.

Disconnecting Means. A device that opens all of the ungrounded circuit conductors from their power source. This includes devices such as switches, attachment plugs and receptacles, and circuit breakers.
▶Figure 100–15

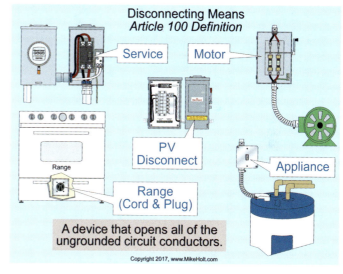
▶Figure 100–15

Effective Ground-Fault Current Path. An intentionally constructed low-impedance conductive path designed to carry fault current from the point of a ground fault to the source for the purpose of opening the circuit overcurrent protective device. ▶Figure 100–16

100 | Definitions

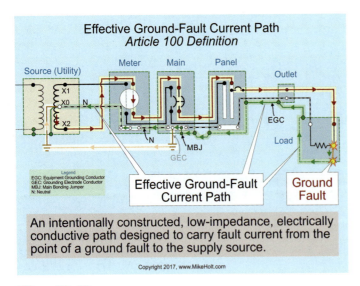
▶Figure 100–16

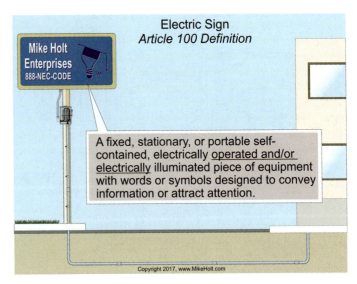
▶Figure 100–17

Author's Comment:

- In the preceding Figure, "EGC" represents the equipment grounding conductor [250.118], "MBJ" represents the main bonding jumper, "N" represents the service neutral conductor (grounded service conductor), and "GEC" represents the grounding electrode conductor.

- The current path shown between the supply source grounding electrode and the grounding electrode at the service main shows that some current will flow through the earth but the earth isn't part of the effective ground-fault current path.

- The effective ground-fault current path is intended to help remove dangerous voltage from a ground fault by opening the circuit overcurrent protection device.

Electric Sign [Article 600]. A fixed, stationary, or portable self-contained, electrically operated and/or electrically illuminated piece of equipment with words or symbols designed to convey information or attract attention. ▶Figure 100–17

Enclosed. Surrounded by a case, housing, fence, or wall(s) that prevents accidental contact with energized parts.

Equipment. A general term including fittings, devices, appliances, luminaires, machinery, and the like as part of, or in connection with, an electrical installation. ▶Figure 100–18

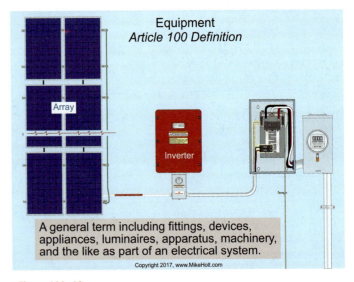
▶Figure 100–18

Exposed (as applied to wiring methods). On or attached to the surface of a building, or behind panels designed to allow access. ▶Figure 100–19

Feeder [Article 215]. The conductors between the service equipment, a separately derived system, or other power supply and the final branch-circuit overcurrent protection device. ▶Figure 100–20

Author's Comment:

- An "other power source" includes a solar PV system or conductors from a generator.

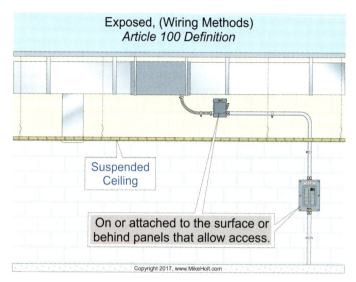
▶Figure 100–19

▶Figure 100–21

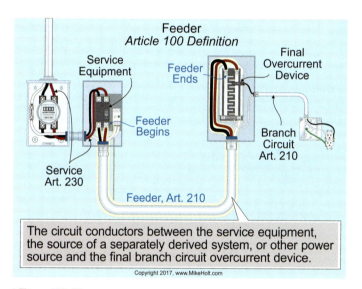
▶Figure 100–20

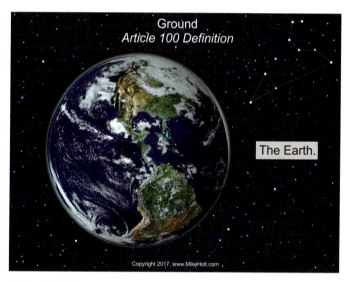
▶Figure 100–22

Fitting. An accessory, such as a locknut, intended to perform a mechanical function. ▶Figure 100–21

Ground. The earth. ▶Figure 100–22

Ground Fault. An unintentional electrical connection between an ungrounded conductor and the metal parts of enclosures, raceways, or equipment. ▶Figure 100–23

Ground-Fault Circuit Interrupter (GFCI). A device intended to protect people by de-energizing a circuit when a current imbalance has been detected that exceeds the value established for a "Class A" device.

Note: Class A ground-fault circuit interrupter opens the circuit when the imbalance current has a value of 6 mA or higher and doesn't trip when the current to ground is less than 4 mA. ▶Figure 100–24

100 | Definitions

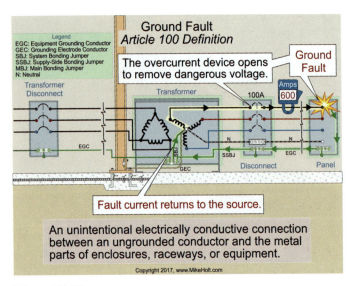

▶ Figure 100–23

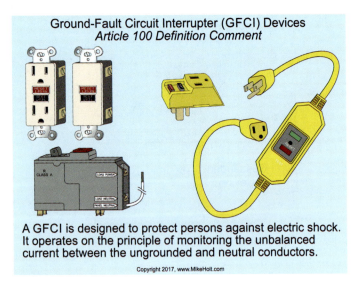

▶ Figure 100–25

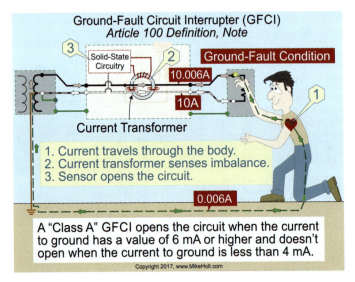

▶ Figure 100–24

Author's Comment:

- A GFCI operates on the principle of monitoring the unbalanced current between the current-carrying circuit conductors. On a 120V circuit, the GFCI will monitor the unbalanced current between the ungrounded and neutral conductors; on 240V GFCIs, this monitoring is between all circuit conductors. GFCI-protective devices are commercially available in receptacles, circuit breakers, cord sets, and other types of devices. ▶ Figure 100–25

Ground-Fault Protection of Equipment. A system intended to provide protection of equipment from damaging ground-fault currents by opening all ungrounded conductors of the faulted circuit. This protection is provided at current levels less than those required to protect conductors from damage through the operation of a supply circuit overcurrent device [215.10, 230.95, and 240.13].

Author's Comment:

- This type of protective device isn't intended to protect people and trips at a higher level than required for "Class A" GFCIs. This type of device is typically referred to as ground-fault protection for equipment, or GFPE, but should never be called a GFCI.

Grounded (Grounding). Connected to ground or to a conductive body that extends the ground connection. ▶ Figure 100–26

Author's Comment:

- An example of a "body that extends the ground (earth) connection" is the termination to structural steel that's connected to the earth either directly or by the termination to another grounding electrode in accordance with 250.52.

Grounded System, Solidly. A power-supply system connected to ground (earth) without inserting any resistor or impedance device between the system and ground. ▶ Figure 100–27

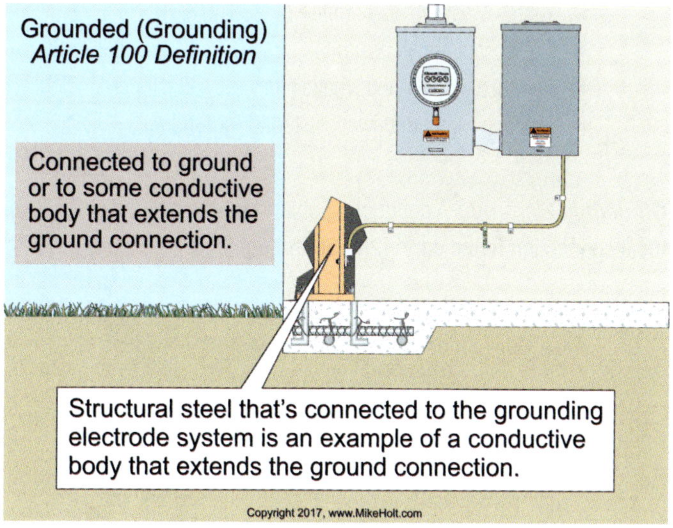

Definitions | 100

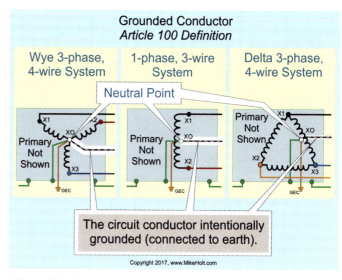
▶Figure 100–26

▶Figure 100–28

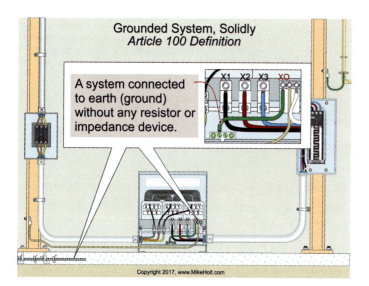
▶Figure 100–27

▶Figure 100–29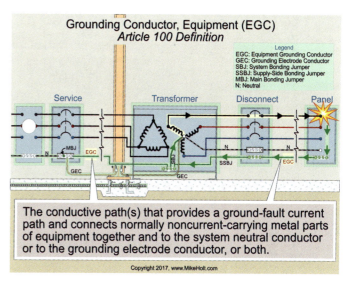

Grounded Conductor [Article 200]. The system or circuit conductor that's intentionally grounded (connected to the earth). ▶Figure 100–28

Grounding Conductor, Equipment (EGC). The conductive path(s) that provides a ground-fault current path and connects metal parts of equipment to the system neutral conductor, to the grounding electrode conductor, or both [250.110 through 250.126]. ▶Figure 100–29

Note 1: The circuit equipment grounding conductor also performs bonding.

Author's Comment:

- To quickly remove dangerous touch voltage on metal parts from a ground fault, the equipment grounding conductor must be connected to the system neutral conductor at the source, and have low enough impedance so fault current will quickly rise to a level that will open the circuit's overcurrent protection device [250.2 and 250.4(A)(3)]. ▶Figure 100–30

Note 2: An equipment grounding conductor can be any one or a combination of the types listed in 250.118. ▶Figure 100–31

Mike Holt Enterprises • www.MikeHolt.com • 888.NEC.CODE (632.2633)   29

100 | Definitions

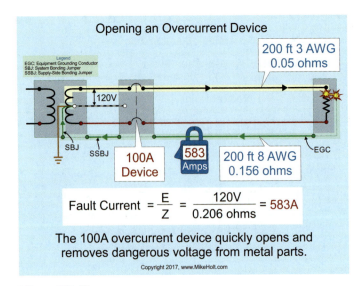

▶Figure 100–30

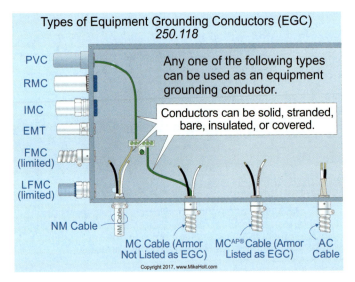

▶Figure 100–31

Author's Comment:

- Equipment grounding conductors include:
  - A bare or insulated conductor
  - Rigid Metal Conduit
  - Intermediate Metal Conduit
  - Electrical Metallic Tubing
  - Listed Flexible Metal Conduit as limited by 250.118(5)
  - Listed Liquidtight Flexible Metal Conduit as limited by 250.118(6)
  - Armored Cable
  - The copper metal sheath of Mineral-Insulated Cable
  - Metal-Clad Cable as limited by 250.118(10)
  - Metal cable trays as limited by 250.118(11) and 392.60
  - Electrically continuous metal raceways listed for grounding
  - Surface Metal Raceways listed for grounding

Grounding Electrode. A conducting object used to make a direct electrical connection to the earth [250.50 through 250.70]. ▶Figure 100–32

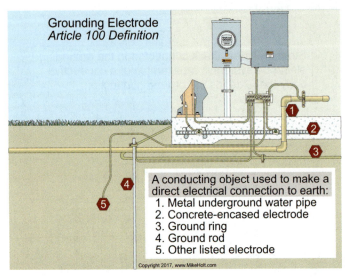

▶Figure 100–32

Grounding Electrode Conductor (GEC). The conductor used to connect the system neutral conductor or the equipment to the grounding electrode system. ▶Figure 100–33

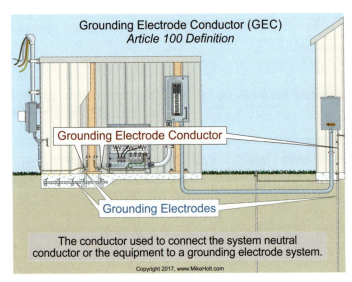

▶Figure 100–33

Handhole Enclosure. An enclosure for underground system use sized to allow personnel to reach into it for the purpose of installing or maintaining equipment or wiring. It may have an open or closed bottom. ▶Figure 100–34

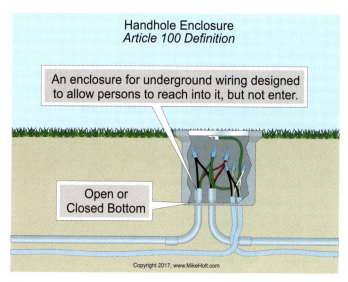

▶Figure 100–34

Author's Comment:

- See 314.30 for the installation requirements for handhole enclosures.

Identified Equipment. Recognized as suitable for a specific purpose, function, or environment by listing, labeling, or other means approved by the authority having jurisdiction. ▶Figure 100–35

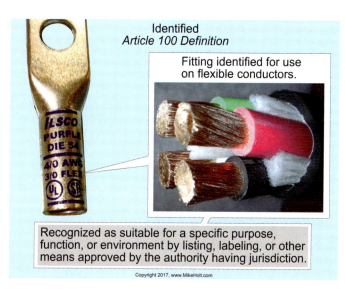

▶Figure 100–35

Author's Comment:

- See 90.4, 90.7, 110.3(A)(1), and the definitions for "Approved," "Labeled," and "Listed" in this article.

Information Technology Equipment (ITE). Equipment used for creation and manipulation of data, voice, and video, but not communications equipment. ▶Figure 100–36

▶Figure 100–36

Interactive Inverter. An inverter used in parallel with an electric utility to supply common loads. ▶Figure 100–37

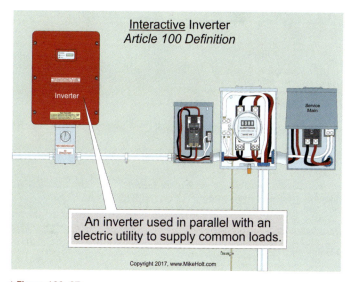

▶Figure 100–37

Intersystem Bonding Termination. A device that provides a means to connect intersystem bonding conductors for communications systems (twisted wire, antennas, and coaxial cable) to the grounding electrode system, in accordance with 250.94. ▶Figure 100–38

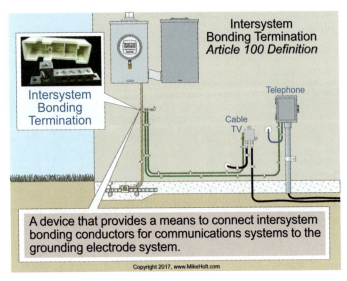

▶Figure 100–38

Labeled. Equipment or materials that have a label, symbol, or other identifying mark in the form of a sticker, decal, printed label, or with the identifying mark molded or stamped into the product by a testing laboratory acceptable to the authority having jurisdiction. ▶Figure 100–39

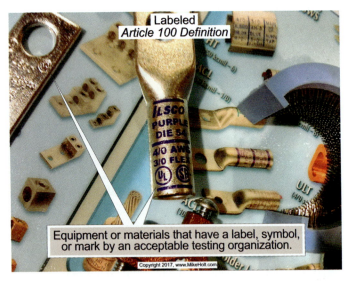

▶Figure 100–39

Author's Comment:

- Labeling and listing of equipment typically provides the basis for equipment approval by the authority having jurisdiction [90.4, 90.7, 110.2, and 110.3].

Listed. Equipment or materials included in a list published by a testing laboratory acceptable to the authority having jurisdiction. The listing organization must periodically inspect the production of listed equipment or material to ensure the equipment or material meets appropriate designated standards and is suitable for a specified purpose.

Author's Comment:

- The *NEC* doesn't require all electrical equipment to be listed, but some *Code* requirements do specifically require product listing. Organizations such as OSHA increasingly require that listed equipment be used when such equipment is available [90.7, 110.2, and 110.3].

Luminaire [Article 410]. A complete lighting unit consisting of a light source with the parts designed to position the light source and connect it to the power supply and distribute the light. A lampholder by itself isn't a luminaire. ▶Figure 100–40

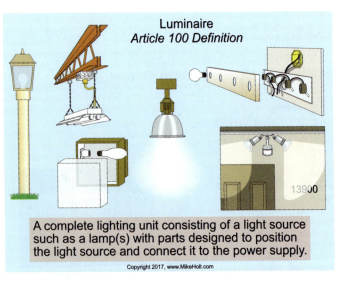

▶Figure 100–40

Multioutlet Assembly [Article 380]. A surface, flush, or freestanding raceway designed to hold conductors and receptacles. ▶Figure 100–41

Definitions | 100

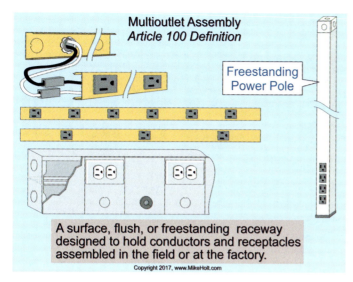
▶Figure 100–41

Neutral Conductor. The conductor connected to the neutral point of a system that's intended to carry current under normal conditions. ▶Figure 100–42

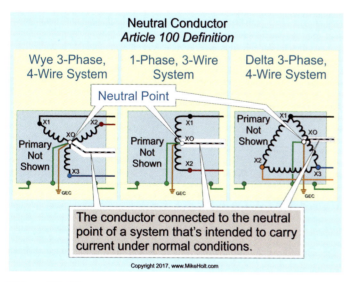
▶Figure 100–42

Author's Comment:

- The neutral conductor of a solidly grounded system is required to be grounded (connected to the earth), therefore this conductor is also called a "grounded conductor."

Neutral Point. The common point of a 4-wire, three-phase, wye-connected system; the midpoint of a 3-wire, single-phase system; or the midpoint of the single-phase portion of a three-phase, delta-connected system. ▶Figure 100–43

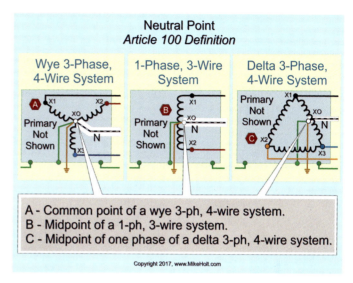
▶Figure 100–43

Panelboard [Article 408]. A distribution point containing overcurrent protection devices and designed to be installed in a cabinet. ▶Figure 100–44

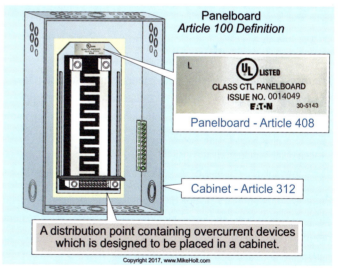
▶Figure 100–44

Mike Holt Enterprises • www.MikeHolt.com • 888.NEC.CODE (632.2633)   33

100 | Definitions

Author's Comment:

- See the definition of "Cabinet" in this article.
- The slang term in the electrical field for a panelboard is "the guts." This is the interior of the panelboard assembly and is covered by Article 408, while the cabinet is covered by Article 312.

2017 CC **Photovoltaic (PV) System.** The combination of all components and subsystems that convert solar energy into electric energy for utilization loads. ▶Figure 100–45

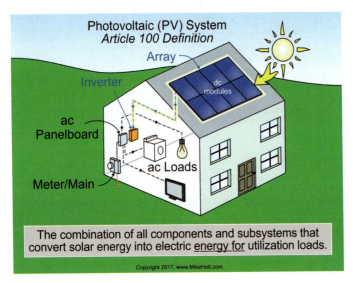

▶Figure 100–45

Premises Wiring. The interior and exterior wiring, including power, lighting, control, and signal circuits, and all associated hardware, fittings, and wiring devices. This includes both permanently and temporarily installed wiring from the service point to the outlets, or where there's no service point, wiring from and including the electric power source, such as a generator, transformer, or PV system to the outlets. ▶Figure 100–46

Premises wiring doesn't include the internal wiring of electrical equipment and appliances, such as luminaires, dishwashers, water heaters, motors, controllers, motor control centers, air-conditioning equipment, and so on [90.7 and 300.1(B)]. ▶Figure 100–47

Note: Electric power sources include, but aren't limited to, interconnected or stand-alone batteries, PV systems, other distributed generation systems, or generators.

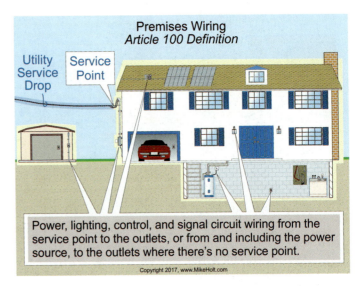

▶Figure 100–46

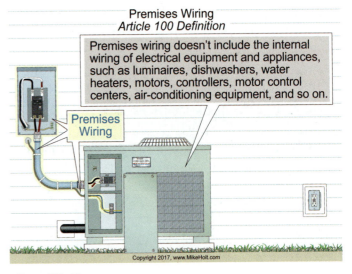

▶Figure 100–47

2017 CC **Raceway.** An enclosed channel designed for the installation of conductors, cables, or busbars.

Author's Comment:

- A cable tray system isn't a raceway; it's a support system for cables and raceways [392.2].

Receptacle [Article 406]. A contact device installed at an outlet for the connection of an attachment plug, or for the direct connection of equipment designed to mate with the contact device (SQL receptacle). ▶Figure 100–48

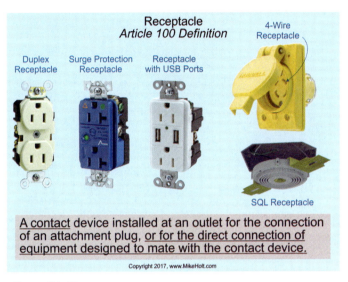

▶Figure 100–48

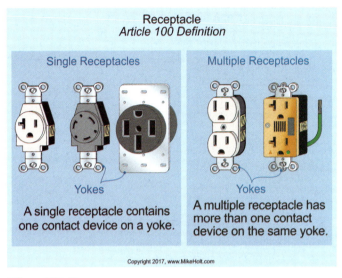

▶Figure 100–49

Author's Comment:

- Outlet boxes are permitted to support listed locking support and mounting receptacles (SQL receptacles) used in combination with compatible attachment fittings [314.27(E)]. For additional information about listed locking, support and mounting receptacles, visit http://www.safetyquicklight.com/.

- See 314.27(E) for the specific *NEC* application for the direct connection of equipment designed to mate with the contact device.

A single receptacle contains one contact device on a yoke; a multiple receptacle has more than one contact device on the same yoke. ▶Figure 100–49

Separately Derived System. An electrical source, other than a service, having no direct connection(s) to circuit conductors of any other electrical source other than those established by grounding and bonding connections. ▶Figure 100–50 and ▶Figure 100–51

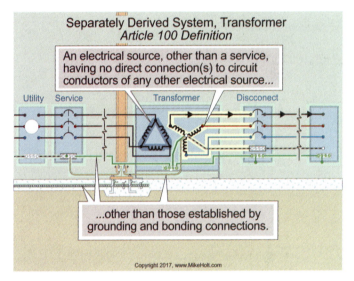

▶Figure 100–50

100 | Definitions

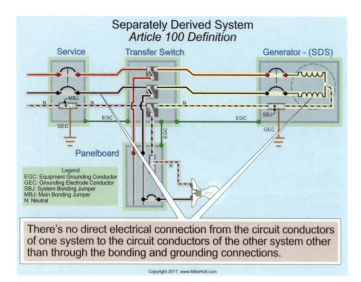
▶Figure 100–51

Author's Comment:

- An alternate alternating-current power source such as an on-site generator isn't a separately derived system if the neutral conductor is solidly interconnected to a service-supplied system neutral conductor. An example is a generator provided with a transfer switch that includes a neutral conductor that's not switched. ▶Figure 100–52

- Separately derived systems are actually much more complicated than the above definition suggests, and understanding them requires additional study. For more information, see 250.30.

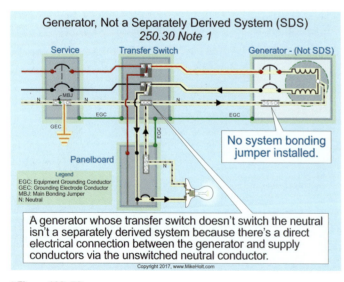
▶Figure 100–52

Service [Article 230]. The conductors and equipment for delivering electric energy from the serving utility to the wiring system of the premises served. ▶Figure 100–53

▶Figure 100–53

Author's Comment:

- Conductors from a UPS system, solar PV system, generator, or transformer aren't service conductors. See the definitions of "Feeder" and "Service Conductors" in this article.

Service Conductors. The conductors from the service point to the service disconnect. ▶Figure 100–54

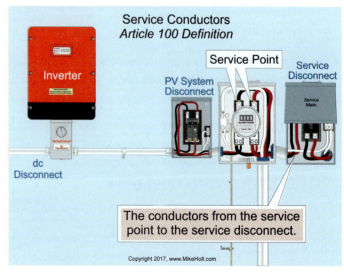
▶Figure 100–54

Author's Comment:

- These conductors fall within the requirements of Article 230, since they're owned by the customer.

Service Equipment [Article 230]. Disconnects such as circuit breaker(s) or switch(es) connected to the load end of service conductors, intended to control and cut off the service supply to the buildings or structure. ▶Figure 100–55

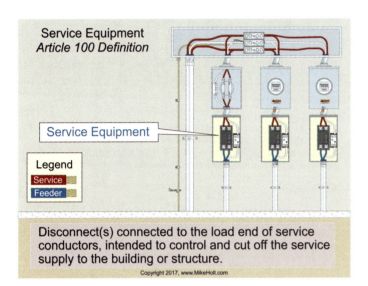

▶Figure 100–55

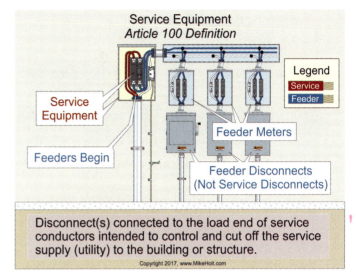

▶Figure 100–56

Author's Comment:

- It's important to know where a service begins and where it ends in order to properly apply the *NEC* requirements. Sometimes the service ends before the metering equipment. ▶Figure 100–56
- Service equipment is often referred to as the "service disconnect" or "service disconnecting means."

Special Permission. Written consent from the authority having jurisdiction.

Author's Comment:

- See the definition of "Authority Having Jurisdiction."

Structure. That which is built or constructed, other than equipment. ▶Figure 100–57

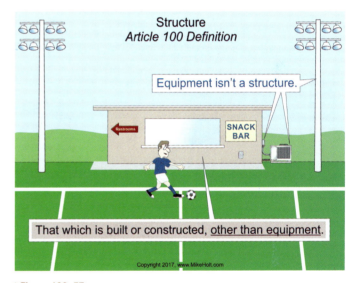

▶Figure 100–57

Switch, General-Use Snap. A switch constructed to be installed in a device box or a box cover.

Ungrounded System. An electrical power system that's not connected to the ground (earth) or a conductive body that extends the ground (earth) connection. ▶Figure 100–58

Voltage (of a circuit). The greatest effective root-mean-square (RMS) difference of voltage between any two conductors of the circuit. ▶Figure 100–59

100 | Definitions

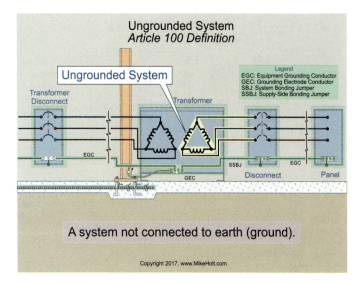

▶Figure 100–58

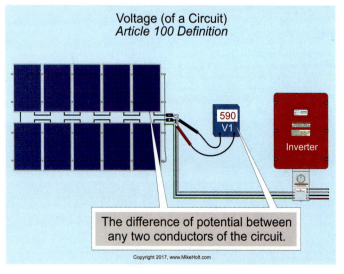

▶Figure 100–59

Voltage to Ground. The greatest difference of voltage (RMS) between an ungrounded conductor and the neutral point of the circuit that's grounded. ▶Figure 100–60

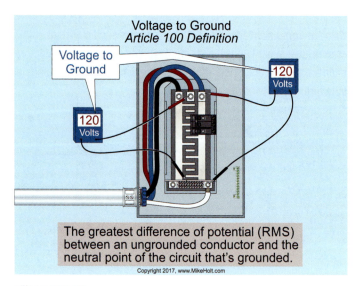

▶Figure 100–60

ARTICLE 110 — REQUIREMENTS FOR ELECTRICAL INSTALLATIONS

Introduction to Article 110—Requirements for Electrical Installations

Article 110 sets the stage for how you'll implement the rest of the *NEC*. This article contains a few of the most important and yet neglected parts of the *Code*. For example:

- How should conductors be terminated?
- What kinds of warnings, markings, and identification does a given installation require?
- What's the right working clearance for a given installation?
- What do the temperature limitations at terminals mean?
- What are the *NEC* requirements for dealing with flash protection?

It's critical that you master Article 110; as you read this article, you're building your foundation for correctly applying the *NEC*. In fact, this article itself is a foundation for much of the *Code*. The purpose for the *National Electrical Code* is to provide a safe installation, but Article 110 is perhaps focused a little more on providing an installation that's safe for the installer and maintenance electrician, so time spent in this article is time well spent.

Part I. General Requirements

110.1 Scope

Article 110 covers the general requirements for the examination and approval, installation and use, access to and spaces about electrical equipment; as well as general requirements for enclosures intended for personnel entry (manholes, vaults, and tunnels).

Note: See Annex J for information regarding ADA accessibility design.

Author's Comment:

- Requirements for people with disabilities include things like mounting heights for switches and receptacles, and requirements for the distance that objects such as wall sconces protrude from a wall.

110.2 Approval of Conductors and Equipment

The authority having jurisdiction must approve all electrical conductors and equipment. ▶Figure 110–1

▶Figure 110–1

110.3 | Requirements for Electrical Installations

Author's Comment:

- For a better understanding of product approval, review 90.4, 90.7, 110.3, and the definitions for "Approved," "Identified," "Labeled," and "Listed" in Article 100.

110.3 Examination, Identification, Installation, Use, and Product Listing (Certification) of Equipment

(A) Guidelines for Approval. The authority having jurisdiction must approve equipment. In doing so, consideration must be given to the following:

(1) Suitability for installation and use in accordance with the *NEC*

Note 1: Equipment may be new, reconditioned, refurbished, or remanufactured.

Note 2: Suitability of equipment use may be identified by a description marked on, or provided with, a product to identify the suitability of the product for a specific purpose, environment, or application. Special conditions of use or other limitations may be marked on the equipment, in the product instructions, or appropriate listing and labeling information. Suitability of equipment may be evidenced by listing or labeling.

(2) Mechanical strength and durability

(3) Wire-bending and connection space

(4) Electrical insulation

(5) Heating effects under all conditions of use

(6) Arcing effects

(7) Classification by type, size, voltage, current capacity, and specific use

(8) Other factors contributing to the practical safeguarding of persons using or in contact with the equipment

(B) Installation and Use. Equipment must be installed and used in accordance with any instructions included in the listing or labeling requirements. ▶Figure 110–2

(C) Product Listing (Certification). Product certification (testing, evaluation, and listing) must be performed by a recognized qualified testing laboratory in accordance with standards that achieve effective safety to comply with the *NEC*.

Note: OSHA recognizes qualified electrical testing laboratories that provide product certification that meets OSHA electrical standards.

▶Figure 110–2

110.5 Conductor Material

Conductors are to be copper or aluminum unless otherwise provided in this *Code*; and when the conductor material isn't specified in a rule, the sizes given in the *NEC* are based on a copper conductor. ▶Figure 110–3

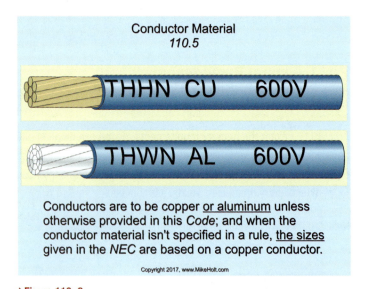

▶Figure 110–3

110.6 Conductor Sizes

Conductor sizes are expressed in American Wire Gage (AWG), typically from 18 AWG up to 4/0 AWG. Conductor sizes larger than 4/0 AWG are expressed in kcmil (thousand circular mils). ▶Figure 110–4

Requirements for Electrical Installations | 110.11

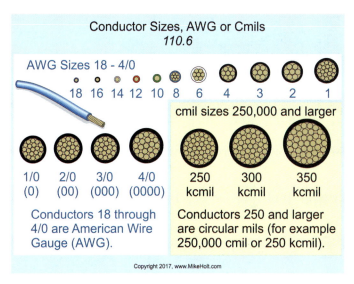

▶Figure 110–4

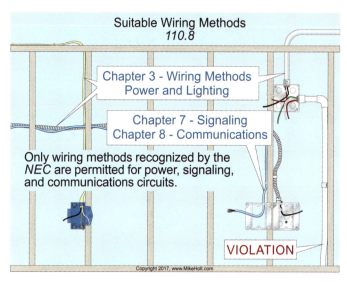

▶Figure 110–6

110.7 Wiring Integrity

Completed installations must be free from short circuits, ground faults, or any connections to ground unless required or permitted by the *Code*.
▶Figure 110–5

Author's Comment:

- See Chapter 3 for power and lighting wiring methods; Chapter 7 for signaling, remote-control, and power-limited circuits; and Chapter 8 for communications circuits.

110.11 Deteriorating Agents

Electrical equipment and conductors must be suitable for the environment and conditions of use. Consideration must also be given to the presence of corrosive gases, fumes, vapors, liquids, or other substances that can have a deteriorating effect on the conductors or equipment.
▶Figure 110–7

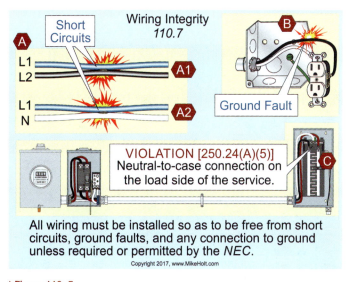

▶Figure 110–5

110.8 Suitable Wiring Methods

Only wiring methods recognized as suitable are included in the *NEC*, and they must be installed in accordance with the *Code*. ▶Figure 110–6

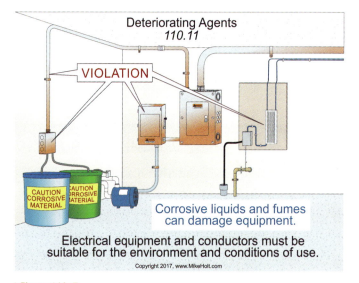

▶Figure 110–7

110.12 | Requirements for Electrical Installations

Author's Comment:

- Conductors aren't permitted to be exposed to ultraviolet rays from the sun unless identified for the purpose [310.10(D)].

Note 1: Raceways, cable trays, cablebus, cable armor, boxes, cable sheathing, cabinets, elbows, couplings, fittings, supports, and support hardware must be of materials that are suitable for the environment in which they're to be installed, in accordance with 300.6. ▶Figure 110–8

▶Figure 110–8

Note 2: Some cleaning and lubricating compounds contain chemicals that can cause deterioration of the plastic used for insulating and structural applications in equipment.

Equipment not identified for outdoor use and equipment identified only for indoor use must be protected against damage from the weather during construction.

Note 3: See Table 110.28 for NEMA enclosure-type designations.

110.12 Mechanical Execution of Work

Electrical equipment must be installed in a neat and workmanlike manner. ▶Figure 110–9

▶Figure 110–9

110.14 Conductor Termination and Splicing

Conductor terminal and splicing devices must be identified for the conductor material and they must be properly installed and used. ▶Figure 110–10

▶Figure 110–10

Author's Comment:

- Switches and receptacles marked "CO/ALR" are designed to ensure a good connection through the use of a larger contact area and compatible materials. The terminal screws are plated with the element called "Indium." Indium is an extremely soft metal that forms a gas-sealed connection with the aluminum conductor.

Connectors and terminals for conductors more finely stranded than Class B and Class C, as shown in Table 10 of Chapter 9, must be identified for the use of finely stranded conductors. ▶Figure 110–11

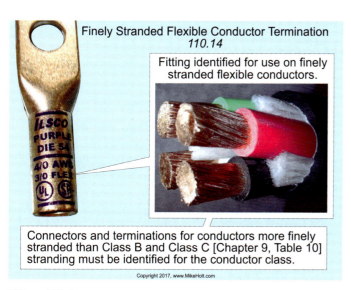

▶Figure 110–11

Author's Comment:

- According to UL Standard 486 A-B, a terminal/lug/connector must be listed and marked for use with other than Class B stranded conductors. With no marking or factory literature/instructions to the contrary, terminals may only be used with Class B stranded conductors.
- See the definition of "Identified" in Article 100.
- Conductor terminations must comply with the manufacturer's instructions as required by 110.3(B). For example, if the instructions for the device state "Suitable for 18-12 AWG Stranded," then only stranded conductors can be used with the terminating device. If the instructions state "Suitable for 18-12 AWG Solid," then only solid conductors are permitted, and if the instructions state "Suitable for 18-12 AWG," then either solid or stranded conductors can be used with the terminating device.

Copper and Aluminum Mixed. Copper and aluminum conductors must not make contact with each other in a device unless the device is listed and identified for this purpose. ▶Figure 110–12

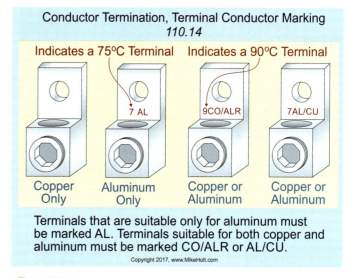

▶Figure 110–12

Author's Comment:

- Few terminations are listed for the mixing of aluminum and copper conductors, but if they are, that will be marked on the product package or terminal device. The reason copper and aluminum shouldn't be in contact with each other is because corrosion develops between the two different metals due to galvanic action, resulting in increased contact resistance at the splicing device. This increased resistance can cause the splice to overheat and cause a fire.

(A) Terminations. Conductor terminals must ensure a good connection without damaging the conductors.

Terminals for more than one conductor and terminals used for aluminum conductors must be identified for this purpose, either within the equipment instructions or on the terminal itself. ▶Figure 110–13

Author's Comment:

- Split-bolt connectors are commonly listed for only two conductors, although some are listed for three conductors. However, it's a common industry practice to terminate as many conductors as possible within a split-bolt connector, even though this violates the *NEC*. ▶Figure 110–14

110.14 | Requirements for Electrical Installations

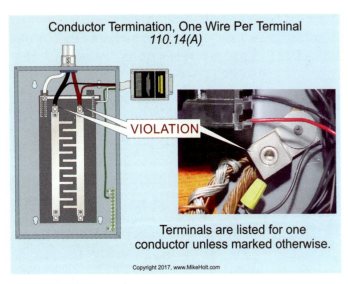
▶Figure 110–13

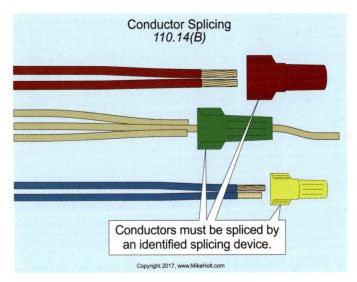
▶Figure 110–15

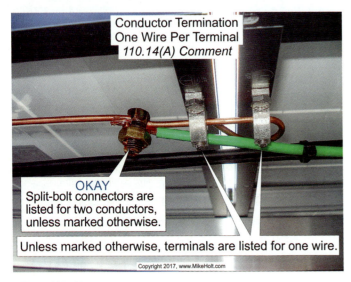
▶Figure 110–14

(B) Conductor Splices. Conductors must be spliced by a splicing device identified for the purpose or by exothermic welding. ▶Figure 110–15

Author's Comment:

- Conductors aren't required to be twisted together prior to the installation of a twist-on wire connector, unless specifically required in the installation instructions. ▶Figure 110–16

- Unused circuit conductors aren't required to be removed. However, to prevent an electrical hazard, the free ends of the conductors must be insulated to prevent the exposed end of the conductor from touching energized parts. This requirement can be met by the use of an insulated twist-on or push-on wire connector. ▶Figure 110–17

- See the definition of "Energized" in Article 100.

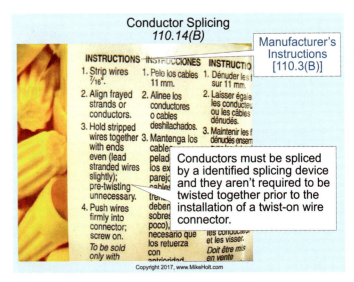
▶Figure 110–16

Requirements for Electrical Installations | 110.14

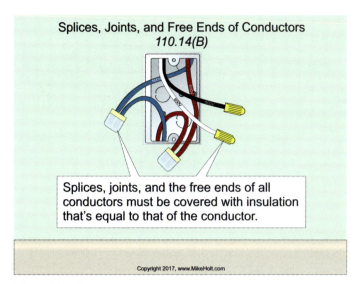

▶Figure 110–17

Underground Splices, Single Conductors. Single direct burial conductors of types UF or USE can be spliced underground without a junction box, but the conductors must be spliced with a device listed for direct burial [300.5(E) and 300.15(G)]. ▶Figure 110–18

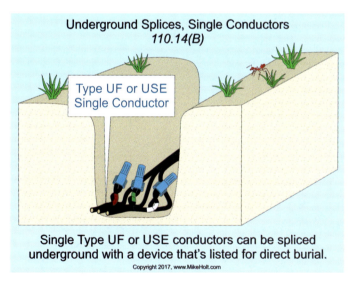

▶Figure 110–18

Underground Splices, Multiconductor Cable. Multiconductor UF or USE cable can have the individual conductors spliced underground without a junction box as long as a listed splice kit that encapsulates the conductors as well as the cable jacket is used.

(D) Torque. Where tightening torque values are indicated on equipment or installation instructions, a calibrated torque tool must be used to achieve the indicated torque value, unless the equipment manufacturer provides an alternative method of achieving the required torque.
▶Figure 110–19

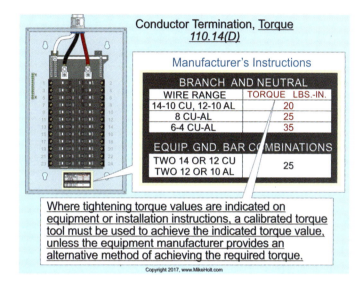

▶Figure 110–19

Author's Comment:

- Conductors must terminate in devices that have been properly tightened in accordance with the manufacturer's torque specifications included with equipment instructions. Failure to torque terminals properly can result in excessive heating of terminals or splicing devices due to a loose connection. A loose connection can also lead to arcing which increases the heating effect and may also lead to a short circuit or ground fault. Any of these can result in a fire or other failure, including an arc-flash event. In addition, this is a violation of 110.3(B), which requires all equipment to be installed in accordance with listing or labeling instructions.

Notes

CHAPTER 1 PRACTICE QUESTIONS

Please use the 2017 *Code* book to answer the following questions.

Article 100. Definitions

1. "_____" means acceptable to the authority having jurisdiction.

   (a) Identified
   (b) Listed
   (c) Approved
   (d) Labeled

2. In many circumstances, the authority having jurisdiction can be a property owner or his/her designated agent.

   (a) True
   (b) False

3. "Bonded" is defined as _____ to establish electrical continuity and conductivity.

   (a) isolated
   (b) guarded
   (c) connected
   (d) separated

4. A reliable conductor that ensures electrical conductivity between metal parts of the electrical installation that are required to be electrically connected is called a(n) "_____."

   (a) grounding electrode
   (b) auxiliary ground
   (c) bonding conductor or jumper
   (d) tap conductor

5. The connection between the grounded circuit conductor and the equipment grounding conductor at the service is accomplished by installing a(n) _____ bonding jumper.

   (a) main
   (b) system
   (c) equipment
   (d) circuit

6. An enclosure designed for either surface mounting or flush mounting provided with a frame in which a door(s) can be hung is called a(n) "_____."

   (a) enclosure
   (b) outlet box
   (c) cutout box
   (d) cabinet

7. A solderless pressure connector is a device that _____ between two or more conductors or between one or more conductors and a terminal by means of mechanical pressure and without the use of solder.

   (a) provides access
   (b) protects the wiring
   (c) is never needed
   (d) establishes a connection

8. A(n) _____ is a device, or group of devices, by which the conductors of a circuit can be disconnected from their source of supply.

   (a) feeder
   (b) enclosure
   (c) disconnecting means
   (d) conductor interrupter

Chapter 1 | Practice Questions

9. As used in the *NEC*, equipment includes _____.
   (a) fittings
   (b) appliances
   (c) machinery
   (d) all of these

10. As applied to wiring methods, "on or attached to the surface, or behind access panels designed to allow access" is known as _____.
    (a) open
    (b) uncovered
    (c) exposed
    (d) bare

11. An accessory, such as a locknut, intended primarily to perform a mechanical function rather than an electrical function best describes _____.
    (a) a part
    (b) equipment
    (c) a device
    (d) a fitting

12. The word "Earth" best describes what *NEC* term?
    (a) Bonded.
    (b) Ground.
    (c) Effective ground-fault current path.
    (d) Guarded.

13. A(n) _____ is an unintentional, electrically conductive connection between an ungrounded conductor of an electrical circuit, and the normally noncurrent-carrying conductors, metallic enclosures, metallic raceways, metallic equipment, or earth.
    (a) grounded conductor
    (b) ground fault
    (c) equipment ground
    (d) bonding jumper

14. Connected (connecting) to ground or to a conductive body that extends the ground connection is called "_____."
    (a) equipment grounding
    (b) bonded
    (c) grounded
    (d) all of these

15. A system or circuit conductor that is intentionally grounded is called a(n) "_____."
    (a) grounding conductor
    (b) unidentified conductor
    (c) grounded conductor
    (d) grounding electrode conductor

16. A device intended for the protection of personnel that functions to de-energize a circuit or portion thereof within an established period of time when the current to ground exceeds the values established for a Class A device, is a(n) "_____."
    (a) dual-element fuse
    (b) inverse time breaker
    (c) ground-fault circuit interrupter
    (d) safety switch

17. A Class A GFCI protection device is designed to trip when the current to ground is _____ or higher.
    (a) 4 mA
    (b) 5 mA
    (c) 6 mA
    (d) 7 mA

18. A ground-fault current path is an electrically conductive path from the point of a ground fault through normally noncurrent-carrying conductors, equipment, or the earth to the _____.
    (a) ground
    (b) earth
    (c) electrical supply source
    (d) none of these

19. A system intended to provide protection of equipment from damaging line-to-ground fault currents by causing a disconnecting means to open all ungrounded conductors of the faulted circuit at current levels less than the supply circuit overcurrent device defines "_____."
    (a) ground-fault protection of equipment
    (b) guarded
    (c) personal protection
    (d) automatic protection

20. The installed conductive path(s) that provide(s) a ground-fault current path and connects normally noncurrent-carrying metal parts of equipment together and to the system grounded conductor or to the grounding electrode conductor, or both, is known as a(n) "_____ conductor."

    (a) grounding electrode
    (b) grounding
    (c) equipment grounding
    (d) none of these

21. A conducting object through which a direct connection to earth is established is a "_____."

    (a) bonding conductor
    (b) grounding conductor
    (c) grounding electrode
    (d) grounded conductor

22. A conductor used to connect the system grounded conductor or the equipment to a grounding electrode or to a point on the grounding electrode system is called the "_____ conductor."

    (a) main grounding
    (b) common main
    (c) equipment grounding
    (d) grounding electrode

23. Recognized as suitable for the specific purpose, function, use, environment, and application is the definition of "_____."

    (a) labeled
    (b) identified (as applied to equipment)
    (c) listed
    (d) approved

24. An interactive inverter is an inverter intended for use in parallel with a(n) _____ to supply common loads that may deliver power to the utility.

    (a) electric utility
    (b) photovoltaic (PV) system
    (c) battery
    (d) none of these

25. A device that provides a means to connect intersystem bonding conductors for _____ systems to the grounding electrode system is an intersystem bonding termination.

    (a) limited-energy
    (b) low-voltage
    (c) communications
    (d) power and lighting

26. Equipment or materials to which a label, symbol, or other identifying mark of a product evaluation organization that is acceptable to the authority having jurisdiction has been attached is known as "_____."

    (a) listed
    (b) labeled
    (c) approved
    (d) identified

27. The term "Luminaire" means a single individual lampholder by itself.

    (a) True
    (b) False

28. A neutral conductor is the conductor connected to the _____ of a system, which is intended to carry current under normal conditions.

    (a) grounding electrode
    (b) neutral point
    (c) intersystem bonding termination
    (d) none of these

29. The common point on a wye-connection in a polyphase system is a "neutral point."

    (a) True
    (b) False

30. A _____ is the total components and subsystem that, in combination, convert solar energy into electric energy for connection to a utilization load.

    (a) photovoltaic system
    (b) solar array
    (c) a and b
    (d) none of these

31. Premises wiring includes _____ wiring from the service point or power source to the outlets.
    (a) interior
    (b) exterior
    (c) underground
    (d) a and b

32. A contact device installed at an outlet for the connection of an attachment plug, or for the direct connection of electrical utilization equipment designed to mate with the corresponding contact device, is known as a(n) "_____."
    (a) attachment point
    (b) tap
    (c) receptacle
    (d) wall plug

33. A single receptacle is a single contact device with no other contact device on the same _____.
    (a) circuit
    (b) yoke
    (c) run
    (d) equipment

34. A(n) _____ system is an electrical source, other than a service, having no direct connection(s) to circuit conductors of any other electrical source other than those established by grounding and bonding connections.
    (a) separately derived
    (b) classified
    (c) direct
    (d) emergency

35. The conductors and equipment for delivering electric energy from the serving utility to the wiring system of the premises served is called a "_____."
    (a) branch circuit
    (b) feeder
    (c) service
    (d) none of these

36. The _____ is the necessary equipment, usually consisting of a circuit breaker(s) or switch(es) and fuse(s) and their accessories, connected to the load end of service conductors, and intended to constitute the main control and cutoff of the supply.
    (a) service equipment
    (b) service
    (c) service disconnect
    (d) service overcurrent device

37. Special permission is the written consent from the _____.
    (a) testing laboratory
    (b) manufacturer
    (c) owner
    (d) authority having jurisdiction

38. "Ungrounded" means not connected to ground or to a conductive body that extends the ground connection.
    (a) True
    (b) False

Article 110. Requirements for Electrical Installations

39. In judging equipment for approval, considerations such as _____ shall be evaluated.
    (a) mechanical strength
    (b) wire-bending space
    (c) arcing effects
    (d) all of these

40. Listed or labeled equipment shall be installed and used in accordance with any instructions included in the listing or labeling.
    (a) True
    (b) False

41. Wiring shall be installed so that the completed system will be free from _____, other than as required or permitted elsewhere in the *Code*.
    (a) short circuits
    (b) ground faults
    (c) connections to the earth
    (d) all of these

42. The *NEC* requires that electrical equipment be _____.

    (a) installed in a neat and workmanlike manner
    (b) installed under the supervision of a licensed person
    (c) completed before being inspected
    (d) all of these

43. Conductor terminal and splicing devices shall be _____ for the conductor material and they shall be properly installed and used.

    (a) listed
    (b) approved
    (c) identified
    (d) all of these

44. Connectors and terminals for conductors more finely stranded than Class B and Class C, as shown in Table 10 of 9, shall be _____ for the specific conductor class or classes.

    (a) listed
    (b) approved
    (c) identified
    (d) all of these

45. Connection of conductors to terminal parts shall ensure a thoroughly good connection without damaging the conductors and shall be made by means of _____.

    (a) solder lugs
    (b) pressure connectors
    (c) splices to flexible leads
    (d) any of these

46. Connection by means of wire-binding screws, studs, and nuts having upturned lugs or the equivalent shall be permitted for _____ AWG or smaller conductors.

    (a) 12
    (b) 10
    (c) 8
    (d) 6

47. Where a tightening torque is indicated as a numeric value on equipment or in installation instructions provided by the manufacturer, a(n) _____ torque tool shall be used to achieve the indicated torque value, unless the equipment manufacturer has provided installation instructions for an alternative method of achieving the required torque.

    (a) calibrated
    (b) identified
    (c) adjustable
    (d) listed

Notes

CHAPTER 2
WIRING AND PROTECTION

Introduction to Chapter 2—Wiring and Protection

Chapter 2 provides general rules for wiring and for the overcurrent protection of conductors. The rules in this chapter apply to all electrical installations covered by the *NEC*—except as modified in Chapters 5, 6, and 7 [90.3].

Communications systems (twisted wire, antennas, and coaxial cable) (Chapter 8 systems) aren't subject to the general requirements of Chapters 1 through 4, or the special requirements of Chapters 5 through 7, unless there's a specific reference in Chapter 8 to a rule in Chapters 1 through 7 [90.3].

As you go through Chapter 2, remember its purpose. It's primarily concerned with correctly sizing and protecting circuits. Every article in this chapter deals with a different aspect of this purpose. This differs from the purpose of Chapter 3, which is to correctly install the conductors that make up those circuits.

Chapter 1 introduced you to the *NEC* and provided a solid foundation for understanding the *Code*. Chapter 2 (Wiring and Protection) and Chapter 3 (Wiring Methods and Materials) continue building the foundation for applying the *NEC*. Chapter 4 applies the preceding chapters to general equipment. It's beneficial to learn the first four chapters of the *Code* in a sequential manner because each of the first four chapters builds on the one before it. Once you've become familiar with the first four chapters, you can learn the next four in any order you wish.

- **Article 250—Grounding and Bonding.** Article 250 covers the grounding requirements for providing a path to the earth to reduce overvoltage from lightning, and the bonding requirements for a low-impedance fault current path necessary to facilitate the operation of overcurrent protection devices in the event of a ground fault.

Notes

ARTICLE 250 GROUNDING AND BONDING

Introduction to Article 250—Grounding and Bonding

No other article can match Article 250 for misapplication, violation, and misinterpretation. Terminology used in this article has been a source for much confusion, but that's improved during the last few *NEC* revisions. It's very important to understand the difference between grounding and bonding in order to correctly apply the provisions of Article 250. Pay careful attention to the definitions that apply to grounding and bonding both here and in Article 100 as you begin the study of this important article. Article 250 covers the grounding requirements for providing a path to the earth to reduce overvoltage from lightning, and the bonding requirements for a low-impedance fault current path back to the source of the electrical supply to facilitate the operation of overcurrent protection devices in the event of a ground fault.

Over the past several *Code* cycles, this article was extensively revised to organize it better and make it easier to understand and implement. It's arranged in a logical manner, so it's a good idea to just read through Article 250 to get a big picture view—after you review the definitions. Next, study the article closely so you understand the details. The illustrations will help you understand the key points.

Part I. General

250.1 Scope

Article 250 contains the following grounding and bonding requirements:

(1) What systems and equipment are required to be grounded.

(3) Location of grounding connections.

(4) Types of electrodes and sizes of grounding and bonding conductors.

(5) Methods of grounding and bonding.

250.2 Definition

Bonding Jumper, Supply-Side. The conductor on the supply side of the service or separately derived system overcurrent protection device that ensures electrical conductivity between metal parts and the grounded conductor. ▶Figure 250–1, ▶Figure 250–2, and ▶Figure 250–3

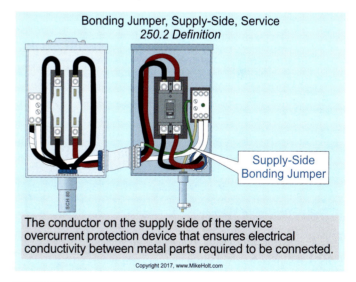

▶Figure 250–1

250.4 | Grounding and Bonding

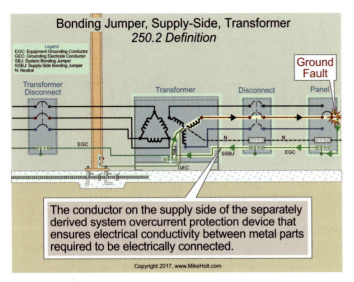

▶Figure 250–2

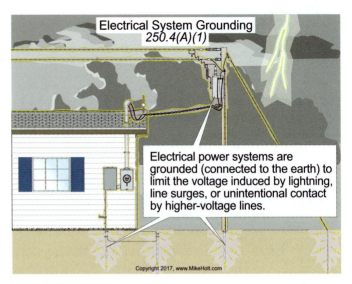

▶Figure 250–4

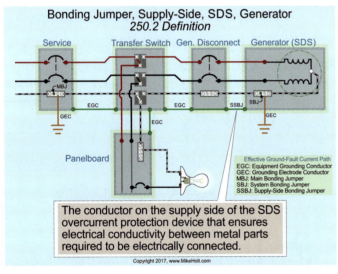

▶Figure 250–3

250.4 Performance Requirements for Grounding and Bonding

(A) Solidly Grounded Systems.

 Scan this QR code for a video of Mike explaining this topic; it's a sample from the DVDs that accompany this textbook.

(1) Electrical System Grounding. Electrical power systems are grounded (connected to the earth) to limit the voltage induced by lightning, line surges, or unintentional contact by higher-voltage lines. ▶Figure 250–4

Author's Comment:

- System grounding helps reduce fires in buildings as well as voltage stress on electrical insulation, thereby ensuring longer insulation life for motors, transformers, and other system components. ▶Figure 250–5

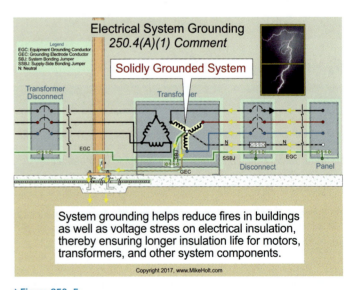

▶Figure 250–5

Note 1: To limit imposed voltage, the grounding electrode conductors shouldn't be any longer than necessary and unnecessary bends and loops should be avoided. ▶Figure 250–6

Grounding and Bonding | 250.4

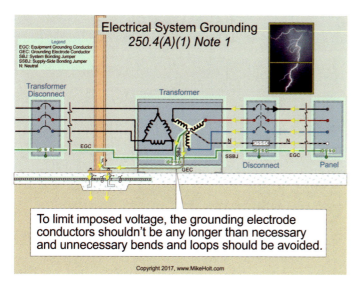

▶Figure 250–6

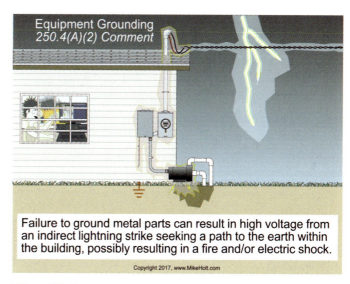

▶Figure 250–8

Note 2: See NFPA 780, *Standard for the Installation of Lightning Protection Systems* for grounding and bonding of lightning protection systems.

(2) Equipment Grounding. Metal parts of electrical equipment are grounded to reduce arcing within the buildings/structures from induced voltage from indirect lightning strikes. ▶Figure 250–7

Author's Comment:

- Grounding metal parts helps drain off static electricity charges before flashover potential is reached. Static grounding is often used in areas where the discharge (arcing) of the voltage buildup (static) can cause dangerous or undesirable conditions [500.4 Note 3].

(3) Equipment Bonding. Metal parts of electrical raceways, cables, enclosures, and equipment must be connected to the supply source via an effective ground-fault current path. ▶Figure 250–9

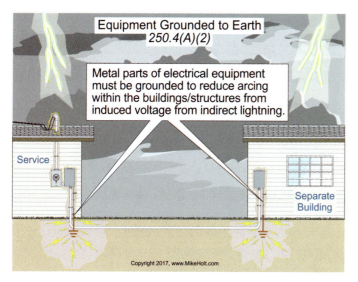

▶Figure 250–7

DANGER: *Failure to ground metal parts to earth can result in induced voltage on metal parts from an indirect lightning strike seeking a path to the earth within the building—possibly resulting in a fire and/or electric shock from a side flash.* ▶Figure 250–8

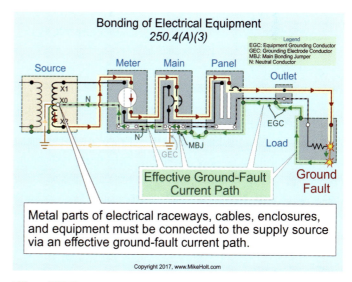

▶Figure 250–9

250.4 | Grounding and Bonding

Author's Comment:

- To quickly remove dangerous voltage on metal parts from a ground fault, the effective ground-fault current path must have sufficiently low impedance to the source so fault current will quickly rise to a level that will open the branch-circuit overcurrent protection device. ▶Figure 250–10

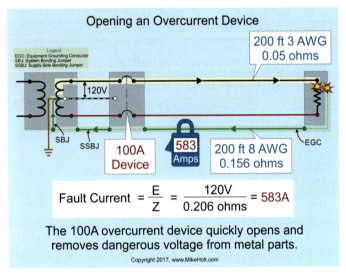

▶Figure 250–10

- The time it takes for an overcurrent protection device to open is dependent on the magnitude of the fault current. A higher fault current value will result in a shorter clearing time for the overcurrent protection device. For example, a 20A overcurrent protection device with an overload of 40A (two times the 20A rating) takes 25 to 150 seconds to open. The same device at 100A (five times the 20A rating) trips in 5 to 20 seconds. ▶Figure 250–11

(4) Bonding Conductive Materials. Electrically conductive materials likely to become energized, such as metal water piping systems, metal sprinkler piping, metal gas piping, and other metal-piping systems, as well as exposed structural steel members, must be connected to the supply source via an effective ground-fault current path. ▶Figure 250–12

Author's Comment:

- The phrase "likely to become energized" is subject to interpretation by the authority having jurisdiction.

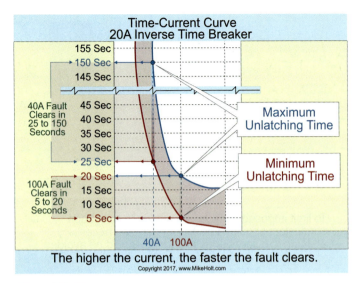

▶Figure 250–11

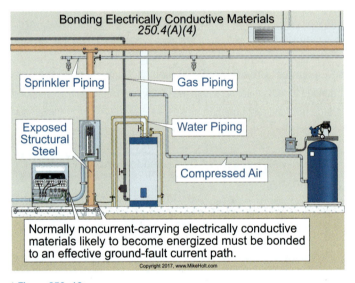

▶Figure 250–12

(5) Effective Ground-Fault Current Path. Metal parts of electrical raceways, cables, enclosures, or equipment must be bonded together and to the supply source in a manner that creates a low-impedance path for ground-fault current that facilitates the operation of the circuit overcurrent protection device. ▶Figure 250–13

Author's Comment:

- To ensure a low-impedance ground-fault current path, all circuit conductors must be grouped together in the same raceway, cable, or trench [300.3(B), 300.5(I), and 300.20(A)]. ▶Figure 250–14

Grounding and Bonding | 250.4

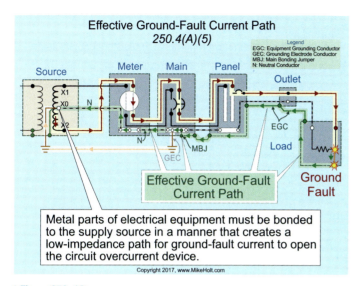

▶Figure 250–13

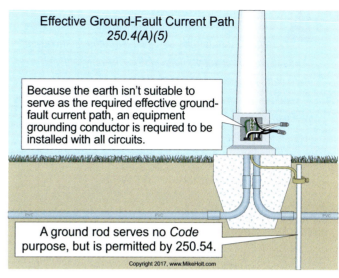

▶Figure 250–15

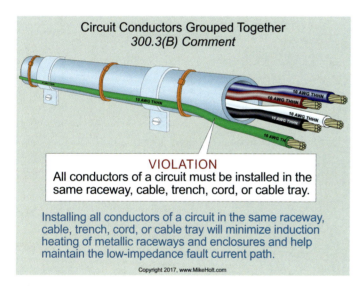

▶Figure 250–14

Because the earth isn't a low impedance path for fault current, it isn't suitable to serve as the required effective ground-fault current path, therefore an equipment grounding conductor of a type recognized in 250.118 is required to be installed with all circuits. ▶Figure 250–15

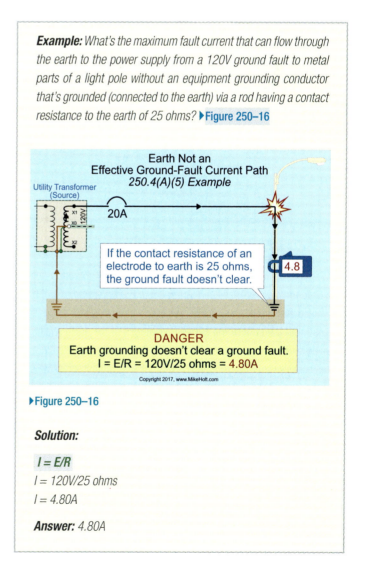

▶Figure 250–16

Solution:

$I = E/R$

$I = 120V/25\ ohms$

$I = 4.80A$

Answer: 4.80A

250.4 | Grounding and Bonding

DANGER: Because the contact resistance of an electrode to the earth is so high, very little fault current returns to the power supply if the earth is the only fault current return path. ▶Figure 250–17

Result—the circuit overcurrent protection device won't open and all metal parts associated with the electrical installation, metal piping, and structural building steel will become and remain energized.

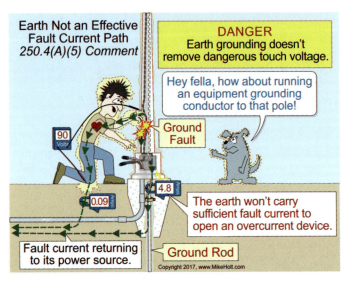

▶Figure 250–17

Since voltage is directly proportional to resistance, the voltage gradient of the earth around an energized rod, assuming a 120V ground fault, will be as follows: ▶Figure 250–18 and ▶Figure 250–19

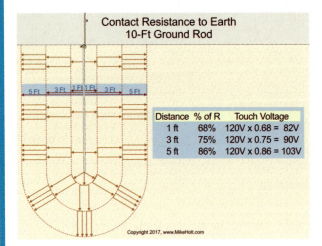

▶Figure 250–18

Earth Shells

According to ANSI/IEEE 142, *Recommended Practice for Grounding of Industrial and Commercial Power Systems* (Green Book) [4.1.1], the resistance of the soil outward from a rod is equal to the sum of the series resistances of the earth shells. The shell nearest the rod has the highest resistance and each successive shell has progressively larger areas and progressively lower resistances. Don't be concerned if you don't understand this statement; just review the table below.

Distance from Rod	Soil Contact Resistance
1 ft (Shell 1)	68% of total contact resistance
3 ft (Shells 1 and 2)	75% of total contact resistance
5 ft (Shells 1, 2, and 3)	86% of total contact resistance

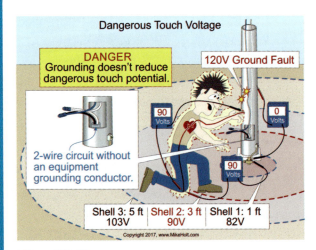

▶Figure 250–19

Distance from Rod	Soil Contact Resistance	Voltage Gradient
1 ft (Shell 1)	68%	82V
3 ft (Shells 1 and 2)	75%	90V
5 ft (Shells 1, 2, and 3)	86%	103V

(B) Ungrounded Systems.

 Scan this QR code for a video of Mike explaining this topic; it's a sample from the DVDs that accompany this textbook.

Author's Comment:

- Ungrounded systems are those systems with no connection to the ground or to a conductive body that extends the ground connection [Article 100]. ▶Figure 250–20

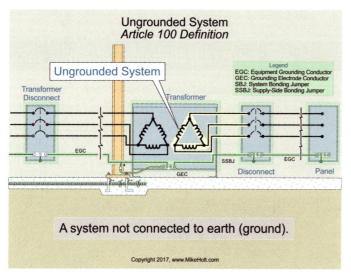

▶Figure 250–20

(1) Equipment Grounding. Metal parts of electrical equipment are grounded (connected to the earth) to reduce induced voltage on metal parts from lightning so as to prevent fires from an arc within the buildings. ▶Figure 250–21

Note 2: See NFPA 780, *Standard for the Installation of Lightning Protection Systems* for grounding and bonding of lightning protection systems.

Author's Comment:

- Grounding metal parts helps drain off static electricity charges before an electric arc takes place (flashover potential). Static grounding is often used in areas where the discharge (arcing) of the voltage buildup (static) can cause dangerous or undesirable conditions [500.4 Note 3].

⚠️ **CAUTION:** *Connecting metal parts to the earth (grounding) serves no purpose in electrical shock protection.*

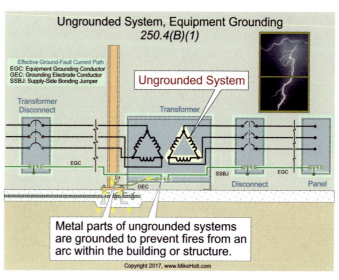

▶Figure 250–21

(2) Equipment Bonding. Metal parts of electrical raceways, cables, enclosures, or equipment must be bonded together in a manner that creates a low-impedance path for ground-fault current to facilitate the operation of the circuit overcurrent protection device. ▶Figure 250–22

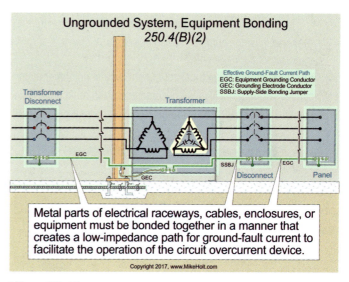

▶Figure 250–22

The fault current path must be capable of safely carrying the maximum ground-fault current likely to be imposed on it from any point on the wiring system should a ground fault occur to the electrical supply source.

(3) Bonding Conductive Materials. Conductive materials such as metal water piping systems, metal sprinkler piping, metal gas piping, and other metal-piping systems, as well as exposed structural steel members

250.6 | Grounding and Bonding

likely to become energized must be bonded together in a manner that creates a low-impedance fault current path that's capable of carrying the maximum fault current likely to be imposed on it. ▶Figure 250–23

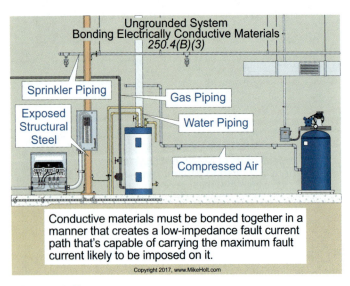

▶Figure 250–23

Author's Comment:

- The phrase "likely to become energized" is subject to interpretation by the authority having jurisdiction.

(4) Fault Current Path. Electrical equipment, wiring, and other electrically conductive material likely to become energized must be installed in a manner that creates a low-impedance fault current path to facilitate the operation of overcurrent protection devices should a second ground fault from a different phase occur. ▶Figure 250–24

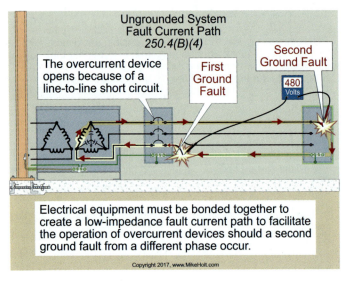

▶Figure 250–24

Author's Comment:

- A single ground fault can't be cleared on an ungrounded system because there's no low-impedance fault current path to the electric power source. The first ground fault simply grounds the system and initiates the ground detector. However, a second ground fault on a different phase results in a line-to-line short circuit between the two ground faults. The conductive path, between the ground faults, provides the low-impedance fault current path necessary so the overcurrent protection device will open.

250.6 Objectionable Current

(A) Preventing Objectionable Current. To prevent a fire, electric shock, or improper operation of circuit overcurrent protection devices or electronic equipment, electrical systems and equipment must be installed in a manner that prevents objectionable neutral current from flowing on metal parts. ▶Figure 250–25

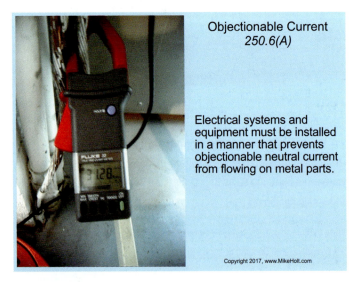

▶Figure 250–25

(B) Stopping Objectionable Current. If the use of multiple grounding connections results in objectionable current and the requirements of 250.4(A)(5) or (B)(4) are met, one or more of the following alterations are permitted:

(1) Discontinue one or more but not all of such grounding connections.

(2) Change the locations of the grounding connections.

(3) Interrupt the continuity of the conductor or conductive path causing the objectionable current.

(4) Take other suitable remedial and approved action.

(C) Temporary Currents Not Classified as Objectionable Currents. Temporary currents from abnormal conditions, such as ground faults, aren't to be classified as objectionable current. ▶Figure 250–26

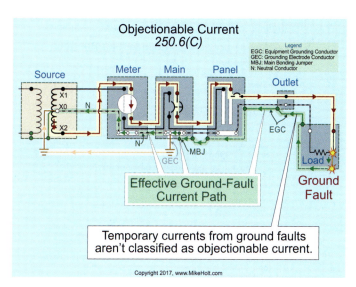

▶Figure 250–26

Objectionable Current

Objectionable neutral current occurs because of improper neutral-to-case connections or wiring errors that violate 250.142(B).

Improper Neutral-to-Case Connection [250.142]

Panelboards. Objectionable neutral current will flow on metal parts and the equipment grounding conductor when the neutral conductor is connected to the metal case of a panelboard on the load side of service equipment. ▶Figure 250–27

Separately Derived Systems. Objectionable neutral current will flow on metal parts if the neutral conductor is connected to the circuit equipment grounding conductor on the load side of the system bonding jumper for a separately derived system. ▶Figure 250–28

Generator. Objectionable neutral current will flow on metal parts and the equipment grounding conductor if a generator is connected to a transfer switch with a solidly connected neutral and a neutral-to-case connection is made at the generator. ▶Figure 250–29

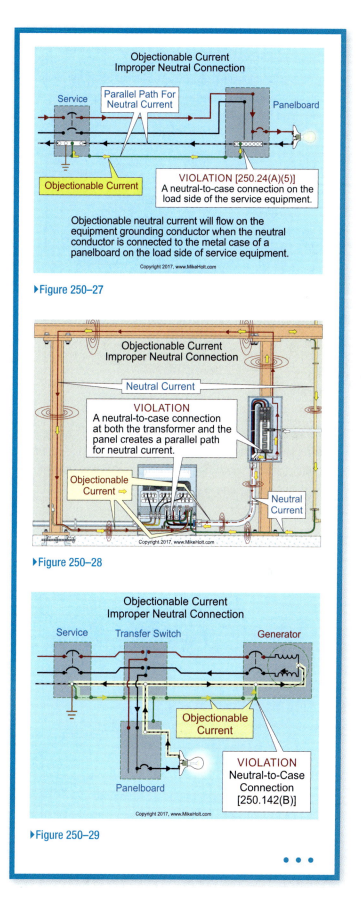

▶Figure 250–27

▶Figure 250–28

▶Figure 250–29

250.6 | Grounding and Bonding

Disconnects. Objectionable neutral current will flow on metal parts and the equipment grounding conductor when the neutral conductor is connected to the metal case of a disconnect that's not part of the service equipment. ▶Figure 250–30

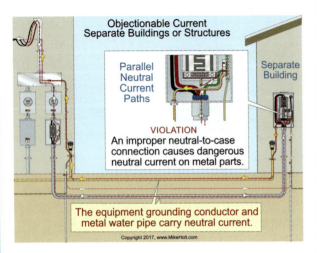

▶Figure 250–30

Wiring Errors. Objectionable neutral current will flow on metal parts and equipment grounding conductors when the neutral conductor from one system is used as the neutral conductor for a different system. ▶Figure 250–31

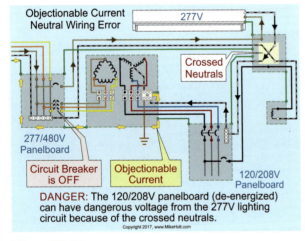

▶Figure 250–31

Objectionable neutral current will flow on the equipment grounding conductor when the circuit equipment grounding conductor is used as a neutral conductor such as where:

- A 230V time-clock motor is replaced with a 115V time-clock motor, and the circuit equipment grounding conductor is used for neutral return current.

- A 115V water filter is wired to a 240V well-pump motor circuit, and the circuit equipment grounding conductor is used for neutral return current. ▶Figure 250–32

- The circuit equipment grounding conductor is used for neutral return current. ▶Figure 250–33

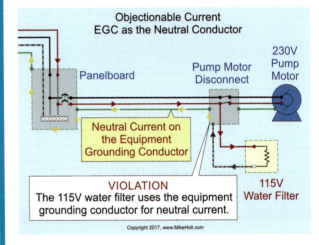

▶Figure 250–32

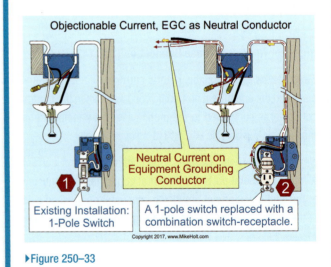

▶Figure 250–33

Dangers of Objectionable Current

Objectionable neutral current on metal parts can cause electric shock, fires, and improper operation of electronic equipment and overcurrent protection devices such as GFPs, GFCIs, and AFCIs.

Shock Hazard. When objectionable neutral current flows on metal parts or the equipment grounding conductor, electric shock and even death can occur from the elevated voltage on those metal parts. ▶Figure 250–34 and ▶Figure 250–35

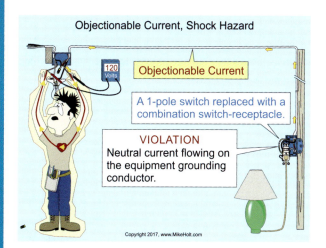

▶Figure 250–34

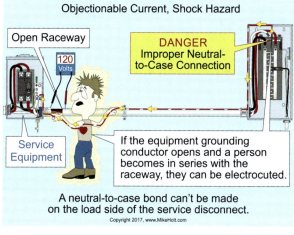

▶Figure 250–35

Fire Hazard. When objectionable neutral current flows on metal parts, a fire can ignite adjacent combustible material. Heat is generated whenever current flows, particularly over high-resistance parts. In addition, arcing at loose connections is especially dangerous in areas containing easily ignitible and explosive gases, vapors, or dust. ▶Figure 250–36

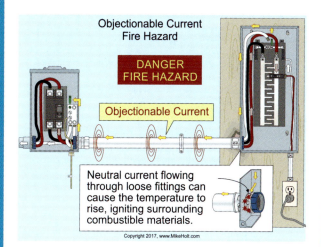

▶Figure 250–36

Improper Operation of Electronic Equipment. Objectionable neutral current flowing on metal parts of electrical equipment and building parts can cause electromagnetic fields which negatively affect the performance of electronic devices, particularly medical equipment. ▶Figure 250–37

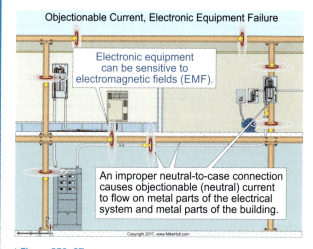

▶Figure 250–37

For more information, visit www.MikeHolt.com, click on the "Technical" link, and then on "Power Quality."

When a solidly grounded system is properly bonded, the voltage of all metal parts to the earth and to each other will be zero. ▶Figure 250–38

250.8 | Grounding and Bonding

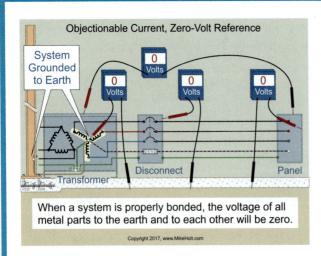

▶Figure 250–38

When objectionable neutral current travels on metal parts and equipment grounding conductors because of the improper bonding of the neutral to metal parts, a difference of voltage will exist between all metal parts. This situation can cause some electronic equipment to operate improperly. ▶Figure 250–39

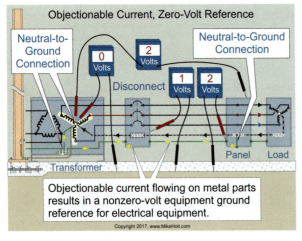

▶Figure 250–39

Operation of Overcurrent Protection Devices. When objectionable neutral current travels on metal parts, tripping of electronic overcurrent protection devices equipped with ground-fault protection can occur because some neutral current flows on the circuit equipment grounding conductor instead of the neutral conductor.

250.8 Termination of Grounding and Bonding Conductors

(A) Permitted Methods. Equipment grounding conductors, grounding electrode conductors, and bonding jumpers must terminate in one or more of the following methods:

(1) Listed pressure connectors

(2) Terminal bars

(3) Pressure connectors listed for grounding and bonding

(4) Exothermic welding

(5) Machine screws that engage at least two threads or are secured with a nut, ▶Figure 250–40

(6) Self-tapping machine screws that engage at least two threads ▶Figure 250–41

(7) Connections that are part of a listed assembly

(8) Other listed means

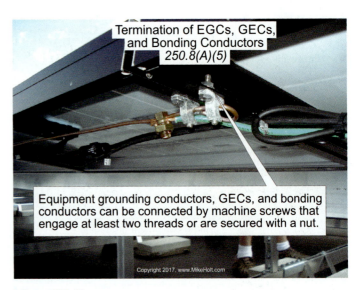

▶Figure 250–40

Grounding and Bonding | 250.20

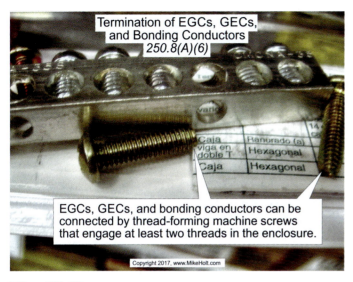

▶Figure 250–41

(B) **Methods Not Permitted.** Connection devices or fittings that depend solely on solder aren't allowed.

250.10 Protection of Fittings

Where subject to physical damage, grounding and bonding fittings must be protected by enclosing the fittings in metal, wood, or an equivalent protective covering. ▶Figure 250–42

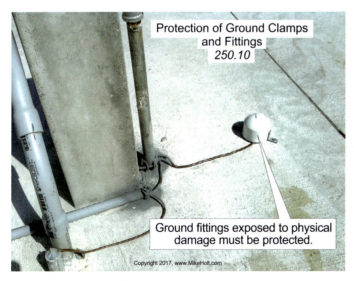

▶Figure 250–42

250.12 Clean Surfaces

Nonconductive coatings, such as paint, must be removed to ensure good electrical continuity, or the termination fittings must be designed so as to make such removal unnecessary [250.53(A) and 250.96(A)].

Author's Comment:

- Tarnish on copper water pipe needn't be removed before making a termination.

Part II. System Grounding and Bonding

250.20 Systems Required to be Grounded

(A) Systems Below 50V. Systems operating below 50V aren't required to be grounded or bonded in accordance with 250.30 unless the transformer's primary supply is from: ▶Figure 250–43

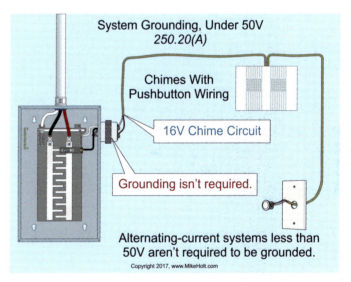

▶Figure 250–43

(1) A 277V or 480V system.

(2) An ungrounded system.

(B) Systems 50V to 1,000V. The following systems must be grounded (connected to the earth):

(1) Single-phase systems where the neutral conductor is used as a circuit conductor. ▶Figure 250–44

250.21 | Grounding and Bonding

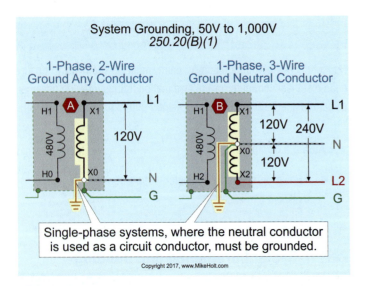

▶Figure 250–44

(2) Three-phase, wye-connected systems where the neutral conductor is used as a circuit conductor. ▶Figure 250–45

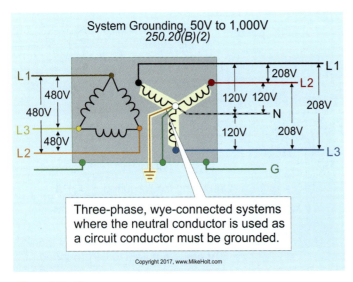

▶Figure 250–45

(3) Three-phase, high-leg delta-connected systems where the neutral conductor is used as a circuit conductor. ▶Figure 250–46

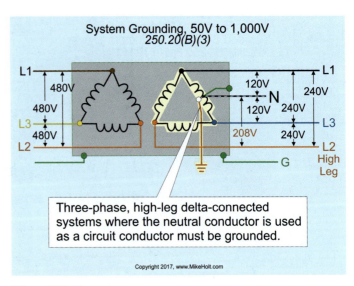

▶Figure 250–46

250.21 Ungrounded Systems

(B) Ground Detectors. Ungrounded systems must have ground detectors installed as close as practicable to where the system receives its supply. ▶Figure 250–47

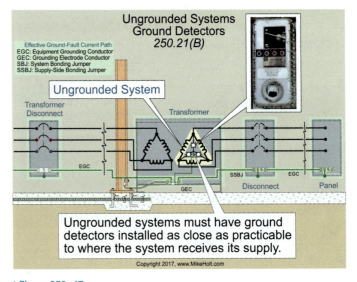

▶Figure 250–47

(C) Marking. Ungrounded systems must be legibly marked "Caution Ungrounded System Operating—____ Volts Between Conductors" at the source or first disconnect of the system, with sufficient durability to withstand the environment involved. ▶Figure 250–48

Grounding and Bonding | 250.24

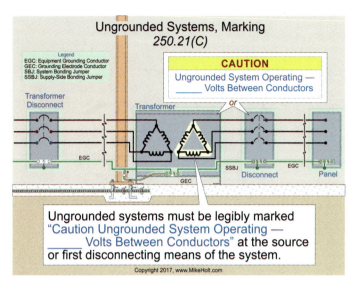

▶Figure 250–48

250.24 Service Equipment— Grounding and Bonding

(A) Grounded System. Service equipment supplied from a grounded system must have the grounding electrode conductor terminate in accordance with (1) through (5).

(1) Grounding Location. A grounding electrode conductor must connect the service neutral conductor to the grounding electrode at any accessible location, from the load end of the overhead service conductors, service drop, underground service conductors, or service lateral, up to and including the service disconnect. ▶Figure 250–49

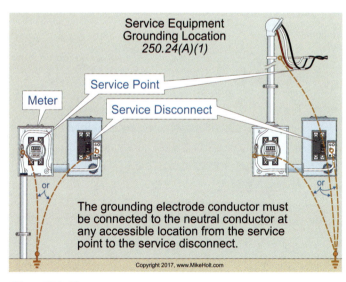

▶Figure 250–49

Author's Comment:

- Some inspectors require the service neutral conductor to be grounded (connected to the earth) from the meter socket enclosure, while other inspectors insist that it be grounded (connected to the earth) only from the service disconnect. Grounding at either location complies with this rule.

(4) Grounding Termination. When the service neutral conductor is connected to the service disconnect [250.24(B)] by a wire or busbar [250.28], the grounding electrode conductor can terminate to either the neutral terminal or the equipment grounding terminal within the service disconnect.

(5) Neutral-to-Case Connection. A neutral-to-case connection isn't permitted on the load side of service equipment, except as permitted by 250.142(B). ▶Figure 250–50

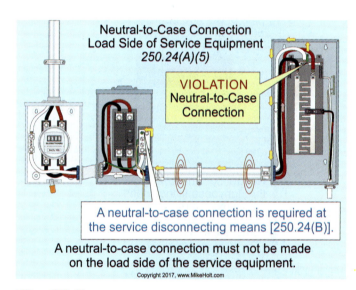

▶Figure 250–50

Author's Comment:

- If a neutral-to-case connection is made on the load side of service equipment, dangerous objectionable neutral current will flow on conductive metal parts of electrical equipment [250.6(A)]. Objectionable neutral current on metal parts of electrical equipment can cause electric shock and even death from ventricular fibrillation, as well as a fire. ▶Figure 250–51 and ▶Figure 250–52

250.24 | Grounding and Bonding

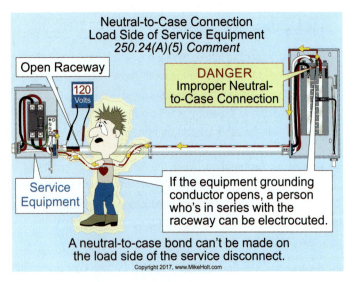
▶Figure 250–51

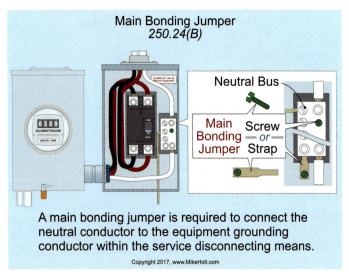
▶Figure 250–53

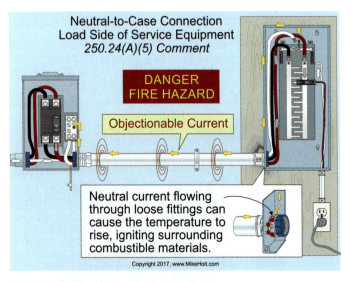
▶Figure 250–52

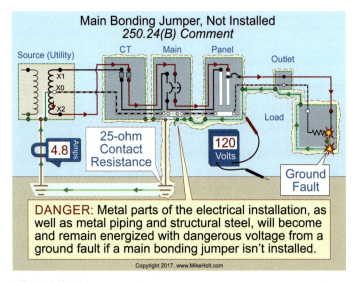
▶Figure 250–54

(B) Main Bonding Jumper. A main bonding jumper [250.28] is required to connect the neutral conductor to the equipment grounding conductor within the service disconnect. ▶Figure 250–53 and ▶Figure 250–54

(C) Neutral Conductor Brought to Service Equipment. A service neutral conductor must be run from the electric utility power supply with the ungrounded conductors and terminate to the service disconnect neutral terminal. A main bonding jumper [250.24(B)] must be installed between the service neutral terminal and the service disconnect enclosure [250.28]. ▶Figure 250–55 and ▶Figure 250–56

Author's Comment:

- The service neutral conductor provides the effective ground-fault current path to the power supply to ensure that dangerous voltage from a ground fault will be quickly removed by opening the overcurrent protection device [250.4(A)(3) and 250.4(A)(5)].
▶Figure 250–57

Grounding and Bonding | 250.24

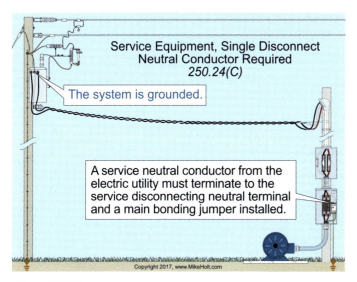

▶Figure 250–55

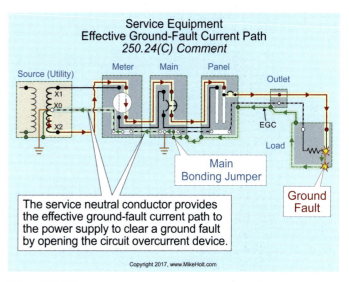

▶Figure 250–57

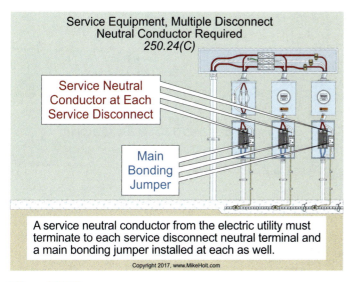

▶Figure 250–56

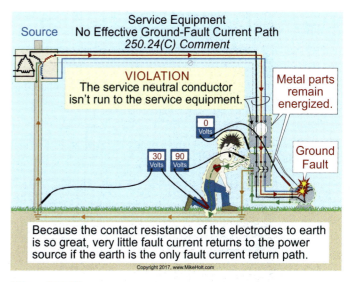

▶Figure 250–58

DANGER: *Dangerous voltage from a ground fault won't be removed from metal parts, metal piping, and structural steel if the service disconnect enclosure isn't connected to the service neutral conductor. This is because the contact resistance of a grounding electrode to the earth is so great that insufficient fault current returns to the power supply if the earth is the only fault current return path to open the circuit overcurrent protection device.* ▶Figure 250–58

Author's Comment:

- If the neutral conductor is opened, dangerous voltage will be present on metal parts under normal conditions, providing the potential for electric shock. If the earth's ground resistance is 25 ohms and the load's resistance is 25 ohms, the voltage drop across each of these resistors will be half of the voltage source. Since the neutral is connected to the service disconnect, all metal parts will be elevated to 60V above the earth's voltage for a 120/240V system. ▶Figure 250–59

250.24 | Grounding and Bonding

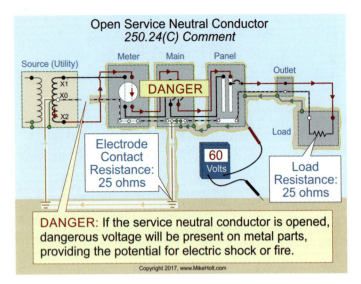

▶Figure 250–59

(1) Neutral Sizing for Single Raceway or Cable. Because the service neutral conductor serves as the effective ground-fault current path to the source for ground faults, the neutral conductor must be sized so it can safely carry the maximum fault current likely to be imposed on it [110.10 and 250.4(A)(5)]. This is accomplished by sizing the neutral conductor not smaller than specified in Table 250.102(C)(1), based on the cross-sectional area of the largest ungrounded service conductor.

▶Figure 250–60

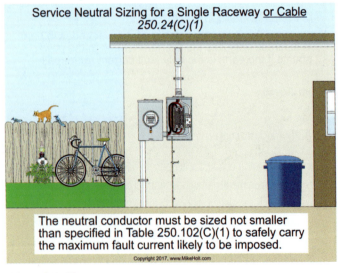

▶Figure 250–60

Author's Comment:

- In addition, the neutral conductors must have the capacity to carry the maximum unbalanced neutral current in accordance with 220.61.

Example: What's the minimum size service neutral conductor required where the ungrounded service conductors are 350 kcmil and the maximum unbalanced load is 100A? ▶Figure 250–61

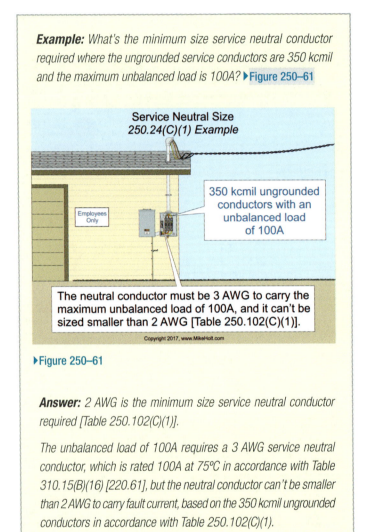

▶Figure 250–61

Answer: 2 AWG is the minimum size service neutral conductor required [Table 250.102(C)(1)].

The unbalanced load of 100A requires a 3 AWG service neutral conductor, which is rated 100A at 75°C in accordance with Table 310.15(B)(16) [220.61], but the neutral conductor can't be smaller than 2 AWG to carry fault current, based on the 350 kcmil ungrounded conductors in accordance with Table 250.102(C)(1).

(2) Neutral Sizing for Parallel Conductors in Two or More Raceways or Cables. If service conductors are paralleled in two or more raceways or cables, a neutral conductor must be installed in each of the parallel raceways or cables. The size of the neutral conductor in each raceway or cable isn't permitted to be smaller than specified in Table 250.102(C)(1), based on the cross-sectional area of the largest ungrounded service conductor in each raceway or cable. In no case can the neutral conductor in each parallel set be sized smaller than 1/0 AWG [310.10(H)(1)].

Mike Holt's Illustrated Guide to Understanding 2017 NEC Requirements for Bonding and Grounding

Grounding and Bonding | 250.28

Author's Comment:

- In addition, the neutral conductors must have the capacity to carry the maximum unbalanced neutral current in accordance with 220.61.

Example: What's the minimum size service neutral conductor required for each of two raceways, where the ungrounded service conductors in each of the raceways are 350 kcmil and the maximum unbalanced load is 100A? ▶Figure 250–62

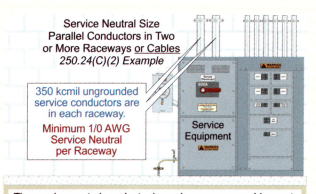

▶Figure 250–62

Answer: The minimum size service neutral conductor required is 1/0 AWG per raceway [Table 250.102(C)(1) and 310.10(H)].

The unbalanced load of 50A in each raceway requires an 8 AWG service neutral conductor, which is rated 50A at 75°C in accordance with Table 310.15(B)(16) [220.61]. Also, Table 250.102(C)(1) requires a minimum of 2 AWG in each raceway, however, 1/0 AWG is the smallest conductor permitted to be paralleled [310.10(H) and Table 310.15(B)(16)].

(D) Grounding Electrode Conductor. A grounding electrode conductor, sized in accordance with 250.66 based on the area of the ungrounded service conductor, must connect the neutral conductor and metal parts of service equipment enclosures to a grounding electrode in accordance with Part III of Article 250.

Example: What's the minimum size grounding electrode conductor for a 400A service where the ungrounded service conductors are sized at 500 kcmil? ▶Figure 250–63

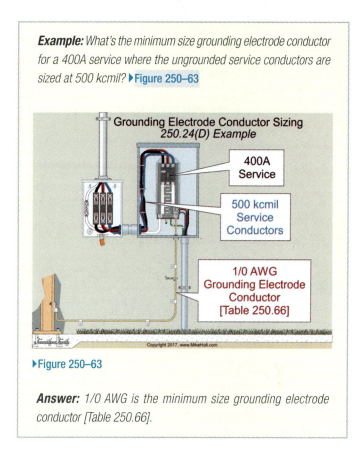

▶Figure 250–63

Answer: 1/0 AWG is the minimum size grounding electrode conductor [Table 250.66].

Author's Comment:

- If the grounding electrode conductor or bonding jumper connects to one or more ground rods [250.52(A)(5)] and doesn't connect to any another type of electrode, the grounding electrode conductor isn't required to be larger than 6 AWG copper.

- If the grounding electrode conductor or bonding jumper is connected to one or more concrete-encased electrodes [250.52(A)(3)] and doesn't connect to another type of electrode that requires a larger size conductor, the grounding electrode conductor isn't required to be larger than 4 AWG copper.

250.28 Main Bonding Jumper and System Bonding Jumper

Main and system bonding jumpers must be installed as follows:

(A) Material. The bonding jumper can be a wire, bus, or screw.

(B) Construction. If the bonding jumper is a screw, it must be identified with a green finish visible with the screw installed.

250.30 | Grounding and Bonding

(C) Attachment. Main and system bonding jumpers must terminate by any of the following means in accordance with 250.8(A):

- Listed pressure connectors
- Terminal bars
- Pressure connectors listed as grounding and bonding equipment
- Exothermic welding
- Machine screw-type fasteners that engage not less than two threads or are secured with a nut
- Thread-forming machine screws that engage not less than two threads in the enclosure
- Connections that are part of a listed assembly
- Other listed means

(D) Size.

(1) Main and system bonding jumpers must be sized not smaller than the sizes shown in Table 250.102(C)(1). ▶Figure 250–64

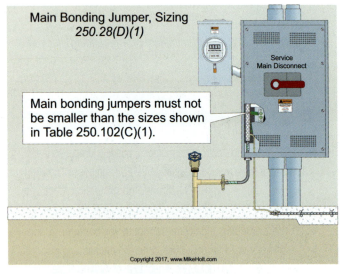

▶Figure 250–64

250.30 Separately Derived Systems—Grounding and Bonding

Note 1: An alternate alternating-current power source such as an on-site generator isn't a separately derived system if the neutral conductor is solidly interconnected to a service-supplied system neutral conductor. An example is a generator provided with a transfer switch that includes a neutral conductor that's not switched. ▶Figure 250–65

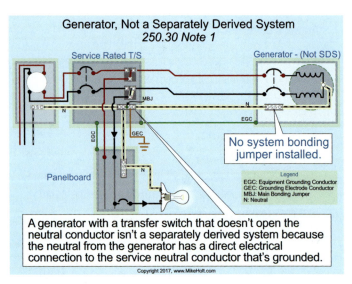

▶Figure 250–65

Author's Comment:

- According to Article 100, a separately derived system is a wiring system whose power is derived from a source, other than the electric utility, where there's no direct electrical connection to the supply conductors of another system, other than through grounding and bonding connections.

- Transformers are separately derived when the primary conductors have no direct electrical connection from circuit conductors of one system to circuit conductors of another system, other than connections through grounding and bonding connections. ▶Figure 250–66

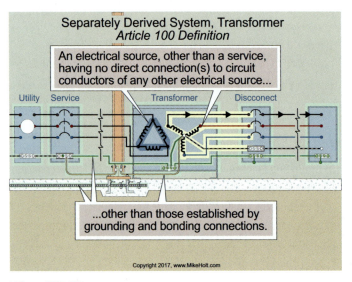

▶Figure 250–66

- A generator having transfer equipment that switches the neutral conductor, or one that has no neutral conductor at all, is a separately derived system and must be grounded and bonded in accordance with 250.30(A). ▶Figure 250–67

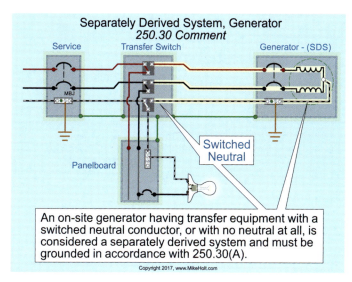

▶Figure 250–67

Note 2: For nonseparately derived systems, see 445.13 for the minimum size neutral conductors necessary to carry fault current. ▶Figure 250–68

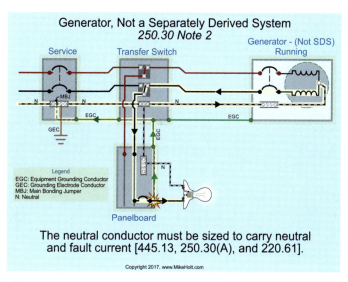

▶Figure 250–68

(A) Grounded Systems. Separately derived systems must be grounded and bonded in accordance with (A)(1) through (A)(8). A neutral-to-case connection isn't permitted to be made on the load side of the system bonding jumper, except as permitted by 250.142(B).

(1) System Bonding Jumper. A system bonding jumper must be installed at the same location where the grounding electrode conductor terminates to the neutral terminal of the separately derived system; either at the separately derived system or the system disconnect, but not at both locations [250.30(A)(5)]. ▶Figure 250–69

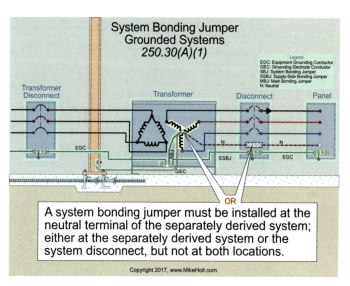

▶Figure 250–69

If the separately derived source is located outside the building or structure supplied, a system bonding jumper must be installed at the grounding electrode connection in accordance with 250.30(C).

Ex. 2: If a building or structure is supplied by a feeder from an outdoor separately derived system, a system bonding jumper at both the source and the first disconnect is permitted. The grounded conductor isn't permitted to be smaller than the size specified for the system bonding jumper, but it's not required to be larger than the ungrounded conductor(s).

(a) System Bonding Jumper at Source. Where the system bonding jumper is installed at the source of the separately derived system, the system bonding jumper must connect the neutral conductor of the derived system to the metal enclosure of the derived system. ▶Figure 250–70

(b) System Bonding Jumper at Disconnect. Where the system bonding jumper is installed at the first disconnect of a separately derived system, the system bonding jumper must connect the neutral conductor of the derived system to the metal disconnect enclosure. ▶Figure 250–71

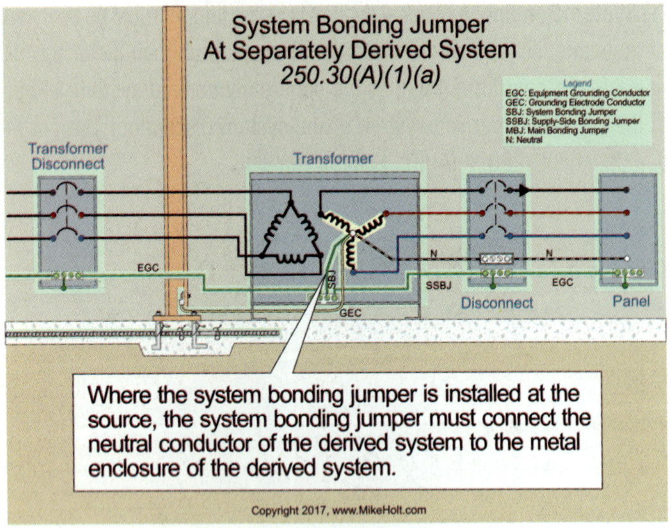

250.30 | Grounding and Bonding

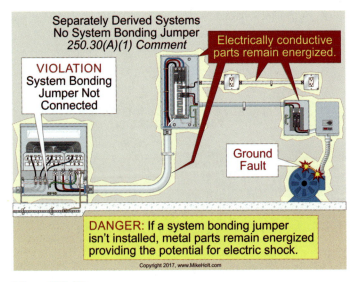

▶Figure 250–72

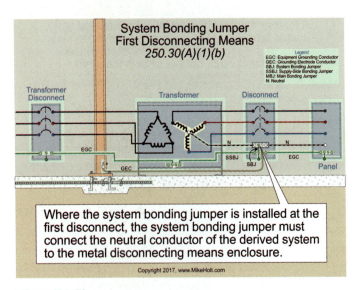

▶Figure 250–70

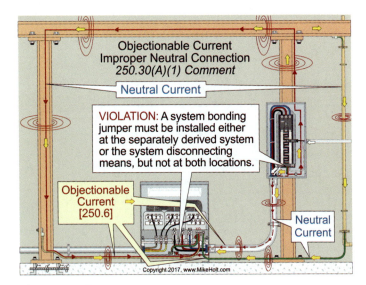

▶Figure 250–71

Author's Comment:

- A system bonding jumper is a conductor, screw, or strap that bonds the metal parts of a separately derived system to the system neutral point [Article 100 Bonding Jumper, System], and it's sized to Table 250.102(C)(1) in accordance with 250.28(D).

DANGER: During a ground fault, metal parts of electrical equipment, as well as metal piping and structural steel, will become and remain energized providing the potential for electric shock and fire if the system bonding jumper isn't installed. ▶Figure 250–72

CAUTION: Dangerous objectionable neutral current will flow on conductive metal parts of electrical equipment as well as metal piping and structural steel, in violation of 250.6(A), if more than one system bonding jumper is installed, or if it's not located where the grounding electrode conductor terminates to the neutral conductor. ▶Figure 250–73

▶Figure 250–73

(2) Supply-Side Bonding Jumper to Disconnect. A supply-side bonding jumper (nonflexible metal raceway or wire) must be run from the derived system to the derived system disconnect.

Mike Holt's Illustrated Guide to Understanding 2017 NEC Requirements for Bonding and Grounding

(a) If the supply-side bonding jumper is of the wire type, it must be sized in accordance with Table 250.102(C)(1), based on the area of the largest ungrounded derived system conductor in the raceway or cable.

Example: What size supply-side bonding jumper is required for flexible metal conduit containing 300 kcmil secondary conductors? ▶Figure 250–74

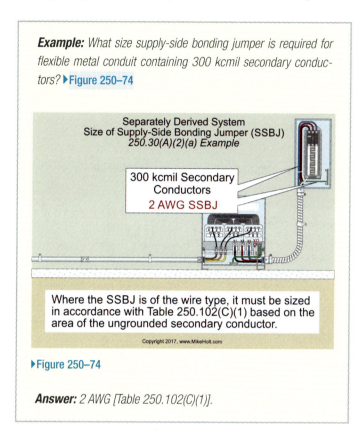

▶Figure 250–74

Answer: 2 AWG [Table 250.102(C)(1)].

(3) Neutral Conductor Size, System Bonding Jumper at Derived System Disconnect. If the system bonding jumper is installed at the disconnect instead of at the source, the following requirements apply:

(a) Sizing for Single Raceway. The neutral conductor must be routed with the ungrounded conductors of the derived system to the disconnect and be sized not smaller than specified in Table 250.102(C)(1), based on the area of the ungrounded conductor of the derived system.
▶Figure 250–75

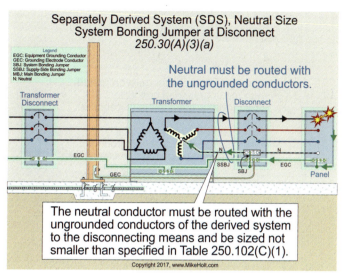

▶Figure 250–75

Example: What size neutral conductor is required for a 75 kVA transformer with 250 kcmil secondary conductors? ▶Figure 250–76

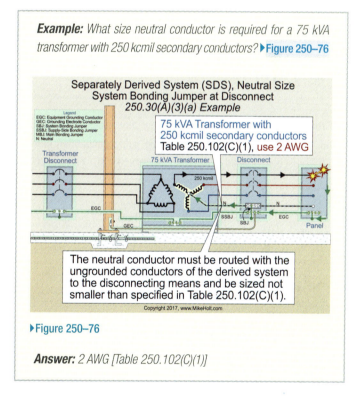

▶Figure 250–76

Answer: 2 AWG [Table 250.102(C)(1)]

(b) Parallel Conductors in Two or More Raceways. If the conductors from the derived system are installed in parallel in two or more raceways, the neutral conductor of the derived system in each raceway or cable must be sized not smaller than specified in Table 250.102(C)(1), based on the area of the largest ungrounded conductor of the derived system in the raceway or cable. In no case is the neutral conductor of the derived system permitted to be smaller than 1/0 AWG [310.10(H)].
▶Figure 250–77

250.30 | Grounding and Bonding

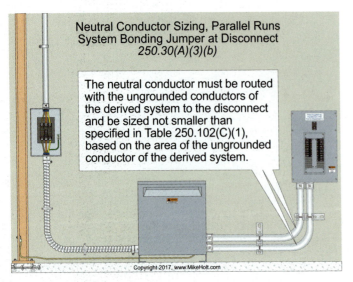

▶Figure 250–77

Example: What size neutral conductor is required for a 112.50 kVA transformer with two sets of 3/0 AWG secondary conductors?

Answer: 1/0 AWG [310.10(H)(1)]

(4) Grounding Electrode. Indoor separately derived systems must use the building or structure grounding electrode; outdoor separately derived systems must be grounded in accordance with 250.30(C). ▶Figure 250–78

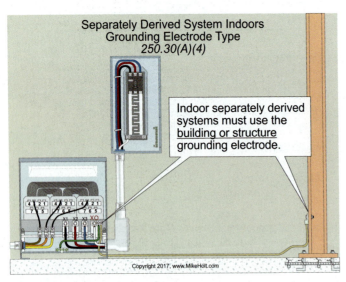

▶Figure 250–78

Note 1: Interior metal water piping in the area served by separately derived systems must be bonded to the separately derived system in accordance with 250.104(D).

Note 2: See 250.50 and 250.58 for requirements for bonding all electrodes together if located at the same building or structure.

(5) Grounding Electrode Conductor, Single Separately Derived System. The grounding electrode conductor for the separately derived system is sized in accordance with 250.66 and it must terminate to the grounding electrode in accordance with 250.30(A)(4).

The grounding electrode conductor is required to terminate to the neutral conductor at the same point on the separately derived system where the system bonding jumper is connected. ▶Figure 250–79

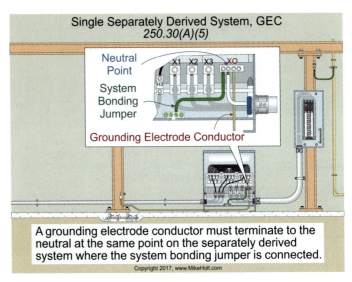

▶Figure 250–79

Author's Comment:

- System grounding helps reduce fires in buildings as well as voltage stress on electrical insulation, thereby ensuring longer insulation life for motors, transformers, and other system components. ▶Figure 250–80

- To prevent objectionable neutral current from flowing [250.6] onto metal parts, the grounding electrode conductor must originate at the same point on the separately derived system where the system bonding jumper is connected [250.30(A)(1)].

Ex 1: If the system bonding jumper [250.30(A)(1)] is a wire or busbar, the grounding electrode conductor is permitted to terminate to the equipment grounding terminal, bar, or bus. ▶Figure 250–81

Ex 3: Separately derived systems rated 1 kVA or less aren't required to be grounded (connected to the earth).

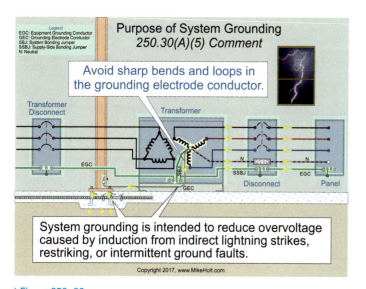

▶Figure 250–80

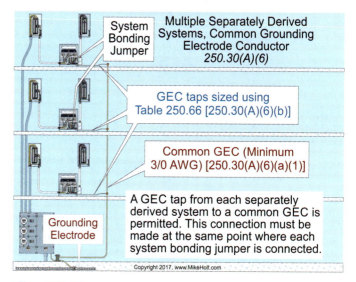

▶Figure 250–82

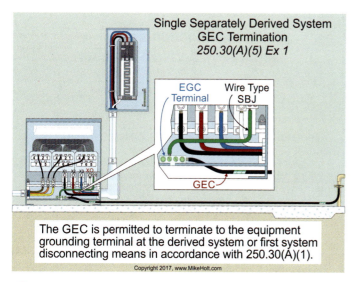

▶Figure 250–81

(6) Grounding Electrode Conductor, Multiple Separately Derived Systems. Where there are multiple separately derived systems, a grounding electrode conductor tap from each separately derived system to a common grounding electrode conductor is permitted. This connection is to be made at the same point on the separately derived system where the system bonding jumper is connected [250.30(A)(1)]. ▶Figure 250–82

Ex 1: If the system bonding jumper is a wire or busbar, the grounding electrode conductor tap can terminate to either the neutral terminal or the equipment grounding terminal, bar, or bus in accordance with 250.30(A)(1).

Ex 2: Separately derived systems rated 1 kVA or less aren't required to be grounded (connected to the earth).

(a) Common Grounding Electrode Conductor. The common grounding electrode conductor can be any of the following:

(1) A conductor not smaller than 3/0 AWG copper or 250 kcmil aluminum.

(2) Interior metal water pipe located not more than 5 ft from the point of entrance to the building [250.68(C)(1)].

(3) The metal frame of the building or structure that complies with 250.68(C)(2) or is connected to the grounding electrode system by a conductor not smaller than 3/0 AWG copper or 250 kcmil aluminum.

(b) Tap Conductor Size. Grounding electrode conductor taps must be sized in accordance with Table 250.66, based on the area of the largest ungrounded conductor of the given derived system.

(c) Connections. Tap connections to the common grounding electrode conductor must be made at an accessible location by any of the following methods:

(1) A connector listed as grounding and bonding equipment.

(2) Listed connections to aluminum or copper busbars not less than ¼ in. thick × 2 in. wide, and of sufficient length to accommodate the terminations necessary for the installation. ▶Figure 250–83

(3) Exothermic welding.

Grounding electrode conductor taps must be connected to the common grounding electrode conductor so the common grounding electrode conductor isn't spliced.

250.30 | Grounding and Bonding

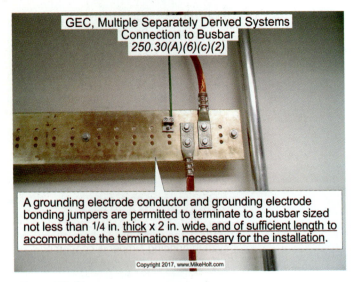

▶Figure 250–83

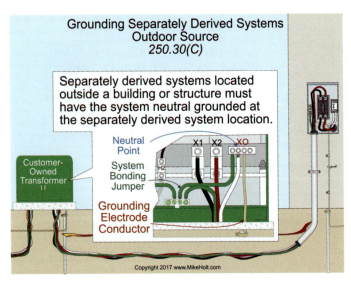

▶Figure 250–84

(7) Installation. The grounding electrode conductor must comply with the following:

- Be of copper where within 18 in. of the surface of the earth [250.64(A)].
- Be securely fastened to the surface on which it's carried [250.64(B)].
- Be adequately protected if exposed to physical damage [250.64(B)].
- Metal enclosures enclosing a grounding electrode conductor must be made electrically continuous from the point of attachment to cabinets or equipment to the grounding electrode [250.64(E)].

(8) Structural Steel and Metal Piping. To ensure dangerous voltage on metal parts from a ground fault is removed quickly, structural steel and metal piping in the area served by a separately derived system must be connected to the neutral conductor at the separately derived system in accordance with 250.104(D).

(C) Outdoor Source. Separately derived systems located outside the building must have the grounding electrode connection made at the separately derived system location. ▶Figure 250–84

**Special Section 250.30
Separately Derived Systems**

Outdoor Installations

Generator System with Integral Disconnect. ▶Figure 250–85

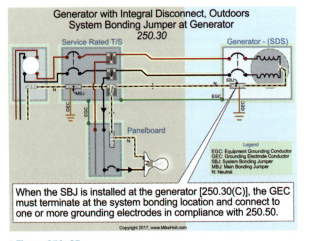

▶Figure 250–85

System Bonding Jumper. Where a separately derived system generator with integral disconnecting means is installed outdoors, a system bonding jumper sized in accordance with Table 250.102(C)(1), is required to be installed at the generator neutral terminal [250.30(A)(1)(a)].

Grounding Electrode Conductor. A grounding electrode conductor, sized in accordance with 250.66, must be run from the generator neutral terminal to one or more grounding electrodes in compliance with 250.50 in accordance with 250.30(C) [250.30(A)(4)].

Where the system bonding jumper is a wire or busbar, the grounding electrode conductor can originate at the generator equipment grounding terminal, bar, or bus [250.30(A)(5) Ex].

Transformer Outdoors. ▶Figure 250–86

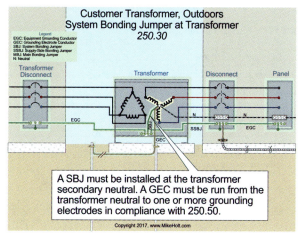

▶Figure 250–86

System Bonding Jumper. Where a separately derived system transformer is installed outdoors, a system bonding jumper sized in accordance with Table 250.102(C)(1), is required to be installed at the transformer secondary neutral [250.30(A)(1)].

Grounding Electrode Conductor. A grounding electrode conductor, sized in accordance with 250.66, must be run from the transformer neutral terminal to one or more grounding electrodes in compliance with 250.50 in accordance with 250.30(C) [250.30(A)(4)].

Where the system bonding jumper is a wire or busbar, the grounding electrode conductor can originate at the generator equipment grounding terminal, bar, or bus [250.30(A)(5) Ex].

Supply-Side Bonding Jumper. A supply-side bonding jumper must be run from the transformer equipment grounding conductor terminal to the secondary disconnect enclosure equipment grounding conductor terminal.

Where the supply-side bonding jumper is of the wire type, it must be sized in accordance with Table 250.102(C)(1), based on the area of the secondary conductor [250.30(A)(2)].

Example: What size system bonding jumper is required to be installed at a 75 kVA transformer having 250 kcmil secondary conductors? ▶Figure 250–87

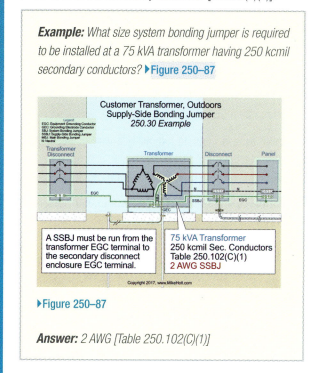

▶Figure 250–87

Answer: 2 AWG [Table 250.102(C)(1)]

Indoor Installations

Generator System Indoor with Integral Disconnect. ▶Figure 250–88

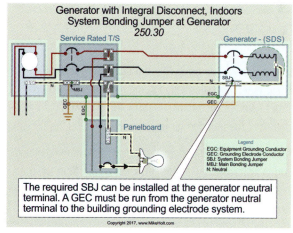

▶Figure 250–88

250.30 | Grounding and Bonding

System Bonding Jumper. Where a separately derived system generator with an integral disconnect is installed indoors, the required system bonding jumper, sized in accordance with Table 250.102(C)(1), can be installed at the generator neutral terminal [250.30(A)(1)(a)].

Grounding Electrode Conductor. A grounding electrode conductor, sized in accordance with 250.66, must be run from the generator neutral terminal to the building or structure grounding electrode system [250.30(A)(4)].

Where the system bonding jumper is a wire or busbar, the grounding electrode conductor can originate at the generator equipment grounding terminal, bar, or bus [250.30(A)(5) Ex].

Transformer System Indoors, System Bonding Jumper at Transformer. ▶Figure 250–89

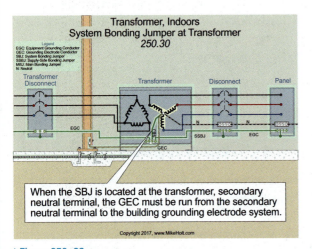

▶Figure 250–89

System Bonding Jumper. Where a separately derived system transformer is installed indoors, the required system bonding jumper, sized in accordance with Table 250.102(C)(1), can be installed at the transformer neutral terminal [250.30(A)(1)(a)].

Grounding Electrode Conductor. A grounding electrode conductor, sized in accordance with 250.66, must be run from the transformer neutral terminal to the building or structure grounding electrode system [250.30(A)(4)].

Where the system bonding jumper is a wire or busbar, the grounding electrode conductor can originate at the generator equipment grounding terminal, bar, or bus [250.30(A)(5) Ex].

Supply-Side Bonding Jumper. A supply-side bonding jumper, sized in accordance with Table 250.102(C)(1), must be run from the transformer equipment grounding conductor terminal to the secondary disconnect enclosure equipment grounding conductor terminal [250.30(A)(2)].

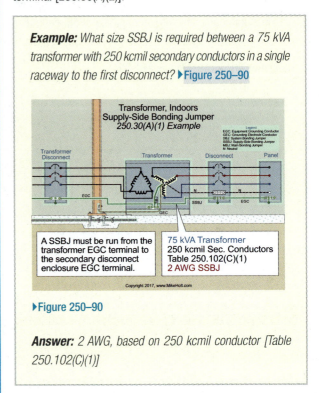

▶Figure 250–90

Answer: 2 AWG, based on 250 kcmil conductor [Table 250.102(C)(1)]

Transformer Indoors, System Bonding Jumper at Secondary Disconnect. ▶Figure 250–91

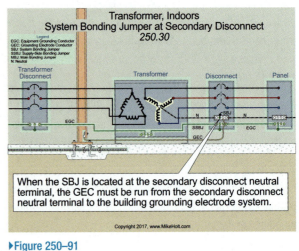

▶Figure 250–91

System Bonding Jumper. Where a separately derived system transformer is installed indoors, the required system bonding jumper, sized in accordance with Table 250.102(C)(1), can be installed at the transformer secondary disconnect [250.30(A)(1)(b)].

Grounding Electrode Conductor. A grounding electrode conductor, sized in accordance with 250.66, must be run from the transformer neutral terminal to the building or structure grounding electrode system [250.30(A)(4)].

Where the system bonding jumper is a wire or busbar, the grounding electrode conductor can originate at the generator equipment grounding terminal, bar, or bus [250.30(A)(5) Ex].

Supply-Side Bonding Jumper. A supply-side bonding jumper, sized in accordance with Table 250.102(C)(1), must be run from the transformer equipment grounding conductor terminal to the secondary disconnect enclosure equipment grounding conductor terminal [250.30(A)(2)].

> **Example:** What size SSBJ is required between a 112.6 kVA transformer paralleled in two raceways with 250 kcmil secondary conductors to the first disconnect?
>
> **Answer:** 1/0 AWG [Table 250.102(C)(1)]. The area of 3/0 AWG is 167,800 circular mills × 2 conductors equals 335,600 circular mills [Chapter 9, Table 8 and Table 250.102(C)(1)].

Neutral Conductor. When the system bonding jumper is installed at a secondary disconnect, a secondary neutral conductor in each raceway, sized no smaller than specified in Table 250.102(C)(1), must be run from the transformer secondary to the secondary disconnect enclosure.

> **Example:** What size neutral conductor is required for a 112.50 kVA transformer paralleled in two raceways with 3/0 AWG secondary conductors in each raceway?
>
> **Answer:** 1/0 AWG [310.10(H)(1)]

Author's Comment:

- When the system bonding jumper is installed at the secondary disconnect, the secondary neutral conductor will serve as part of the effective ground-fault current path.

250.32 Buildings Supplied by a Feeder

(A) Equipment Grounding Electrode. Building feeder disconnects must be connected to a grounding electrode system for the purpose of reducing induced voltages on the metal parts from nearby lightning strikes [250.4(A)(1)]. ▶Figure 250–92

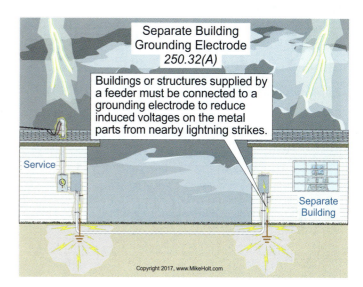

▶Figure 250–92

Ex: A grounding electrode isn't required for a building disconnect supplied by a branch circuit. ▶Figure 250–93

(B) Equipment Grounding Conductor.

(1) Building Supplied by a Feeder. To quickly clear a ground fault and remove dangerous voltage from metal parts, the building disconnect must be connected to the circuit equipment grounding conductor, of the type(s) described in 250.118. ▶Figure 250–94

250.32 | Grounding and Bonding

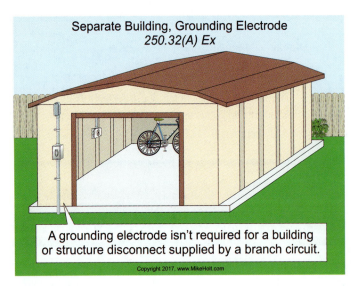

▶Figure 250–93

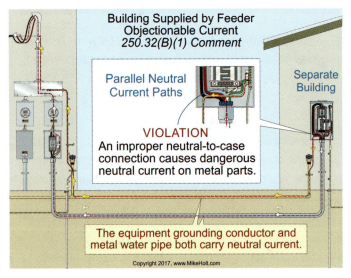

▶Figure 250–95

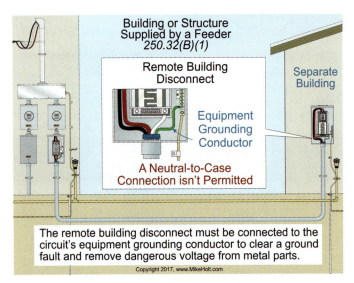

▶Figure 250–94

Where the supply circuit equipment grounding conductor is of the wire type, it must be sized in accordance with 250.122, based on the rating of the overcurrent protection device.

⚡ **CAUTION:** *To prevent dangerous objectionable neutral current from flowing on metal parts [250.6(A)], the supply circuit neutral conductor isn't permitted to be connected to the remote building disconnect [250.142(B)].* ▶Figure 250–95

Ex 1: The neutral conductor can serve as the ground-fault return path for the building disconnect for existing installations where there are no continuous metallic paths between buildings and structures, ground-fault protection of equipment isn't installed on the supply side of the circuit, and the neutral conductor is sized no smaller than the larger of:

(1) The maximum unbalanced neutral load in accordance with 220.61.

(2) The minimum equipment grounding conductor size in accordance with 250.122.

(E) Grounding Electrode Conductor Size. The grounding electrode conductor must terminate to the equipment grounding terminal of the disconnect (not the neutral terminal), and it must be sized in accordance with 250.66, based on the conductor area of the ungrounded feeder conductor.

Example: *What size grounding electrode conductor is required for a building disconnect supplied with a 3/0 AWG feeder?* ▶Figure 250–96

Answer: *A 4 AWG grounding electrode conductor is required [Table 250.66].*

Grounding and Bonding | 250.35

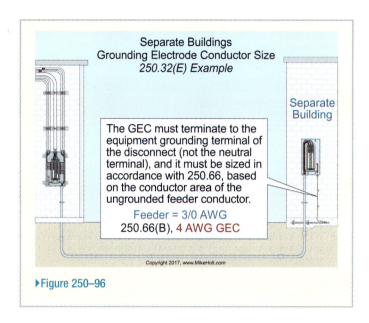
▶Figure 250–96

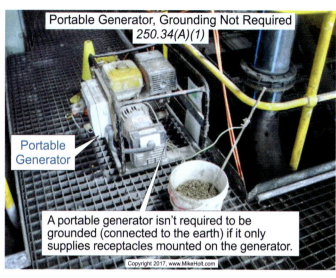
▶Figure 250–97

Author's Comment:

- If the grounding electrode conductor is connected to a rod(s), the portion of the conductor that connects only to the rod(s) isn't required to be larger than 6 AWG copper [250.66(A)]. If the grounding electrode conductor is connected to a concrete-encased electrode(s), the portion of the conductor that connects only to the concrete-encased electrode(s) isn't required to be larger than 4 AWG copper [250.66(B)].

250.34 Generators—Portable and Vehicle-Mounted

(A) Portable Generators. A portable generator isn't required to be grounded (connected to the earth) if all of the following apply:

(1) The generator only supplies equipment or receptacles mounted on the generator ▶Figure 250–97

(2) The metal parts of the generator and the receptacle grounding terminal are connected to the generator frame.

(B) Vehicle-Mounted Generators. A vehicle-mounted generator isn't required to be grounded (connected to the earth) if all of the following apply:

(1) The generator frame is bonded to the vehicle frame

(2) The generator only supplies equipment or receptacles mounted on the vehicle or generator ▶Figure 250–98

▶Figure 250–98

(3) The metal parts of the generator and the receptacle grounding terminal are connected to the generator frame.

250.35 Permanently Installed Generators

(A) Separately Derived System Generators. If the generator is installed as a separately derived system, the system must be grounded and bonded in accordance with the requirements contained in 250.30.

250.36 High-Impedance Grounded Systems

High-impedance grounded systems are only permitted for three-phase systems up to 1000V, where all of the following conditions are met:
▸Figure 250–99

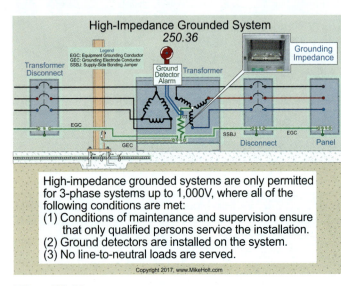

▸Figure 250–99

(1) Conditions of maintenance and supervision ensure that only qualified persons service the installation.

(2) Ground detectors are installed on the system [250.21(B)].

(3) Line-to-neutral loads aren't served.

Author's Comment:

- High-impedance grounded systems are generally referred to as "high-resistance grounded systems" in the industry.

(A) Grounding Impedance Location. To limit fault current to a very low value, high-impedance grounded systems must have a resistor installed between the neutral point of the derived system and the grounding electrode conductor. ▸Figure 250–100

Note: For more information on this topic see IEEE 142—*Recommended Practice for Grounding of Industrial and Commercial Power Systems* (Green Book).

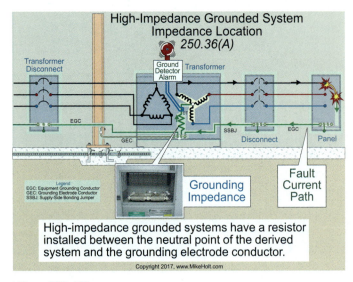

▸Figure 250–100

Part III. Grounding Electrode System and Grounding Electrode Conductor

250.50 Grounding Electrode System

Any grounding electrodes described in 250.52(A)(1) through (A)(7) that are present at a building must be bonded together to form the grounding electrode system. ▸Figure 250–101

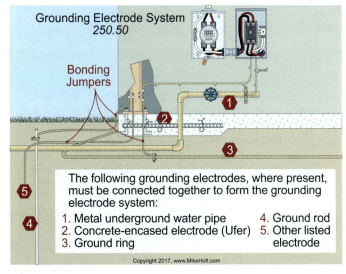

▸Figure 250–101

Ex: Concrete-encased electrodes aren't required for existing buildings where the conductive steel reinforcing bars aren't accessible without chipping up the concrete. ▸Figure 250–102

Grounding and Bonding | 250.52

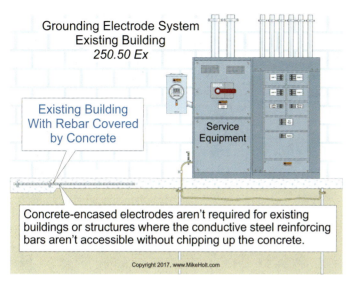

▶Figure 250–102

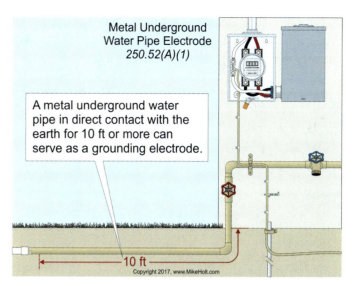

▶Figure 250–104

Author's Comment:

- When a concrete-encased electrode is used at a building that doesn't have an underground metal water pipe electrode, no additional electrode is required. ▶Figure 250–103

Author's Comment:

- Controversy about using metal underground water piping as a grounding electrode has existed since the early 1900s. The water industry believes that neutral current flowing on water piping corrodes the metal. For more information, contact the American Water Works Association about their report—*Effects of Electrical Grounding on Pipe Integrity and Shock Hazard*, Catalog No. 90702, 1.800.926.7337. ▶Figure 250–105

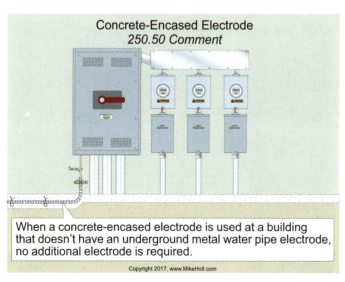

▶Figure 250–103

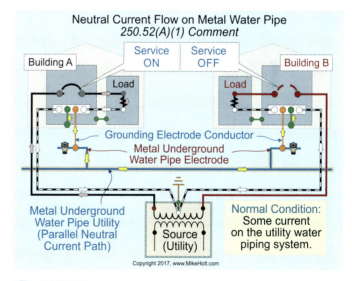

▶Figure 250–105

250.52 Grounding Electrode Types

(A) Electrodes Permitted for Grounding.

(1) Underground Metal Water Pipe Electrode. Underground metal water pipe in direct contact with the earth for 10 ft or more can serve as a grounding electrode. ▶Figure 250–104

(2) Metal In-Ground Support Structure(s). Metal in-ground support structure(s) in direct contact with the earth vertically for 10 ft or more can serve as a grounding electrode. ▶Figure 250–106

▶Figure 250–106

Note: Metal in-ground support structures include, but aren't limited to, pilings, casings, and other structural metal.

(3) Concrete-Encased Electrode. ▶Figure 250–107

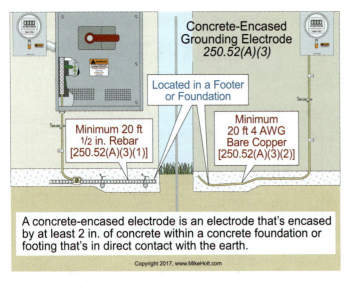

▶Figure 250–107

(1) One or more electrically conductive steel reinforcing bars of not less than ½ in. in diameter, mechanically connected together by steel tie wires, or other effective means to create a 20 ft or greater length can serve as a grounding electrode. ▶Figure 250–108

▶Figure 250–108

(2) Bare copper conductor not smaller than 4 AWG of 20 ft or greater length.

The reinforcing bars or bare copper conductor must be encased by at least 2 in. of concrete located horizontally within a concrete footing or vertically within a concrete foundation that's in direct contact with the earth can serve as a grounding electrode.

Where multiple concrete-encased electrodes are present at a building, only one is required to serve as a grounding electrode. ▶Figure 250–109

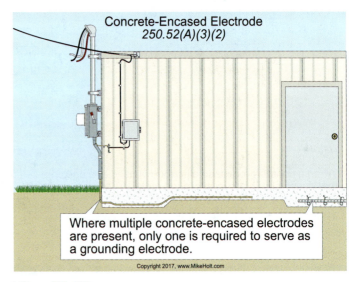

▶Figure 250–109

Note: Concrete separated from the earth because of insulation, vapor barriers, or similar items isn't considered to be in direct contact with the earth. ▶Figure 250–110

Grounding and Bonding | 250.52

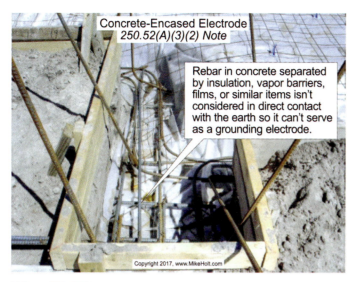

▶Figure 250–110

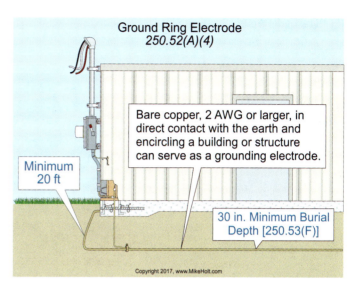

▶Figure 250–111

Author's Comment:

- The grounding electrode conductor to a concrete-encased grounding electrode isn't required to be larger than 4 AWG copper [250.66(B)].

- The concrete-encased grounding electrode is also called a "Ufer Ground," named after a consultant working for the U.S. Army during World War II. The technique Mr. Ufer came up with was necessary because the site needing grounding had no underground water table and little rainfall. The desert site was a series of bomb storage vaults in the area of Flagstaff, Arizona. This type of grounding electrode generally offers the lowest ground resistance for the cost.

(4) Ground Ring Electrode. A ground ring consisting of at least 20 ft of bare copper conductor not smaller than 2 AWG buried in the earth encircling a building, can serve as a grounding electrode. ▶Figure 250–111

(5) Rod Electrode. Rod electrodes must have at less 8 ft in length in contact with the earth [250.53(G)].

(b) Rod-type electrodes must have a diameter of at least ⅝ in., unless listed. ▶Figure 250–112

Author's Comment:

- The grounding electrode conductor, if it's the sole connection to the rod(s), isn't required to be larger than 6 AWG copper [250.66(A)].

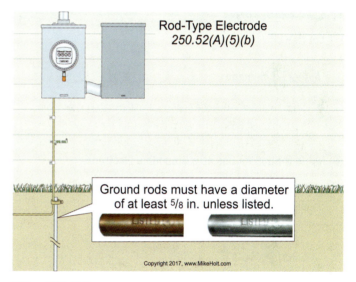

▶Figure 250–112

- The diameter of a rod has an insignificant effect on the contact resistance of a rod(s) to the earth. However, larger diameter rods (¾ in. and 1 in.) are sometimes installed where mechanical strength is desired, or to compensate for the loss of the electrode's metal due to corrosion.

(6) Listed Electrode. Other listed grounding electrodes can serve as a grounding electrode.

(7) Plate Electrode. Bare or electrically conductive coated iron or steel plate with not less than ¼ in. of thickness, or a solid uncoated copper metal plate not less than 0.06 in. of thickness, with an exposed surface area of not less than 2 sq ft can serve as a grounding electrode.

(8) Metal Underground Systems. Metal underground systems, piping, and well casings can serve as a grounding electrode. ▶Figure 250–113

▶Figure 250–113

Author's Comment:

- The grounding electrode conductor to the metal underground system must be sized in accordance with Table 250.66.

(B) Not Permitted for Use as a Grounding Electrode.

(1) Underground metal gas-piping systems aren't permitted to be used as a grounding electrode. ▶Figure 250–114

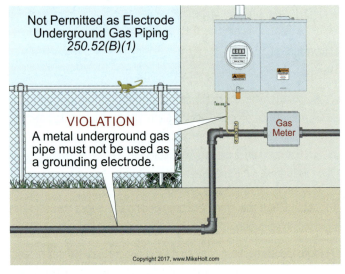

▶Figure 250–114

(2) Aluminum isn't permitted to be used as a grounding electrode.

(3) Swimming pool reinforcing steel for equipotential bonding in accordance with 680.26(B)(1) and 680.26(B)(2) isn't permitted to be used as a grounding electrode. ▶Figure 250–115

▶Figure 250–115

250.53 Grounding Electrode Installation Requirements

(A) Rod Electrodes.

(1) Below Permanent Moisture Level. If practicable, pipe electrodes must be embedded below the permanent moisture level and be free from nonconductive coatings such as paint or enamel.

(2) Supplemental Electrode. A rod electrode must be supplemented by an additional electrode that's bonded to: ▶Figure 250–116

(1) Another rod electrode

(2) The grounding electrode conductor

(3) The service neutral conductor

(4) A nonflexible metal service raceway

(5) The service disconnect

Ex: A single rod electrode having a contact resistance to the earth of 25 ohms or less isn't required to have a supplemental electrode.
▶Figure 250–117

Grounding and Bonding | 250.53

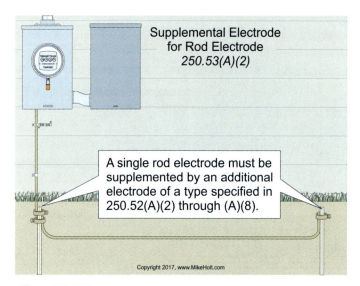
▶Figure 250–116

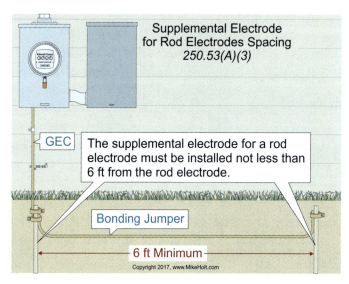
▶Figure 250–118

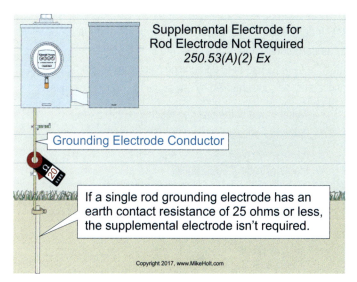
▶Figure 250–117

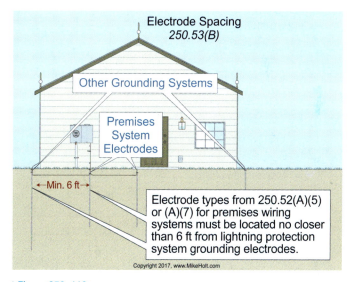
▶Figure 250–119

(3) Spacing. The supplemental electrode for a rod electrode must be installed not less than 6 ft from the rod electrode. ▶Figure 250–118

(B) Electrode Spacing. Electrodes for premises systems must be located no closer than 6 ft from lightning protection system grounding electrodes. Two or more grounding electrodes that are bonded together are considered a single grounding electrode system. ▶Figure 250–119

(C) Grounding Electrode Bonding Jumper. Grounding electrode bonding jumpers must be copper when within 18 in. of the earth [250.64(A)], be securely fastened to the surface, and be protected from physical damage [250.64(B)]. The bonding jumper to each electrode must be sized in accordance with 250.66. ▶Figure 250–120

250.53 | Grounding and Bonding

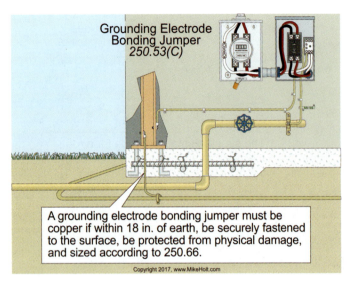
▶Figure 250–120

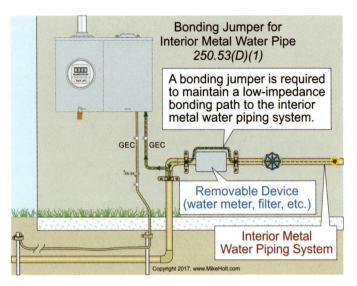
▶Figure 250–121

Author's Comment:

- The grounding electrode bonding jumpers must terminate by any of the following means in accordance with 250.8(A):
  - Listed pressure connectors
  - Terminal bars
  - Pressure connectors listed as grounding and bonding equipment
  - Exothermic welding
  - Machine screw-type fasteners that engage not less than two threads or are secured with a nut
  - Thread-forming machine screws that engage not less than two threads in the enclosure
  - Connections that are part of a listed assembly
  - Other listed means

When the termination is encased in concrete or buried, the termination fittings must be listed for this purpose [250.70].

(D) Underground Metal Water Pipe Electrode.

(1) Interior Metal Water Piping. The bonding connection for the interior metal water piping system, as required by 250.104(A), isn't permitted to be dependent on water meters, filtering devices, or similar equipment likely to be disconnected for repairs or replacement. When necessary, a bonding jumper must be installed around insulated joints and equipment likely to be disconnected for repairs or replacement. ▶Figure 250–121

(2) Underground Metal Water Pipe Supplemental Electrode. When an underground metal water pipe grounding electrode is present, it must be used as part of the grounding electrode system [250.52(A)(1)], and it must be supplemented by any of the following electrodes:

- Metal frame of the building electrode [250.52(A)(2)]
- Concrete-encased electrode [250.52(A)(3)]
  ▶Figure 250–122
- Rod electrode [250.52(A)(5)]
- Other listed electrode [250.52(A)(6)]
- Metal underground piping electrode [250.52(A)(8)]

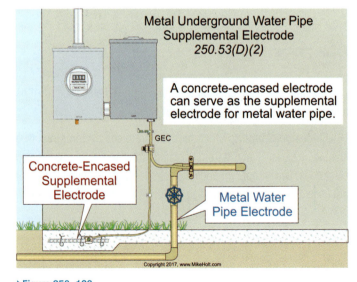
▶Figure 250–122

The supplemental grounding electrode conductor must terminate to any of the following: ▶Figure 250–123

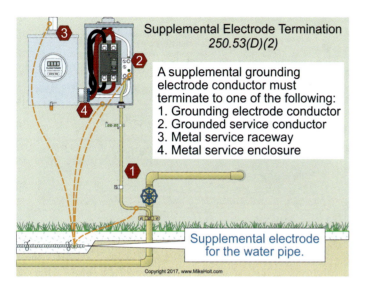

▶Figure 250–123

(1) Grounding electrode conductor

(2) Service neutral conductor

(3) Metal service raceway

(4) Service equipment enclosure

Ex: The supplemental electrode can be bonded to interior metal water piping located not more than 5 ft from the point of entrance to the building [250.68(C)(1)].

(E) Supplemental Rod Electrode. The grounding electrode conductor to a rod(s) that serves as a supplemental electrode isn't required to be larger than 6 AWG copper.

(F) Ground Ring. A bare 2 AWG or larger copper conductor installed not less than 30 in. below the surface of the earth encircling the building [250.52(A)(4)]. ▶Figure 250–124

(G) Rod Electrodes. Rod electrodes must be installed so that not less than 8 ft of length is in contact with the soil. If rock bottom is encountered, the rod must be driven at an angle not to exceed 45 degrees from vertical. If rock bottom is encountered at an angle up to 45 degrees from vertical, the rod can be buried in a minimum 30 in. below the surface of the earth. ▶Figure 250–125

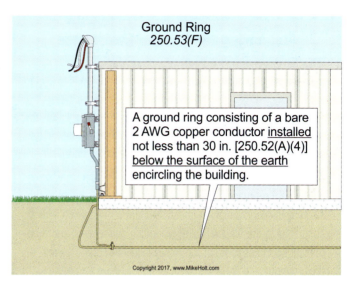

▶Figure 250–124

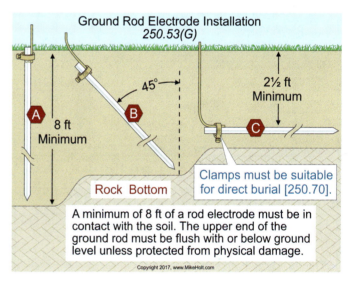

▶Figure 250–125

The upper end of the rod must be flush with or underground unless the grounding electrode conductor attachment is protected against physical damage as specified in 250.10.

Author's Comment:

■ When the grounding electrode attachment fitting is located underground, it must be listed for direct soil burial [250.68(A) Ex 1 and 250.70].

250.53 | Grounding and Bonding

Measuring the Ground Resistance

 Scan this QR code for a video of Mike explaining this topic; it's a sample from the DVDs that accompany this textbook.

A ground resistance clamp meter, or a three-point fall-of-potential ground resistance meter, can be used to measure the contact resistance of a grounding electrode to the earth.

Ground Clamp Meter. The ground resistance clamp meter measures the contact resistance of the grounding electrode system to the earth by injecting a high-frequency signal via the service neutral conductor to the electric utility grounding connection, and then measuring the strength of the return signal through the earth to the grounding electrode being measured. ▶Figure 250–126

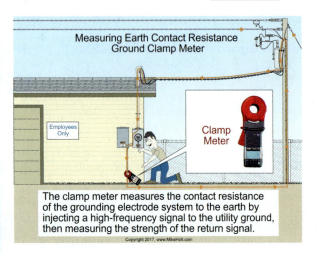

▶Figure 250–126

Fall-of-Potential Ground Resistance Meter. The three-point fall-of-potential ground resistance meter determines the contact resistance of a single grounding electrode to the earth by using Ohm's Law: $R = E/I$. ▶Figure 250–127

This meter divides the voltage difference between the electrode to be measured and a driven voltage test stake (P) by the current flowing between the electrode to be measured and a driven current test stake (C). The test stakes are typically made of ¼ in. diameter steel rods, 24 in. long, driven two-thirds of their length into the earth.

The distance and alignment between the voltage and current test stakes, and the electrode, is extremely important to the validity of the earth contact resistance measurements. For an 8-ft rod, the accepted practice is to space the current test stake (C) 80 ft from the electrode to be measured.

▶Figure 250–127

The voltage test stake (P) is positioned in a straight line between the electrode to be measured and the current test stake (C). The voltage test stake should be located at approximately 62 percent of the distance the current test stake is located from the electrode. Since the current test stake (C) for an 8-ft rod is located 80 ft from the grounding electrode, the voltage test stake (P) will be about 50 ft from the electrode to be measured.

Example: If the voltage between the rod and the voltage test stake (P) is 3V and the current between the rod and the current test stake (C) is 0.20A, what will be the earth contact resistance of the electrode to the earth? ▶Figure 250–128

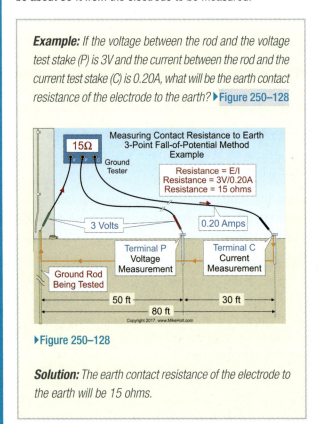

▶Figure 250–128

Solution: The earth contact resistance of the electrode to the earth will be 15 ohms.

Grounding and Bonding | 250.54

Resistance = Voltage/Current
E (Voltage) = 3V
I (Current) = 0.20A

R = E/I
Resistance = 3V/0.20A
Resistance = 15 ohms

Answer: 15 ohms

Author's Comment:

- The three-point fall-of-potential meter should only be used to measure the contact resistance of one electrode to the earth at a time, and this electrode must be independent and not connected to any part of the electrical system. The contact resistance of two electrodes bonded together must not be measured until they've been separated. The contact resistance of two separate electrodes to the earth can be thought of as two resistors in parallel, if they're outside each other's sphere of influence.

Soil Resistivity

The earth's ground resistance is directly impacted by soil resistivity, which varies throughout the world. Soil resistivity is influenced by electrolytes, which consist of moisture, minerals, and dissolved salts. Because soil resistivity changes with moisture content, the resistance of any grounding system varies with the seasons of the year. Since moisture is stable at greater distances below the surface of the earth, grounding systems are generally more effective if the grounding electrode can reach the water table. In addition, placing the grounding electrode below the frost line helps to ensure less deviation in the system's contact resistance to the earth year round.

The contact resistance to the earth can be lowered by chemically treating the earth around the grounding electrodes with electrolytes designed for this purpose.

250.54 Auxiliary Grounding Electrodes

 Scan this QR code for a video of Mike explaining this topic; it's a sample from the DVDs that accompany this textbook.

Auxiliary electrodes are permitted, but they have no *Code* requirements since they serve no purpose related to electrical safety addressed by the *NEC*. ▶Figure 250–129

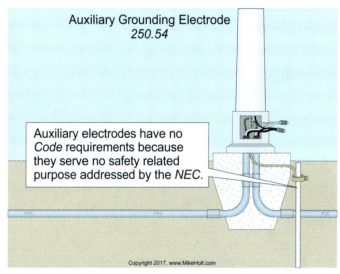

▶Figure 250–129

If an auxiliary electrode is installed, it's not required to be bonded to the building grounding electrode system, required to have the grounding conductor sized to 250.66, or comply with the 25-ohm requirement of 250.53(A)(2) Ex. ▶Figure 250–130

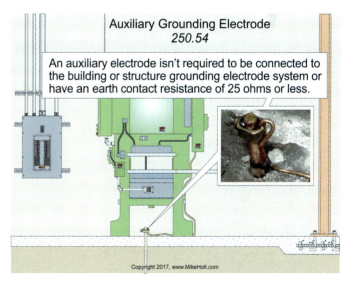

▶Figure 250–130

250.58 | Grounding and Bonding

CAUTION: An auxiliary electrode typically serves no useful purpose, and in some cases it may actually cause equipment failures by providing a path for lightning to travel through electronic equipment. ▶Figure 250–131

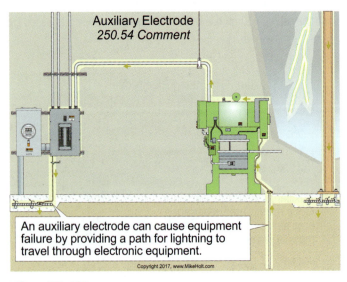

▶Figure 250–131

DANGER: Because the contact resistance of an electrode to the earth is so great, very little fault current returns to the power supply if the earth is the only fault current return path. Result—the circuit overcurrent protection device won't open and clear the ground fault, and all metal parts associated with the electrical installation, metal piping, and structural building steel will become and remain energized.

250.58 Common Grounding Electrode

Where an ac system is connected to a grounding electrode in or at a building or structure, the same grounding electrode must be used. If separate services, feeders, or branch circuits supply a building, the same grounding electrode must be used. ▶Figure 250–132

Two or more grounding electrodes that are bonded together will be considered as a single grounding electrode system in this sense.

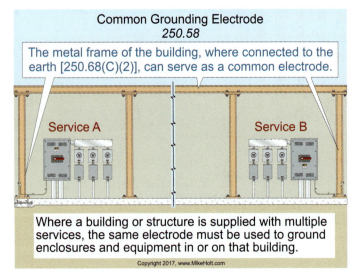

▶Figure 250–132

Author's Comment:

- Metal parts of the electrical installation are grounded (connected to the earth) to reduce induced voltage on the metal parts from lightning so as to prevent fires from a surface arc within the building/structure. Grounding electrical equipment doesn't serve the purpose of providing a low-impedance fault current path to open the circuit overcurrent device in the event of a ground fault.

CAUTION: Potentially dangerous objectionable neutral current flows on the metal parts when multiple service disconnecting means are connected to the same electrode. This is because neutral current from each service can return to the utility via the common grounding electrode and its conductors. This is especially a problem if a service neutral conductor is opened. ▶Figure 250–133

250.60 Lightning Protection Electrode

The lightning protection electrode isn't permitted to be used for the building or structure grounding electrode system required for service equipment [250.24] and remote building feeder disconnecting means [250.32(A)]. ▶Figure 250–134

Grounding and Bonding | 250.62

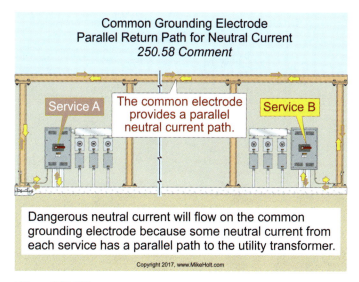
▶Figure 250–133

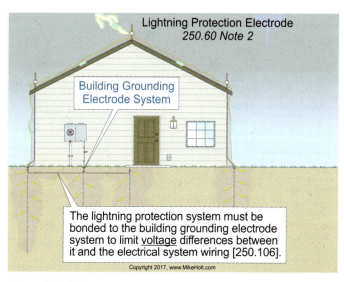
▶Figure 250–135

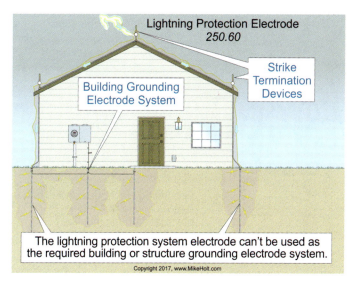
▶Figure 250–134

▶Figure 250–136

Note 1: See 250.106 for the bonding requirements of the lightning protection system to the building or structure grounding electrode system.

Note 2: If a lightning protection system is installed, the lightning protection system must be bonded to the building grounding electrode system so as to limit voltage differences between it and the electrical system wiring. ▶Figure 250–135

Author's Comment:

- A lightning protection system installed in accordance with NFPA 780 is intended to protect the structure from lighting damage. ▶Figure 250–136

250.62 Grounding Electrode Conductor

Grounding electrode conductors of the wire type must be solid or stranded, insulated or bare, and must be copper if within 18 in. of the earth [250.64(A)]. ▶Figure 250–137

250.64 | Grounding and Bonding

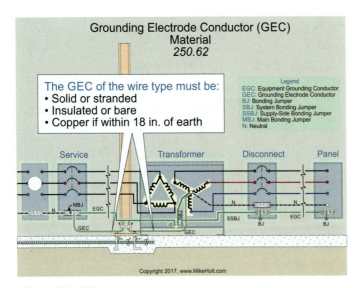
▶Figure 250–137

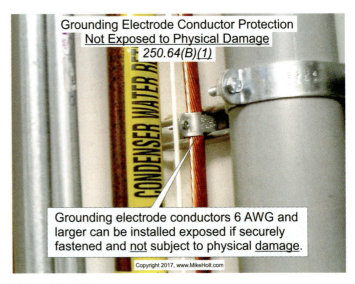
▶Figure 250–138

250.64 Grounding Electrode Conductor Installation

Grounding electrode conductors must be installed as specified in (A) through (F).

(A) Aluminum Conductors. Bare or covered aluminum grounding electrode conductors aren't permitted to be in contact with masonry, the earth, or subject to corrosive conditions. Where used outside, aluminum grounding electrode conductors aren't permitted within 18 in. of the earth.

(B) Conductor Protection. Where exposed, a grounding electrode conductor or its enclosure must be securely fastened to the surface on which it's carried.

(1) Not Exposed to Physical Damage. Grounding electrode conductors 6 AWG and larger can be installed exposed along the surface of the building if securely fastened and not exposed to physical damage.
▶Figure 250–138

(2) Exposed to Physical Damage. Grounding electrode conductors 6 AWG and larger subject to physical damage must be installed in rigid metal conduit, intermediate metal conduit, rigid polyvinyl chloride conduit, Type XW reinforced thermosetting resin conduit (RTRC-XW), electrical metallic tubing, or cable armor. ▶Figure 250–139

(3) Smaller than 6 AWG. Grounding electrode conductors sized 8 AWG must be protected by installing them in rigid metal conduit, intermediate metal conduit, PVC conduit, electrical metallic tubing, Type XW reinforced thermosetting resin conduit (RTRC-XW), or cable armor.

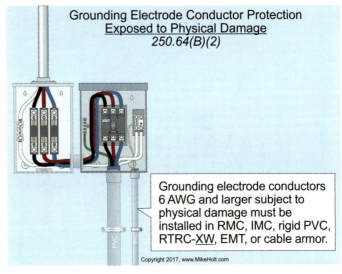
▶Figure 250–139

Author's Comment:

■ A ferrous metal raceway containing a grounding electrode conductor must be made electrically continuous by bonding each end of the raceway to the grounding electrode conductor [250.64(E)], so it's best to use nonmetallic conduit.

(4) In Contact with the Earth. Grounding electrode conductors and bonding jumpers in contact with the earth aren't required to comply with the cover requirements of 300.5, but must be protected if subject to physical damage. ▶Figure 250–140

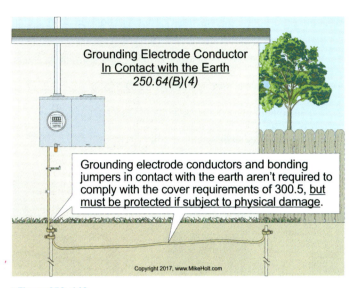

▶Figure 250–140

Author's Comment:

- Grounding and bonding fittings must be protected from physical damage by enclosing the fittings in metal, wood, or an equivalent protective covering [250.10].

(C) Continuous. Grounding electrode conductor(s) must be installed without a splice or joint except by: ▶Figure 250–141

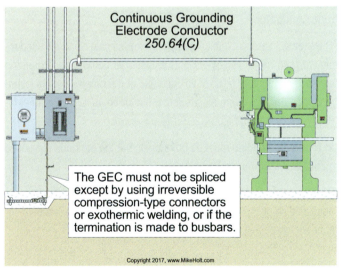

▶Figure 250–141

(1) Irreversible compression-type connectors or exothermic welding.

(2) Busbars connected together.

(3) Bolted, riveted, or welded connections of structural metal frames of buildings.

(4) Threaded, welded, brazed, soldered, or bolted-flange connections of metal water piping.

(D) Grounding Electrode Conductor for Multiple Building or Structure Disconnects. If a building or structure contains two or more building disconnects in separate enclosures, the grounding electrode connections must be made in any of the following methods:

(1) Common Grounding Electrode Conductor and Taps. A grounding electrode conductor tap must extend to the inside of each disconnect enclosure.

The common grounding electrode conductor must be sized in accordance with 250.66, based on the sum of the circular mil area of the largest ungrounded conductor supplying the equipment. ▶Figure 250–142

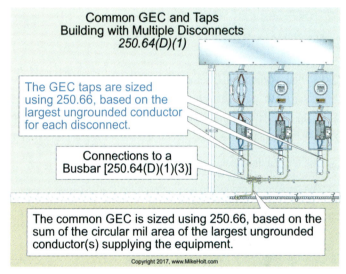

▶Figure 250–142

A grounding electrode conductor must extend from each disconnect, sized no smaller than specified in Table 250.66, based on the area of the largest ungrounded conductor for each disconnect.

The grounding electrode tap conductors must be connected to the common grounding electrode conductor, without splicing the common grounding electrode conductor, by any of the following methods:

(1) Exothermic welding.

(2) Connectors listed as grounding and bonding equipment.

(3) Connections to a busbar of sufficient length and not less than ¼ in. thick × 2 in. wide that's securely fastened and installed in an accessible location. ▶Figure 250–143

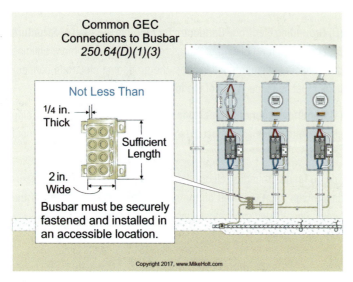

▶Figure 250–143

(2) Individual Grounding Electrode Conductors. A grounding electrode conductor, sized in accordance with 250.66 based on the ungrounded conductor(s) supplying the individual disconnect, must be connected between the grounding electrode system and one or more of the following:

(1) The service neutral conductor ▶Figure 250–144

(2) The equipment grounding conductor of the feeder circuit

(3) The supply-side bonding jumper

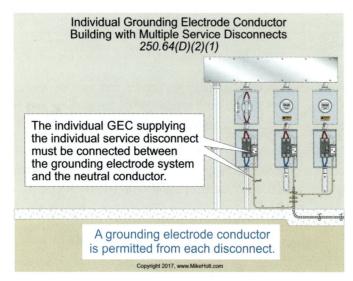

▶Figure 250–144

(3) Common Grounding Electrode Conductor Location. A grounding electrode conductor can be connected from an accessible enclosure on the supply side of the disconnect to one or more of the following locations:

(1) The service neutral conductor ▶Figure 250–145

(2) The equipment grounding conductor of the feeder circuit

(3) The supply-side bonding jumper

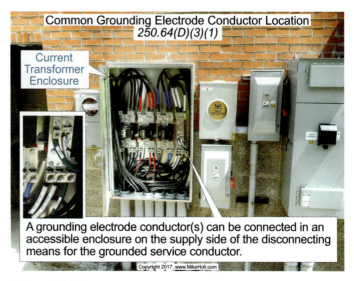

▶Figure 250–145

(E) Ferrous Enclosures and Raceways Containing Grounding Electrode Conductor.

(1) General. To prevent inductive choking of grounding electrode conductors, ferrous metal raceways and enclosures containing grounding electrode conductors must have each end of the raceway or enclosure bonded to the grounding electrode conductor so as to create an electrically parallel path. ▶Figure 250–146

(2) Methods. Bonding must be done by one of the methods discussed in 250.92(B)(2) through (B)(4).

(3) Size. Bonding jumpers must be the same size or larger than the required size of the grounding electrode conductor in the raceway or other enclosure.

Author's Comment:

- Nonferrous metal raceways, such as aluminum rigid metal conduit, enclosing the grounding electrode conductor aren't required to meet the "bonding each end of the raceway to the grounding electrode conductor" provisions of this section.

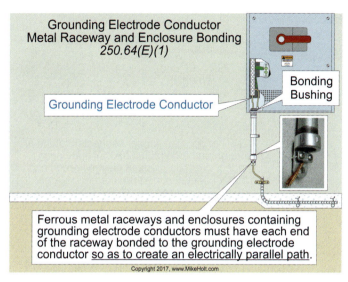

▶Figure 250–146

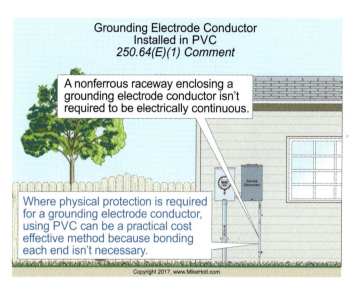

▶Figure 250–147

⚠ **CAUTION:** *The effectiveness of a grounding electrode is significantly reduced if a ferrous metal raceway containing a grounding electrode conductor isn't bonded to the ferrous metal raceway at both ends. This is because a single conductor carrying high-frequency induced lightning current in a ferrous raceway causes the raceway to act as an inductor, which severely limits (chokes) the current flow through the grounding electrode conductor. ANSI/IEEE 142—Recommended Practice for Grounding of Industrial and Commercial Power Systems (Green Book) states: "An inductive choke can reduce the current flow by 97 percent."*

Author's Comment:

- To save a lot of time and effort, install the grounding electrode conductor exposed if it's not subject to physical damage [250.64(B)], or enclose it in nonmetallic conduit suitable for the application [352.10(F)]. ▶Figure 250–147

(F) Termination to Grounding Electrode.

(1) Single Grounding Electrode Conductor. A single grounding electrode conductor can terminate to any grounding electrode of the grounding electrode system. ▶Figure 250–148

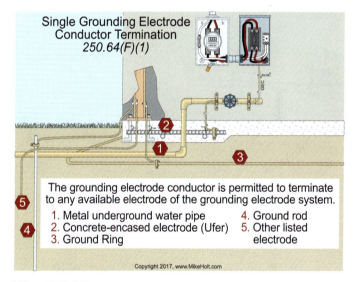

▶Figure 250–148

(2) Multiple Grounding Electrode Conductors. When multiple grounding electrode conductors are installed [250.64(D)(2)], each grounding electrode conductor can terminate to any grounding electrode of the grounding electrode system. ▶Figure 250–149

(3) Termination to Busbar. Grounding electrode conductors and grounding electrode bonding jumpers are permitted to terminate to a busbar not less than ¼ in. thick × 2 in. wide, and of sufficient length to accommodate the terminations necessary for the installation. The busbar must be securely fastened and be installed an accessible location. ▶Figure 250–150

250.66 | Grounding and Bonding

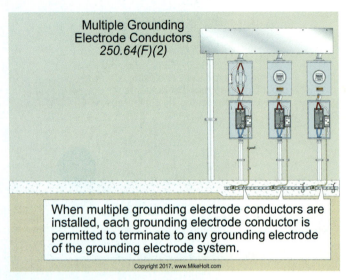
▶Figure 250–149

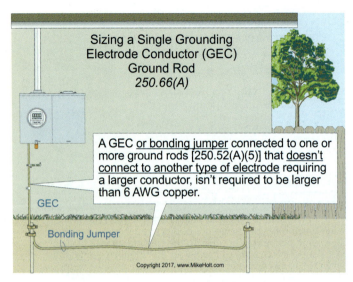
▶Figure 250–151

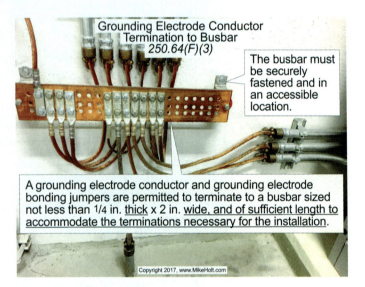
▶Figure 250–150

(B) Concrete-Encased Grounding Electrode. If the grounding electrode conductor or bonding jumper is connected to one or more concrete-encased electrodes [250.52(A)(3)] and doesn't connect to another type of electrode that requires a larger size conductor, the grounding electrode conductor isn't required to be larger than 4 AWG copper. ▶Figure 250–152

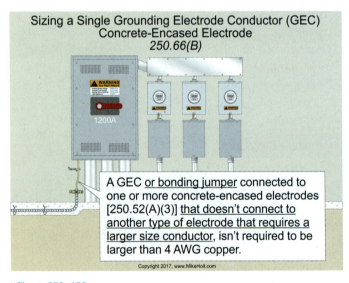
▶Figure 250–152

250.66 Sizing Grounding Electrode Conductor

Except as permitted in (A) through (C), the grounding electrode conductor must be sized in accordance with Table 250.66.

(A) Rod. If the grounding electrode conductor or bonding jumper connects to one or more ground rods [250.52(A)(5)] and doesn't connect to another type of electrode that requires a larger conductor, the grounding electrode conductor isn't required to be larger than 6 AWG copper. ▶Figure 250–151

Table 250.66 Sizing Grounding Electrode Conductor	
Conductor or Area of Parallel Conductors	Copper Grounding Electrode Conductor
12 through 2 AWG	8 AWG
1 or 1/0 AWG	6 AWG
2/0 or 3/0 AWG	4 AWG
Over 3/0 through 350 kcmil	2 AWG
Over 350 through 600 kcmil	1/0 AWG
Over 600 through 1,100 kcmil	2/0 AWG
Over 1,100 kcmil	3/0 AWG

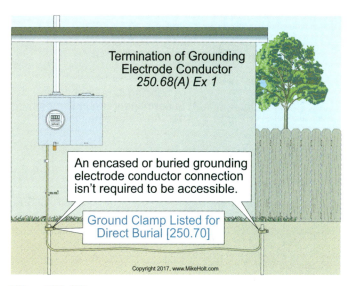

▶Figure 250–154

250.68 Termination to the Grounding Electrode

(A) Accessibility. The mechanical elements used to terminate a grounding electrode conductor or bonding jumper to a grounding electrode must be accessible. ▶Figure 250–153

Author's Comment:

- If the grounding electrode attachment fitting is encased in concrete or buried in the earth, it must be listed for direct soil burial or concrete encasement [250.70].

Ex 2: Exothermic or irreversible compression connections, together with the mechanical means used to attach to fireproofed structural metal, aren't required to be accessible.

(B) Integrity of Underground Metal Water Pipe Electrode. A bonding jumper must be installed around insulated joints and equipment likely to be disconnected for repairs or replacement for an underground metal water piping system used as a grounding electrode. The bonding jumper must be of sufficient length to allow the removal of such equipment while retaining the integrity of the grounding path. ▶Figure 250–155

(C) Grounding Electrode Conductor Connections. Grounding electrode conductors and bonding jumpers are permitted to terminate and use the following to extend the connection to another electrode(s):

(1) Interior metal water piping that's electrically continuous with a metal underground water pipe electrode and is located not more than 5 ft from the point of entrance to the building can be used to extend the connection to electrodes. Interior metal water piping located more than 5 ft from the point of entrance to the building isn't permitted to be used as a conductor to interconnect electrodes of the grounding electrode system. ▶Figure 250–156

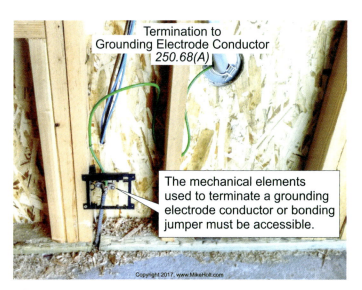

▶Figure 250–153

Ex 1: The termination isn't required to be accessible if the termination to the electrode is encased in concrete or buried in the earth. ▶Figure 250–154

250.68 | Grounding and Bonding

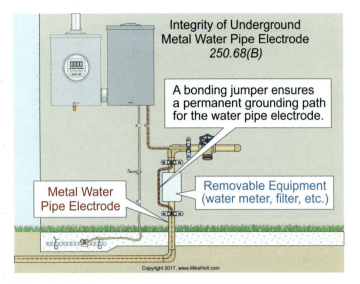
▶Figure 250–155

▶Figure 250–157

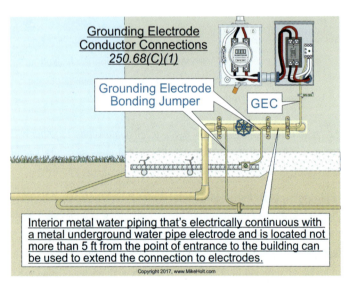
▶Figure 250–156

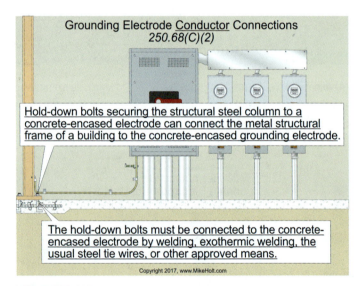
▶Figure 250–158

(2) The metal structural frame of a building can be used as a conductor to interconnect electrodes that are part of the grounding electrode system, or as a grounding electrode conductor. Hold-down bolts securing the structural steel column to a concrete-encased electrode [250.52(A)(3)] can connect the metal structural frame of a building to the concrete-encased grounding electrode. The hold-down bolts must be connected to the concrete-encased electrode by welding, exothermic welding, the usual steel tie wires, or other approved means. ▶Figure 250–157 and ▶Figure 250–158

(3) A rebar-type concrete-encased electrode [250.52(A)(3)] with an additional rebar section to an accessible location above the concrete, where not in contact with the earth or subject to corrosion, can be used for the connection of the grounding electrode conductors and bonding jumpers. ▶Figure 250–159

Grounding and Bonding | 250.70

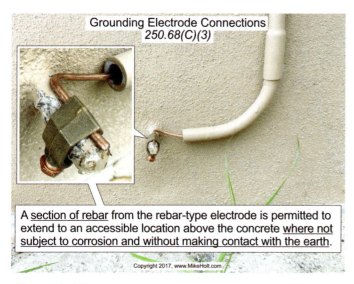

▶Figure 250–159

250.70 Grounding Electrode Conductor Termination Fittings

The grounding electrode conductor must terminate to the grounding electrode by exothermic welding, listed lugs, listed pressure connectors, listed clamps, or other listed means. In addition, fittings terminating to a grounding electrode must be listed for the materials of the grounding electrode and the grounding electrode conductor. ▶Figure 250–160

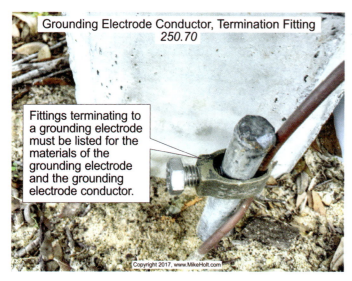

▶Figure 250–160

When the termination to a grounding electrode is buried in the earth or encased in concrete, the termination fitting must be listed for direct soil burial or concrete encasement. ▶Figure 250–161

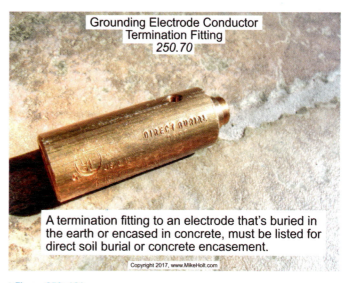

▶Figure 250–161

No more than one conductor can terminate on a single clamp or fitting unless the clamp or fitting is listed for multiple connections. ▶Figure 250–162

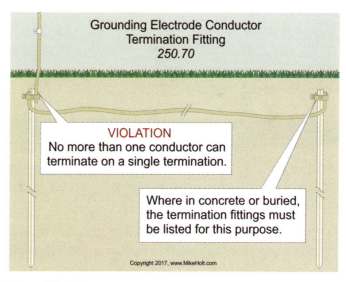

▶Figure 250–162

Part IV. Grounding Enclosure, Raceway, and Service Cable Connections

250.80 Service Raceways and Enclosures

Metal enclosures and raceways containing service conductors must be bonded to the neutral conductor at service equipment if the electrical system is grounded, or to the grounding electrode conductor for electrical systems that aren't grounded.

Ex: Metal components installed in a run of an underground nonmetallic raceway having a minimum cover of 18 in. isn't required to be bonded to the service neutral, supply-side bonding jumper, or grounding electrode conductor. ▶Figure 250–163

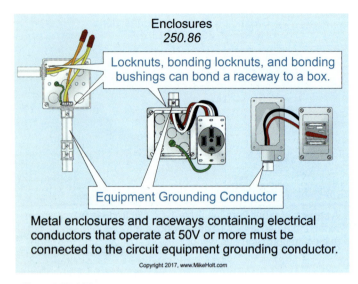

▶Figure 250–164

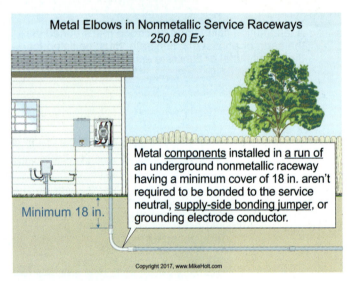

▶Figure 250–163

250.86 Other Enclosures

Metal raceways and enclosures containing electrical conductors operating at 50V or more [250.20(A)] must be connected to the circuit equipment grounding conductor. ▶Figure 250–164

Ex 2: Short sections of metal raceways used for the support or physical protection of cables aren't required to be connected to the circuit equipment grounding conductor. ▶Figure 250–165

Ex 3: Metal components aren't required to be connected to the circuit equipment grounding conductor or supply-side bonding jumper where either of the following conditions exist:

(1) The metal components are installed in a run of an underground nonmetallic raceway and isolated from possible contact by a minimum cover of 18 in. to any part of the metal components. ▶Figure 250–166

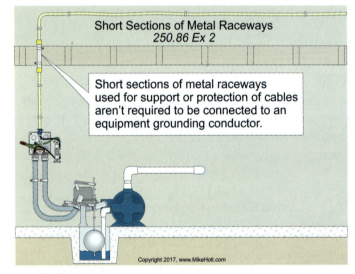

▶Figure 250–165

(2) The metal components are part of an installation of nonmetallic raceway(s) and are isolated from possible contact to any part of the metal components by being enclosed in not less than 2 in. of concrete.

Part V. Bonding

250.90 General

Bonding must be provided to ensure electrical continuity and the capacity to conduct safely any fault current likely to be imposed.

Grounding and Bonding | 250.92

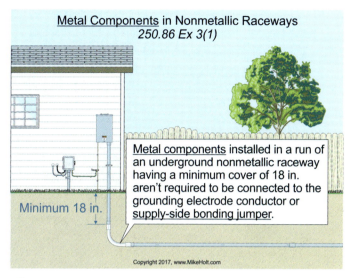

▶Figure 250–166

250.92 Bonding Equipment for Services

(A) Bonding Requirements for Equipment for Services. The metal parts of equipment indicated below must be bonded together in accordance with 250.92(B). ▶Figure 250–167

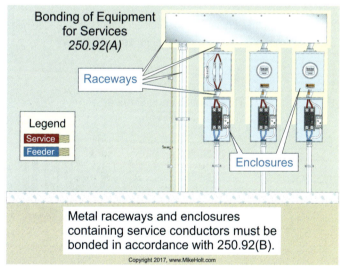

▶Figure 250–167

(1) Metal raceways containing service conductors.

(2) Metal enclosures containing service conductors.

Author's Comment:

- Metal raceways or metal enclosures containing feeder and branch-circuit conductors must be connected to the circuit equipment grounding conductor in accordance with 250.86.
  ▶Figure 250–168

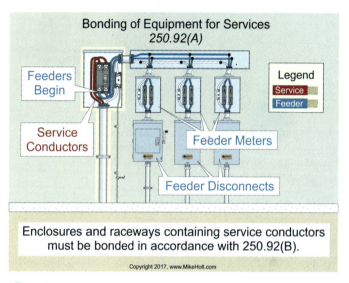

▶Figure 250–168

(B) Methods of Bonding. Bonding jumpers around reducing washers or oversized, concentric, or eccentric knockouts are required. ▶Figure 250–169

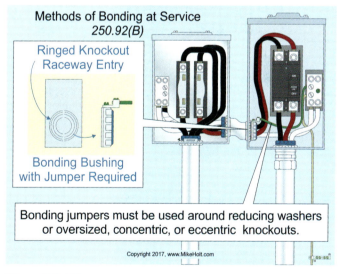

▶Figure 250–169

250.92 | Grounding and Bonding

Standard locknuts are permitted to make a mechanical connection to the raceway(s), but they can't serve as the bonding means required by this section. ▶Figure 250–170

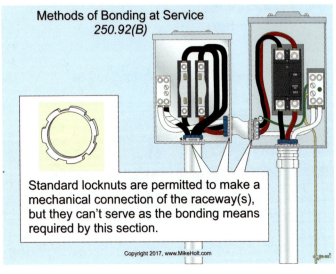

▶Figure 250–170

Electrical continuity at service equipment, service raceways, and service conductor enclosures must be ensured by any of the following methods:

(1) Bonding the metal parts to the service neutral conductor. ▶Figure 250–171

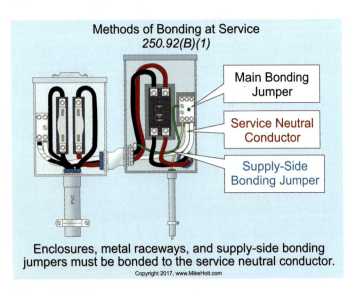

▶Figure 250–171

Author's Comment:

- A main bonding jumper is required to bond the service disconnect to the service neutral conductor [250.24(B) and 250.28].

- At service equipment, the service neutral conductor provides the effective ground-fault current path to the power supply [250.24(C)]; therefore, a supply-side bonding jumper (SSBJ) isn't required to be installed within PVC conduit containing service-entrance conductors [250.142(A)(1) and 352.60 Ex 2]. ▶Figure 250–172

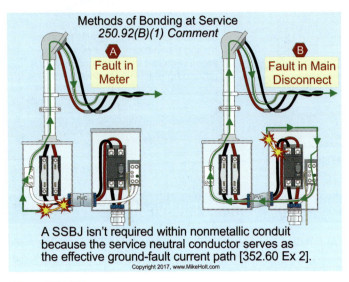

▶Figure 250–172

(2) Terminating metal raceways to metal enclosures by threaded hubs on enclosures if made up wrenchtight. ▶Figure 250–173

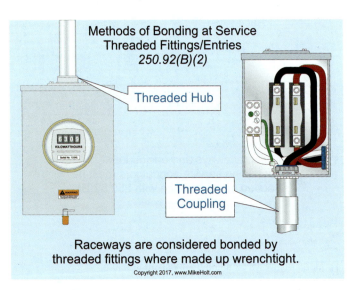

▶Figure 250–173

(3) Terminating metal raceways to metal enclosures by threadless fittings if made up tight. ▶Figure 250–174

Grounding and Bonding | 250.92

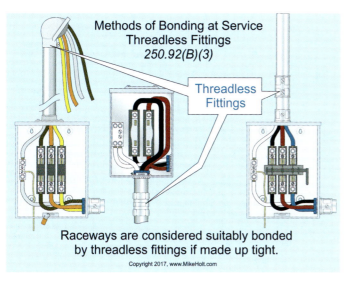

▶Figure 250–174

(4) Other listed devices, such as bonding-type locknuts, bushings, wedges, or bushings with bonding jumpers.

Author's Comment:

- A listed bonding wedge or bushing with a bonding jumper to the service neutral conductor is required when a metal raceway containing service conductors terminates to a ringed knockout. ▶Figure 250–175

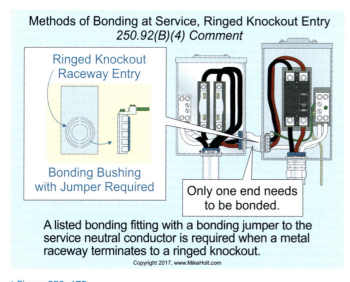

▶Figure 250–175

- The bonding jumper used for this purpose must be sized in accordance with Table 250.102(C)(1), based on the area of the largest ungrounded service conductors within the raceway [250.102(C)].

- A bonding-type locknut can be used for a metal raceway containing service conductors that terminates to an enclosure without a ringed knockout. ▶Figure 250–176

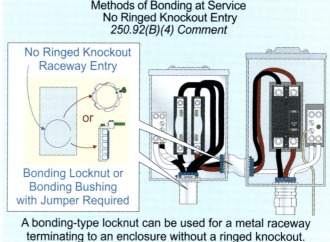

▶Figure 250–176

- A bonding locknut differs from a standard locknut in that it contains a bonding screw with a sharp point that drives into the metal enclosure to ensure a solid connection.
- Bonding one end of a service raceway to the service neutral provides the necessary low-impedance fault current path to the source. ▶Figure 250–177

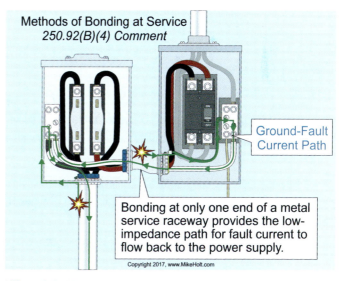

▶Figure 250–177

Note: The use of an intersystem bonding termination device can assist in reducing electrical noise on communications systems.

Mike Holt Enterprises • www.MikeHolt.com • 888.NEC.CODE (632.2633)   109

250.94 Bonding Communications Systems

Where communications systems (twisted wire, antennas, and coaxial cable) are likely to be used in a building or structure, communications system bonding terminations must be provided in accordance with (A) or (B) at service equipment or building disconnects supplied by a feeder.

(A) Intersystem Bonding Termination Device. Where an intersystem bonding termination device is required, it must meet the following requirements:

(1) Be accessible for connection and inspection. ▶Figure 250–178

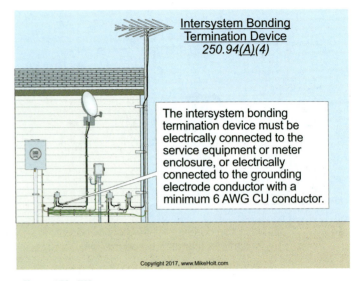

▶Figure 250–179

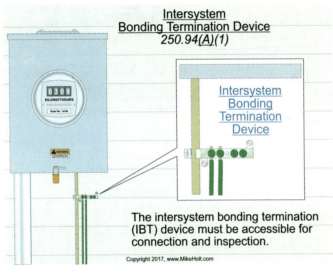

▶Figure 250–178

(2) Have a capacity for connection of at least three intersystem bonding conductors.

(3) Installed so that it doesn't interfere with opening any enclosure.

(4) Be securely mounted and electrically connected to the service equipment or meter enclosure, or grounding electrode conductor with a minimum 6 AWG copper conductor. ▶Figure 250–179

(5) Be securely mounted and electrically connected to the building's disconnect, or grounding electrode conductor with a minimum 6 AWG copper conductor.

(6) The terminals are listed as grounding and bonding equipment.

Author's Comment:

- According to Article 100, an intersystem bonding termination is a device that provides a means to connect communications systems (twisted wire, antennas, and coaxial cable) bonding conductors to the building grounding electrode system.

Ex: At existing buildings, an external accessible means for bonding communications systems (twisted wire, antennas, and coaxial cable) together can be by the use of a:

(1) Nonflexible metallic raceway,

(2) Grounding electrode conductor, or

(3) Connection approved by the authority having jurisdiction.

Note 2: Communications systems (twisted wire, antennas, and coaxial cable) must be bonded to the intersystem bonding termination in accordance with the following requirements: ▶Figure 250–180

- Antennas/Satellite Dishes, 810.15 and 810.21
- Coaxial Circuits, 820.100
- Telephone Circuits, 800.100

Author's Comment:

- External communications systems (twisted wire, antennas, and coaxial cable) must be connected to the intersystem bonding termination to minimize the damage to them from induced voltage differences between the systems from a lightning event. ▶Figure 250–181

Grounding and Bonding | 250.96

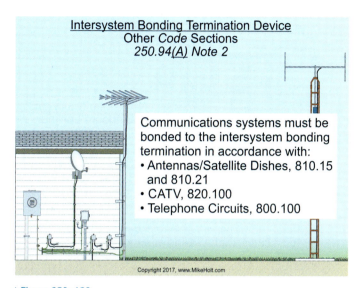
▶Figure 250–180

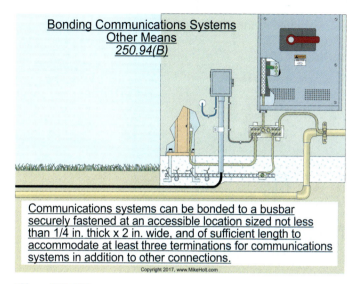
▶Figure 250–182

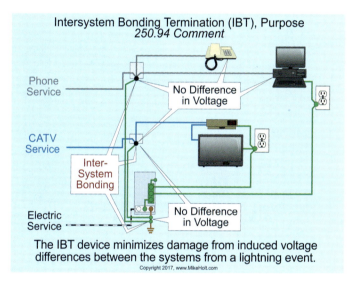
▶Figure 250–181

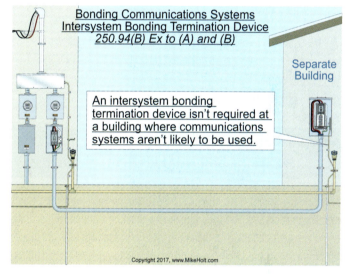
▶Figure 250–183

(B) Other Means. A busbar securely fastened at an accessible location sized not less than ¼ in. thick × 2 in. wide, and of sufficient length to accommodate at least three terminations for communications systems in addition to other connections. ▶Figure 250–182

Ex to (A) and (B): An intersystem bonding termination device isn't required where communications systems (twisted wire, antennas, and coaxial cable) aren't likely to be used. ▶Figure 250–183

250.96 Bonding Other Enclosures

(A) Maintaining Effective Ground-Fault Current Path. Metal parts intended to serve as equipment grounding conductors, including raceways, cables, equipment, and enclosures, must be bonded together to ensure they have the capacity to conduct safely any fault current likely to be imposed on them [110.10, 250.4(A)(5), and Note to Table 250.122]. ▶Figure 250–184

Nonconductive coatings such as paint, lacquer, and enamel on equipment must be removed to ensure an effective ground-fault current path, or the termination fittings must be designed so as to make such removal unnecessary [250.12].

250.97 | Grounding and Bonding

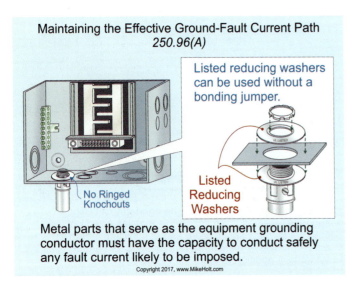

▶Figure 250–184

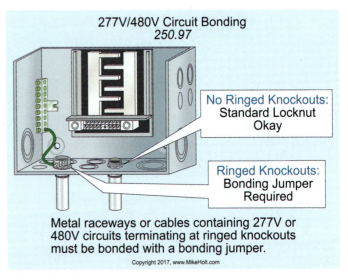

▶Figure 250–185

Author's Comment:

- The practice of driving a locknut tight with a screwdriver and pliers is considered sufficient in removing paint and other nonconductive finishes to ensure an effective ground-fault current path.

250.97 Bonding Metal Parts Containing 277V and 480V Circuits

Metal raceways or cables containing 277V and/or 480V feeder or branch circuits terminating at ringed knockouts must be bonded to the metal enclosure with a bonding jumper sized in accordance with 250.122, based on the rating of the circuit overcurrent protection device [250.102(D)].
▶Figure 250–185

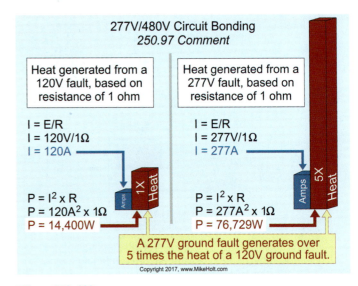

▶Figure 250–186

Ex: A bonding jumper isn't required where ringed knockouts aren't encountered, knockouts are totally punched out, or if the box is listed to provide a reliable bonding connection. ▶Figure 250–187

Author's Comment:

- Bonding jumpers for raceways and cables containing 277V or 480V circuits are required at ringed knockout terminations to ensure the ground-fault current path has the capacity to safely conduct the maximum ground-fault current likely to be imposed [110.10, 250.4(A)(5), and 250.96(A)].

- Ringed knockouts aren't listed to withstand the heat generated by a 277V ground fault, which generates five times as much heat as a 120V ground fault. ▶Figure 250–186

Grounding and Bonding | 250.102

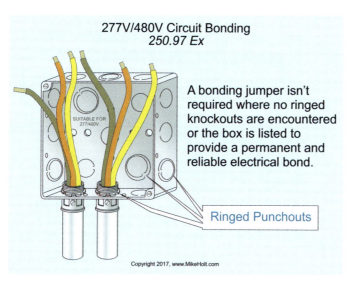

▸Figure 250–187

250.98 Bonding Loosely Jointed Metal Raceways

Expansion fittings and telescoping sections of metal raceways must be made electrically continuous by equipment bonding jumpers.
▸Figure 250–188

▸Figure 250–188

250.102 Grounded Conductor, Bonding Conductors, and Jumpers

(A) Material. Equipment bonding jumpers can be of copper, aluminum, or other corrosion-resistant material.

(B) Termination. Equipment bonding jumpers must terminate by any of the following means in accordance with 250.8(A):

- Listed pressure connectors
- Terminal bars
- Pressure connectors listed as grounding and bonding equipment
- Exothermic welding
- Machine screw-type fasteners that engage not less than two threads or are secured with a nut
- Thread-forming machine screws that engage not less than two threads in the enclosure
- Connections that are part of a listed assembly
- Other listed means

(C) Supply-Side Bonding Jumper Sizing.

(1) Single Raceway or Cable Installations. The supply-side bonding jumper is sized in accordance with Table 250.102(C)(1), based on the largest ungrounded conductor within the raceway or cable.
▸Figure 250–189

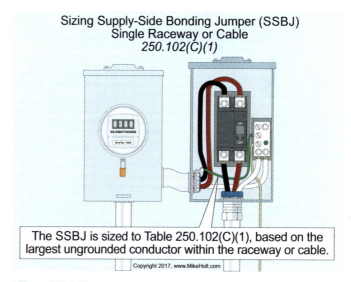

▸Figure 250–189

Mike Holt Enterprises • www.MikeHolt.com • 888.NEC.CODE (632.2633)   113

250.102 | Grounding and Bonding

(2) Parallel Conductor Installations in Two or More Raceways or Cables. If the ungrounded supply conductors are paralleled in two or more raceways or cables, the size of the supply-side bonding jumper for each raceway or cable is sized in accordance with Table 250.102(C)(1), based on the size of the largest ungrounded conductors in each raceway or cable. ▶Figure 250–190

Note 1: The term "supply conductors" includes ungrounded conductors that don't have overcurrent protection on their supply side and terminate at service equipment or the first disconnect of a separately derived system.

Note 2: See Chapter 9, Table 8, for the circular mil area of conductors 18 AWG through 4/0 AWG.

▶Figure 250–190

Table 250.102(C)(1) Grounded Conductor, Main Bonding Jumper, System Bonding Jumper, and Supply-Side Bonding Jumper

Size of Largest Ungrounded Conductor Per Raceway or Equivalent Area for Parallel Conductors		Size of Bonding Jumper or Grounded Conductor
Copper	Aluminum or Copper-Clad Aluminum	Copper-Aluminum
2 or smaller	1/0 or smaller	8—6
1 or 1/0	2/0 or 3/0	6—4
2/0 or 3/0	Over 3/0 250 kcmil	4—2
Over 3/0 through 350 kcmil	Over 250 through 500 kcmil	2—1/0
Over 350 through 600 kcmil	Over 500 through 900 kcmil	1/0—3/0

Example: What size single supply-side bonding jumper is required for three metal raceways, each containing 400 kcmil service conductors? ▶Figure 250–191

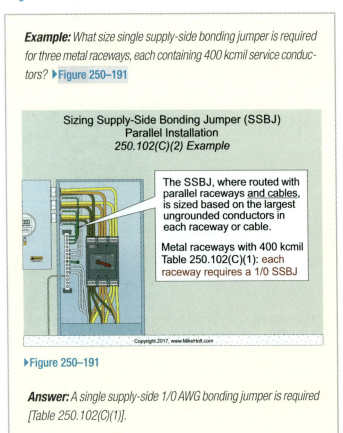

▶Figure 250–191

Answer: A single supply-side 1/0 AWG bonding jumper is required [Table 250.102(C)(1)].

(D) Load-Side Bonding Jumper Sizing. Bonding jumpers on the load side of feeder and branch-circuit overcurrent protection devices are sized in accordance with 250.122, based on the rating of the circuit overcurrent protection device. ▶Figure 250–192

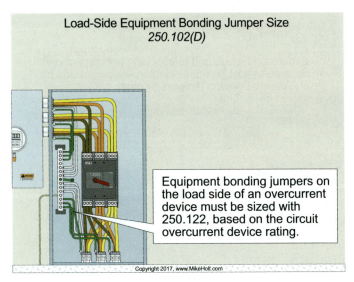

▶Figure 250–192

Grounding and Bonding | 250.104

Example: What size equipment bonding jumper is required for each metal raceway where the circuit conductors are protected by a 1,200A overcurrent protection device? ▶Figure 250–193

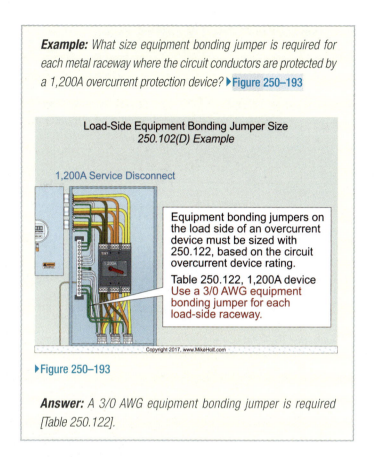

▶Figure 250–193

Answer: A 3/0 AWG equipment bonding jumper is required [Table 250.122].

If a single bonding jumper is used to bond two or more raceways, it must be sized in accordance with 250.122, based on the rating of the largest circuit overcurrent protection device. ▶Figure 250–194

▶Figure 250–194

(E) Installation of Bonding Jumpers.

(1) Inside Raceway. Bonding jumpers installed inside a raceway must be identified in accordance with 250.119 and must terminate to the enclosure in accordance with 250.148.

(2) Outside Raceway. Bonding jumpers installed outside a raceway must be routed with the raceway and can't exceed 6 ft in length. ▶Figure 250–195

▶Figure 250–195

250.104 Bonding of Piping Systems and Exposed Structural Metal

Author's Comment:

- To remove dangerous voltage on metal parts from a ground fault, electrically conductive metal water piping systems, metal sprinkler piping, metal gas piping, as well as exposed structural metal members likely to become energized, must be connected to an effective ground-fault current path [250.4(A)(4)].

(A) Metal Water Piping System. Metal water piping systems that are interconnected to form a mechanically and electrically continuous system must be bonded in accordance with 250.104(A)(1), (A)(2), or (A)(3).

(1) Buildings Supplied by a Service. The metal water piping system, including the metal sprinkler water piping system, of a building supplied with service conductors must be bonded to any of the following: ▶Figure 250–196

250.104 | Grounding and Bonding

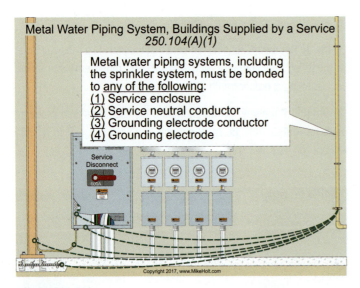
▶Figure 250–196

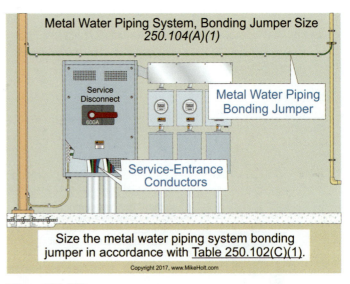
▶Figure 250–197

(1) Service equipment enclosure,

(2) Neutral at service equipment,

(3) Grounding electrode conductor if of sufficient size, or

(4) One of the grounding electrodes of the grounding electrode system if the grounding electrode conductor or bonding jumper to the electrode is of sufficient size.

The bonding jumper must be copper where within 18 in. of the surface of earth [250.64(A)], must be adequately protected if exposed to physical damage [250.64(B)], and all points of attachment must be accessible. A ferrous metal raceway containing a grounding electrode conductor must be made electrically continuous by bonding each end of the raceway to the grounding electrode conductor [250.64(E)], so it's best to use nonmetallic conduit.

The metal water piping system bonding jumper must be sized in accordance with Table 250.102(C)(1), based on the cross-sectional area of the ungrounded service conductors. ▶Figure 250–197

Example: What size bonding jumper is required for a metal water piping system, if the 300 kcmil service conductors are paralleled in two raceways? ▶Figure 250–198

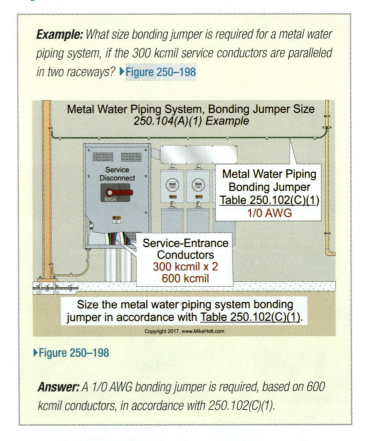
▶Figure 250–198

Answer: A 1/0 AWG bonding jumper is required, based on 600 kcmil conductors, in accordance with 250.102(C)(1).

Author's Comment:

- If hot and cold metal water pipes are electrically connected, only one bonding jumper is required, either to the cold or hot water pipe. Bonding isn't required for isolated sections of metal water piping connected to a nonmetallic water piping system.
▶Figure 250–199

Grounding and Bonding | 250.104

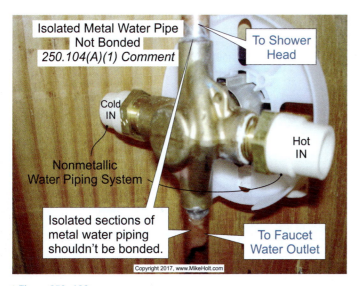

▶Figure 250–199

(2) Multiple Occupancy Building. When a metal water piping system in an individual occupancy is metallically isolated from other occupancies, the metal water piping system for that occupancy can be bonded to the equipment grounding terminal of the occupancy's switchgear, switchboard, or panelboard. The bonding jumper must be sized based on the rating of the circuit overcurrent protection device sized in accordance with 250.122 [250.102(D)]. ▶Figure 250–200

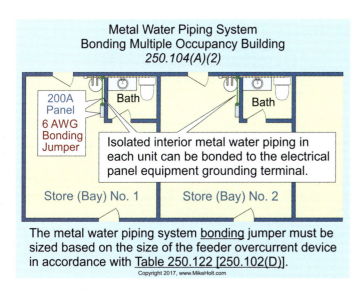

▶Figure 250–200

(3) Buildings Supplied by a Feeder. The metal water piping system of a building supplied by a feeder must be bonded to one of the following:

(a) The equipment grounding terminal of the building disconnect enclosure,

(b) The feeder equipment grounding conductor, or

(c) One of the building grounding electrodes of the grounding electrode system if the grounding electrode or bonding jumper to the electrode is of sufficient size.

The bonding jumper is sized to Table 250.102(C)(1), based on the cross-sectional area of the feeder conductor.

(B) Other Metal-Piping Systems. Metal-piping systems in or attached to a building that are likely to become energized must be bonded to one of the following:

(1) Equipment grounding conductor for the circuit that's likely to energize the piping system ▶Figure 250–201

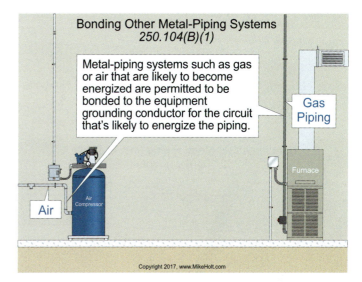

▶Figure 250–201

(2) Service equipment enclosure

(3) Neutral conductor at the service equipment

(4) Grounding electrode conductor, if of sufficient size

(5) One of the grounding electrodes of the grounding electrode system if the grounding electrode conductor or bonding jumper to the electrode is of sufficient size

The bonding jumper is sized to Table 250.122, based on the cross-sectional area of the feeder conductor, and equipment grounding conductors are sized to Table 250.122 using the rating of the circuit that's likely to energize the piping system(s). The points of attachment of the bonding jumper(s) must be accessible.

Note 1: Bonding all piping and metal air ducts within the premises will provide additional safety. ▶Figure 250–202

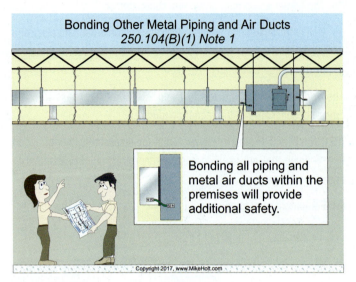
▶Figure 250–202

Note 2: The *National Fuel Gas Code*, NFPA 54, Section 7.13 contains further information about bonding gas piping. ▶Figure 250–203

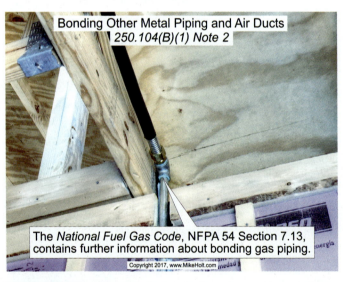
▶Figure 250–203

Author's Comment

- Informational Notes in the *NEC* are for information purposes only and aren't enforceable as a requirement of the *Code* [90.5(C)].

(C) Structural Metal. Exposed structural metal that's interconnected to form a metal building frame and is likely to become energized must be bonded to any of the following: ▶Figure 250–204

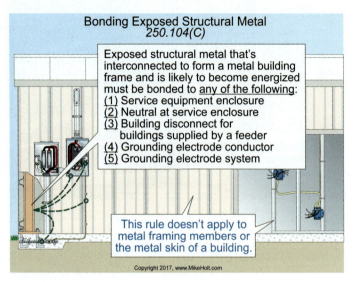
▶Figure 250–204

(1) The service equipment enclosure,

(2) The neutral at the service equipment,

(3) The building disconnect enclosure for buildings supplied by a feeder,

(4) The grounding electrode conductor where of sufficient size, or

(5) One of the grounding electrodes of the grounding electrode system if the grounding electrode conductor or bonding jumper to the electrode is of sufficient size.

The structural metal bonding conductor or jumper must be sized in accordance with Table 250.102(C)(1), based on the area of the ungrounded supply conductors. The bonding jumper must be copper where within 18 in. of the surface of the earth [250.64(A)], be securely fastened to the surface on which it's carried [250.64(B)], and be adequately protected if exposed to physical damage [250.64(B)]. In addition, all points of attachment must be accessible, except as permitted in 250.68(A) Ex.

Author's Comment:

- This rule doesn't require the bonding of sheet metal framing members (studs) or the metal skin of a wood-frame building.

(D) Separately Derived Systems. Metal water piping systems and structural metal that's interconnected to form a building frame must be bonded to the separately derived system in accordance with 250.104(D)(1) through (D)(3).

(1) Metal Water Pipe. If metal water piping systems exists in the area served by a separately derived system, it must be bonded to the neutral point of the separately derived system where the grounding electrode conductor is connected. ▶Figure 250–205

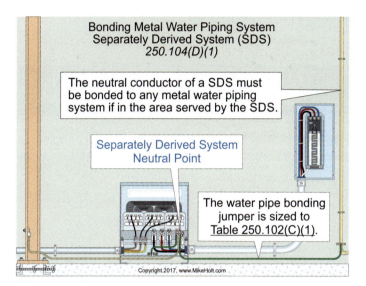

▶Figure 250–205

The bonding jumper must be sized in accordance with Table 250.102(C)(1), based on the area of the ungrounded conductor of the derived system.

Ex 2: The metal water piping system can be bonded to the structural metal building frame if it serves as the grounding electrode [250.52(A)(1)] for the separately derived system. ▶Figure 250–206

(2) Structural Metal. Exposed structural metal that's interconnected to form the building frame located in the area served by a separately derived system must be bonded to the neutral conductor where the grounding electrode conductor is connected at the separately derived system.

The bonding jumper must be sized in accordance with Table 250.102(C)(1), based on the largest ungrounded conductor of the separately derived system.

Ex 1: Bonding to the separately derived system isn't required if the metal serves as the grounding electrode [250.52(A)(2)] for the separately derived system.

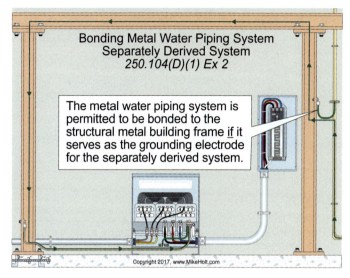

▶Figure 250–206

(3) Common Grounding Electrode Conductor. If a common grounding electrode conductor is installed for multiple separately derived systems as permitted by 250.30(A)(6), and exposed structural metal that's interconnected to form the building frame or interior metal piping exists in the area served by the separately derived system, the metal piping and the structural metal member can be bonded to the common grounding electrode conductor in the area served by the separately derived system.

Ex: A separate bonding jumper from each derived system to metal water piping and to structural metal members isn't required if the metal water piping and the structural metal members in the area served by the separately derived system are bonded to the common grounding electrode conductor.

250.106 Lightning Protection System

When a lightning protection system is installed in accordance with NFPA 780, the lightning protection electrode system must be bonded to the building grounding electrode system. ▶Figure 250–207

Note 1: See NFPA 780—*Standard for the Installation of Lightning Protection Systems*, which contains detailed information on grounding, bonding, and side-flash distance from lightning protection systems.

Note 2: To minimize the likelihood of arcing between metal parts because of induced voltage, metal raceways, enclosures, and other metal parts of electrical equipment may require bonding or spacing from the lightning protection conductors in accordance with NFPA 780—*Standard for the Installation of Lightning Protection Systems*. ▶Figure 250–208

250.110 | Grounding and Bonding

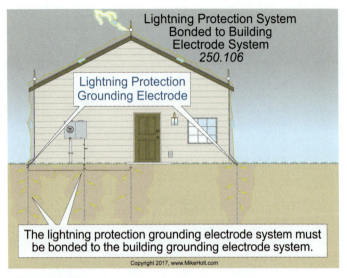

▶Figure 250–207

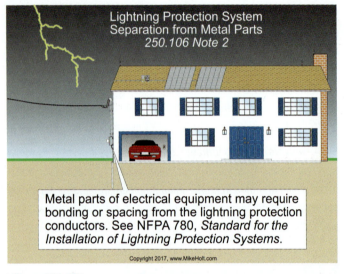

▶Figure 250–208

Part VI. Equipment Grounding and Equipment Grounding Conductors

250.110 Fixed Equipment Connected by Permanent Wiring Methods—General

Exposed metal parts of fixed equipment likely to become energized must be connected to the circuit equipment grounding conductor where the equipment is:

(1) Within 8 ft vertically or 5 ft horizontally from the surface of the earth or a grounded metal object

(2) Located in a wet or damp location

(3) In electrical contact with metal

(4) In a hazardous (classified) location [Articles 500 through 517]

(5) Supplied by a wiring method that provides an equipment grounding conductor

(6) Supplied by a 277V or 480V circuit

Ex 3: Listed double-insulated equipment isn't required to be connected to the circuit equipment grounding conductor.

250.112 Specific Equipment Fastened in Place or Connected by Permanent Wiring Methods

To remove dangerous voltage from a ground fault, metal parts must be connected to the circuit equipment grounding conductor. ▶Figure 250–209

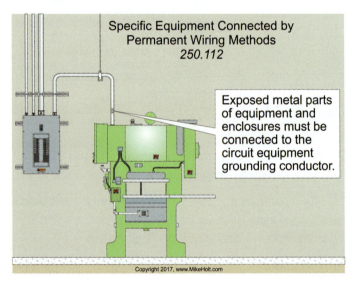

▶Figure 250–209

(I) Low-Voltage Circuits. Equipment supplied by circuits operating at less than 50V isn't required to be connected to the circuit equipment grounding conductor. ▶Figure 250–210

250.114 Cord-and-Plug-Connected Equipment

To remove dangerous voltage from a ground fault, metal parts must be connected to the circuit equipment grounding conductor. ▶Figure 250–211

Grounding and Bonding | 250.118

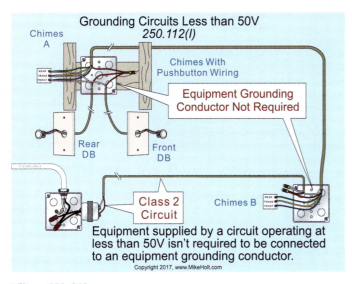

▶Figure 250–210

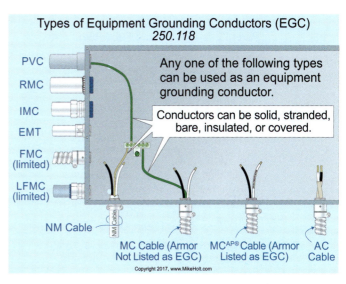

▶Figure 250–212

▶Figure 250–211

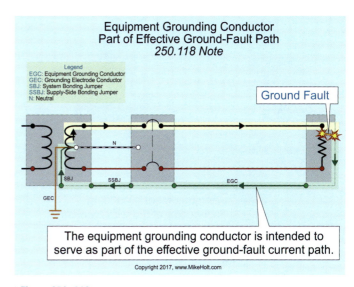

▶Figure 250–213

Ex: Listed double-insulated equipment isn't required to be connected to the circuit equipment grounding conductor.

250.118 Types of Equipment Grounding Conductors

An equipment grounding conductor can be any one or a combination of the following: ▶Figure 250–212

Note: The equipment grounding conductor is intended to serve as part of the effective ground-fault current path. See 250.2. ▶Figure 250–213

Author's Comment:

- The effective ground-fault path is an intentionally constructed low-impedance conductive path designed to carry fault current from the point of a ground fault on a wiring system to the electrical supply source. Its purpose is to quickly remove dangerous voltage from a ground fault by opening the circuit overcurrent protection device [250.2]. ▶Figure 250–214

(1) An equipment grounding conductor of the wire type can be a bare or insulated copper or aluminum conductor. ▶Figure 250–215

Mike Holt Enterprises • www.MikeHolt.com • 888.NEC.CODE (632.2633)   121

250.118 | Grounding and Bonding

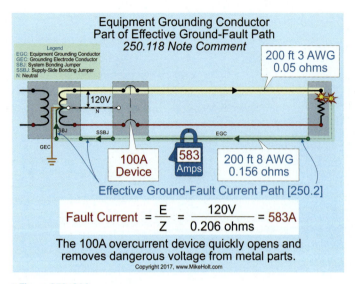

▶Figure 250–214

▶Figure 250–216

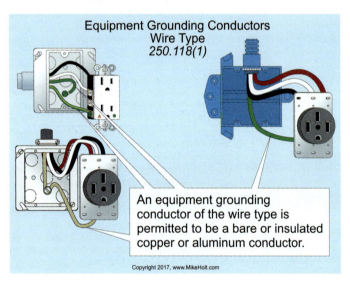

▶Figure 250–215

(2) Rigid metal conduit can serve as an equipment grounding conductor.

(3) Intermediate metal conduit can serve as an equipment grounding conductor.

(4) Electrical metallic tubing can serve as an equipment grounding conductor.

(5) Listed flexible metal conduit (FMC) can serve as an equipment grounding conductor where: ▶Figure 250–216

   a. The raceway terminates in listed fittings.

   b. The circuit conductors are protected by an overcurrent protection device rated 20A or less.

   c. The size of the flexible metal conduit doesn't exceed trade size 1¼.

   d. The combined length of the flexible conduit in the same ground-fault current path doesn't exceed 6 ft.

   e. If flexibility is required to minimize the transmission of vibration from equipment or to provide flexibility for equipment that requires movement after installation, an equipment grounding conductor of the wire type must be installed with the circuit conductors in accordance with 250.102(E), and it must be sized in accordance with 250.122, based on the rating of the circuit overcurrent protection device. ▶Figure 250–217

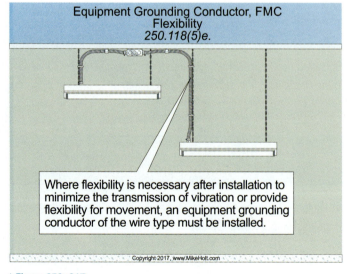

▶Figure 250–217

Grounding and Bonding | 250.118

(6) Listed liquidtight flexible metal conduit (LFMC) can serve as an equipment grounding conductor where: ▶Figure 250–218

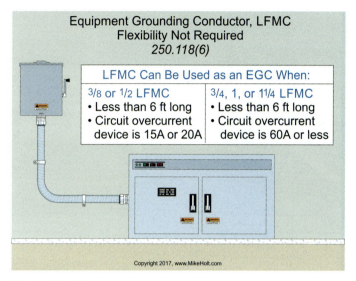

▶Figure 250–218

a. The raceway terminates in listed fittings.

b. For ⅜ in. through ½ in., the circuit conductors are protected by an overcurrent protection device rated 20A or less.

c. For ¾ in. through 1¼ in., the circuit conductors are protected by an overcurrent protection device rated 60A or less.

d. The combined length of the flexible conduit in the same ground-fault current path doesn't exceed 6 ft.

e. If flexibility is required to minimize the transmission of vibration from equipment or to provide flexibility for equipment that requires movement after installation, an equipment grounding conductor of the wire type must be installed with the circuit conductors in accordance with 250.102(E), and it must be sized in accordance with 250.122, based on the rating of the circuit overcurrent protection device.

(8) The sheath of Type AC cable containing an aluminum bonding strip can serve as an equipment grounding conductor. ▶Figure 250–219

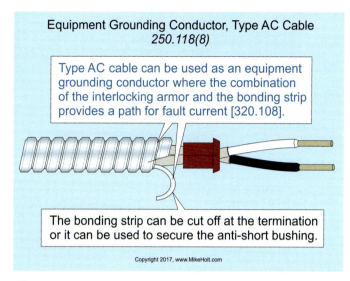

▶Figure 250–219

Author's Comment:

- The internal aluminum bonding strip isn't an equipment grounding conductor, but it allows the interlocked armor to serve as an equipment grounding conductor because it reduces the impedance of the armored spirals to ensure that a ground fault will be cleared. It's the aluminum bonding strip in combination with the cable armor that creates the circuit equipment grounding conductor. Once the bonding strip exits the cable, it can be cut off because it no longer serves any purpose.

- The effective ground-fault current path must be maintained by the use of fittings specifically listed for Type AC cable [320.40]. See 300.12, 300.15, and 320.100.

(9) The copper sheath of Type MI cable can serve as an equipment grounding conductor.

(10) Type MC cable

a. The interlock type cable that contains an insulated or uninsulated equipment grounding conductor in accordance with 250.118(1) can serve as an equipment grounding conductor. ▶Figure 250–220

b. The combined metallic sheath and uninsulated equipment grounding/bonding conductor of interlocked metal that's listed and identified as an equipment grounding conductor can serve as an equipment grounding conductor. ▶Figure 250–221

250.118 | Grounding and Bonding

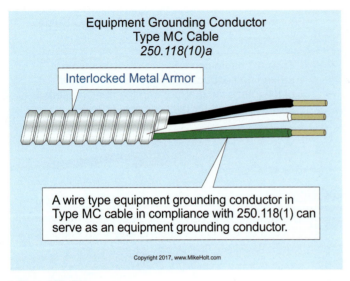

▶Figure 250–220

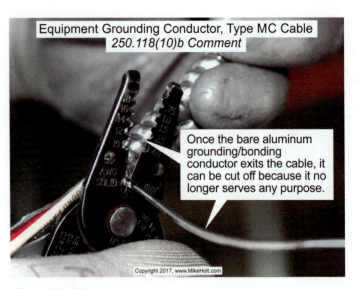

▶Figure 250–222

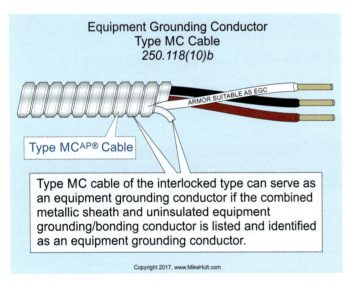

▶Figure 250–221

Author's Comment:

- Once the bare aluminum grounding/bonding conductor exits the cable, it can be cut off because it no longer serves any purpose. The effective ground-fault current path must be maintained by the use of fittings specifically listed for Type MC^{AP}® cable [330.40]. See 300.12, 300.15, and 330.100.
▶Figure 250–222

c. The metallic sheath of the smooth or corrugated tube-type MC cable that's listed and identified as an equipment grounding conductor can serve as an equipment grounding conductor.

(11) Metal cable trays can serve as an equipment grounding conductor if continuous maintenance and supervision ensure only qualified persons will service the cable tray, with cable tray and fittings identified for grounding and the cable tray, fittings [392.10], and raceways are bonded together using bolted mechanical connectors or bonding jumpers sized and installed in accordance with 250.102 [392.60]. ▶Figure 250–223

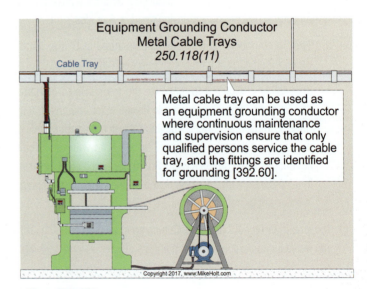

▶Figure 250–223

(13) Listed electrically continuous metal raceways, such as metal wireways [Article 376] or strut-type channel raceways [384.60] can serve as an equipment grounding conductor. ▶Figure 250–224

Grounding and Bonding | 250.119

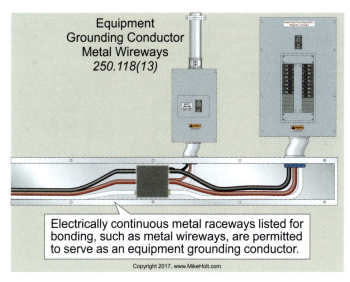
▶Figure 250–224

(14) Surface metal raceways listed for grounding [Article 386] can serve as an equipment grounding conductor.

250.119 Identification of Equipment Grounding Conductors

Unless required to be insulated, equipment grounding conductors can be bare or covered. Insulated equipment grounding conductors 6 AWG and smaller must have a continuous outer finish that's either green or green with one or more yellow stripes. ▶Figure 250–225

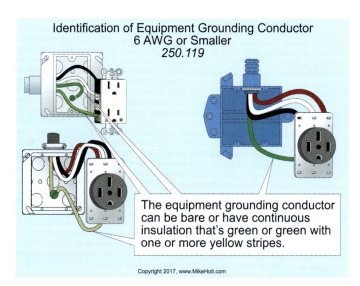
▶Figure 250–225

Conductors with insulation that's green, or green with one or more yellow stripes, aren't permitted be used for an ungrounded or neutral conductor. ▶Figure 250–226

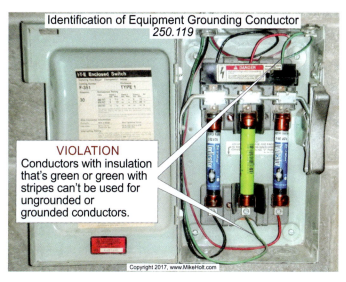
▶Figure 250–226

Author's Comment:

- The *NEC* neither requires nor prohibits the use of the color green for the identification of grounding electrode conductors. ▶Figure 250–227

▶Figure 250–227

250.120 | Grounding and Bonding

Ex 3: Conductors with green insulation can be used as ungrounded signal conductors for traffic signal control and traffic signal indicating heads. The circuit must still include an equipment grounding conductor, and if it's of the wire type it must be bare or green with one or more yellow stripes.

(A) Conductors 4 AWG and Larger.

(1) Identified if Accessible. Insulated equipment grounding conductors 4 AWG and larger can be permanently reidentified at the time of installation at every point where the conductor is accessible. ▶Figure 250–228

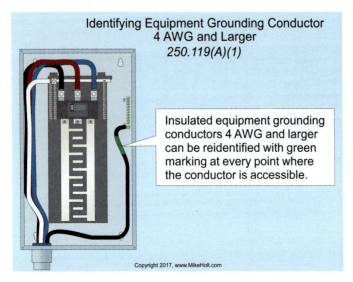
▶Figure 250–228

Ex: Identification of equipment grounding conductors 4 AWG and larger in conduit bodies isn't required.

(2) Identification Method. ▶Figure 250–229

   a. Removing the insulation at termination

   b. Coloring the insulation green at termination

   c. Marking the insulation at termination with green tape or green adhesive labels

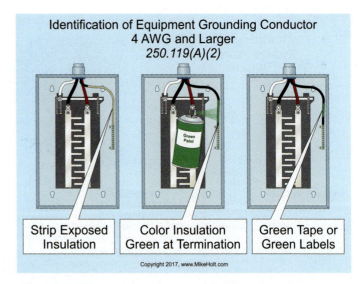
▶Figure 250–229

250.120 Equipment Grounding Conductor Installation

An equipment grounding conductor must be installed as follows:

(A) Raceway, Cable Trays, Cable Armor, Cablebus, or Cable Sheaths. If it consists of a raceway, cable tray, cable armor, cablebus framework, or cable sheath, fittings for joints and terminations must be made tight using suitable tools.

(B) Aluminum Conductors. Aluminum equipment grounding conductors must comply with the following:

(1) Bare or covered aluminum equipment grounding conductors are not permitted to be in contact with masonry or earth.

(2) Aluminum equipment grounding conductors within 18 in. of the earth are permitted to terminate within listed enclosures identified for outdoor use.

(3) Aluminum equipment grounding conductors located outdoors must be insulated when within 18 in. of the earth. The terminal must be listed as a sealed wire-connector system for grounding and bonding equipment.

(C) Equipment Grounding Conductors Smaller Than 6 AWG. If not routed with circuit conductors as permitted in 250.130(C) and 250.134(B) Ex 2, equipment grounding conductors smaller than 6 AWG must be installed within a raceway or cable if subject to physical damage. ▶Figure 250–230

Grounding and Bonding | 250.122

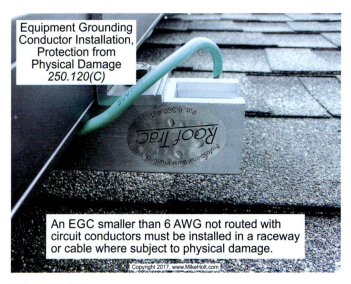

▶Figure 250–230

250.121 Use of Equipment Grounding Conductors

An equipment grounding conductor isn't permitted to be used as a grounding electrode conductor. ▶Figure 250–231

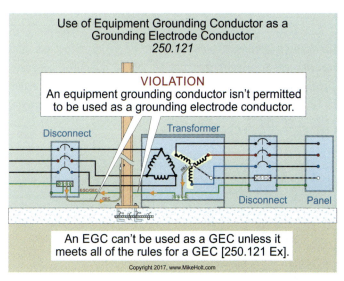

▶Figure 250–231

Ex: Equipment grounding conductors of the wire type can be used as a grounding electrode conductor provided they meet all of the rules for both.

250.122 Sizing Equipment Grounding Conductor

(A) General. Equipment grounding conductors of the wire type must be sized not smaller than shown in Table 250.122, based on the rating of the circuit overcurrent protection device; however, the circuit equipment grounding conductor isn't required to be larger than the circuit conductors. ▶Figure 250–232 and ▶Figure 250–233

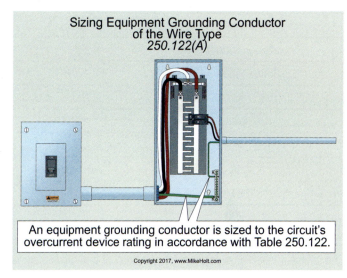

▶Figure 250–232

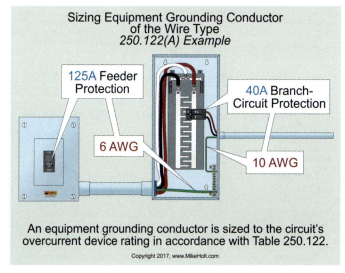

▶Figure 250–233

250.122 | Grounding and Bonding

Table 250.122 Sizing Equipment Grounding Conductor	
Overcurrent Protection Device Rating	Copper Conductor
15A	14 AWG
20A	12 AWG
25A—60A	10 AWG
70A—100A	8 AWG
110A—200A	6 AWG
225A—300A	4 AWG
350A—400A	3 AWG
450A—500A	2 AWG
600A	1 AWG
700A—800A	1/0 AWG
1,000A	2/0 AWG
1,200A	3/0 AWG

(B) Increased in Size. If ungrounded conductors are increased in size for any reason from the minimum size that has sufficient ampacity for the intended installation before the application of any adjustment or correction factor(s), wire-type equipment grounding conductors must be at least proportionately increased in size according to the circular mil area of the ungrounded conductors.

Author's Comment:

- Ungrounded conductors are sometimes increased in size to accommodate conductor voltage drop, harmonic current heating, short-circuit rating, or simply for future capacity.

Example: If the ungrounded conductors for a 40A circuit (with 75°C terminals) are increased in size from 8 AWG to 6 AWG due to voltage drop, the circuit equipment grounding conductor must be increased in size from 10 AWG to what size? ▶Figure 250–234

Solution: The circuit equipment grounding conductor must be increased to size 8 AWG.

Conductor Size = 10,380 Cmil × 1.59
Conductor Size = 16,504 Cmil

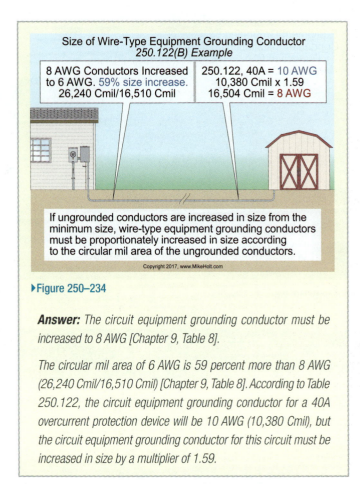

▶Figure 250–234

Answer: The circuit equipment grounding conductor must be increased to 8 AWG [Chapter 9, Table 8].

The circular mil area of 6 AWG is 59 percent more than 8 AWG (26,240 Cmil/16,510 Cmil) [Chapter 9, Table 8]. According to Table 250.122, the circuit equipment grounding conductor for a 40A overcurrent protection device will be 10 AWG (10,380 Cmil), but the circuit equipment grounding conductor for this circuit must be increased in size by a multiplier of 1.59.

(C) Multiple Circuits. When multiple circuits are installed in the same raceway, cable, or cable tray, one equipment grounding conductor sized in accordance with 250.122, based on the rating of the largest circuit overcurrent protection device is sufficient. ▶Figure 250–235 and ▶Figure 250–236

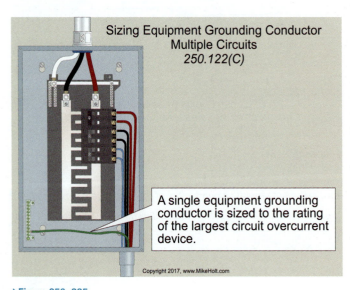

▶Figure 250–235

Grounding and Bonding | 250.122

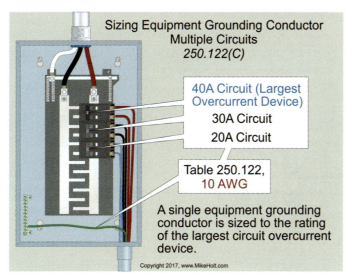

▶Figure 250–236

(D) Motor Branch Circuits.

(1) General. The equipment grounding conductor of the wire type must be sized in accordance with Table 250.122, based on the rating of the motor circuit branch-circuit short-circuit and ground-fault overcurrent protection device, but this conductor isn't required to be larger than the circuit conductors [250.122(A)]. ▶Figure 250–237

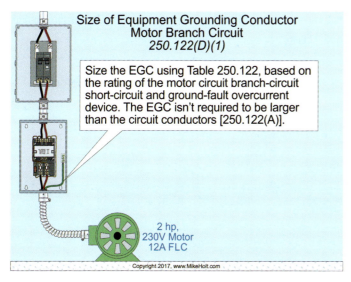

▶Figure 250–237

Example: What size equipment grounding conductor of the wire type is required for a 14 AWG motor branch circuit [430.22], protected with a 2-pole, 30A circuit breaker in accordance with 430.22 and 430.52(C)(1)? ▶Figure 250–238

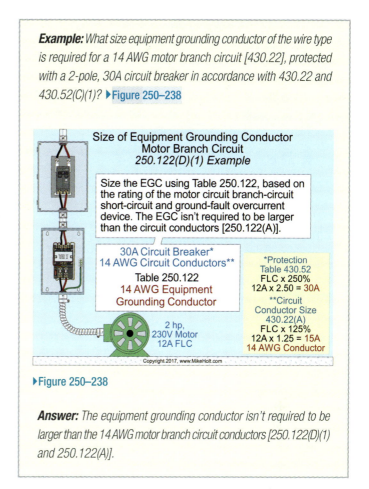

▶Figure 250–238

Answer: The equipment grounding conductor isn't required to be larger than the 14 AWG motor branch circuit conductors [250.122(D)(1) and 250.122(A)].

(F) Parallel Runs. If circuit conductors are installed in parallel as permitted by 310.10(H), an equipment grounding conductor must be installed for each parallel conductor set in accordance with the following:

(1) Raceways or Cable Trays.

(a) Parallel Feeder Runs in a Single Raceway or Cable Tray. The single wire-type equipment grounding conductor is required in each raceway or cable tray. It must be sized in accordance with Table 250.122, based on the rating of the circuit overcurrent protection device.

(b) Parallel Feeder Runs in Multiple Raceways. The equipment grounding conductor in each parallel run raceway must be sized in accordance with Table 250.122, based on the rating of the feeder overcurrent protection device. ▶Figure 250–239 and ▶Figure 250–240

(2) Parallel Feeder Runs Using Multiconductor Cables.

(a) Multiconductor cables used in parallel must have the equipment grounding conductors of all cables electrically paralleled with each other.

250.122 | Grounding and Bonding

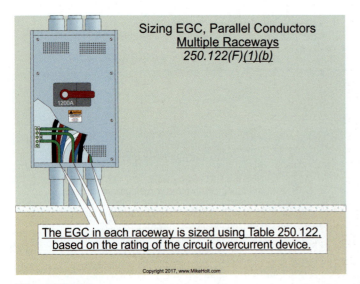

▶Figure 250–239

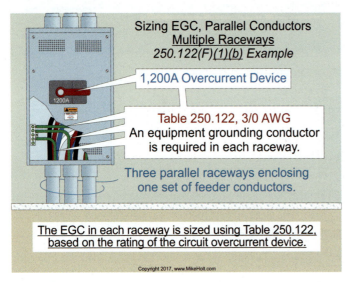

▶Figure 250–240

(b) Parallel multiconductor cables in a single raceway or cable tray are permitted to have a single equipment grounding conductor connected to the equipment grounding conductors within the multiconductor cables. This single equipment grounding conductor must be sized in accordance with 250.122, based on the rating of the feeder overcurrent protection device.

(c) Equipment grounding conductors installed in cable trays must comply with 392.10(B)(1)(c).

(d) Parallel multiconductor cables not installed in a raceway or cable tray must have an equipment grounding conductor of the wire type in each cable sized in accordance with 250.122, based on the rating of the circuit overcurrent protection device. ▶Figure 250–241

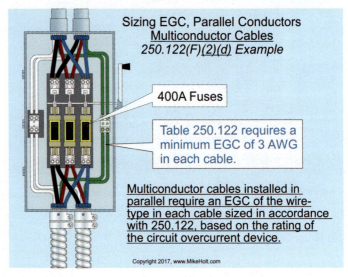

▶Figure 250–241

(G) Feeder Tap Conductors. Equipment grounding conductors for feeder taps must be sized in accordance with Table 250.122, based on the ampere rating of the overcurrent protection device ahead of the feeder, but in no case is it required to be larger than the feeder tap conductors. ▶Figure 250–242

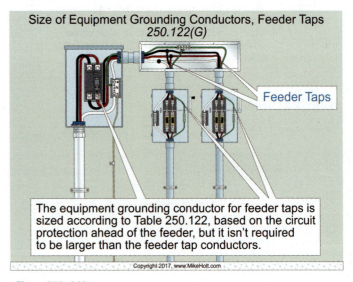

▶Figure 250–242

Part VII. Methods of Equipment Grounding

250.130 Equipment Grounding Conductor Connections

(C) Nongrounding Receptacle Replacement or Branch-Circuit Extension. If a grounding-type receptacle is installed or a branch circuit extension is made from an outlet box that doesn't contain an equipment grounding conductor, the grounding contacts of a grounding-type receptacle must be connected to any of the following: ▶Figure 250–243 and ▶Figure 250–244

(1) The grounding electrode system [250.50]

(2) The grounding electrode conductor

(3) The panelboard equipment grounding terminal

(4) An equipment grounding conductor that's part of a different circuit, if both circuits originate from the same panel

(5) The service neutral conductor

Note: A grounding-type receptacle can replace a nongrounding-type receptacle, without having the grounding terminal connected to an equipment grounding conductor, if the receptacle is GFCI protected and marked in accordance with 406.4(D)(2).

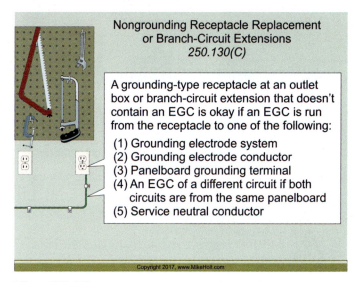

▶Figure 250–243

250.134 Equipment Connected by Permanent Wiring Methods

Except as permitted for services or separately derived systems [250.142(A)], metal parts of equipment, raceways, and enclosures must be connected to an equipment grounding conductor by any of the following methods:

(A) Equipment Grounding Conductor Types. By connecting to one of the equipment grounding conductors identified in 250.118.

(B) With Circuit Conductors. If an equipment grounding conductor of the wire type is installed, it must be in the same raceway, cable tray, trench, cable, or flexible cord with the circuit conductors in accordance with 300.3(B). ▶Figure 250–245

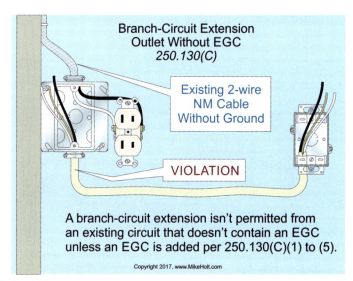

▶Figure 250–244

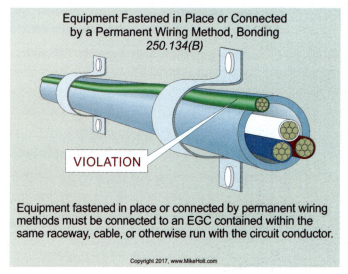

▶Figure 250–245

250.136 | Grounding and Bonding

Author's Comment:

- Conductors of a circuit must be installed in the same raceway, cable, trench, cord, or cable tray to minimize induction heating of ferrous metal raceways and enclosures, and to maintain a low-impedance ground-fault current path [250.4(A)(3)].

Ex 1: As provided in 250.130(C), the equipment grounding conductor is permitted to be run separately from the circuit conductors.

Ex 2: For dc circuits, the equipment grounding conductor is permitted to be run separately from the circuit conductors. ▶Figure 250–246

▶Figure 250–246

250.136 Equipment Considered Grounded

(A) Equipment Secured to Grounded Metal Supports. The structural metal frame of a building isn't permitted to be used as the required equipment grounding conductor.

250.138 Cord-and-Plug-Connected

(A) Equipment Grounding Conductor. Metal parts of cord-and-plug-connected equipment must be connected to an equipment grounding conductor that terminates to a grounding-type attachment plug.

250.140 Ranges, Ovens, and Clothes Dryers

The frames of electric ranges, wall-mounted ovens, counter-mounted cooking units, clothes dryers, and outlet boxes that are part of the circuit for these appliances must be connected to the equipment grounding conductor [250.134(A)]. ▶Figure 250–247

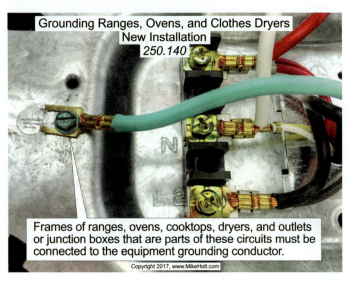

▶Figure 250–247

CAUTION: Ranges, dryers, and ovens have their metal cases connected to the neutral conductor at the factory. This neutral-to-case connection must be removed when these appliances are installed in new construction, and a 4-wire flexible cord and receptacle must be used [250.142(B)]. ▶Figure 250–248

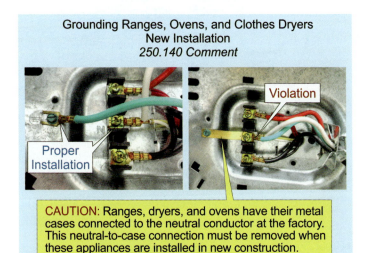

▶Figure 250–248

Ex: For existing installations if an equipment grounding conductor isn't present in the outlet box, the frames of electric ranges, wall-mounted ovens, counter-mounted cooking units, clothes dryers, and outlet boxes that are part of the circuit for these appliances may be connected to the neutral conductor. ▶Figure 250–249

▶Figure 250–249

250.142 Use of Neutral Conductor for Equipment Grounding (Bonding)

(A) Supply-Side Equipment.

(1) Service Equipment. The neutral conductor can be used as the circuit equipment grounding conductor on the supply side or within the enclosure of the service disconnecting means in accordance with 250.24(B). ▶Figure 250–250

(B) Load-Side Equipment. The neutral conductor isn't permitted to serve as an equipment grounding conductor on the load side of service equipment except as permitted for separately derived system transformers and generators in accordance with 250.30(A)(1). ▶Figure 250–251

Ex 1: In existing installations, the frames of ranges, wall-mounted ovens, counter-mounted cooking units, and clothes dryers can be connected to the neutral conductor in accordance with 250.140 Ex.

Ex 2: The neutral conductor can be connected to meter socket enclosures on the load side of the service disconnecting means if: ▶Figure 250–252

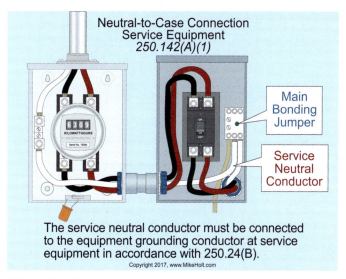

▶Figure 250–250

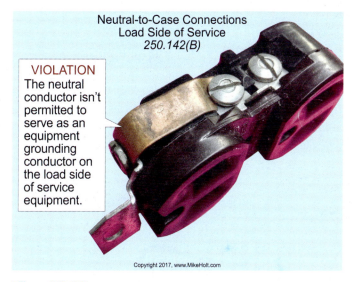

▶Figure 250–251

(1) Ground-fault protection isn't provided on service equipment,

(2) Meter socket enclosures are immediately adjacent to the service disconnect, and

(3) The neutral conductor is sized in accordance with 250.122, based on the ampere rating of the occupancy's feeder overcurrent protection device.

250.146 | Grounding and Bonding

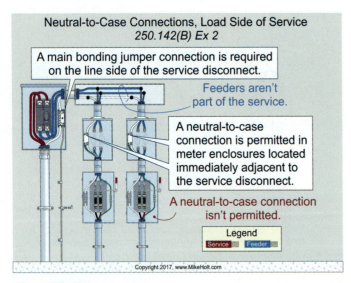

▶Figure 250–252

250.146 Connecting Receptacle Grounding Terminal to Metal Enclosure

Except as permitted for (A) through (D), an equipment bonding jumper sized in accordance with 250.122, based on the rating of the circuit overcurrent protection device, must connect the grounding terminal of a receptacle to a metal box. ▶Figure 250–253

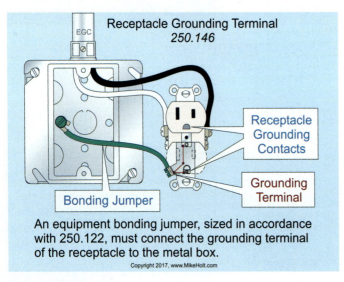

▶Figure 250–253

Author's Comment:

- The *NEC* doesn't restrict the position of the receptacle grounding terminal; it can be up, down, or sideways. *Code* proposals to specify the mounting position of receptacles have always been rejected. ▶Figure 250–254

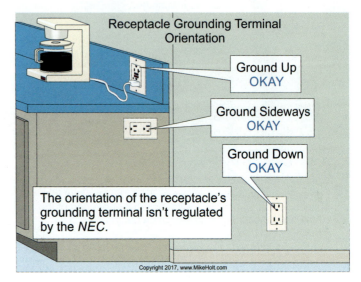

▶Figure 250–254

(A) Surface-Mounted Box. An equipment bonding jumper from a receptacle to a metal box that's surface mounted isn't required if there's direct metal-to-metal contact between the device yoke and the metal box. To ensure a suitable bonding path between the device yoke and a metal box, at least one of the insulating retaining washers on the yoke screw must be removed. ▶Figure 250–255

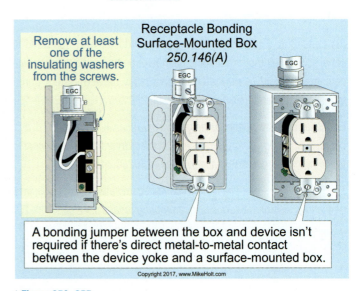

▶Figure 250–255

An equipment bonding jumper isn't required for receptacles attached to listed exposed work covers when the receptacle is attached to the cover with at least two fasteners that have a thread locking or screw or nut locking means, and the cover mounting holes are located on a flat non-raised portion of the cover. ▶Figure 250–256

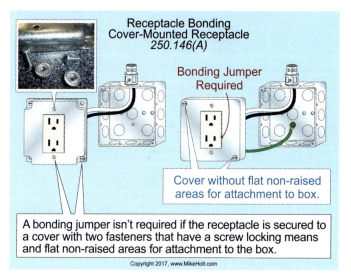

▶Figure 250–256

(B) Self-Grounding Receptacles. Receptacle yokes listed as self-grounding are designed to establish the equipment bonding between the device yoke and a metal box via the metal mounting screws. ▶Figure 250–257

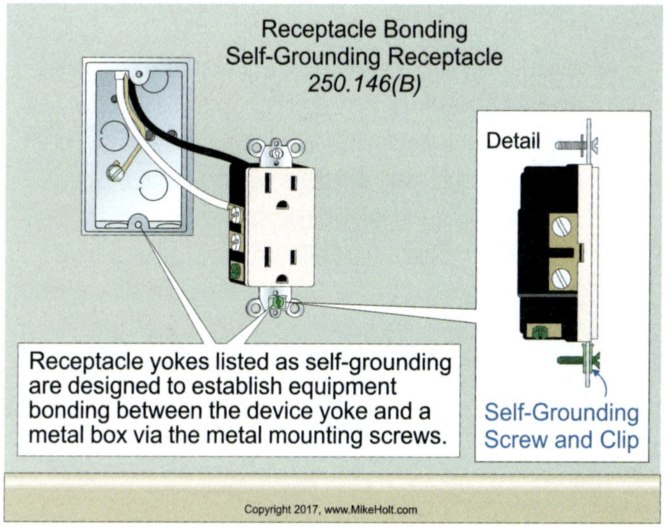

(C) Floor Boxes. Listed floor boxes are designed to establish the bonding path between the device yoke and a metal box.

(D) Isolated Ground Receptacles. The grounding terminal of an isolated ground receptacle must be connected to an insulated equipment grounding conductor run with the circuit conductors. ▶Figure 250–258

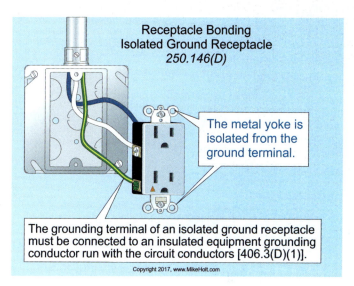

▶Figure 250–258

The circuit equipment grounding conductor can pass through panelboards [408.40 Ex], boxes, wireways, or other enclosures without a connection to the enclosure [250.148 Ex].

Author's Comment:

- Type AC Cable—Type AC cable containing an insulated equipment grounding conductor of the wire type can be used to supply receptacles having insulated grounding terminals because the metal armor of the cable is listed as an equipment grounding conductor [250.118(8)]. ▶Figure 250–259

- The armor assembly of interlocked Type MC$^{AP®}$ cable with a 10 AWG bare aluminum grounding/bonding conductor running just below the metal armor is listed to serve as an equipment grounding conductor in accordance with 250.118(10)(b). ▶Figure 250–260

▶Figure 250–257

250.146 | Grounding and Bonding

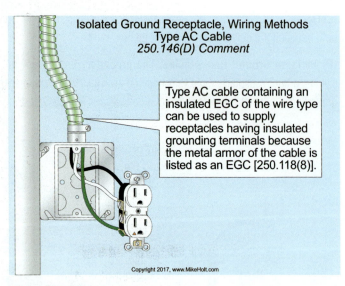

▶Figure 250–259

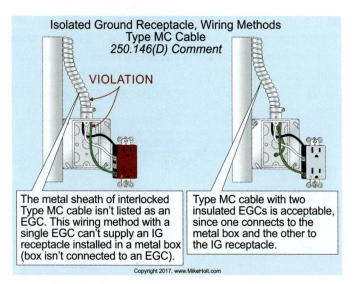

▶Figure 250–261

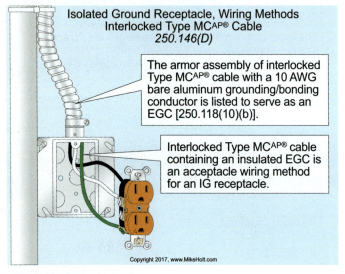

▶Figure 250–260

⚡ CAUTION: Type MC Cable. The metal armor sheath of interlocked Type MC cable containing an insulated equipment grounding conductor isn't listed as an equipment grounding conductor. Therefore, this wiring method with a single equipment grounding conductor can't supply an isolated ground receptacle installed in a metal box (because the box isn't connected to an equipment grounding conductor). However, Type MC cable with two insulated equipment grounding conductors is acceptable, since one equipment grounding conductor connects to the metal box and the other to the isolated ground receptacle. ▶Figure 250–261

Author's Comment:

- When should an isolated ground receptacle be installed and how should the isolated ground system be designed? These questions are design issues and must not be answered based on the *NEC* alone [90.1(A)]. In most cases, using isolated ground receptacles is a waste of money. For example, IEEE 1100— *Powering and Grounding Electronic Equipment (Emerald Book)* states, "The results from the use of the isolated ground method range from no observable effects, the desired effects, or worse noise conditions than when standard equipment bonding configurations are used to serve electronic load equipment [8.5.3.2]."

- In reality, few electrical installations truly require an isolated ground system. For those systems that can benefit from an isolated ground system, engineering opinions differ as to what's a proper design. Making matters worse—of those properly designed, few are correctly installed and even fewer are properly maintained. For more information on how to properly ground electronic equipment, go to: www.MikeHolt.com, click on the "Technical" link, and then visit the "Power Quality" page.

Grounding and Bonding | 250.148

250.148 Continuity and Attachment of Equipment Grounding Conductors in Metal Boxes

If circuit conductors are spliced or terminated on equipment within a box, all equipment grounding conductor associated with any of the spliced or terminated circuits must be connected together or to the metal box in accordance (A) through (E). ▶Figure 250–262

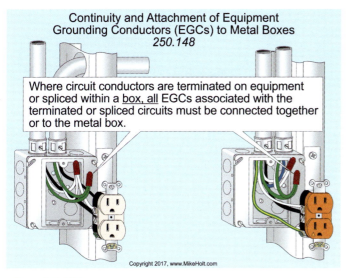

▶Figure 250–262

Ex: The circuit equipment grounding conductor for an isolated ground receptacle installed in accordance with 250.146(D) isn't required to terminate to a metal box. ▶Figure 250–263

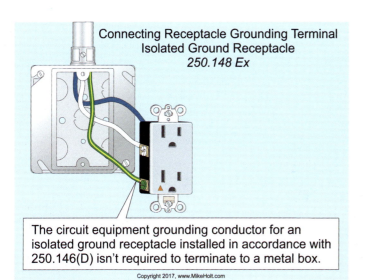

▶Figure 250–263

(A) Splicing. Equipment grounding conductors must be spliced together with a device identified for the purpose [110.14(B)]. ▶Figure 250–264

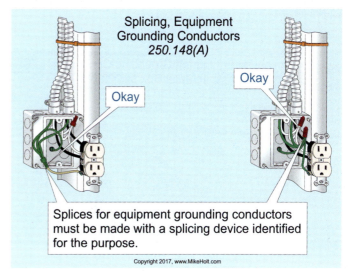

▶Figure 250–264

Author's Comment:

- Wire connectors of any color can be used with equipment grounding conductor splices, but green wire connectors can only be used with equipment grounding conductors since they're only tested for that application.

(B) Grounding Continuity. Equipment grounding conductors must terminate in a manner such that the disconnection or the removal of a receptacle, luminaire, or other device won't interrupt the grounding continuity. ▶Figure 250–265

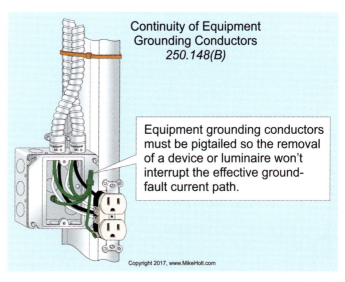

▶Figure 250–265

137

250.148 | Grounding and Bonding

(C) Metal Boxes. Terminating equipment grounding conductors within metal boxes must be with a grounding screw that's not used for any other purpose, a fitting listed for grounding, or a listed grounding device such as a ground clip. ▶Figure 250–266

Author's Comment:

- Equipment grounding conductors aren't permitted to terminate to a screw that secures a plaster ring. ▶Figure 250–267

▶Figure 250–266

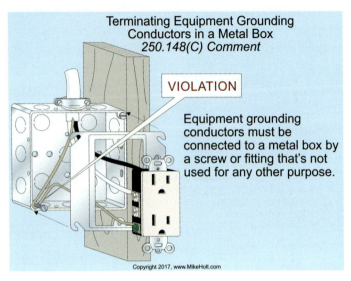

▶Figure 250–267

CHAPTER 2

PRACTICE QUESTIONS

Please use the 2017 *Code* book to answer the following questions.

Article 250. Grounding and Bonding

Part I. General

1. Grounded electrical systems shall be connected to earth in a manner that will _____.

   (a) limit voltages due to lightning, line surges, or unintentional contact with higher-voltage lines
   (b) stabilize the voltage-to-ground during normal operation
   (c) facilitate overcurrent device operation in case of ground faults
   (d) a and b

2. An important consideration for limiting imposed voltage on electrical systems is to remember that bonding and grounding electrode conductors should not be any longer than necessary and unnecessary bends and loops should be avoided.

   (a) True
   (b) False

3. NFPA 780, *Standard for the Installation of Lightning Protection Systems* provides information on the installation of _____ for lightning protection systems [250.4(A)(1)].

   (a) grounding
   (b) bonding
   (c) a and b
   (d) none of these

4. For grounded systems, normally noncurrent-carrying conductive materials enclosing electrical conductors or equipment shall be connected to earth so as to limit the voltage-to-ground on these materials.

   (a) True
   (b) False

5. In grounded systems, normally noncurrent-carrying electrically conductive materials that are likely to become energized shall be connected _____ in a manner that establishes an effective ground-fault current path.

   (a) together
   (b) to the electrical supply source
   (c) to the closest grounded conductor
   (d) a and b

6. For grounded systems, electrical equipment and other electrically conductive material likely to become energized shall be installed in a manner that creates a _____ from any point on the wiring system where a ground fault may occur to the electrical supply source.

   (a) circuit facilitating the operation of the overcurrent device
   (b) low-impedance circuit
   (c) circuit capable of safely carrying the ground-fault current likely to be imposed on it
   (d) all of these

Mike Holt Enterprises • www.MikeHolt.com • 888.NEC.CODE (632.2633)   139

Chapter 2 | Practice Questions

7. For grounded systems, electrical equipment and electrically conductive material likely to become energized, shall be installed in a manner that creates a low-impedance circuit capable of safely carrying the maximum ground-fault current likely to be imposed on it from where a ground fault may occur to the _____.

   (a) ground
   (b) earth
   (c) electrical supply source
   (d) none of these

8. For ungrounded systems, noncurrent-carrying conductive materials enclosing electrical conductors or equipment shall be connected to the _____ in a manner that will limit the voltage imposed by lightning or unintentional contact with higher-voltage lines.

   (a) raceway
   (b) earth
   (c) electrical supply source
   (d) none of these

9. NFPA 780, *Standard for the Installation of Lightning Protection Systems* provides information on the installation of _____ for lightning protection systems [250.4(B)(1)].

   (a) grounding
   (b) bonding
   (c) a and b
   (d) none of these

10. For ungrounded systems, noncurrent-carrying conductive materials enclosing electrical conductors or equipment, or forming part of such equipment, shall be connected together and to the supply system grounded equipment in a manner that creates a low-impedance path for ground-fault current that is capable of carrying _____.

    (a) the maximum branch-circuit current
    (b) at least twice the maximum ground-fault current
    (c) the maximum fault current likely to be imposed on it
    (d) the equivalent of the main service rating

11. Electrically conductive materials that are likely to _____ in ungrounded systems shall be connected together and to the supply system grounded equipment in a manner that creates a low-impedance path for ground-fault current that is capable of carrying the maximum fault current likely to be imposed on it.

    (a) become energized
    (b) require service
    (c) be removed
    (d) be coated with paint or nonconductive materials

12. The grounding of electrical systems, circuit conductors, surge arresters, surge-protective devices, and conductive normally noncurrent-carrying metal parts of equipment shall be installed and arranged in a manner that will prevent objectionable current.

    (a) True
    (b) False

13. If the use of multiple grounding connections results in objectionable current and the requirements of 250.4(A)(5) or (B)(4) are met, it shall be permitted to _____.

    (a) discontinue one or more but not all of such grounding connections
    (b) change the locations of the grounding connections
    (c) interrupt the continuity of the conductor or conductive path causing the objectionable current
    (d) any of these

14. Temporary currents resulting from abnormal conditions, such as ground faults, are not considered to be objectionable currents.

    (a) True
    (b) False

15. Currents that introduce noise or data errors in electronic equipment are considered objectionable currents in the context of 250.6(d) of the *NEC*.

    (a) True
    (b) False

16. Grounding and bonding connection devices that depend solely on _____ shall not be used.

    (a) pressure connections
    (b) solder
    (c) lugs
    (d) approved clamps

17. Ground clamps and fittings that are exposed to physical damage shall be enclosed in ____ or equivalent protective covering.

    (a) metal
    (b) wood
    (c) concrete
    (d) a or b

18. ____ on equipment to be grounded shall be removed from contact surfaces to ensure good electrical continuity.

    (a) Paint
    (b) Lacquer
    (c) Enamel
    (d) any of these

Part II. System Grounding and Bonding

19. Alternating-current systems of 50V to 1,000V that supply premises wiring systems shall be grounded where the system is three-phase, 4-wire, wye-connected, with the neutral conductor used as a circuit conductor.

    (a) True
    (b) False

20. Alternating-current systems of 50V to 1,000V that supply premises wiring systems shall be grounded where supplied by a three-phase, 4-wire, delta-connected system in which the midpoint of one phase winding is used as a circuit conductor.

    (a) True
    (b) False

21. ____ alternating-current systems operating at 480V shall have ground detectors installed on the system.

    (a) Grounded
    (b) Solidly grounded
    (c) Effectively grounded
    (d) Ungrounded

22. Ungrounded alternating-current systems from 50V to 1,000V or less that are not required to be grounded in accordance with 250.20(b) shall have ____.

    (a) ground detectors installed for ac systems operating at not less than 120V and at 1,000V or less
    (b) the ground detection sensing equipment connected as close as practicable to where the system receives its supply
    (c) a and b
    (d) ground fault protection for equipment

23. The grounding electrode conductor shall be connected to the grounded service conductor at the ____.

    (a) load end of the service drop
    (b) load end of the service lateral
    (c) service disconnecting means
    (d) any of these

24. Where the main bonding jumper is installed from the grounded conductor terminal bar to the equipment grounding terminal bar in service equipment, the ____ conductor is permitted to be connected to the equipment grounding terminal bar.

    (a) grounding
    (b) grounded
    (c) grounding electrode
    (d) none of these

25. For a grounded system, an unspliced ____ shall be used to connect the equipment grounding conductor(s) and the service disconnect enclosure to the grounded conductor of the system within the enclosure for each service disconnect.

    (a) grounding electrode
    (b) main bonding jumper
    (c) busbar
    (d) insulated copper conductor

26. Where an alternating-current system operating at 1,000V or less is grounded at any point, the ____ conductor(s) shall be routed with the ungrounded conductors to each service disconnecting means and shall be connected to each disconnecting means grounded conductor(s) terminal or bus.

    (a) ungrounded
    (b) grounded
    (c) grounding
    (d) none of these

27. The grounded conductor brought to service equipment shall be routed with the phase conductors and shall not be smaller than specified in Table _____ when the service-entrance conductors are 1,100 kcmil copper and smaller.

    (a) 250.102(C)(1)
    (b) 250.122
    (c) 310.16
    (d) 430.52

28. Where service-entrance conductors are installed in parallel in two or more raceways or cables, the size of the grounded conductor in each raceway or cable shall be based on the total circular mil area of the parallel ungrounded service-entrance conductors in the raceway or cable, sized in accordance with 250.24(C)(1), but not smaller than _____ AWG.

    (a) 1/0
    (b) 2/0
    (c) 3/0
    (d) 4/0

29. A grounding electrode conductor, sized in accordance with 250.66, shall be used to connect the equipment grounding conductors, the service-equipment enclosures, and, where the system is grounded, the grounded service conductor to the grounding electrode(s).

    (a) True
    (b) False

30. A main bonding jumper shall be a _____ or similar suitable conductor.

    (a) wire
    (b) bus
    (c) screw
    (d) any of these

31. Main bonding jumpers and system bonding jumpers shall not be smaller than specified in _____.

    (a) Table 250.102(C)(1)
    (b) Table 250.122
    (c) Table 310.15(B)(16)
    (d) Chapter 9, Table 8

32. Where the supply conductors are larger than 1,100 kcmil copper or 1,750 kcmil aluminum, the main bonding jumper shall have an area that is _____ the area of the largest phase conductor when of the same material.

    (a) at least equal to
    (b) at least 50 percent of
    (c) not less than 12½ percent of
    (d) not more than 12½ percent of

33. A grounded conductor shall not be connected to normally noncurrent-carrying metal parts of equipment on the _____ side of the system bonding jumper of a separately derived system except as otherwise permitted in Article 250.

    (a) supply
    (b) grounded
    (c) high-voltage
    (d) load

34. An unspliced _____ that is sized based on the derived phase conductors shall be used to connect the grounded conductor and the supply-side bonding jumper, or the equipment grounding conductor, or both, at a separately derived system.

    (a) system bonding jumper
    (b) equipment grounding conductor
    (c) grounded conductor
    (d) grounding electrode conductor

35. If a building or structure is supplied by a feeder from an outdoor separately derived system, a system bonding jumper at both the source and the first disconnecting means shall be permitted if doing so does not establish a _____ path for the grounded conductor.

    (a) series
    (b) parallel
    (c) series-parallel
    (d) none of these

36. Where a supply-side bonding jumper of the wire type is run with the derived phase conductors from the source of a separately derived system to the first disconnecting means, it shall be sized in accordance with 250.102(C), based on _____.

    (a) the size of the primary conductors
    (b) the size of the secondary overcurrent protection
    (c) the size of the derived ungrounded conductors
    (d) one third the size of the primary grounded conductor

37. The building or structure grounding electrode system shall be used as the _____ electrode for the separately derived system.

    (a) grounding
    (b) bonding
    (c) grounded
    (d) bonded

38. For a single separately derived system, the grounding electrode conductor connects the grounded conductor of the derived system to the grounding electrode at the same point on the separately derived system where the _____ is connected.

    (a) metering equipment
    (b) transfer switch
    (c) system bonding jumper
    (d) largest circuit breaker

39. Grounding electrode conductor taps from a separately derived system to a common grounding electrode conductor are permitted when a building or structure has multiple separately derived systems, provided that the taps terminate at the same point as the system bonding jumper.

    (a) True
    (b) False

40. The common grounding electrode conductor installed for multiple separately derived systems shall not be smaller than _____ AWG copper when using a wire-type conductor.

    (a) 1/0
    (b) 2/0
    (c) 3/0
    (d) 4/0

41. The common grounding electrode conductor installed for multiple separately derived systems shall be permitted to be a _____ pipe that complies with 250.68(C)(1).

    (a) metal gas
    (b) metal water
    (c) PVC water
    (d) any of these

42. The common grounding electrode conductor installed for multiple separately derived systems shall be permitted to be the metal structural frame of the building or structure that complies with 250.68(C)(2) or is connected to the grounding electrode system by a conductor not smaller than _____.

    (a) 3/0 AWG copper
    (b) 250 kcmil aluminum
    (c) a or b
    (d) none of these

43. Tap connections to a common grounding electrode conductor for multiple separately derived systems shall be made at an accessible location by _____.

    (a) a connector listed as grounding and bonding equipment
    (b) listed connections to aluminum or copper busbars
    (c) the exothermic welding process
    (d) any of these

44. Tap connections to a common grounding electrode conductor for multiple separately derived systems may be made to a copper or aluminum busbar that is _____ and of sufficient length to accommodate the number of terminations necessary for the installation.

    (a) smaller than ¼ in. thick × 4 in. wide
    (b) not smaller than ¼ in. thick × 2 in. wide
    (c) not smaller than ½ in. thick × 2 in. wide
    (d) a and c

45. In an area served by a separately derived system, the _____ shall be connected to the grounded conductor of the separately derived system.

    (a) structural steel
    (b) metal piping
    (c) metal building skin
    (d) a and b

46. A grounding electrode shall be required if a building or structure is supplied by a feeder.

    (a) True
    (b) False

Chapter 2 | Practice Questions

47. When supplying a grounded system at a separate building or structure, an equipment grounding conductor shall be run with the supply conductors and connected to the building or structure disconnecting means and to the grounding electrode(s).

    (a) True
    (b) False

48. For a separate building or structure supplied by a feeder or branch circuit, the grounded conductor can serve as the ground-fault return path for the building/structure disconnecting means for existing installations made in compliance with previous editions of the *Code* as long as the installation continues to meet the condition(s) that ____.

    (a) there are no continuous metallic paths between buildings and structures
    (b) ground-fault protection of equipment is not installed on the supply side of the feeder
    (c) the neutral conductor is sized no smaller than the larger required by 220.61 or 250.122
    (d) all of these

49. For a separate building or structure supplied by a separately derived system when overcurrent protection is provided where the conductors originate, the supply conductors shall contain a(n) ____.

    (a) equipment grounding conductor
    (b) copper conductors only
    (c) GFI protection for the feeder
    (d) all of these

50. For a separate building or structure supplied by a separately derived system when overcurrent protection is not provided for the supply conductors to the building/structure as permitted by 240.21(C)(4), the installation shall be ____ in accordance with 250.30(A).

    (a) AFCI protected
    (b) grounded and bonded
    (c) isolated
    (d) all of these

51. The frame of a portable generator shall not be required to be connected to a(n) ____ if the generator only supplies equipment mounted on the generator, cord-and-plug connected equipment using receptacles mounted on the generator, or both.

    (a) grounding electrode
    (b) grounded conductor
    (c) ungrounded conductor
    (d) equipment grounding conductor

52. The frame of a vehicle-mounted generator shall not be required to be connected to a(n) ____ if the generator only supplies equipment mounted on the vehicle or cord-and-plug connected equipment, using receptacles mounted on the vehicle.

    (a) grounding electrode
    (b) grounded conductor
    (c) ungrounded conductor
    (d) equipment grounding conductor

53. When a permanently installed generator ____, the requirements of 250.30 shall apply.

    (a) is a separately derived system
    (b) is not a separately derived system
    (c) supplies only cord-and-plug-connected loads
    (d) none of these

Part III. Grounding Electrode System and Grounding Electrode Conductor

54. Concrete-encased electrodes of ____ shall not be required to be part of the grounding electrode system where the steel reinforcing bars or rods aren't accessible for use without disturbing the concrete.

    (a) hazardous (classified) locations
    (b) health care facilities
    (c) existing buildings or structures
    (d) agricultural buildings with equipotential planes

55. In order for a metal underground water pipe to be used as a grounding electrode, it shall be in direct contact with the earth for ____.

    (a) 5 ft
    (b) 10 ft or more
    (c) less than 10 ft
    (d) 20 ft or more

56. One or more metal in-ground support structure(s) in direct contact with the earth vertically for _____ ft or more, with or without concrete encasement is permitted to be a grounding electrode in accordance with 250.52.

    (a) 4
    (b) 6
    (c) 8
    (d) 10

57. A bare 4 AWG copper conductor installed horizontally near the bottom or vertically, and within that portion of a concrete foundation or footing that is in direct contact with the earth, can be used as a grounding electrode when the conductor is at least _____ ft in length.

    (a) 10
    (b) 15
    (c) 20
    (d) 25

58. An electrode encased by at least 2 in. of concrete, located horizontally near the bottom or vertically and within that portion of a concrete foundation or footing that is in direct contact with the earth, shall be permitted as a grounding electrode when it consists of _____.

    (a) at least 20 ft of ½ in. or larger steel reinforcing bars or rods
    (b) at least 20 ft of bare copper conductor of 4 AWG or larger
    (c) a or b
    (d) none of these

59. Reinforcing bars for use as a concrete-encased electrode can be bonded together by the usual steel tie wires or other effective means.

    (a) True
    (b) False

60. Where more than one concrete-encased electrode is present at a building or structure, it shall be permitted to bond to only one into the grounding electrode system.

    (a) True
    (b) False

61. Grounding electrodes of the rod type less than _____ in diameter shall be listed.

    (a) ½ in.
    (b) ⅝ in.
    (c) ¾ in.
    (d) 1 in.

62. A buried iron or steel plate used as a grounding electrode shall expose not less than _____ sq ft of surface area to exterior soil.

    (a) 2
    (b) 4
    (c) 9
    (d) 10

63. Grounding electrodes of bare or electrically conductive coated iron or steel plates shall be at least _____ in. thick.

    (a) ⅛
    (b) ¼
    (c) ½
    (d) ¾

64. Local metal underground systems or structures such as _____ are permitted to serve as grounding electrodes.

    (a) piping systems
    (b) underground tanks
    (c) underground metal well casings that are not bonded to a metal water pipe
    (d) all of these

65. Swimming pool structures and structural _____ [680.26(B)(1) and (B)(2)] shall not be used as a grounding electrode.

    (a) reinforcing steel
    (b) equipotential planes
    (c) a or b
    (d) none of these

66. Where practicable, rod, pipe, and plate electrodes shall be installed _____.

    (a) directly below the electrical meter
    (b) on the north side of the building
    (c) below permanent moisture level
    (d) all of these

Chapter 2 | Practice Questions

67. Where the resistance-to-ground of 25 ohms or less is not achieved for a single rod electrode, _____.
    (a) other means besides electrodes shall be used in order to provide grounding
    (b) the single rod electrode shall be supplemented by one additional electrode
    (c) no additional electrodes are required
    (d) none of these

68. Two or more grounding electrodes bonded together are considered a single grounding electrode system.
    (a) True
    (b) False

69. Where the supplemental electrode is a rod, that portion of the bonding jumper that is the sole connection to the supplemental grounding electrode shall not be required to be larger than _____ AWG copper wire.
    (a) 8
    (b) 6
    (c) 4
    (d) 1

70. When a ground ring is used as a grounding electrode, it shall be installed at a depth below the earth's surface of not less than _____.
    (a) 18 in.
    (b) 24 in.
    (c) 30 in.
    (d) 8 ft

71. Ground rod electrodes shall be installed so that at least _____ of the length is in contact with the soil.
    (a) 5 ft
    (b) 8 ft
    (c) one-half
    (d) 80 percent

72. Where rock bottom is encountered when driving a ground rod at an angle up to 45 degrees, the electrode can be buried in a trench that is at least _____ deep.
    (a) 18 in.
    (b) 30 in.
    (c) 4 ft
    (d) 8 ft

73. Auxiliary grounding electrodes can be connected to the _____.
    (a) equipment grounding conductor
    (b) grounded conductor
    (c) a and b
    (d) none of these

74. When installing auxiliary electrodes, the earth shall not be used as an effective ground-fault current path.
    (a) True
    (b) False

75. Buildings or structures supplied by multiple services or feeders shall use the same _____ to ground enclosures and equipment in or on that building.
    (a) service
    (b) disconnect
    (c) grounding electrode system
    (d) any of these

76. The grounding electrode used for grounding strike termination devices of a lightning protection system can be used as a grounding electrode system for the buildings or structures.
    (a) True
    (b) False

77. Where used outside, aluminum or copper-clad aluminum grounding electrode conductors shall not be terminated within _____ in. of the earth.
    (a) 6
    (b) 12
    (c) 15
    (d) 18

78. Bare aluminum or copper-clad aluminum grounding electrode conductors shall not be used where in direct contact with _____ or where subject to corrosive conditions.
    (a) masonry or the earth
    (b) bare copper conductors
    (c) wooden framing members
    (d) all of these

79. Grounding electrode conductors that are not subject to physical damage can be run exposed along the surface of the building construction if securely fastened to the surface on which they are carried.

    (a) True
    (b) False

80. Grounding electrode conductors _____ AWG and larger that are not exposed to physical damage can be run along the surface of the building construction without metal covering or protection.

    (a) 10
    (b) 8
    (c) 6
    (d) 4

81. Grounding electrode conductors smaller than _____ AWG shall be protected in rigid metal conduit, IMC, PVC conduit, electrical metallic tubing, or cable armor.

    (a) 10
    (b) 8
    (c) 6
    (d) 4

82. Grounding electrode conductors and grounding electrode bonding jumpers in contact with _____ shall not be required to comply with 300.5, but shall be buried or otherwise protected if subject to physical damage.

    (a) water
    (b) the earth
    (c) metal
    (d) all of these

83. Grounding electrode conductors shall be installed in one continuous length without a splice or joint, unless spliced by _____.

    (a) connecting together sections of a busbar
    (b) irreversible compression-type connectors listed as grounding and bonding equipment
    (c) the exothermic welding process
    (d) any of these

84. If a building or structure is supplied by a service or feeder with _____ or more disconnecting means in separate enclosures, the grounding electrode connections shall be made in accordance with 250.64(D)(1), 250.64(D)(2), or 250.64(D)(3).

    (a) one
    (b) two
    (c) three
    (d) four

85. Ferrous metal raceways and enclosures for grounding electrode conductors shall be electrically continuous from the point of attachment to cabinets or equipment to the grounding electrode.

    (a) True
    (b) False

86. Ferrous metal raceways and enclosures for grounding electrode conductors shall be bonded at each end of the raceway or enclosure to the grounding electrode or grounding electrode conductor to create a(n) _____ parallel path.

    (a) mechanically
    (b) electrically
    (c) physically
    (d) none of these

87. A grounding electrode conductor shall be permitted to be run to any convenient grounding electrode available in the grounding electrode system where the other electrode(s), if any, is connected by bonding jumpers that are installed in accordance with 250.53(C).

    (a) True
    (b) False

88. Bonding jumper(s) from grounding electrode(s) shall be permitted to be connected to an aluminum or copper busbar not less than _____ and of sufficient length to accommodate the number of terminations necessary for the installation in accordance with 250.64(F).

    (a) ⅛ in. thick × 1 in. wide
    (b) ⅛ in. thick × 2 in. wide
    (c) ¼ in. thick × 1 in. wide
    (d) ¼ in. thick × 2 in. wide

Chapter 2 | Practice Questions

89. The largest size grounding electrode conductor required is _____ copper.
    (a) 6 AWG
    (b) 1/0 AWG
    (c) 3/0 AWG
    (d) 250 kcmil

90. What size copper grounding electrode conductor is required for a service that has three sets of 600 kcmil copper conductors per phase?
    (a) 1 AWG
    (b) 1/0 AWG
    (c) 2/0 AWG
    (d) 3/0 AWG

91. If the grounding electrode conductor or bonding jumper connected to a single or multiple rod, pipe, or plate electrode(s), or any combination thereof, as described in 250.52(A)(5) or (A)(7), does not extend on to other types of electrodes that require a larger size conductor, the grounding electrode conductor shall not be required to be larger than _____ AWG copper wire.
    (a) 10
    (b) 8
    (c) 6
    (d) 4

92. In an ac system, if the size of the grounding electrode conductor or bonding jumper connected to a concrete-encased electrode does not extend on to other types of electrodes that require a larger size of conductor, the grounding electrode conductor shall not be required to be larger than _____ AWG copper.
    (a) 10
    (b) 8
    (c) 6
    (d) 4

93. An encased or buried connection to a concrete-encased, driven, or buried grounding electrode shall be accessible.
    (a) True
    (b) False

94. The connection of the grounding electrode conductor to a buried grounding electrode (driven ground rod) shall be made with a listed terminal device that is accessible.
    (a) True
    (b) False

95. Exothermic or irreversible compression connections, together with the mechanical means used to attach to fireproofed structural metal, shall not be required to be accessible.
    (a) True
    (b) False

96. When an underground metal water piping system is used as a grounding electrode, bonding shall be provided around insulated joints and around any equipment that is likely to be disconnected for repairs or replacement.
    (a) True
    (b) False

97. Interior metal water piping that is electrically continuous with a metal underground water pipe electrode and is located more than _____ ft from the point of entrance to the building shall not be used as a conductor to interconnect electrodes of the grounding electrode system.
    (a) 2
    (b) 4
    (c) 5
    (d) 6

98. Where conditions of maintenance and supervision ensure only qualified persons service the installation in _____ buildings, the entire length of the metal water piping system can be used for grounding purposes, provided the entire length, other than short sections passing through walls, floors, or ceilings, is exposed.
    (a) industrial
    (b) institutional
    (c) commercial
    (d) all of these

99. The metal structural frame of a building shall be permitted to be used as a conductor to interconnect electrodes that are part of the grounding electrode system, or as a grounding electrode conductor. Hold-down bolts securing the structural steel column that are connected to a concrete-encased electrode that complies with 250.52(A)(3) and is located in the support footing or foundation shall be permitted to connect the metal structural frame of a building or structure to the concrete encased grounding electrode.

    (a) True
    (b) False

100. The grounding conductor connection to the grounding electrode shall be made by _____.

    (a) listed lugs
    (b) exothermic welding
    (c) listed pressure connectors
    (d) any of these

Part IV. Grounding Enclosure, Raceway, and Service Cable Connections

101. Metal enclosures and raceways containing service conductors shall be connected to the grounded system conductor if the electrical system is grounded.

    (a) True
    (b) False

102. Metal components in a run of underground nonmetallic raceway and isolated from possible contact by a minimum cover of _____ in. to all parts of the metal components shall not be required to be connected to the grounded system conductor, supply-side bonding jumper, or grounding electrode conductor.

    (a) 6
    (b) 12
    (c) 18
    (d) 24

103. Short sections of metal enclosures or raceways used to provide support or protection of _____ from physical damage shall not be required to be connected to the equipment grounding conductor.

    (a) conduit
    (b) feeders under 600V
    (c) cable assemblies
    (d) none of these

104. Metal components shall not be required to be connected to the equipment grounding conductor or supply-side bonding jumper where the metal components are _____.

    (a) installed in a run of nonmetallic raceway(s) and isolated from possible contact by a minimum cover of 18 in. to any part of the metal components
    (b) part of an installation of nonmetallic raceway(s) and are isolated from possible contact to any part of the metal components by being encased in not less than 2 in. of concrete
    (c) a or b
    (d) none of these

Part V. Bonding

105. Bonding shall be provided where necessary to ensure _____ and the capacity to conduct safely any fault current likely to be imposed.

    (a) electrical continuity
    (b) fiduciary responsibility
    (c) listing requirements are met
    (d) sufficient electrical demand

106. Bonding jumpers for service raceways shall be used around impaired connections such as _____.

    (a) oversized concentric knockouts
    (b) oversized eccentric knockouts
    (c) reducing washers
    (d) any of these

107. Electrical continuity at service equipment, service raceways, and service conductor enclosures shall be ensured by _____.

    (a) bonding equipment to the grounded service conductor
    (b) connections utilizing threaded couplings on enclosures, if made up wrenchtight
    (c) other listed bonding devices, such as bonding-type locknuts, bushings, or bushings with bonding jumpers
    (d) any of these

108. Service raceways threaded into metal service equipment such as bosses (hubs) are considered to be effectively _____ to the service metal enclosure.

    (a) attached
    (b) bonded
    (c) grounded
    (d) none of these

Chapter 2 | Practice Questions

109. Service metal raceways and metal-clad cables are considered effectively bonded when using threadless couplings and connectors that are _____.

    (a) nonmetallic
    (b) made up tight
    (c) sealed
    (d) classified

110. The intersystem bonding termination shall _____.

    (a) be accessible for connection and inspection
    (b) consist of a set of terminals with the capacity for connection of not less than three intersystem bonding conductors
    (c) not interfere with opening the enclosure for a service, building/structure disconnecting means, or metering equipment
    (d) all of these

111. The intersystem bonding termination shall _____.

    (a) be securely mounted and electrically connected to service equipment, the meter enclosure, or exposed nonflexible metallic service raceway, or be mounted at one of these enclosures and be connected to the enclosure or grounding electrode conductor with a minimum 6 AWG copper conductor
    (b) be securely mounted to the building/structure disconnecting means, or be mounted at the disconnecting means and be connected to the metallic enclosure or grounding electrode conductor with a minimum 6 AWG copper conductor
    (c) have terminals that are listed as grounding and bonding equipment
    (d) all of these

112. At existing buildings or structures, an intersystem bonding termination is not required if other acceptable means of bonding exists. An external accessible means for bonding communications systems together can be by the use of a(n) _____.

    (a) nonflexible metallic raceway
    (b) exposed grounding electrode conductor
    (c) connection to a grounded raceway or equipment approved by the authority having jurisdiction
    (d) any of these

113. Communications system bonding termination connections to an aluminum or copper busbar shall not be less than ¼ in. thick × 2 in. wide and of sufficient length to accommodate at least _____ terminations for communications systems in addition to other connections.

    (a) two
    (b) three
    (c) four
    (d) five

114. When bonding enclosures, metal raceways, frames, and fittings, any nonconductive paint, enamel, or similar coating shall be removed at _____.

    (a) contact surfaces
    (b) threads
    (c) contact points
    (d) all of these

115. Where installed to reduce electrical noise for electronic equipment on the grounding circuit, a metal raceway can terminate to a(n) _____ nonmetallic fitting(s) or spacer on the electronic equipment. The metal raceway shall be supplemented by an internal insulated equipment grounding conductor.

    (a) listed
    (b) labeled
    (c) identified
    (d) marked

116. For circuits over 250 volts-to-ground, electrical continuity can be maintained between a box or enclosure where no oversized, concentric or eccentric knockouts are encountered, and a metal conduit by _____.

    (a) threadless fittings for cables with metal sheaths
    (b) double locknuts on threaded conduit (one inside and one outside the box or enclosure)
    (c) fittings that have shoulders that seat firmly against the box with a locknut on the inside or listed fittings
    (d) all of these

117. Equipment bonding jumpers shall be of copper, aluminum, copper-clad aluminum, or other corrosion-resistant material.

    (a) True
    (b) False

118. The supply-side bonding jumper on the supply side of services shall be sized according to the ____.

    (a) overcurrent device rating
    (b) ungrounded supply conductor size
    (c) service-drop size
    (d) load to be served

119. What is the minimum size copper supply-side bonding jumper for a service raceway containing 4/0 THHN aluminum conductors?

    (a) 6 AWG aluminum
    (b) 4 AWG aluminum
    (c) 4 AWG copper
    (d) 3 AWG copper

120. Where ungrounded supply conductors are paralleled in two or more raceways or cables, the bonding jumper for each raceway or cable shall be based on the size of the ____ in each raceway or cable.

    (a) overcurrent protection for conductors
    (b) grounded conductors
    (c) ungrounded supply conductors
    (d) sum of all conductors

121. A service is supplied by three metal raceways, each containing 600 kcmil ungrounded conductors. Determine the copper supply-side bonding jumper size for each service raceway.

    (a) 1/0 AWG
    (b) 3/0 AWG
    (c) 250 kcmil
    (d) 500 kcmil

122. An equipment bonding jumper can be installed on the outside of a raceway, providing the length of the equipment bonding jumper is not more than ____ in. and the equipment bonding jumper is routed with the raceway.

    (a) 12
    (b) 24
    (c) 36
    (d) 72

123. Metal water piping system(s) shall be bonded to the ____, or to one or more grounding electrodes used, if the grounding electrode conductor or bonding jumper to the grounding electrode is of sufficient size.

    (a) grounded conductor at the service
    (b) service equipment enclosure
    (c) grounding electrode conductor if of sufficient size
    (d) any of these

124. The bonding jumper used to bond the metal shall be installed in accordance with 250.64(A), 250.64(B), and 250.64(E) and the points of attachment of the bonding jumper(s) shall be ____.

    (a) readily accessible
    (b) accessible
    (c) a or b
    (d) none of these

125. The bonding jumper used to bond the metal water piping system shall be sized in accordance with ____ except as permitted in 250.104(A)(2) and 250.104(A)(3).

    (a) Table 250.102(C)(1)
    (b) Table 250.122
    (c) Table 310.15(B)(16)
    (d) Table 310.15(B)(6)

126. The metal water piping system(s) installed in or attached to a building or structure [250.104(A)(3)] shall be bonded to ____.

    (a) the building or structure disconnecting means enclosure where located at the building or structure
    (b) the equipment grounding conductor run with the supply conductors
    (c) one or more grounding electrodes used
    (d) any of these

127. A building or structure shall have the interior metal water piping system bonded with a bonding jumper sized in accordance with ____.

    (a) Table 250.102(C)(1)
    (b) Table 250.122
    (c) Table 310.15(B)(16)
    (d) none of these

Chapter 2 | Practice Questions

128. Metal gas piping shall be considered bonded by the equipment grounding conductor for the circuit that is likely to energize the piping system.

    (a) True
    (b) False

129. Metal gas piping installed in or attached to a building shall be considered bonded when one or more grounding electrodes are used, if the grounding electrode conductor or bonding jumper to the grounding electrode is of sufficient size.

    (a) True
    (b) False

130. Exposed structural metal interconnected to form a metal building frame that is not intentionally grounded or bonded and is likely to become energized shall be considered bonded when one or more grounding electrodes are used, if the grounding electrode conductor or bonding jumper to the grounding electrode is of sufficient size.

    (a) True
    (b) False

131. Metal water piping systems and structural metal that is interconnected to form a building frame shall be bonded to separately derived systems in accordance with 250.104(D)(1) through 250.104(D)(3).

    (a) True
    (b) False

132. The grounded conductor of each separately derived system shall be bonded to the nearest available point of the metal water piping system(s) in the area served by each separately derived system and each bonding jumper shall be sized in accordance with Table 250.102(C)(1) based on the largest ungrounded conductor of the separately derived system.

    (a) True
    (b) False

133. A separate water piping bonding jumper shall be required if the metal frame of a building or structure is used as the grounding electrode for a separately derived system and is bonded to the metal water piping in the area served by the separately derived system.

    (a) True
    (b) False

134. A separate bonding jumper to the building structural metal shall not be required if the metal frame of a building or structure is used as the _____ for the separately derived system.

    (a) bonding jumper
    (b) ground-fault current path
    (c) grounding electrode
    (d) none of these

135. If a common grounding electrode conductor is installed for multiple separately derived systems as permitted by 250.30(A)(6), and exposed structural metal that is interconnected to form the building frame or interior metal piping exists in the area served by the separately derived system, the metal piping and the structural metal member shall be bonded to the common grounding electrode conductor in the area served by the separately derived system.

    (a) True
    (b) False

136. A separate bonding jumper from each derived system to metal water piping and to structural metal members shall not be required if the metal water piping and the structural metal members in the area served by the separately derived system are _____ to the common grounding electrode conductor.

    (a) grounded
    (b) bonded
    (c) a and b
    (d) none of these

137. Lightning protection system ground terminals _____ be bonded to the building or structure grounding electrode system.

    (a) shall
    (b) shall not
    (c) shall be permitted to
    (d) none of these

Part VI. Equipment Grounding and Equipment Grounding Conductors

138. Exposed normally noncurrent-carrying metal parts of fixed equipment likely to become energized shall be connected to the equipment grounding conductor where located _____.

    (a) within 8 ft vertically or 5 ft horizontally of ground or grounded metal objects and subject to contact by persons
    (b) in wet or damp locations and not isolated
    (c) in electrical contact with metal
    (d) any of these

139. Electrical equipment permanently mounted on skids, and the skids themselves, shall be connected to the equipment grounding conductor sized as required by _____.

    (a) 250.50
    (b) 250.66
    (c) 250.122
    (d) 310.15

140. Which of the following appliances installed in residential occupancies need not be connected to an equipment grounding conductor?

    (a) A toaster.
    (b) An aquarium.
    (c) A dishwasher.
    (d) A refrigerator.

141. Listed FMC can be used as the equipment grounding conductor if the length in any ground return path does not exceed 6 ft and the circuit conductors contained in the conduit are protected by overcurrent devices rated at _____ or less.

    (a) 15A
    (b) 20A
    (c) 30A
    (d) 60A

142. Listed FMC and LFMC shall contain an equipment grounding conductor if the raceway is installed for the reason of _____.

    (a) physical protection
    (b) flexibility after installation
    (c) minimizing transmission of vibration from equipment
    (d) b or c

143. The *Code* requires the installation of an equipment grounding conductor of the wire type in _____.

    (a) rigid metal conduit (RMC)
    (b) intermediate metal conduit (IMC)
    (c) electrical metallic tubing (EMT)
    (d) none of these

144. Listed liquidtight flexible metal conduit (LFMC) is acceptable as an equipment grounding conductor when it terminates in listed fittings and is protected by an overcurrent device rated 60A or less for trade sizes ⅜ through ½.

    (a) True
    (b) False

145. Type MC cable provides an effective ground-fault current path and is recognized by the *NEC* as an equipment grounding conductor when _____.

    (a) it contains an insulated or uninsulated equipment grounding conductor in compliance with 250.118(1)
    (b) the combined metallic sheath and uninsulated equipment grounding/bonding conductor of interlocked metal tape-type MC cable is listed and identified as an equipment grounding conductor
    (c) only when it is hospital grade Type MC cable
    (d) a or b

146. An equipment grounding conductor shall be identified by _____.

    (a) a continuous outer finish that is green
    (b) being bare
    (c) a continuous outer finish that is green with one or more yellow stripes
    (d) any of these

147. Conductors with the color _____ insulation shall not be used for ungrounded or grounded conductors.

    (a) green
    (b) green with one or more yellow stripes
    (c) a or b
    (d) white

148. A wire-type equipment grounding conductor is permitted to be used as a grounding electrode conductor if it meets all of the requirements of Parts II, III, and VI of Article 250.

    (a) True
    (b) False

149. When ungrounded circuit conductors are increased in size to account for voltage drop, the wire-type equipment grounding conductor shall be proportionately increased in size according to the increase in size of the ungrounded conductors using their _____.

    (a) ampacity
    (b) circular mil area
    (c) diameter
    (d) none of these

150. When a single equipment grounding conductor is used for multiple circuits in the same raceway, cable, or cable tray, the single equipment grounding conductor shall be sized according to the _____.

    (a) combined rating of all the overcurrent devices
    (b) largest overcurrent device of the multiple circuits
    (c) combined rating of all the loads
    (d) any of these

151. Equipment grounding conductors for motor branch circuits shall be sized in accordance with Table 250.122, based on the rating of the _____ device.

    (a) motor overload
    (b) motor over-temperature
    (c) branch-circuit short-circuit and ground-fault protective
    (d) feeder overcurrent protection

152. If conductors are installed in parallel in the same raceway or cable tray, a single wire-type conductor shall be permitted as the equipment grounding conductor and sized in accordance with 250.122, based on the _____.

    (a) feeder
    (b) branch circuit
    (c) overcurrent protective device
    (d) none of these

153. If multiconductor cables are installed in parallel in the same raceway, auxiliary gutter, or cable tray, _____ equipment grounding conductor(s) that is(are) sized in accordance with 250.122 shall be permitted in combination with the equipment grounding conductors provided within the multiconductor cables and shall all be connected together.

    (a) one
    (b) two
    (c) three
    (d) four

154. Except as provided in 250.122(F)(2)(b) for raceway or cable tray installations, the equipment grounding conductor in each multi-conductor cable shall be sized in accordance with 250.122 based on the _____.

    (a) largest circuit conductor
    (b) overcurrent protective device for the feeder or branch circuit
    (c) smallest branch circuit conductor
    (d) overcurrent protective device for the service

155. Equipment grounding conductors for feeder taps are not required to be larger than the tap conductors.

    (a) True
    (b) False

156. The terminal of a wiring device for the connection of the equipment grounding conductor shall be identified by a green-colored, _____.

    (a) not readily removable terminal screw with a hexagonal head
    (b) hexagonal, not readily removable terminal nut
    (c) pressure wire connector
    (d) any of these

Part VII. Methods of Equipment Grounding

157. The structural metal frame of a building can be used as the required equipment grounding conductor for ac equipment.

    (a) True
    (b) False

158. Metal parts of cord-and-plug-connected equipment, if grounded, shall be connected to an equipment grounding conductor that terminates to a grounding-type attachment plug.

    (a) True
    (b) False

159. A grounded circuit conductor is permitted to ground noncurrent-carrying metal parts of equipment, raceways, and other enclosures on the supply side or within the enclosure of the ac service disconnecting means.

    (a) True
    (b) False

160. It shall be permissible to ground meter enclosures immediately adjacent to the service disconnecting means to the _____ circuit conductor on the load side of the service disconnect, if service ground-fault protection is not provided.

    (a) grounding
    (b) bonding
    (c) grounded
    (d) phase

161. Where the box is mounted on the surface, direct metal-to-metal contact between the device yoke and the box shall be permitted to ground the receptacle to the box if at least _____ of the insulating washers of the receptacle is (are) removed.

    (a) one
    (b) two
    (c) three
    (d) four

162. A listed exposed work cover can be the grounding and bonding means when the device is attached to the cover with at least _____ permanent fastener(s) and the cover mounting holes are located on a non-raised portion of the cover.

    (a) one
    (b) two
    (c) three
    (d) four

163. Receptacle yokes designed and _____ as self-grounding can, in conjunction with the supporting screws, establish the equipment bonding between the device yoke and a flush-type box.

    (a) approved
    (b) advertised
    (c) listed
    (d) installed

164. The receptacle grounding terminal of an isolated ground receptacle shall be connected to a(n) _____ equipment grounding conductor run with the circuit conductors.

    (a) insulated
    (b) covered
    (c) bare
    (d) solid

165. A connection between equipment grounding conductors and a metal box shall be by _____.

    (a) a grounding screw used for no other purpose
    (b) equipment listed for grounding
    (c) a listed grounding device
    (d) any of these

Notes

CHAPTER 3

WIRING METHODS AND MATERIALS

Chapter 3—Wiring Methods and Materials

Chapter 3 covers wiring methods and materials, and provides some very specific installation requirements for conductors, cables, boxes, raceways, and fittings. This chapter includes detailed information about the installation and restrictions involved with wiring methods.

It may be because of those details that many people incorrectly apply the rules from this chapter. Be sure to pay careful attention to the details, and be sure you make your installation comply with the rules in the *NEC*, not just completing it in the manner you may have been taught or because "it's always been done that way." This is especially true when it comes to applying the Tables.

Violations of the rules for wiring methods found in Chapter 3 can result in problems with power quality and can lead to fire, shock, and other hazards.

The type of wiring method you'll use depends on several factors; job specifications, *Code* requirements, the environment, need, and cost are among them.

Chapter 3 begins with rules that are common to most wiring methods [Article 300]. It then covers conductors [Article 310] and enclosures [Articles 312 and 314]. The articles that follow become more specific and deal more in-depth with individual wiring methods such as specific types of cables [Articles 320 through 340] and various raceways [Articles 342 through 390]. The chapter winds up with Article 392, a support system, and the final articles [Articles 394 through 398] for open wiring.

Notice as you read through the various wiring methods that the *Code* attempts to use similar subsection numbering for similar topics from one article to the next, using the same digits after the decimal point in the section number for the same topic. This makes it easier to locate specific requirements in a particular article. For example, the rules for securing and supporting can be found in the section that ends with ".30" of each article. In addition to this, you'll find a "uses permitted" and "uses not permitted" section in nearly every article.

Wiring Method Articles

- **Article 300—General Requirements for Wiring Methods and Materials.** Article 300 contains the general requirements for all wiring methods included in the *NEC*, except for signaling and communications systems (twisted wire, antennas, and coaxial cable), which are covered in Chapters 7 and 8.

- **Article 314—Outlet, Device, Pull, and Junction Boxes; Conduit Bodies; Fittings; and Handhole Enclosures.** Installation requirements for outlet boxes, pull and junction boxes, as well as conduit bodies, and handhole enclosures are contained in this article.

Cable Articles

Articles 320 through 340 address specific types of cables. If you take the time to become familiar with the various types of cables, you'll:

- Understand what's available for doing the work.
- Recognize cable types that have special *NEC* requirements.
- Avoid buying cable that you can't install due to *Code* requirements you can't meet with that particular wiring method.

Here's a brief overview of each one:

- **Article 320—Armored Cable (Type AC).** Armored cable is an assembly of insulated conductors, 14 AWG through 1 AWG, individually wrapped with waxed paper. The conductors are contained within a flexible spiral metal (steel or aluminum) sheath that interlocks at the edges. Armored cable looks like flexible metal conduit. Many electricians call this metal cable "BX®."

- **Article 330—Metal-Clad Cable (Type MC).** Metal-clad cable encloses insulated conductors in a metal sheath of either corrugated or smooth copper or aluminum tubing, or spiral interlocked steel or aluminum. The physical characteristics of Type MC cable make it a versatile wiring method permitted in almost any location and for almost any application. The most commonly used Type MC cable is the interlocking kind, which looks similar to armored cable or flexible metal conduit.

- **Article 334—Nonmetallic-Sheathed Cable (Type NM).** Nonmetallic-sheathed cable encloses two, three, or four insulated conductors, 14 AWG through 2 AWG, within a nonmetallic outer jacket. Because this cable is nonmetallic, it contains a separate equipment grounding conductor. Nonmetallic-sheathed cable is a common wiring method used for residential and commercial branch circuits. Many electricians call this plastic-sheathed cable "Romex®."

Raceway Articles

Articles 342 through 390 address specific types of raceways. Refer to Article 100 for the definition of a raceway. If you take the time to become familiar with the various types of raceways, you'll:

- Understand what's available for doing the work.
- Recognize raceway types that have special *Code* requirements.
- Avoid buying a raceway that you can't install due to *NEC* requirements you can't meet with that particular wiring method.

Here's a brief overview of each one:

- **Article 348—Flexible Metal Conduit (Type FMC).** Flexible metal conduit is a raceway of circular cross section made of a helically wound, interlocked metal strip of either steel or aluminum. It's commonly called "Greenfield" or "Flex."

- **Article 350—Liquidtight Flexible Metal Conduit (Type LFMC).** Liquidtight flexible metal conduit is a raceway of circular cross section with an outer liquidtight, nonmetallic, sunlight-resistant jacket over an inner flexible metal core, with associated couplings, connectors, and fittings. It's listed for the installation of electrical conductors. Liquidtight flexible metal conduit is commonly called "Sealtite®" or simply "liquidtight." Liquidtight flexible metal conduit is of similar construction to flexible metal conduit, but it has an outer thermoplastic covering.

- **Article 352—Rigid Polyvinyl Chloride Conduit (Type PVC).** Rigid polyvinyl chloride conduit is a nonmetallic raceway of circular cross section with integral or associated couplings, connectors, and fittings. It's listed for the installation of electrical conductors.

- **Article 356—Liquidtight Flexible Nonmetallic Conduit (Type LFNC).** Liquidtight flexible nonmetallic conduit is a raceway of circular cross section with an outer liquidtight, nonmetallic, sunlight-resistant jacket over an inner flexible core, with associated couplings, connectors, and fittings.

- **Article 358—Electrical Metallic Tubing (EMT).** Electrical metallic tubing is a nonthreaded thinwall raceway of circular cross section designed for the physical protection and routing of conductors and cables. Compared to rigid metal conduit and intermediate metal conduit, electrical metallic tubing is relatively easy to bend, cut, and ream. EMT isn't threaded, so all connectors and couplings are of the threadless type. It's available in a range of colors, such as red and blue.

- **Article 362—Electrical Nonmetallic Tubing (ENT).** Electrical nonmetallic tubing is a pliable, corrugated, circular raceway made of PVC. It's often called "Smurf Pipe" or "Smurf Tube," because it was available only in blue when it came out at the time the children's cartoon characters "The Smurfs" were popular. It's now available in multiple colors such as red and yellow as well as blue.

- **Article 386—Surface Metal Raceways.** A surface metal raceway is a metal raceway intended to be mounted to the surface with associated accessories, in which conductors are placed after the raceway has been installed as a complete system.

Cable Tray

- **Article 392—Cable Trays.** A cable tray system is a unit or assembly of units or sections with associated fittings that form a structural system used to securely fasten or support cables and raceways. A cable tray isn't a raceway; it's a support system for raceways, cables, and enclosures.

Notes

ARTICLE 300 — GENERAL REQUIREMENTS FOR WIRING METHODS AND MATERIALS

Introduction to Article 300—General Requirements for Wiring Methods and Materials

Article 300 contains the general requirements for all wiring methods included in the *NEC*. However, it doesn't apply to communications systems (twisted wire, antennas, and coaxial cable), which are covered in Chapter 8, except when Article 300 is specifically referenced in Chapter 8.

This article is primarily concerned with how to install, route, splice, protect, and secure conductors and raceways. How well you conform to the requirements of Article 300 will generally be evident in the finished work, because many of the requirements tend to determine the appearance of the installation. Because of this, it's often easy to spot Article 300 problems if you're looking for *Code* violations. For example, you can easily see when someone runs an equipment grounding conductor outside a raceway instead of grouping all conductors of a circuit together, as required by 300.3(B).

A good understanding of Article 300 will start you on the path to correctly installing the wiring methods included in Chapter 3. Be sure to carefully consider the accompanying illustrations, and refer to the definitions in Article 100 as needed.

Part I. General

300.1 Scope

(A) Wiring Installations. Article 300 contains the general requirements for wiring methods and materials for power and lighting. ▶Figure 300–1

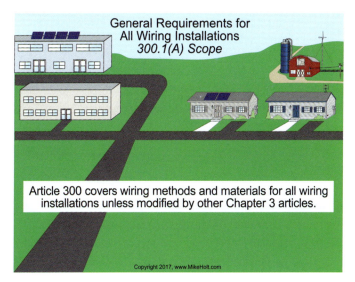

▶Figure 300–1

Author's Comment:

- The requirements contained in Article 300 don't apply to the wiring methods for Class 2 and 3 circuits, fire alarm circuits, and communications systems (twisted wire, antennas, and coaxial cable), except where there's a specific reference in Chapters 7 or 8 to a rule in Article 300.
    - Class 2 and 3 Remote Control and Signaling, 725.3
    - Communications Cables and Raceways, 800.133(A)(2)
    - Coaxial Circuits, 820.3
    - Fire Alarm Circuits, 760.3

(B) Integral Parts of Equipment. The requirements contained in Article 300 don't apply to the internal parts of electrical equipment. ▶Figure 300–2

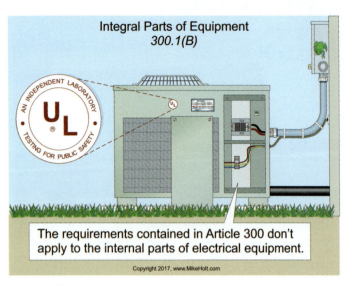
▶Figure 300–2

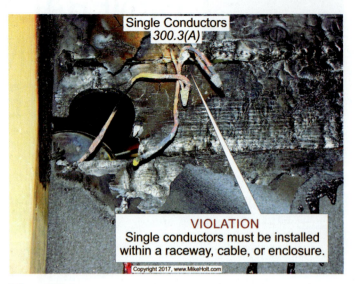
▶Figure 300–3

(C) Trade Sizes. Designators for raceway trade sizes are given in Table 300.1(C).

Author's Comment:

- Industry practice is to describe raceways using inch sizes, such as ½ in., 2 in., and so on; however, the proper reference is to use "Trade Size ½," or "Trade Size 2." In this textbook we use the term "Trade Size."

300.3 Conductors

(A) Conductors. Single conductors must be installed within a Chapter 3 wiring method, such as a raceway, cable, or enclosure. ▶Figure 300–3

Ex: Overhead conductors can be installed in accordance with 225.6.

(B) Circuit Conductors Grouped Together. Conductors of a circuit and, where used, the neutral and equipment grounding and bonding conductors must be installed in the same raceway, cable, trench, cord, or cable tray, except as permitted by (1) through (4).

(1) Paralleled Installations. Conductors installed in parallel in accordance with 310.10(H) must have all circuit conductors within the same raceway, cable tray, trench, or cable. ▶Figure 300–4

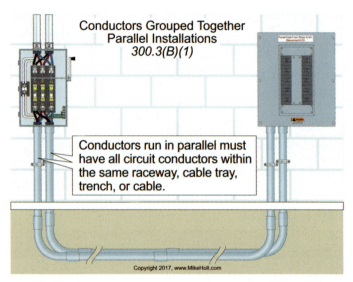
▶Figure 300–4

Author's Comment:

- To minimize induction heating of ferrous metal raceways and ferrous metal enclosures for alternating-current circuits, and to maintain an effective ground-fault current path, all conductors of a circuit must be installed in the same raceway, cable, trench, cord, or cable tray. See 250.102(E), 300.3(B), 300.5(I), 300.20(A), and 392.8(D). ▶Figure 300–5 and ▶Figure 300–6

Ex: Parallel phase and neutral conductors can be installed in individual underground nonmetallic raceways (Phase A in raceway 1, Phase B in raceway 2, and so forth) as permitted by 300.5(I) Ex 2, if the installation complies with 300.20(B). ▶Figure 300–7

General Requirements for Wiring Methods and Materials | 300.3

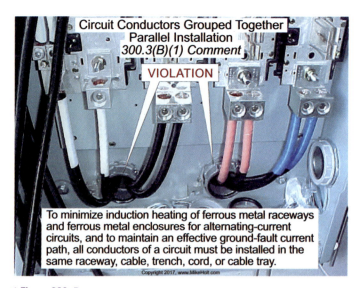
▶Figure 300–5

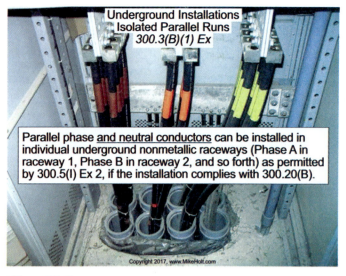
▶Figure 300–7

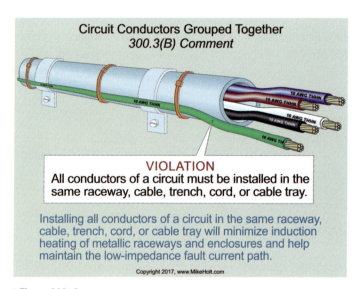
▶Figure 300–6

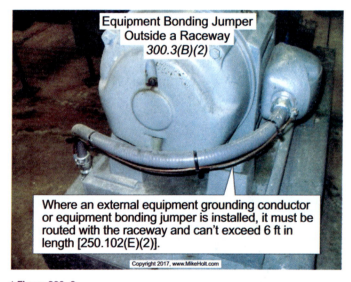
▶Figure 300–8

(2) Outside a Raceway or an Enclosure. Equipment grounding jumpers can be located outside of a flexible raceway if the bonding jumper is installed in accordance with 250.102(E)(2). ▶Figure 300–8

For dc circuits, the equipment grounding conductor can be run separately from the circuit conductors in accordance with 250.134(B) Ex 2.
▶Figure 300–9

(3) Nonferrous Wiring Methods. Circuit conductors can be installed in different raceways (Phase A in raceway 1, Phase B in raceway 2, and so on) if, in order to reduce or eliminate inductive heating, the raceway is nonmetallic or nonmagnetic and the installation complies with 300.20(B). See 300.3(B)(1) and 300.5(I) Ex 2.

300.10 | General Requirements for Wiring Methods and Materials

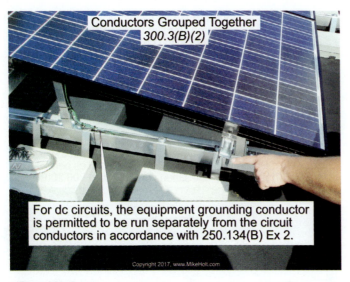

▶Figure 300–9

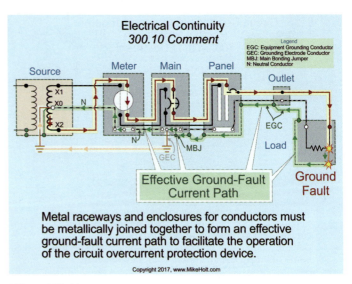

▶Figure 300–11

300.10 Electrical Continuity

Metal raceways, cable armor, and other metal enclosures must be metallically joined together into a continuous electrical conductor to provide effective electrical continuity [110.10 and 250.4(A)(3)]. ▶Figure 300–10

Ex 1: Short lengths of metal raceways used for the support or protection of cables aren't required to be electrically continuous, nor are they required to be connected to an equipment grounding conductor [250.86 Ex 2 and 300.12 Ex]. ▶Figure 300–12

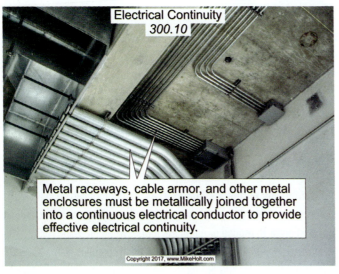

▶Figure 300–10

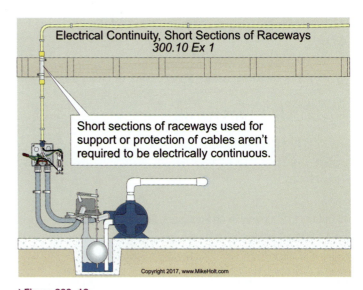

▶Figure 300–12

Author's Comment:

- The purpose of effective electrical continuity is to establish an effective ground-fault current path necessary to facilitate the operation of the circuit overcurrent protection device in the event of a ground fault [250.4(A)(3)]. ▶Figure 300–11

ARTICLE 314 — OUTLET, DEVICE, PULL, AND JUNCTION BOXES; CONDUIT BODIES; AND HANDHOLE ENCLOSURES

Introduction to Article 314—Outlet, Device, Pull, and Junction Boxes; Conduit Bodies; and Handhole Enclosures

Article 314 contains installation requirements for outlet boxes, pull and junction boxes, conduit bodies, and handhole enclosures. As with the cabinets covered in Article 312, the conditions of use have a bearing on the type of material and equipment selected for a particular installation. If a raceway is installed in a wet location, for example, the correct fittings and the proper installation methods must be used.

The information here will help you size an outlet box using the proper cubic-inch capacity as well as calculating the minimum dimensions for larger pull boxes. There are limits on the amount of weight that can be supported by an outlet box and rules on how to support a device or outlet box to various surfaces. Article 314 will help you understand these types of rules so that your installation will be compliant with the *NEC*. As always, the clear illustrations in this article will help you visualize the finished installation.

Part I. Scope and General

314.1 Scope

Article 314 contains the installation requirements for outlet boxes, conduit bodies, pull and junction boxes, and handhole enclosures. ▶Figure 314–1

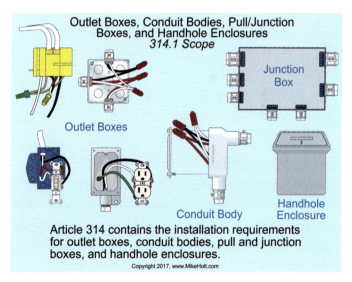

▶Figure 314–1

314.3 Nonmetallic Boxes

Nonmetallic boxes can only be used with nonmetallic cables and raceways.

Ex 1: Metal raceways and metal cables can be used with nonmetallic boxes if all raceways are bonded together in the nonmetallic box. ▶Figure 314–2

314.4 Metal Boxes

Metal boxes containing circuits that operate at 50V or more must be connected to an equipment grounding conductor of a type listed in 250.118 [250.112(I) and 250.148]. ▶Figure 314–3

314.25 | Outlet, Device, Pull, and Junction Boxes; Conduit Bodies; and Handhole Enclosures

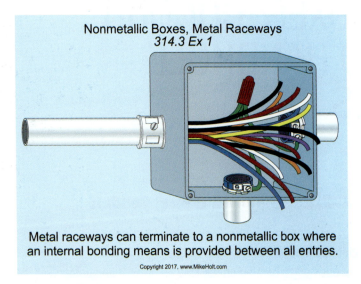

▶Figure 314–2

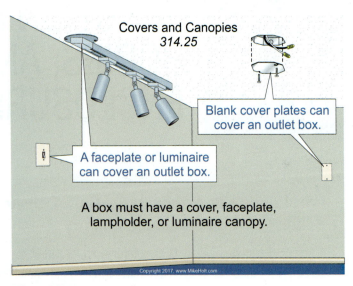

▶Figure 314–4

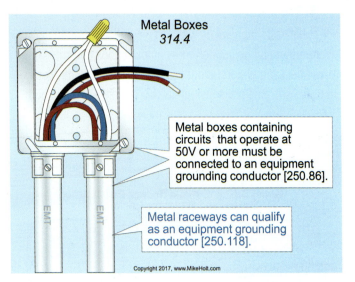

▶Figure 314–3

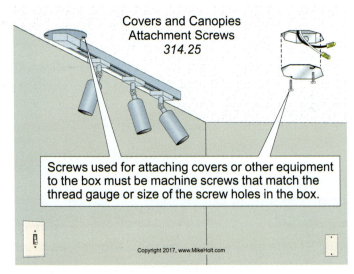

▶Figure 314–5

Part II. Installation

314.25 Covers and Canopies

When the installation is complete, each outlet box must be provided with a cover or faceplate, unless covered by a fixture canopy, lampholder, or similar device. ▶Figure 314–4

Screws used for attaching covers or other equipment to the box must be machine screws that match the thread gage or size of the screw holes in the box or they must be in accordance with the manufacturer's instructions. ▶Figure 314–5

(A) Metal Covers. Metal covers are only permitted if they can be connected to an equipment grounding conductor of a type recognized in 250.118 [250.110]. ▶Figure 314–6

Author's Comment:

- Metal switch faceplates [404.9(B)] and metal receptacle faceplates [406.6(A)] must be connected to an equipment grounding conductor.

Outlet, Device, Pull, and Junction Boxes; Conduit Bodies; and Handhole Enclosures | 314.30

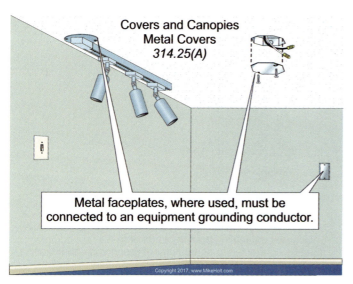

▶Figure 314–6

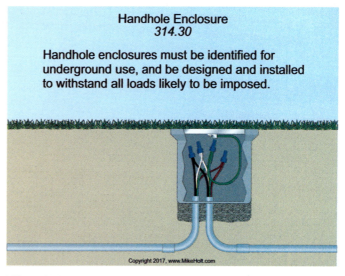

▶Figure 314–8

314.28 Sizing Conductors 4 AWG and Larger

(C) Covers. Pull boxes and junction boxes must have a cover suitable for the conditions. Metal covers must be connected to an equipment grounding conductor of a type recognized in 250.118, in accordance with 250.110 [250.4(A)(3)]. ▶Figure 314–7

(D) Covers. Handhole enclosure covers must have an identifying mark or logo that prominently identifies the function of the enclosure, such as "electric." Handhole enclosure covers must require the use of tools to open, or they must weigh over 100 lb. ▶Figure 314–9 and ▶Figure 314–10

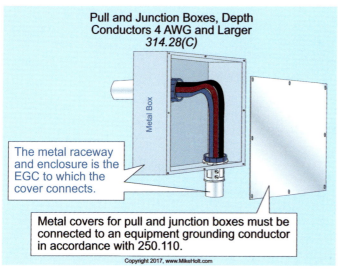

▶Figure 314–7

▶Figure 314–9

314.30 Handhole Enclosures

Handhole enclosures must be identified for underground use, and be designed and installed to withstand all loads likely to be imposed on them. ▶Figure 314–8

314.30 | Outlet, Device, Pull, and Junction Boxes; Conduit Bodies; and Handhole Enclosures

▶Figure 314–10

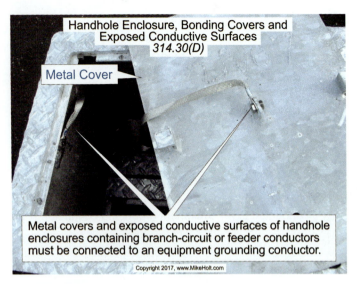
▶Figure 314–11

Metal covers and exposed conductive surfaces of handhole enclosures containing branch-circuit or feeder conductors must be connected to an equipment grounding conductor sized in accordance with 250.122, based on the rating of the overcurrent protection device [250.102(D)].
▶Figure 314–11

Metal covers and exposed conductive surfaces of handhole enclosures containing service conductors must be connected to a supply-side bonding jumper sized in accordance with Table 250.102(C)(1), based on the size of service conductors [250.92 and 250.102(C)].

ARTICLE 320 ARMORED CABLE (TYPE AC)

Introduction to Article 320—Armored Cable (Type AC)

Armored cable is an assembly of insulated conductors, 14 AWG through 1 AWG, individually wrapped within waxed paper and contained within a flexible spiral metal sheath. The outside appearance of armored cable looks like flexible metal conduit as well as metal-clad cable to the casual observer. This cable has been referred to as "BX®" cable over the years and used in residential wiring in some areas of the country.

320.1 Scope

This article covers the use, installation, and construction specifications of armored cable, Type AC. ▶Figure 320–1

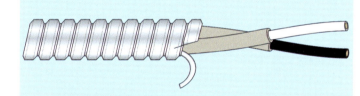

▶Figure 320–1

320.2 Definition

Armored Cable (Type AC). A fabricated assembly of conductors in a flexible interlocked metal armor with an internal bonding strip in intimate contact with the armor for its entire length. ▶Figure 320–2

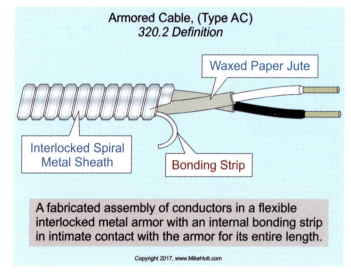

▶Figure 320–2

Author's Comment:

- The conductors are contained within a flexible metal sheath that interlocks at the edges with an internal aluminum bonding strip, giving the cable an outside appearance similar to that of flexible metal conduit. Many electricians call this metal cable "BX®." The advantages the use of any flexible cables, as compared to raceway wiring methods, are that there's no limit to the number of bends between terminations and the cable can be quickly installed.

320.108 Equipment Grounding Conductor

Type AC cable can serve as an equipment grounding conductor [250.118(8)]. ▶Figure 320–3

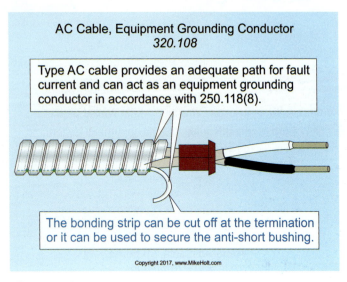

▶Figure 320–3

Author's Comment:

- The internal aluminum bonding strip isn't an equipment grounding conductor, but it allows the interlocked armor to serve as an equipment grounding conductor because it reduces the impedance of the armored spirals to ensure that a ground fault will be cleared. It's the combination of the aluminum bonding strip and the cable armor that creates the equipment grounding conductor. Once the bonding strip exits the cable, it can be cut off because it no longer serves any purpose. The effective ground-fault current path must be maintained by the use of fittings specifically listed for Type AC cable [320.40]. See 300.12, 300.15, and 300.10.

ARTICLE 330 METAL-CLAD CABLE (TYPE MC)

Introduction to Article 330—Metal-Clad Cable (Type MC)

Metal-clad cable encloses insulated conductors in a metal sheath of either corrugated or smooth copper or aluminum tubing, or spiral interlocked steel or aluminum. The physical characteristics of Type MC cable make it a versatile wiring method that you can use in almost any location, and for almost any application. The most commonly used Type MC cable is the interlocking kind, which looks similar to armored cable or flexible metal conduit. Traditional interlocked Type MC cable isn't permitted to serve as an equipment grounding conductor, therefore this cable must contain an equipment grounding conductor in accordance with 250.118(1). There's a fairly new product available called interlocked Type MC^AP® cable that contains a bare aluminum grounding/bonding conductor running just below the metal armor, which allows the sheath to serve as an equipment grounding conductor [250.118(10)(b)].

330.1 Scope

Article 330 covers the use, installation, and construction specifications of metal-clad cable. ▶Figure 330–1

330.2 Definition

Metal-Clad Cable (Type MC). A factory assembly of insulated circuit conductors, with or without optical fiber members, enclosed in an armor of interlocking metal tape; or a smooth or corrugated metallic sheath. ▶Figure 330–2

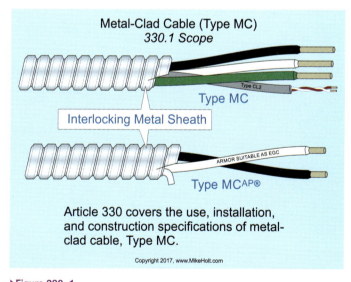

▶Figure 330–1

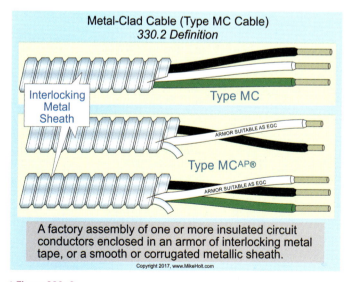

▶Figure 330–2

330.108 | Metal-Clad Cable (Type MC)

Author's Comment:

- Because the outer sheath of interlocked Type MC cable isn't listed as an equipment grounding conductor, it contains an equipment grounding conductor [330.108].

330.108 Equipment Grounding Conductor

If Type MC cable is to serve as an equipment grounding conductor, it must comply with 250.118 and 250.122.

Author's Comment:

- The outer sheath of:
  - Traditional interlocked Type MC cable isn't permitted to serve as an equipment grounding conductor, therefore this cable must contain an insulated equipment grounding conductor in accordance with 250.118(1). ▶Figure 330–3
  - Interlocked Type MC^{AP} cable containing an aluminum grounding/bonding conductor running just below the metal armor is listed to serve as an equipment grounding conductor [250.118(10)(b)]. ▶Figure 330–4
  - Smooth or corrugated-tube Type MC cable is listed to serve as an equipment grounding conductor [250.118(10)(c)].

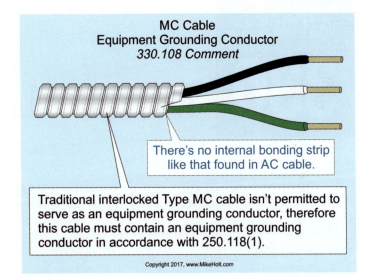

▶Figure 330–3

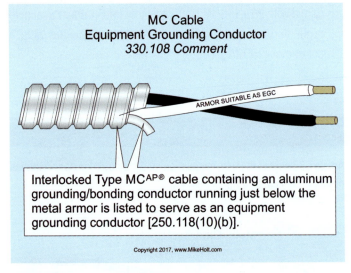

▶Figure 330–4

ARTICLE 334 — NONMETALLIC-SHEATHED CABLE (TYPES NM AND NMC)

Introduction to Article 334—Nonmetallic-Sheathed Cable (Types NM and NMC)

Nonmetallic-sheathed cable is flexible, inexpensive, and easily installed. It provides very limited physical protection for the conductors, so the installation restrictions are stringent. Its low cost and relative ease of installation make it a common wiring method for residential and commercial branch circuits. In the field, Type NM cable is typically referred to as "Romex®."

334.1 Scope

Article 334 covers the use, installation, and construction specifications of nonmetallic-sheathed cable. ▶Figure 334–1

- NM cable has insulated conductors enclosed within an overall nonmetallic jacket.
- NMC cable has insulated conductors enclosed within an overall, corrosion-resistant, nonmetallic jacket.

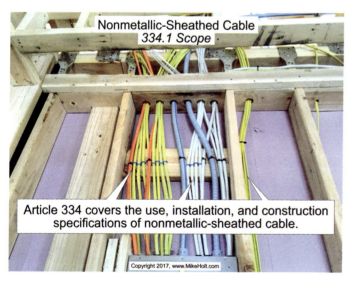

▶Figure 334–1

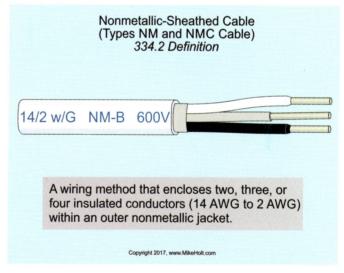

▶Figure 334–2

334.2 Definition

Nonmetallic-Sheathed Cable (Types NM and NMC). A wiring method that encloses two or more insulated conductors, 14 AWG through 2 AWG, within a nonmetallic jacket. ▶Figure 334–2

Author's Comment:

- It's the generally accepted practice in the electrical industry to call Type NM cable "Romex®," a registered trademark of the Southwire Company.

334.108 Equipment Grounding Conductor

Type NM cable must have an insulated, covered, or bare equipment grounding conductor. ▶Figure 334–3

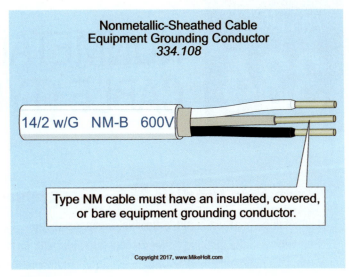

▶Figure 334–3

ARTICLE 348 — FLEXIBLE METAL CONDUIT (TYPE FMC)

Introduction to Article 348—Flexible Metal Conduit (Type FMC)

Flexible metal conduit (FMC), commonly called "Greenfield" or "flex," is a raceway of an interlocked metal strip of either steel or aluminum. It's primarily used for the final 6 ft or less of raceways between a more rigid raceway system and equipment that moves, shakes, or vibrates. Examples of such equipment include pump motors and industrial machinery.

348.1 Scope

Article 348 covers the use, installation, and construction specifications for flexible metal conduit and associated fittings. ▶Figure 348–1

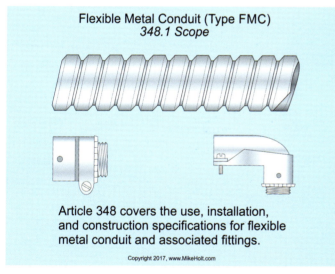

▶Figure 348–1

348.2 Definition

Flexible Metal Conduit (Type FMC). A raceway of circular cross section made of a helically wound, formed, interlocked metal strip. ▶Figure 348–2

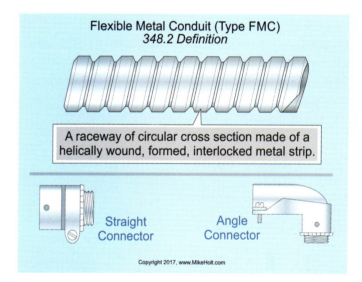

▶Figure 348–2

348.60 Grounding and Bonding

If flexibility is necessary to minimize the transmission of vibration from equipment or to provide flexibility for equipment that requires movement after installation, an equipment grounding conductor of the wire type must be installed with the circuit conductors in accordance with 250.118(5), sized in accordance with 250.122, based on the rating of the overcurrent protection device. ▶Figure 348–3

348.60 | Flexible Metal Conduit (Type FMC)

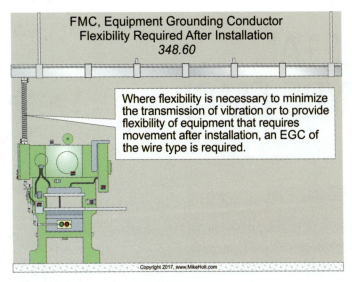

▶Figure 348–3

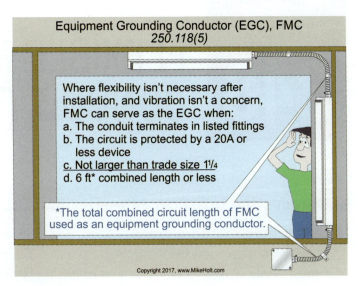

▶Figure 348–4

If flexibility isn't necessary after installation, and vibration isn't a concern, the metal armor of flexible metal conduit can serve as an equipment grounding conductor if the circuit conductors contained in the raceway are protected by an overcurrent protection device rated 20A or less, and the combined length of the flexible metal raceway in the same ground-fault return path doesn't exceed 6 ft [250.118(5)]. ▶Figure 348–4

If an equipment bonding jumper is installed outside of a raceway, the length of the equipment bonding jumper must not exceed 6 ft, and it must be routed with the raceway or enclosure in accordance with 250.102(E)(2).

ARTICLE 350 — LIQUIDTIGHT FLEXIBLE METAL CONDUIT (TYPE LFMC)

Introduction to Article 350—Liquidtight Flexible Metal Conduit (Type LFMC)

Liquidtight flexible metal conduit (LFMC), with its associated connectors and fittings, is a flexible raceway commonly used for connections to equipment that vibrates or is required to move occasionally. Liquidtight flexible metal conduit is commonly called "Sealtight®" or "liquidtight." Liquidtight flexible metal conduit is of similar construction to flexible metal conduit, but it also has an outer liquidtight thermoplastic covering. It has the same primary purpose as flexible metal conduit, but it also provides protection from moisture and some corrosive effects.

350.1 Scope

Article 350 covers the use, installation, and construction specifications of liquidtight flexible metal conduit and associated fittings. ▶Figure 350–1

▶Figure 350–1

350.2 Definition

Liquidtight Flexible Metal Conduit (Type LFMC). A raceway of circular cross section, having an outer liquidtight, nonmetallic, sunlight-resistant jacket over an inner flexible metal core, with associated connectors and fittings for the installation of electric conductors. ▶Figure 350–2

▶Figure 350–2

350.60 | Liquidtight Flexible Metal Conduit (Type LFMC)

350.60 Grounding and Bonding

If flexibility is necessary to minimize the transmission of vibration from equipment or to provide flexibility for equipment that requires movement after installation, an equipment grounding conductor of the wire type must be installed with the circuit conductors in accordance with 250.118(6), sized in accordance with 250.122, based on the rating of the overcurrent protection device. ▶Figure 350–3

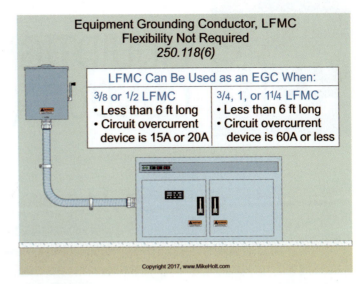

▶Figure 350–4

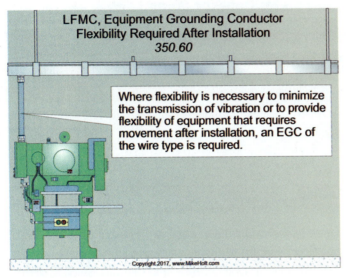

▶Figure 350–3

If flexibility isn't necessary after installation, and vibration isn't a concern, the metal armor of flexible metal conduit can serve as an equipment grounding conductor if the circuit conductors contained in the raceway are protected by an overcurrent protection device rated 20A or less, and the combined length of the flexible metal raceway in the same ground-fault return path doesn't exceed 6 ft [250.118(6)]. ▶Figure 350–4

If an equipment bonding jumper is installed outside of a raceway, the length of the equipment bonding jumper must not exceed 6 ft, and it must be routed with the raceway or enclosure in accordance with 250.102(E)(2). ▶Figure 350–5

▶Figure 350–5

ARTICLE 352 — RIGID POLYVINYL CHLORIDE CONDUIT (TYPE PVC)

Introduction to Article 352—Rigid Polyvinyl Chloride Conduit (Type PVC)

Rigid polyvinyl chloride conduit is a rigid nonmetallic conduit that provides many of the advantages of rigid metal conduit, while allowing installation in areas that are wet or corrosive. It's an inexpensive raceway, and easily installed. It's lightweight, easily cut and glued together, and relatively strong. However, conduits manufactured from polyvinyl chloride (PVC) are brittle when cold, and they sage when hot. This type of conduit is commonly used as an underground raceway because of its low cost, ease of installation, and resistance to corrosion and decay.

352.1 Scope

Article 352 covers the use, installation, and construction specifications of PVC conduit and associated fittings. ▶Figure 352–1

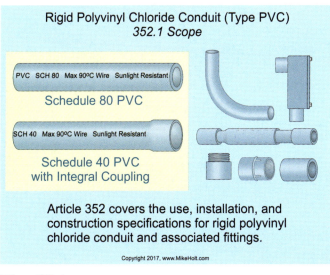

▶Figure 352–1

352.2 Definition

Rigid Polyvinyl Chloride Conduit (PVC). A rigid nonmetallic raceway of circular cross section with integral or associated couplings, listed for the installation of electrical conductors and cables. ▶Figure 352–2

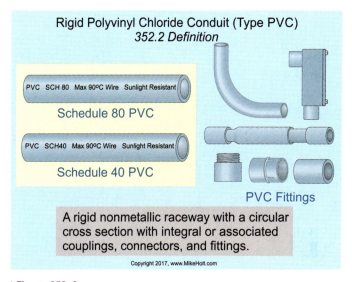

▶Figure 352–2

352.60 Equipment Grounding Conductor

If equipment grounding is required, a separate equipment grounding conductor of the wire type must be installed within the conduit [300.2(B)]. ▶Figure 352–3

Ex 2: An equipment grounding conductor isn't required in PVC conduit if the neutral conductor is used to ground service equipment, as permitted in 250.142(A) [250.24(C)]. ▶Figure 352–4

352.60 | Rigid Polyvinyl Chloride Conduit (Type PVC)

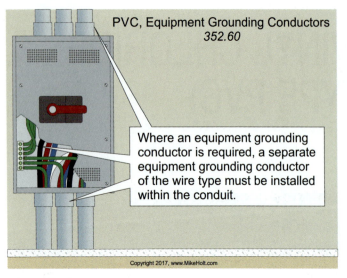

▶Figure 352–3

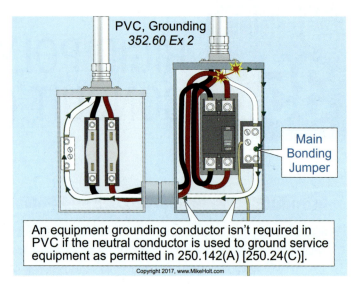

▶Figure 352–4

ARTICLE 356 — LIQUIDTIGHT FLEXIBLE NONMETALLIC CONDUIT (TYPE LFNC)

Introduction to Article 356—Liquidtight Flexible Nonmetallic Conduit (Type LFNC)

Liquidtight flexible nonmetallic conduit (LFNC) is a listed raceway of circular cross section having an outer liquidtight, nonmetallic, sunlight-resistant jacket over an inner flexible core with associated couplings, connectors, and fittings.

356.1 Scope

Article 356 covers the use, installation, and construction specifications of liquidtight flexible nonmetallic conduit and associated fittings.
▶Figure 356–1

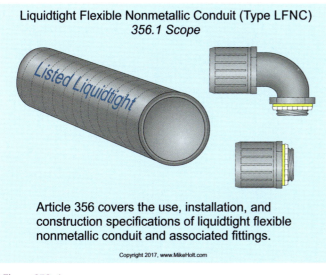

▶Figure 356–1

356.2 Definition

Liquidtight Flexible Nonmetallic Conduit (Type LFNC). A listed raceway of circular cross section, having an outer liquidtight, nonmetallic, sunlight-resistant jacket over a flexible inner core, with associated couplings, connectors, and fittings, listed for the installation of electrical conductors.
▶Figure 356–2

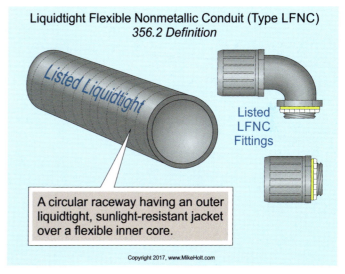

▶Figure 356–2

(1) Type LFNC-A (orange color). A smooth seamless inner core and cover having reinforcement layers between the core and cover.

(2) Type LFNC-B (gray color). A smooth inner surface with integral reinforcement within the raceway wall.

(3) Type LFNC-C (black color). A corrugated internal and external surface without integral reinforcement.

356.60 Equipment Grounding Conductor

If equipment grounding is required, a separate equipment grounding conductor of the wire type must be installed within the conduit [250.134(B)]. ▶Figure 356–3

▶Figure 356–3

Author's Comment:

- An equipment grounding conductor is not required to be installed in a nonmetallic raceway supplying nonmetallic equipment.

If an equipment bonding jumper is installed outside of a raceway, the length of the equipment bonding jumper must not exceed 6 ft, and it must be routed with the raceway or enclosure in accordance with 250.102(E)(2).

ARTICLE 358 — ELECTRICAL METALLIC TUBING (TYPE EMT)

Introduction to Article 358—Electrical Metallic Tubing (Type EMT)

Electrical metallic tubing is a lightweight raceway that's relatively easy to bend, cut, and ream. Because it isn't threaded, all connectors and couplings are of the threadless type and provide quick, easy, and inexpensive installation when compared to other metallic conduit systems, which makes it very popular. Electrical metallic tubing is manufactured in both galvanized steel and aluminum; the steel type is used the most.

358.1 Scope

Article 358 covers the use, installation, and construction specifications of electrical metallic tubing and associated fittings. ▶Figure 358–1

▶Figure 358–1

358.2 Definition

Electrical Metallic Tubing (Type EMT). A metallic tubing of circular cross section used for the installation and physical protection of electrical conductors when joined together with fittings. ▶Figure 358–2

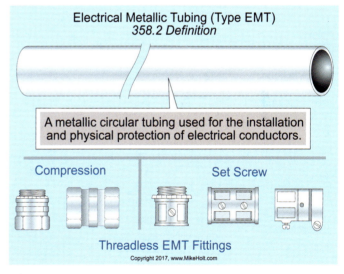

▶Figure 358–2

358.60 | Electrical Metallic Tubing (Type EMT)

358.60 Grounding

EMT can serve as an equipment grounding conductor [250.118(4)].
▶Figure 358–3 and ▶Figure 358–4

▶Figure 358–3

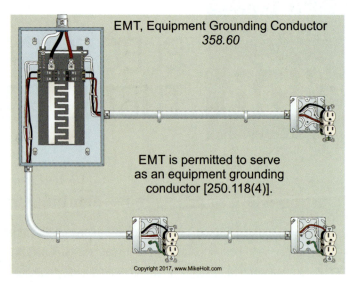

▶Figure 358–4

ARTICLE 362 — ELECTRICAL NONMETALLIC TUBING (TYPE ENT)

Introduction to Article 362—Electrical Nonmetallic Tubing (Type ENT)

Electrical nonmetallic tubing (ENT) is a pliable, corrugated, circular raceway made of polyvinyl chloride. In some parts of the country, the field name for electrical nonmetallic tubing is "Smurf Pipe" or "Smurf Tube," because it was only available in blue when it originally came out when the children's cartoon characters "The Smurfs" were most popular. Today, the raceway is available in many colors such as white, yellow, red, green, and orange, and is sold in both fixed lengths and on reels.

362.1 Scope

Article 362 covers the use, installation, and construction specifications of electrical nonmetallic tubing and associated fittings. ▶Figure 362–1

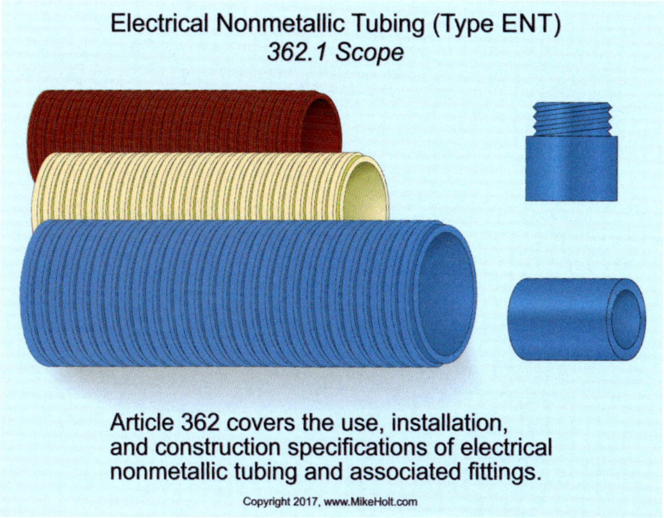

▶Figure 362–1

362.2 Definition

Electrical Nonmetallic Tubing (Type ENT). A pliable corrugated raceway of circular cross section, with integral or associated couplings, connectors, and fittings listed for the installation of electrical conductors. ENT is composed of a material that's resistant to moisture and chemical atmospheres and is flame retardant. ▶Figure 362–2

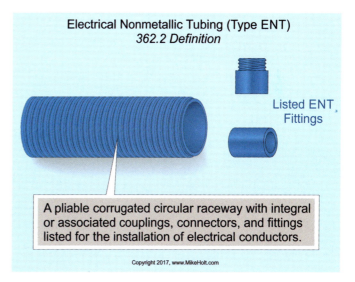

▶Figure 362–2

Electrical nonmetallic tubing can be bent by hand with a reasonable force, but without other assistance.

362.60 Equipment Grounding Conductor

If equipment grounding is required, a separate equipment grounding conductor of the wire type must be installed within the raceway.

▶Figure 362–3

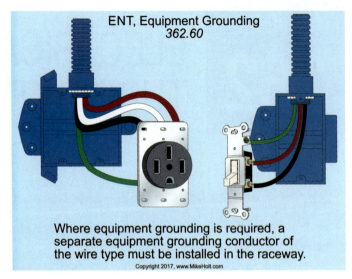

▶Figure 362–3

ARTICLE 386 | SURFACE METAL RACEWAYS

Introduction to Article 386—Surface Metal Raceways

A surface metal raceway is a common method of adding a raceway when exposed traditional raceway systems aren't acceptable, and concealing the raceway isn't economically feasible. It comes in several colors, and is now available with colored or real wood inserts designed to make it look like molding rather than a raceway. A surface metal raceway is commonly known as "Wiremold®" in the field.

386.1 Scope

This article covers the use, installation, and construction specifications of surface metal raceways and associated fittings.

386.2 Definition

Surface Metal Raceway. A metal raceway intended to be mounted to the surface, with associated accessories, in which conductors are placed after the raceway has been installed as a complete system [300.18(A)]. ▶Figure 386–1

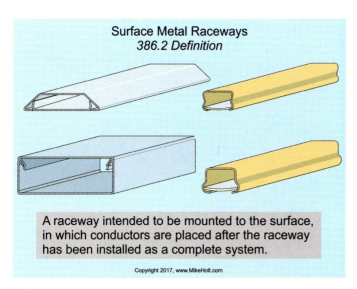

▶Figure 386–1

Author's Comment:

- Surface metal raceways are available in different shapes and sizes and can be mounted on walls, ceilings, or floors. Some surface metal raceways have two or more separate compartments, which permit the separation of power and lighting conductors from low-voltage or limited-energy conductors or cables (control, signaling, and communications cables and conductors) [386.70].

386.60 Equipment Grounding Conductor

Surface metal raceways that allow a transition to another wiring method, such as knockouts for connecting raceways, must have a means for the termination of an equipment grounding conductor.

Author's Comment:

- Surface metal raceway fittings must be mechanically and electrically joined together in a manner that doesn't subject the conductors to abrasion. A listed surface metal raceway is considered suitable as an equipment grounding conductor in accordance with 250.118(14). ▶Figure 386–2

386.70 | Surface Metal Raceways

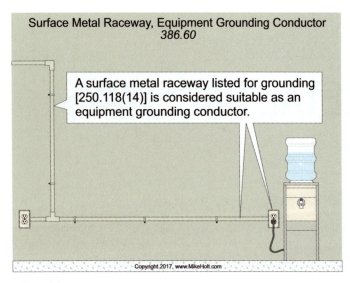

▶Figure 386–2

386.70 Separate Compartments

Where surface metal raceways have separate compartments within a single raceway, power and lighting conductors can occupy one compartment, and the other compartment may contain control, signaling, or communications wiring. Stamping, imprinting, or color coding of the interior finish must identify the separate compartments, and the same relative position of compartments must be maintained throughout the premises.

Author's Comment:

- Separation from power conductors is required by the *NEC* for the following low-voltage and limited-energy systems:
    - Communications, 800.133(A)(1)
    - Control and Signaling, 725.136(B)
    - Fire Alarms, 760.136(B)
    - Intrinsically Safe Systems, 504.30(A)(2)
    - Radio and Television, 810.18(C)
    - Sound Systems, 640.9(C)

- Nonconductive optical fiber cables can occupy the same cable tray or raceway as conductors for electric light, power, Class 1, or nonpower-limited fire alarm circuits [770.133(A)].

ARTICLE 392 CABLE TRAYS

Introduction to Article 392—Cable Trays

A cable tray system is a unit or an assembly of units or sections with associated fittings that forms a structural system used to securely fasten or support cables and raceways. A cable tray isn't a raceway.

Cable tray systems include ladder, ventilated trough, ventilated channel, solid bottom, and other similar structures. Cable trays are manufactured in many forms, from a simple hanger or wire mesh to a substantial, rigid, steel support system. Cable trays are designed and manufactured to support specific wiring methods, as identified in 392.10(A).

392.1 Scope

Article 392 covers cable tray systems, including ladder, ventilated trough, ventilated channel, solid bottom, and other similar structures. ▶Figure 392–1

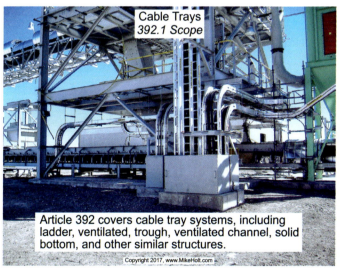

▶Figure 392–1

392.2 Definition

Cable Tray System. A unit or assembly of units or sections with associated fittings forming a rigid structural system used to securely fasten or support cables, raceways, and boxes. ▶Figure 392–2

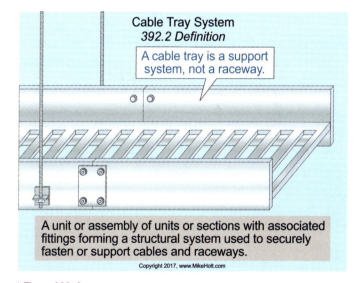

▶Figure 392–2

Author's Comment:

- Cable tray isn't a type of raceway. It's a support system for cables and raceways.

392.60 Equipment Grounding Conductor

(A) Used As Equipment Grounding Conductor. Metal cable trays can be used as equipment grounding conductors where continuous maintenance and supervision ensure that only qualified persons service the cable tray system. ▶Figure 392–3

▶Figure 392–3

Metal cable trays containing single conductors must be bonded together to ensure they have the capacity to conduct safely any fault current likely to be imposed in accordance with 250.96(A).

Metal cable trays containing communications, data, and signaling conductors and cables must be electrically continuous through approved connections or the use of a bonding jumper. ▶Figure 392–4

▶Figure 392–4

(B) Serve as Equipment Grounding Conductor. Metal cable trays can serve as equipment grounding conductors where the following requirements have been met [392.10(C)]:

(1) Metal cable trays and fittings are identified as an equipment grounding conductor. ▶Figure 392–5

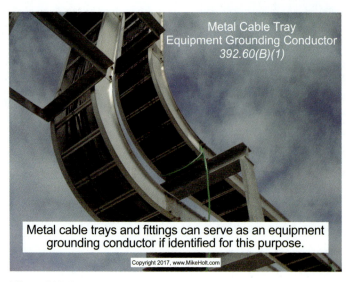

▶Figure 392–5

(4) Cable tray sections, fittings, and connected raceways are effectively bonded to each other to ensure electrical continuity and the capacity to conduct safely any fault current likely to be imposed on them [250.96(A)]. This is accomplished by using bolted mechanical connectors or bonding jumpers sized in accordance with 250.102. ▶Figure 392–6

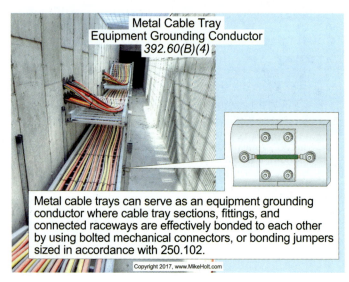

▶Figure 392–6

CHAPTER 3 PRACTICE QUESTIONS

Please use the 2017 *Code* book to answer the following questions.

Article 300. General Requirements for Wiring Methods and Materials

1. All conductors of the same circuit, including the grounded and equipment grounding conductors and bonding conductors shall be contained within the same _____, unless otherwise permitted elsewhere in the *Code*.

    (a) raceway
    (b) cable
    (c) trench
    (d) all of these

2. Metal raceways, cable armor, and other metal enclosures shall be _____ joined together into a continuous electric conductor so as to provide effective electrical continuity.

    (a) electrically
    (b) permanently
    (c) metallically
    (d) none of these

Article 314. Outlet, Device, Pull, and Junction Boxes; Conduit Bodies; Fittings; and Handhole Enclosures

3. Nonmetallic boxes can be used with _____.

    (a) nonmetallic sheaths
    (b) nonmetallic raceways
    (c) flexible cords
    (d) all of these

4. In completed installations, each outlet box shall have a _____.

    (a) cover
    (b) faceplate
    (c) canopy
    (d) any of these

5. Handhole enclosure covers shall have an identifying _____ that prominently identifies the function of the enclosure, such as "electric."

    (a) mark
    (b) logo
    (c) manual
    (d) a or b

Article 320. Armored Cable (Type AC)

6. Type _____ cable is a fabricated assembly of insulated conductors in a flexible interlocked metallic armor.

    (a) AC
    (b) MC
    (c) NM
    (d) b and c

Article 330. Metal-Clad Cable (Type MC)

7. Type _____ cable is a factory assembly of insulated circuit conductors within an armor of interlocking metal tape, or a smooth or corrugated metallic sheath.

    (a) AC
    (b) MC
    (c) NM
    (d) b and c

Article 334. Nonmetallic-Sheathed Cable (Types NM and NMC)

8. Type _____ cable is a factory assembly that encloses two or more insulated conductors within a nonmetallic jacket.

    (a) AC
    (b) MC
    (c) NM
    (d) b and c

Article 348. Flexible Metal Conduit (Type FMC)

9. _____ is a raceway of circular cross section made of a helically wound, formed, interlocked metal strip.

    (a) Type MC cable
    (b) Type AC cable
    (c) LFMC
    (d) FMC

10. When FMC is used where flexibility is necessary to minimize the transmission of vibration from equipment or to provide flexibility for equipment that requires movement after installation, _____ shall be installed.

    (a) an equipment grounding conductor
    (b) an expansion fitting
    (c) flexible nonmetallic connectors
    (d) none of these

Article 350. Liquidtight Flexible Metal Conduit (Type LFMC)

11. _____ is a raceway of circular cross section having an outer liquidtight, nonmetallic, sunlight-resistant jacket over an inner flexible metal core.

    (a) FMC
    (b) LFNMC
    (c) LFMC
    (d) none of these

12. Where flexibility _____, liquidtight flexible metal conduit shall be permitted to be used as an equipment grounding conductor when installed in accordance with 250.118(6).

    (a) is required after installation
    (b) is not required after installation
    (c) a or b
    (d) is optional

Article 356. Liquidtight Flexible Nonmetallic Conduit (Type LFNC)

13. When LFNC is used, and equipment grounding is required, a separate _____ shall be installed in the conduit.

    (a) equipment grounding conductor
    (b) expansion fitting
    (c) flexible nonmetallic connector
    (d) none of these

Article 358. Electrical Metallic Tubing (Type EMT)

14. _____ is an unthreaded thinwall raceway of circular cross section designed for the routing and physical protection of electrical conductors and cables when joined together with listed fittings.

    (a) LFNC
    (b) EMT
    (c) NUCC
    (d) RTRC

Article 392. Cable Trays

15. A cable tray is a unit or assembly of units or sections and associated fittings forming a _____ system used to securely fasten or support cables and raceways.

    (a) structural
    (b) flexible
    (c) movable
    (d) secure

16. Metal cable trays containing only nonpower conductors (such as communications, data, and signaling conductors and cables) shall be electrically continuous through approved connections or the use of a(n) _____.

    (a) grounding electrode conductor
    (b) bonding jumper
    (c) equipment grounding conductor
    (d) grounded conductor

17. Steel or aluminum cable tray systems shall be permitted to be used as an equipment grounding conductor, provided the cable tray sections and fittings are identified as _____, among other requirements.

    (a) an equipment grounding conductor
    (b) special
    (c) industrial
    (d) all of these

Notes

CHAPTER 4
EQUIPMENT FOR GENERAL USE

Introduction to Chapter 4—Equipment for General Use

With the first three chapters behind you, the final chapter in the *NEC* necessary for building a solid foundation in general work is Chapter 4. This chapter helps you apply the first three to installations involving general equipment. These first four chapters follow a natural sequential progression. Each of the next four chapters—5, 6, 7, and 8—build upon the first four, but in no particular order. You need to understand all of the first four chapters to properly apply any of the next ones.

As in the preceding chapters, Chapter 4 is also arranged logically. Here are the groupings:

- Flexible cords and flexible cables, and fixture wires.
- Switches and receptacles.
- Switchboards, switchgear, and panelboards.
- Lamps and luminaires.
- Appliances and space heaters.
- Motors, refrigeration equipment, generators, and transformers.
- Batteries, capacitors, and other components.

This logical arrangement of the *NEC* is something to keep in mind when you're searching for a particular item. You know, for example, that transformers are general equipment. So you'll find the *Code* requirements for them in Chapter 4. You know they're wound devices, so you'll find transformer requirements located somewhere near motor requirements.

- **Article 404—Switches.** The requirements of Article 404 apply to switches of all types. These include snap (toggle) switches, dimmer switches, fan switches, knife switches, circuit breakers used as switches, and automatic switches such as time clocks, timers, and switches and circuit breakers used for disconnecting means.

- **Article 406—Receptacles, Cord Connectors, and Attachment Plugs (Caps).** This article covers the rating, type, and installation of receptacles, cord connectors, and attachment plugs (cord caps). It also covers flanged surface inlets.

- **Article 408—Switchboards, Switchgear, and Panelboards.** Article 408 covers specific requirements for switchboards, panelboards, switchgear, and distribution boards that supply lighting and power circuits.

Author's Comment:

- See Article 100 for the definitions of "Panelboard," "Switchboard," and "Switchgear."

Chapter 4 | Equipment for General Use

- **Article 410—Luminaires, Lampholders, and Lamps.** This article contains the requirements for luminaires, lampholders, and lamps. Because of the many types and applications of luminaires, manufacturer's instructions are very important and helpful for proper installation. Underwriters Laboratories produces a pamphlet called the *Luminaire Marking Guide*, which provides information for properly installing common types of incandescent, fluorescent, and high-intensity discharge (HID) luminaires.

- **Article 440—Air-Conditioning and Refrigeration Equipment.** Article 440 applies to electrically driven air-conditioning and refrigeration equipment with a motorized hermetic refrigerant compressor. The requirements in this article are in addition to, or amend, the requirements in Article 430 and others.

- **Article 450—Transformers.** This article covers the installation of transformers.

ARTICLE 404 — SWITCHES

Introduction to Article 404—Switches

The requirements of Article 404 apply to switches of all types, including snap (toggle) switches, dimmer switches, fan switches, knife switches, circuit breakers used as switches, and automatic switches, such as time clocks and timers.

404.1 Scope

The requirements of Article 404 apply to all types of switches, switching devices, and circuit breakers used as switches. ▶Figure 404–1

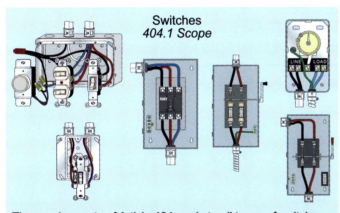

▶Figure 404–1

404.9 Switch Faceplates

 Scan this QR code for a video of Mike explaining this topic; it's a sample from the DVDs that accompany this textbook.

(A) Mounting. Faceplates for switches must be installed so they completely cover the outlet box opening and, where flush mounted, the faceplate must seat against the wall surface.

(B) Grounding. The metal mounting yokes for switches, dimmers, and similar control switches must be connected to an equipment grounding conductor. Metal faceplates must be grounded. Snap switches are considered to be part of an effective ground-fault current path if either of the following conditions is met:

(1) Metal Boxes. The switch is mounted with metal screws to a metal box or a metal cover that's connected to an equipment grounding conductor in accordance with 250.148. ▶Figure 404–2

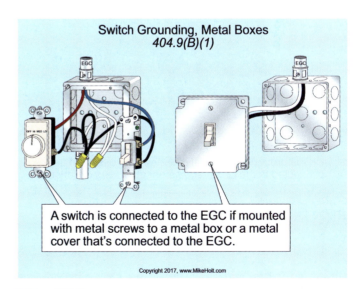

▶Figure 404–2

Mike Holt Enterprises • www.MikeHolt.com • 888.NEC.CODE (632.2633) 197

404.12 | Switches

Author's Comment:

- Direct metal-to-metal contact between the device yoke of a switch and the box isn't required. ▶Figure 404–3

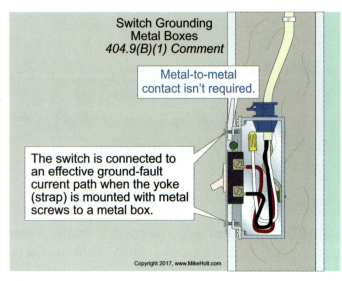

▶Figure 404–3

(2) Nonmetallic Boxes. The grounding terminal of the switch yoke must be connected to the circuit equipment grounding conductor. ▶Figure 404–4

▶Figure 404–4

Ex 1: The metal mounting yoke of a replacement switch isn't required to be connected to an equipment grounding conductor if the wiring at the existing switch doesn't contain an equipment grounding conductor and the switch faceplate is nonmetallic with nonmetallic screws, or the replacement switch is GFCI protected.

Ex 2: Listed assemblies aren't required to be connected to an equipment grounding conductor if all of the following conditions are met:

(1) The device is provided with a nonmetallic faceplate that can't be installed on any other type of device,

(2) The device doesn't have mounting means to accept other configurations of faceplates,

(3) The device is equipped with a nonmetallic yoke, and

(4) Parts of the device that are accessible after installation of the faceplate are manufactured of nonmetallic material.

Ex 3: A snap switch with an integral nonmetallic enclosure complying with 300.15(E).

404.12 Grounding of Enclosures

Metal enclosures for switches and circuit breakers used as switches must be connected to an equipment grounding conductor of a type recognized in 250.118 [250.4(A)(3)]. Nonmetallic boxes for switches must be installed using a wiring method that includes an equipment grounding conductor.

ARTICLE 406 — RECEPTACLES, CORD CONNECTORS, AND ATTACHMENT PLUGS (CAPS)

Introduction to Article 406—Receptacles, Cord Connectors, and Attachment Plugs (Caps)

This article covers the rating, type, and installation of receptacles, flexible cord connectors, and attachment plugs (cord caps). It also addresses their grounding requirements. Some key points to remember include:

- Following the grounding requirements of the specific type of device you're using.
- Providing GFCI protection where specified by 406.4(D)(3).
- Mounting receptacles according to the requirements of 406.5.

406.1 Scope

Article 406 covers the rating, type, and installation of receptacles, flexible cord connectors, and attachment plugs (cord caps). ▶Figure 406–1

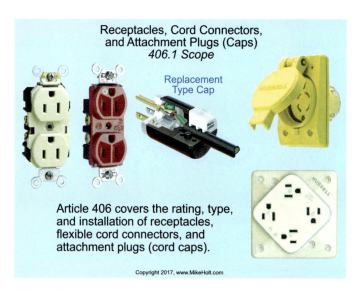

▶Figure 406–1

406.3 Receptacle Rating and Type

(D) Isolated Ground Receptacles. Receptacles of the isolated grounding conductor type must be identified by an orange triangle marking on the face of the receptacle. ▶Figure 406–2

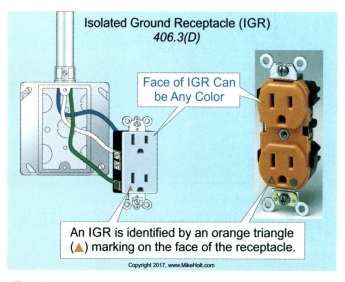

▶Figure 406–2

406.4 | Receptacles, Cord Connectors, and Attachment Plugs (Caps)

(1) Isolated ground receptacles must have the grounding contact connected to an insulated equipment grounding conductor installed with the circuit conductors, in accordance with 250.146(D). ▶Figure 406–3

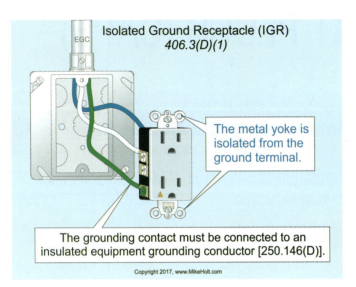

▶Figure 406–3

2017 CC 406.4 General Installation Requirements

(A) Grounding Type. Receptacles installed on 15A and 20A branch circuits must be of the grounding type, unless used for replacements as permitted in (D)(2). ▶Figure 406–4

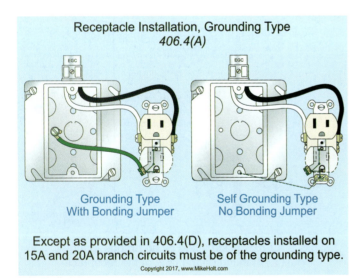

▶Figure 406–4

Receptacles must be installed on circuits for which they're rated, except as permitted in Table 210.21(B)(2) and Table 210.21(B)(3). ▶Figure 406–5

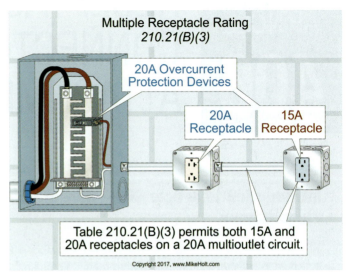

▶Figure 406–5

Table 210.21(B)(3) Receptacle Ratings	
Circuit Rating	Receptacle Rating
15A	15A
20A	15A or 20A
30A	30A
40A	40A or 50A
50A	50A

(C) Methods of Equipment Grounding. The grounding contacts for receptacles must be connected to an equipment grounding conductor supplied with the branch-circuit wiring. ▶Figure 406–6

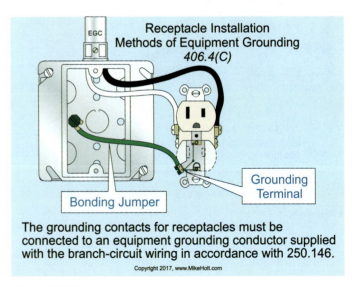

The grounding contacts for receptacles must be connected to an equipment grounding conductor supplied with the branch-circuit wiring in accordance with 250.146.

▶Figure 406–6

Receptacles, Cord Connectors, and Attachment Plugs (Caps) | 406.4

Author's Comment:

- See 250.146 for the specific requirements on connecting the grounding terminals of receptacles to the circuit equipment grounding conductor.

(D) Receptacle Replacement. Arc-fault circuit-interrupter type and ground-fault circuit interrupter type receptacles must be installed at a readily accessible location.

(1) Grounding-Type Receptacles. If an equipment grounding conductor exists, grounding-type receptacles must replace nongrounding-type receptacles and the receptacle's grounding terminal must be connected to the circuit equipment grounding conductor in accordance with 250.130(C) or 406.4(C).

(2) Nongrounding-Type Receptacles. If an equipment grounding conductor doesn't exist in the outlet box, the existing nongrounding-type receptacles can be replaced with:

(a) A nongrounding-type receptacle.

(b) A GFCI-type receptacle with the receptacle or <u>cover plate</u> marked "No Equipment Ground." ▶Figure 406–7

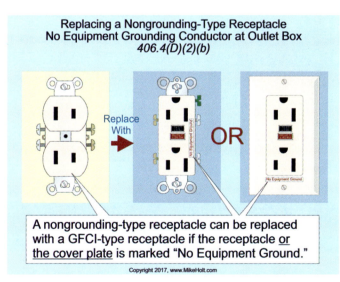

▶Figure 406–7

(c) A GFCI-protected grounding-type receptacle with the <u>receptacle or cover plate marked</u> "GFCI Protected" and "No Equipment Ground" <u>and be visible after installation.</u> ▶Figure 406–8

Note 1: Where equipment instructions require an equipment grounding conductor, a nongrounding type receptacle isn't permitted.

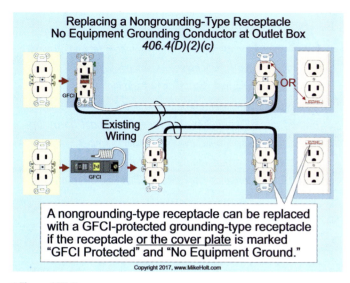

▶Figure 406–8

Note 2: Where an equipment grounding conductor is required by 250.114, a nongrounding type receptacle isn't permitted.

Author's Comment:

- GFCI protection functions properly on a 2-wire circuit without an equipment grounding conductor because the circuit equipment grounding conductor serves no role in the operation of the GFCI-protection device. See the definition of "Ground-Fault Circuit Interrupter" for more information. ▶Figure 406–9

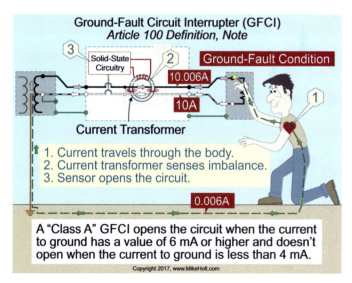

▶Figure 406–9

406.6 | Receptacles, Cord Connectors, and Attachment Plugs (Caps)

⚠️ **CAUTION:** The permission to replace nongrounding-type receptacles with GFCI-protected grounding-type receptacles doesn't apply to new receptacle outlets that extend from an existing outlet box that's not connected to an equipment grounding conductor. Once you add a receptacle outlet (branch-circuit extension), the receptacle must be of the grounding type and it must have its grounding terminal connected to an equipment grounding conductor of a type recognized in 250.118, in accordance with 250.130(C). ▶Figure 406–10

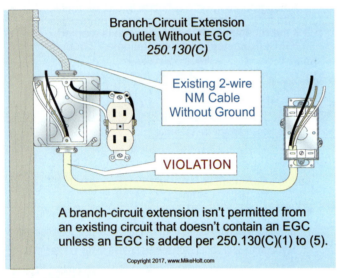

▶Figure 406–10

406.6 Receptacle Faceplates

Faceplates for receptacles must completely cover the outlet openings.
▶Figure 406–11

(B) Grounding. Metal faceplates for receptacles must be connected to the circuit equipment grounding conductor. ▶Figure 406–12

Author's Comment:

- The *NEC* doesn't specify how this is accomplished, but 517.13(B) Ex 1 for health care facilities permits the metal mounting screw(s) securing the faceplate to a metal outlet box or wiring device to be suitable for this purpose.

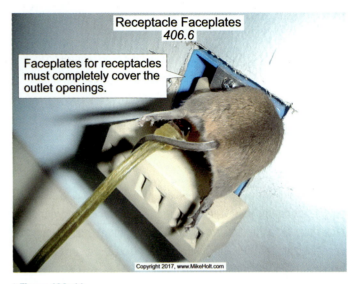

▶Figure 406–11

▶Figure 406–12

406.11 Connecting Receptacle Grounding Terminal to Equipment Grounding Conductor

The grounding terminal of receptacles must be connected to an equipment grounding conductor in accordance with 250.146.

ARTICLE 408 — SWITCHBOARDS, SWITCHGEAR, AND PANELBOARDS

Introduction to Article 408—Switchboards, Switchgear, and Panelboards

Article 408 covers the specific requirements for switchboards, switchgear, and panelboards that control power and lighting circuits. There's a tendency among some people in the industry to use the terms switchboard and switchgear interchangeably. Switchgear is manufactured and tested to more exacting standards and is configured differently than switchboards. For example, in switchgear there are physical barriers between breakers, and between the breakers and the bus. Switchgear is more durable and fault resistant, and is commonly selected for larger applications where low-voltage power circuit breakers and selective coordination are applied, such as computer data centers, manufacturing, and process facilities [Source NCCER].

As you study this article, remember some of these key points:

- One objective of Article 408 is that the installation prevents contact between current-carrying conductors and people or equipment.
- The circuit directory of a panelboard must clearly identify the purpose or use of each circuit that originates in the panelboard.
- You must understand the detailed grounding and overcurrent protection requirements for panelboards.

408.1 Scope

Article 408 covers the specific requirements for switchboards, switchgear, and panelboards that control power and lighting circuits. ▶Figure 408–1

408.40 Equipment Grounding Conductor

Metal panelboard cabinets and frames must be connected to an equipment grounding conductor of a type recognized in 250.118 [215.6 and 250.4(A)(3)]. Where a panelboard cabinet contains equipment grounding conductors, a terminal bar for the equipment grounding conductors must be bonded to the metal cabinet or be connected to the feeder equipment grounding conductor. ▶Figure 408–2

Ex: Insulated equipment grounding conductors for receptacles having insulated grounding terminals (isolated ground receptacles) [250.146(D)] are permitted to pass through the panelboard without terminating onto the equipment grounding terminal of the panelboard cabinet.

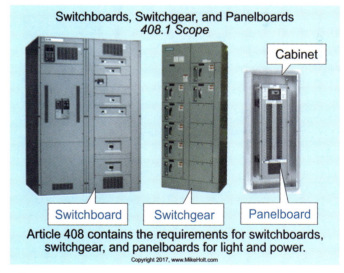

▶Figure 408–1

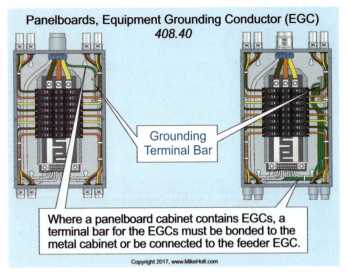

▶Figure 408–2

Author's Comment:

- See the definition of "Separately Derived System" in Article 100.

CAUTION: Most panelboards are rated for use as service equipment, which means they're supplied with a main bonding jumper [250.28]. This screw or strap must not be installed except when the panelboard is used for service equipment [250.24(A)(5)] or a separately derived system [250.30(A)(1)]. In addition, a panelboard marked "suitable only for use as service equipment" means the neutral bar or terminal of the panelboard has been bonded to the case at the factory, and this panelboard is restricted to being used only for service equipment or on separately derived systems in accordance with 250.142(A).

Equipment grounding conductors aren't permitted to terminate on the neutral terminal bar, and neutral conductors aren't permitted to terminate on the equipment grounding terminal bar, except as permitted by 250.142 for services and separately derived systems. ▶Figure 408–3

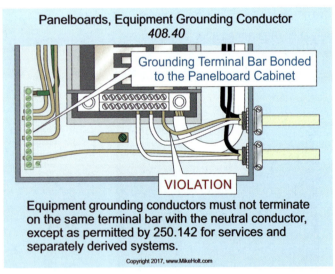

▶Figure 408–3

ARTICLE 410 — LUMINAIRES, LAMPHOLDERS, AND LAMPS

Introduction to Article 410—Luminaires, Lampholders, and Lamps

This article covers luminaires, lampholders, lamps, decorative lighting products, and lighting accessories for temporary seasonal and holiday use, including portable flexible lighting products, and the wiring and equipment of such products and lighting installations. Even though Article 410 is highly detailed, it's broken down into 16 parts. The first five are sequential, and apply to all luminaires, lampholders, and lamps:

- Part I. General
- Part II. Locations
- Part III. Outlet Boxes and Covers
- Part IV. Supports
- Part V. Equipment Grounding Conductors

The first five parts contain mostly mechanical information, and aren't hard to follow or absorb. Part VI, Wiring, ends the sequence. The seventh, ninth, and tenth parts provide requirements for manufacturers to follow—use only equipment that conforms to these requirements. Part VIII provides requirements for installing lampholders. The rest of Article 410 addresses specific types of lighting.

Author's Comment:

- Article 411 addresses "Low-Voltage Lighting" which are lighting systems and their associated components that operate at no more than 30V alternating current, or 60V direct current.

410.1 Scope

This article covers luminaires, lampholders, lamps, decorative lighting products, lighting accessories for temporary seasonal and holiday use, portable flexible lighting products, and the wiring and equipment of such products and lighting installations. ▶Figure 410–1

Author's Comment:

- Because of the many types and applications of luminaires, manufacturers' instructions are very important and helpful for proper installation. UL produces a pamphlet called the *Luminaire Marking Guide*, which provides information for properly installing common types of incandescent, fluorescent, and high-intensity discharge (HID) luminaires.

410.30 | Luminaires, Lampholders, and Lamps

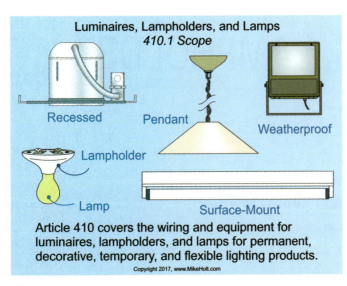

▶Figure 410–1

410.30 Supports

(B) Poles. Poles are permitted to be used to support luminaires and as a raceway to enclose supply conductors where the following conditions are met:

Author's Comment:

- With security being a high priority, many owners want to install security cameras on existing parking lot poles. However, 820.133(A)(1)(b) prohibits the mixing of power and communications conductors in the same raceway. ▶Figure 410–2

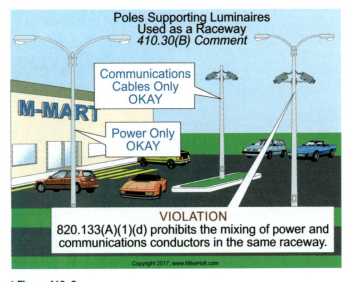

▶Figure 410–2

(1) The pole must have an accessible 2 in. × 4 in. handhole with a cover suitable for use in wet locations that provides access to the supply conductors within the pole. ▶Figure 410–3

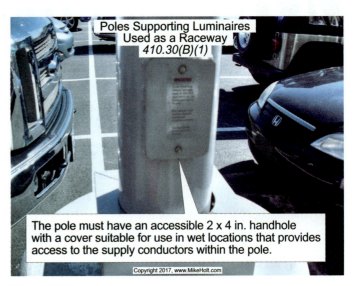

▶Figure 410–3

Ex 1: The handhole isn't required for a pole that's 8 ft or less in height, if the supply conductors for the luminaire are accessible by removing the luminaire. ▶Figure 410–4

▶Figure 410–4

Ex 2: The handhole can be omitted on poles that are 20 ft or less in height, if the pole is provided with a hinged base.

(2) When the supply raceway or cable doesn't enter the pole, a threaded fitting or nipple must be welded, brazed, or attached to the pole opposite the handhole opening for the supply conductors.

(3) A metal pole must have an equipment grounding terminal accessible from the handhole.

Ex: A grounding terminal isn't required in a pole that's 8 ft or less in height above grade if the splices are accessible by removing the luminaire.

(5) Metal poles used for the support of luminaires must be connected to an equipment grounding conductor of a type recognized in 250.118 [250.4(A)(5)]. ▶Figure 410–5

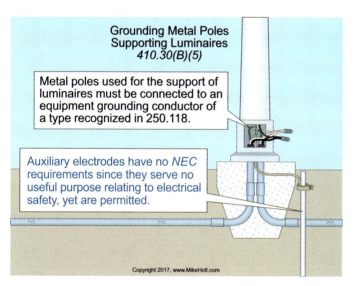

▶Figure 410–5

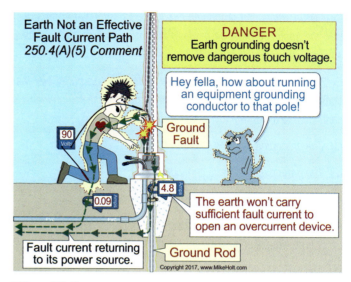

▶Figure 410–6

DANGER: *Because the contact resistance of an electrode to the earth is so high, very little fault current returns to the power supply if the earth is the only fault current return path. Result—the circuit overcurrent protection device won't open and clear the ground fault, and the metal pole will become and remain energized by the circuit voltage.* ▶Figure 410–6

(6) Conductors in vertical metal poles must be supported when the vertical rise exceeds 100 ft [Table 300.19(A)].

Author's Comment:

■ When provided by the manufacturer of roadway lighting poles, so-called J-hooks must be used to support conductors, as they're part of the listing instructions [110.3(B)].

410.44 Methods of Grounding

The metal parts of luminaires must be connected to an equipment grounding conductor of a type recognized in 250.118. If the equipment grounding conductor is of the wire type, the conductor must be sized in accordance with 250.122, based on the rating of the overcurrent protection device. ▶Figure 410–7

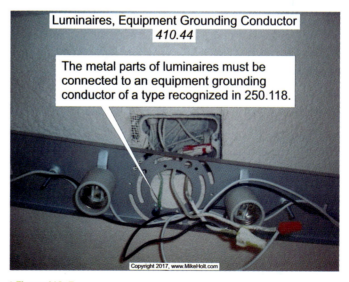

▶Figure 410–7

Ex 1: If an equipment grounding conductor isn't present in the outlet box, the luminaire must be made of insulating material and not have any exposed conductive parts.

Ex 2: Replacement luminaires can be installed in an outlet box that doesn't contain an equipment grounding conductor if the luminaire is connected to any of the following [250.130(C)]:

(1) The grounding electrode system [250.50],

(2) The grounding electrode conductor,

(3) The panelboard equipment grounding terminal,

(4) An equipment grounding conductor that's part of a different circuit, if both circuits originate from the same panel, or

(5) The service neutral conductor.

Ex 3: GFCI-protected replacement luminaires aren't required to be connected to an equipment grounding conductor if no equipment grounding conductor exists at the outlet box.

Author's Comment:

- This is similar to the rule for receptacle replacements in locations where an equipment grounding conductor isn't present in the outlet box [406.4(D)(3)].

ARTICLE 440 — AIR-CONDITIONING AND REFRIGERATION EQUIPMENT

Introduction to Article 440—Air-Conditioning and Refrigeration Equipment

This article applies to electrically driven air-conditioning and refrigeration equipment. The rules in this article add to, or amend, the rules in Article 430 and other articles.

Each equipment manufacturer has the motor for a given air-conditioning unit built to its own specifications. Cooling and other characteristics are different from those of nonhermetic motors. For each motor, the manufacturer has worked out all of the details and supplied the correct protection, conductor sizing, and other information on the nameplate. So when wiring an air conditioner, trust the information on the nameplate and don't try to over-complicate the situation. The math for sizing the overcurrent protection and conductor minimum ampacity has already been done for you.

Part I. General

440.1 Scope

Article 440 applies to electrically driven air-conditioning and refrigeration equipment. ▶Figure 440–1

440.2 Definitions

Rated-Load Current. The current resulting when the motor-compressor operates at its rated load and rated voltage.

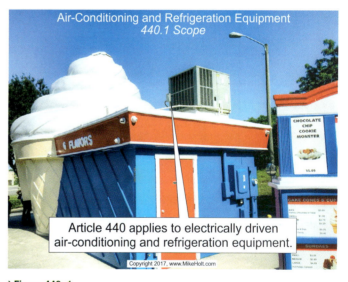

▶Figure 440–1

440.9 | Air-Conditioning and Refrigeration Equipment

440.9 Grounding and Bonding

 Scan this QR code for a video of Mike explaining this topic; it's a sample from the DVDs that accompany this textbook.

Where equipment is installed using a metal raceway is run exposed on a roof for air-conditioning and refrigeration equipment, an equipment grounding conductor of the wire type must be installed within the outdoor portions of metal raceways that use non-threaded fittings. ▶Figure 440–2

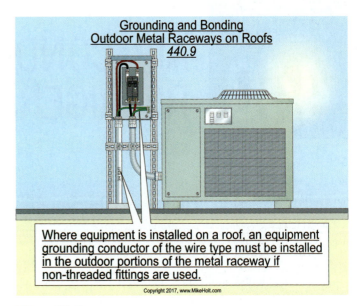

▶Figure 440–2

ARTICLE 450 TRANSFORMERS

Introduction to Article 450—Transformers

Article 450 opens by saying, "This article covers the installation of all transformers." Then it lists eight exceptions. So what does it really cover? Essentially, Article 450 covers power transformers and most kinds of lighting transformers.

A major concern with transformers is preventing overheating. The *Code* doesn't completely address this issue. Article 90 explains that the *NEC* isn't a design manual, and it assumes that anyone using the *Code* has a certain level of expertise. Proper transformer selection is an important part of preventing it from overheating.

The *NEC* assumes you've already selected a transformer suitable to the load characteristics. For the *Code* to tell you how to do that would push it into the realm of a design manual. Article 450 then takes you to the next logical step—providing overcurrent protection and the proper connections. But this article doesn't stop there; 450.9 provides ventilation requirements, and 450.13 contains accessibility requirements.

Part I contains the general requirements such as guarding, marking, and accessibility, Part II contains the requirements for different types of transformers, and Part III covers transformer vaults.

Part I. General

450.1 Scope

Article 450 covers the installation requirements of transformers.
▶Figure 450–1

450.10 Grounding and Bonding

(A) Dry-Type Transformer Enclosures. Where separate equipment grounding conductors and supply-side bonding jumpers are installed, a terminal bar for these conductors must be installed inside the enclosure. The terminal bar must not cover any ventilation openings. ▶Figure 450–2

Ex: Where a dry-type transformer is equipped with wire-type connections (leads), the terminal bar isn't required.

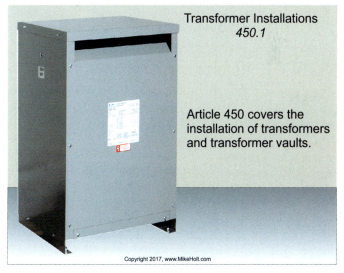

Transformer Installations
450.1

Article 450 covers the installation of transformers and transformer vaults.

▶Figure 450–1

450.10 | Transformers

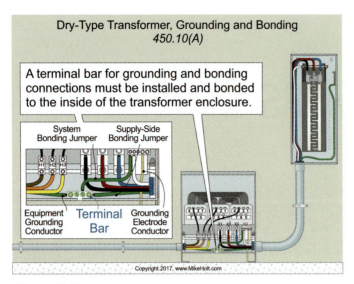

▶Figure 450–2

CHAPTER 4 PRACTICE QUESTIONS

Please use the 2017 *Code* book to answer the following questions.

Article 404. Switches

1. Snap switches, including dimmer and similar control switches, shall be connected to an equipment grounding conductor and shall provide a means to connect metal faceplates to the equipment grounding conductor, whether or not a metal faceplate is installed.

    (a) True
    (b) False

2. Metal faceplates for snap switches, including dimmer and similar control switches, shall be _____.

    (a) bonded to the grounded electrode
    (b) grounded
    (c) a and b
    (d) none of these

3. Snap switches are considered to be part of the effective ground-fault current path when _____.

    (a) the switch is connected to the intersystem bonding termination
    (b) the switch is mounted with metal screws to a metal box or a metal cover that is connected to an equipment grounding conductor
    (c) an equipment grounding conductor or equipment bonding jumper is connected to the equipment grounding termination of the snap switch
    (d) b or c

4. The metal mounting yoke of a replacement switch is not required to be connected to an equipment grounding conductor if the wiring at the existing switch does not contain an equipment grounding conductor, and the _____.

    (a) switch faceplate is nonmetallic with nonmetallic screws
    (b) replacement switch is GFCI protected
    (c) a or b
    (d) circuit is AFCI protected

5. Snap switches in listed assemblies are not required to be connected to an equipment grounding conductor if _____.

    (a) the device is provided with a nonmetallic faceplate that cannot be installed on any other type of device and the device does not have mounting means to accept other configurations of faceplates
    (b) the device is equipped with a nonmetallic yoke
    (c) all parts of the device that are accessible after installation of the faceplate are manufactured of nonmetallic material
    (d) all of these

6. A snap switch with an integral nonmetallic enclosure complying with 300.15(E) is required to be connected to an equipment grounding conductor.

    (a) True
    (b) False

Chapter 4 | Practice Questions

7. Metal enclosures for switches or circuit breakers shall be connected to the circuit _____.

    (a) grounded conductor
    (b) grounding conductor
    (c) equipment grounding conductor
    (d) any of these

Article 406. Receptacles, Cord Connectors, and Attachment Plugs (Caps)

8. Receptacles incorporating an isolated grounding conductor connection intended for the reduction of electrical noise shall be identified by _____ on the face of the receptacle.

    (a) an orange triangle
    (b) a green triangle
    (c) the color orange
    (d) the engraved word "ISOLATED"

9. Where a grounding means exists in the receptacle enclosure a(n) _____-type receptacle shall be used.

    (a) isolated ground
    (b) grounding
    (c) GFCI
    (d) dedicated

10. When non-grounding-type receptacles are replaced by GFCI-type receptacles where attachment to an equipment grounding conductor does not exist in the receptacle enclosure, _____ shall be marked "No Equipment Ground."

    (a) these receptacles
    (b) their cover plates
    (c) a or b
    (d) none of these

11. Where attachment to an equipment grounding conductor does not exist in the receptacle enclosure, a non-grounding-type receptacle(s) shall be permitted to be replaced with a GFCI-type receptacle(s) where supplied through a ground-fault circuit interrupter and _____ shall be marked "GFCI Protected" and "No Equipment Ground," visible after installation.

    (a) the receptacle(s)
    (b) their cover plates
    (c) a or b
    (d) none of these

12. Where attachment to an equipment grounding conductor does not exist in the receptacle enclosure, a non-grounding-type receptacle shall be permitted to be replaced with a GFCI-type receptacle; however, some equipment or appliance manufacturers require that the _____ to the equipment or appliance includes an equipment grounding conductor.

    (a) feeder
    (b) branch circuit
    (c) small-appliance circuit
    (d) none of these

13. Where attachment to an equipment grounding conductor does not exist in the receptacle enclosure, a non-grounding-type receptacle(s) shall be permitted to be replaced with a GFCI-type receptacle(s) where supplied through a ground-fault circuit interrupter; however, some cord-and-plug-connected equipment or appliances require an equipment grounding conductor and are listed in 250.114.

    (a) True
    (b) False

14. Metal faceplates for receptacles shall be grounded.

    (a) True
    (b) False

Article 408. Switchboards, Switchgear, and Panelboards

15. When separate equipment grounding conductors are provided in panelboards, a _____ shall be secured inside the cabinet.

    (a) grounded conductor
    (b) terminal lug
    (c) terminal bar
    (d) none of these

Article 410. Luminaires, Lampholders, and Lamps

16. Article 410 covers luminaires, portable luminaires, lampholders, pendants, incandescent filament lamps, arc lamps, electric-discharge lamps, and _____, and the wiring and equipment forming part of such products and lighting installations.

    (a) decorative lighting products
    (b) lighting accessories for temporary seasonal and holiday use
    (c) portable flexible lighting products
    (d) all of these

17. Luminaires and equipment shall be mechanically connected to an equipment grounding conductor as specified in 250.118 and shall be sized in accordance with _____.

    (a) Table 250.66
    (b) Table 250.122
    (c) Table 310.16
    (d) a and c

18. Replacement luminaires are not required to be connected to an equipment grounding conductor if no equipment grounding conductor exists at the outlet box and the luminaire is _____.

    (a) more than 20 years old
    (b) mounted to the box using nonmetallic fittings and screws
    (c) mounted more than 6 ft above the floor
    (d) GFCI protected

Article 440. Air-Conditioning and Refrigeration Equipment

19. Where multimotor and combination-load equipment for air-conditioning and refrigeration is installed outdoors on a roof, a(n) _____ conductor of the wire type shall be installed in outdoor portions of metallic raceway systems that use non-threaded fittings.

    (a) equipment grounding
    (b) grounding
    (c) equipment bonding
    (d) bonding

Notes

CHAPTER 5
SPECIAL OCCUPANCIES

Introduction to Chapter 5—Special Occupancies

Chapter 5, which covers special occupancies, is the first of four *NEC* chapters that deals with special topics.

Chapters 6 and 7 cover special equipment, and special conditions, respectively. Remember, the first four chapters of the *Code* are sequential and form a foundation for each of the subsequent three chapters. Chapter 8 covers communications systems (twisted wire, antennas, and coaxial cable) and isn't subject to the requirements of Chapters 1 through 7 except where the requirements are specifically referenced in Chapter 8 [90.3].

What exactly is a "Special Occupancy"? It's a location where a facility, or its use, creates specific conditions that require additional measures to ensure the "practical safeguarding of people and property" purpose of the *NEC*, as put forth in Article 90.

The *Code* groups these special occupancies logically, as you might expect. Here are the general groupings:

- General environments that pose explosion or fire hazards. Articles 500 through 510.
- Specific types of environments that pose explosion or fire hazards. Articles 511 through 516—Examples include motor fuel dispensing facilities, aircraft hangars, and bulk storage plants.
- Facilities that pose evacuation difficulties. Articles 517 through 525—Examples include hospitals, theaters, and carnivals.
- Motion picture related facilities. Articles 530 and 540.
- Specific types of buildings. Articles 545 through 553—Examples include park trailers and floating buildings.
- Marinas, Boatyards, and Commercial and Noncommercial Docking Facilities. Article 555.
- Temporary Installations. Article 590.

Many people struggle to understand the requirements for special occupancies, mostly because of the narrowness of application. However, if you study the illustrations and explanations here, you'll clearly understand them.

- **Article 501—Class I Hazardous (Classified) Locations.** A Class I hazardous (classified) location is an area where flammable or combustible liquid-produced vapors or flammable gases may present the hazard of a fire or explosion.

- **Article 502—Class II Hazardous (Classified) Locations.** A Class II hazardous (classified) location is an area where the possibility of fire or explosion may exist due to the presence of combustible dust.

Chapter 5 | Special Occupancies

- **Article 503—Class III Hazardous (Classified) Locations.** Class III locations are hazardous because fire or explosion risks may exist due to easily ignitible fibers/flyings. These include materials such as cotton and rayon, which are found in textile mills and clothing manufacturing plants. They can also include establishments and industries such as sawmills and woodworking plants.

- **Article 517—Health Care Facilities.** This article applies to electrical wiring in human health care facilities such as hospitals, nursing homes, limited-care facilities, clinics, medical and dental offices, and ambulatory care, whether permanent or movable. It doesn't apply to animal veterinary facilities.

- **Article 525—Carnivals, Circuses, Fairs, and Similar Events.** This article covers the installation of portable wiring and equipment for temporary carnivals, circuses, exhibitions, fairs, traveling attractions, and similar functions, including wiring in or on structures.

- **Article 547—Agricultural Buildings.** Article 547 covers agricultural buildings or those parts of buildings or adjacent areas where excessive dust or dust with water may accumulate, or where a corrosive atmosphere exists.

- **Article 555—Marinas, Boatyards, and Commercial and Noncommercial Docking Facilities.** This article covers the installation of wiring and equipment in the areas that comprise fixed or floating piers, wharves, docks, and other areas in marinas, boatyards, boat basins, boathouses, and similar locations used, or intended to be used, for repair, berthing, launching, storing, or fueling of small craft, and the mooring of floating buildings.

ARTICLE 501
CLASS I HAZARDOUS (CLASSIFIED) LOCATIONS

Introduction to Article 501—Class I Hazardous (Classified) Locations

If flammable or combustible gases, vapors, or liquids are, or may be, present in quantities sufficient to produce an explosive or ignitible mixture, you have a Class I location. Examples of such locations include some fuel storage areas, certain solvent storage areas, grain processing facilities (where hexane is used), plastic extrusion areas where oil removal is part of the process, refineries, and paint storage areas.

501.1 Scope

Article 501 covers requirements for electrical and electronic equipment and wiring in Class I, Division 1 and Division 2 locations where flammable gases, flammable liquid-produced vapors, or flammable liquid-produced vapors may be present in the air and in quantities sufficient to produce explosive or ignitible mixtures [500.5(B)]. ▶Figure 501–1

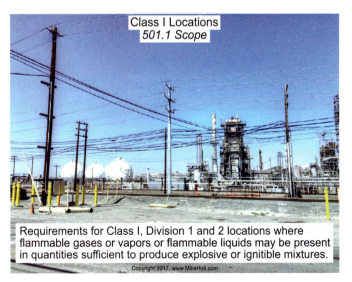

▶Figure 501–1

501.30 Grounding and Bonding

Because of the explosive conditions associated with electrical installations in hazardous (classified) locations [500.5], electrical continuity of metal parts of equipment and raceways must be ensured regardless of the voltage of the circuit.

(A) Bonding. Locknuts aren't suitable for bonding purposes in hazardous (classified) locations, therefore bonding jumpers or other approved means of bonding must be used. Such means of bonding apply to all intervening raceways, fittings, boxes, enclosures, and so forth between Class I locations and service equipment. ▶Figure 501–2

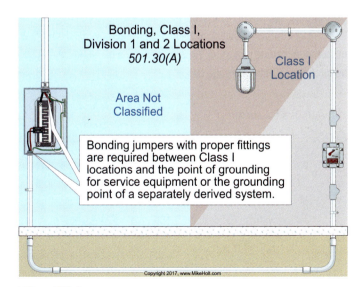

▶Figure 501–2

501.30 | Class I Hazardous (Classified) Locations

Author's Comment:

- Regardless of the circuit voltage, electrical continuity of metal parts of equipment and raceways in hazardous (classified) locations must be ensured by bonding-type locknuts, bushings, wedges, or bushings with bonding jumpers [250.92(B)(4)]; whether or not equipment grounding conductors of the wire type are installed in the raceway [250.100].

- A separate equipment grounding conductor isn't required if a metal raceway is used for equipment grounding. Threaded couplings and hubs made up wrenchtight provide a suitable low-impedance fault current path [250.100]. ▶Figure 501–3

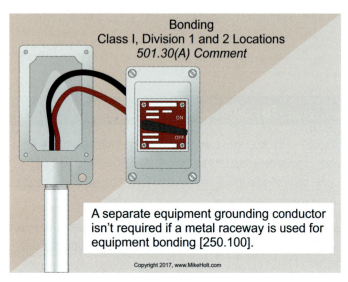

▶Figure 501–3

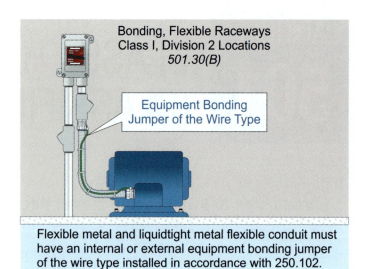

▶Figure 501–4

▶Figure 501–5

(B) Bonding—Flexible Raceway. Where flexible metal conduit or liquidtight flexible metal conduit is installed as permitted by 501.10(B)(2), an equipment bonding jumper of the wire type must be installed in accordance with 250.102. ▶Figure 501–4

Author's Comment:

- Bonding jumpers are sized in accordance with Table 250.122, based on the rating of the overcurrent protection device [250.102(D)]. Where installed outside a raceway, the length of bonding jumpers must not exceed 6 ft and they must be routed with the raceway [250.102(E)(2)]. ▶Figure 501–5

ARTICLE 502 — CLASS II HAZARDOUS (CLASSIFIED) LOCATIONS

Introduction to Article 502—Class II Hazardous (Classified) Locations

If an area has sufficient combustible dust present, it may be classified as a Class II location.

Examples of such locations include flour mills, grain silos, coal bins, wood pulp storage areas, and munitions plants.

Article 502 follows a logical arrangement similar to that of Article 501 and provides guidance in selecting equipment and wiring methods for Class II locations, including distinctions between Class II, Division 1 and Class II, Division 2 requirements.

502.1 Scope

Article 502 covers the requirements for electrical and electronic equipment and wiring in Class II, Division 1 and 2 locations where fire or explosion hazards may exist due to the presence of combustible dust, combustible metal dusts, coal, carbon black, charcoal, coke, flour, grain, wood, plastic, and chemicals in the air in quantities sufficient to produce explosive or ignitible mixtures [500.5(C) and 500.8]. ▶Figure 502–1

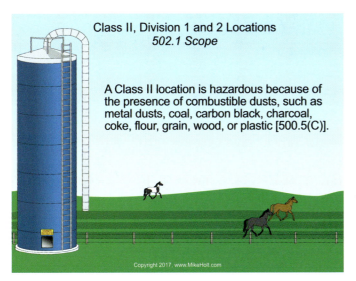

▶Figure 502–1

502.30 Grounding and Bonding

Because of the explosive conditions associated with electrical installations in hazardous (classified) locations [500.5], electrical continuity of metal parts of equipment and raceways must be ensured regardless of the voltage of the circuit.

(A) Bonding. Locknuts aren't suitable for bonding purposes in hazardous (classified) locations, therefore bonding jumpers or other approved means of bonding must be used. Such means of bonding apply to all intervening raceways, fittings, boxes, enclosures, and so forth between Class II locations and service equipment. ▶Figure 502–2

Author's Comment:

- A separate equipment grounding conductor isn't required if a metal raceway is used for equipment grounding. Threaded couplings and hubs made up wrenchtight provide a suitable low-impedance fault current path [250.100]. ▶Figure 502–3

(B) Bonding—Flexible Raceway. Where flexible metal conduit or liquidtight flexible metal conduit is installed as permitted by 501.10(A)(4), an equipment bonding jumper of the wire type must be installed in accordance with 250.102. ▶Figure 502–4

502.30 | Class II Hazardous (Classified) Locations

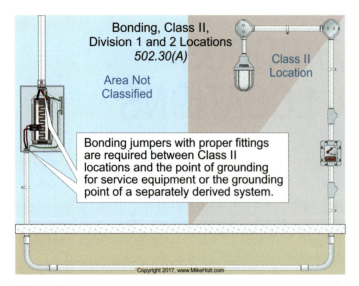

▶Figure 502–2

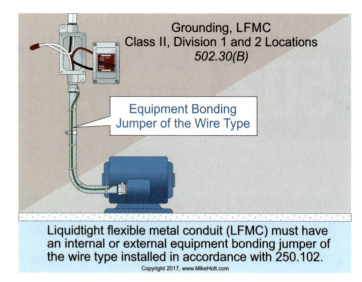

▶Figure 502–4

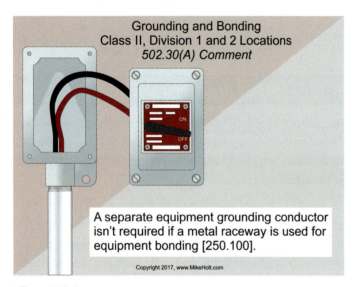

▶Figure 502–3

▶Figure 502–5

Author's Comment:

- Bonding jumpers must be sized in accordance with 250.122, based on the rating of the overcurrent protection device [250.102(D)], and where installed outside a raceway, the length of the bonding jumpers must not exceed 6 ft and they must be routed with the raceway [250.102(E)(2)]. ▶Figure 502–5

ARTICLE 503 — CLASS III HAZARDOUS (CLASSIFIED) LOCATIONS

Introduction to Article 503—Class III Hazardous (Classified) Locations

The Class III location scope is cumbersome, and many people have a hard time grasping what it means. If you have easily ignitible fibers/flyings present, you may have a Class III location. Examples of such locations include sawmills, textile mills, and fiber processing plants. In many cases, the distinction between Class II and Class III locations may simply be the size of the particles. The definition of "Combustible Dust" in Article 100 defines it based on the size of the particles, so the same material (such as sawdust) may be subject to Article 503 if the predominant material is "larger" than the definition.

503.1 Scope

Article 503 covers the requirements for electrical and electronic equipment and wiring for all voltages in Class III, Division 1 and 2 locations. These are locations where fire or explosion hazards may exist because easily ignitible fibers or materials producing combustible flyings are handled, manufactured, or used but aren't likely to be suspended in the air in quantities sufficient to produce ignitible mixtures [500.5(D)].

503.30 Grounding and Bonding

Because of the explosive conditions associated with electrical installations in hazardous (classified) locations [500.5], electrical continuity of metal parts of equipment and raceways must be ensured regardless of the voltage of the circuit.

(A) Bonding. Locknuts aren't suitable for bonding purposes in hazardous (classified) locations, therefore bonding jumpers or other approved means of bonding must be used. Such means of bonding apply to all intervening raceways, fittings, boxes, and enclosures between Class III locations and service equipment.

(B) Bonding—Flexible Raceway. Where flexible metal conduit or liquidtight flexible metal conduit is installed as permitted by 503.10(A)(3), an equipment bonding jumper of the wire type must be installed in accordance with 250.102. ▶Figure 503–1

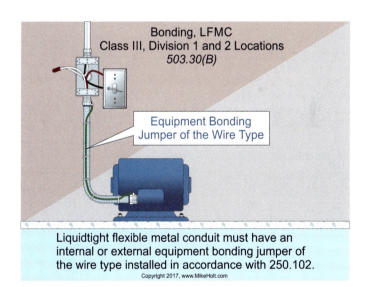

▶Figure 503–1

503.30 | Class III Hazardous (Classified) Locations

Author's Comment:

- Bonding jumpers must be sized in accordance with 250.122, based on the rating of the overcurrent protection device [250.102(D)], and where installed outside a raceway, the length of bonding jumpers must not exceed 6 ft and they must be routed with the raceway [250.102(E)(2)]. ▶Figure 503–2

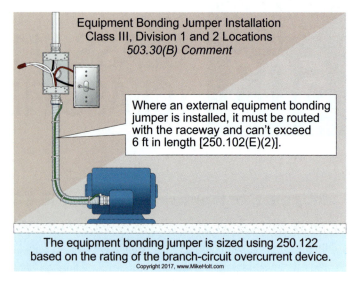

▶Figure 503–2

ARTICLE 517 HEALTH CARE FACILITIES

Introduction to Article 517—Health Care Facilities

Health care facilities differ from other types of buildings in many important ways. Article 517 is primarily concerned with those parts of health care facilities where patients are examined and treated. Whether those facilities are permanent or movable, they still fall under this article. However, Article 517 wiring and protection requirements don't apply to business offices or waiting rooms. They don't apply to animal veterinary facilities either.

This article contains many specialized definitions that only apply to health care facilities. While you don't need to be able to quote these definitions, you should have a clear understanding of what the terms mean. As you study Parts II and III, keep in mind the special requirements of hospitals and why these requirements exist. The requirements in Parts II and III are highly detailed and not intuitively obvious. These are three of the main objectives of Article 517, Parts II and III:

- Maximize the physical and electromagnetic protection of wiring by requiring metal raceways.
- Minimize electrical hazards by keeping the voltage between patients' bodies and medical equipment low. This involves many specific steps, beginning with 517.11.
- Minimize the negative effects of power interruptions by establishing specific requirements for essential electrical systems.

Part IV addresses gas anesthesia stations. The primary objective of Part IV is to prevent ignition. Part V addresses X-ray installations and really has two main objectives:

- Provide adequate ampacity and overcurrent protection for the branch circuits.
- Address the safety issues inherent in high-voltage equipment installations.

Part VI provides requirements for low-voltage communications systems (twisted wire, antennas, and coaxial cable), such as fire alarms and intercoms. The primary objective there is to prevent compromising those systems with inductive couplings or other sources of interference. Part VII provides requirements for isolated power systems where the main objective is to keep them actually isolated.

Be aware that the *NEC* is just one of the standards that apply to health care locations, and there may be additional requirements from other standards and special requirements for sophisticated equipment.

517.1 | Health Care Facilities

Part I. General

517.1 Scope

Article 517 applies to electrical wiring in health care facilities, such as hospitals, nursing homes, limited care and supervisory care facilities, clinics, medical and dental offices, and ambulatory care facilities that provide services to human beings. ▶Figure 517–1

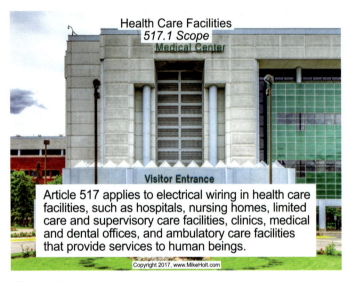

▶Figure 517–1

Author's Comment:

- This article doesn't apply to animal veterinary facilities.

517.2 Definitions

Health Care Facilities. Buildings, portions of buildings, or mobile enclosures in which medical, dental, psychiatric, nursing, obstetrical, or surgical care are provided for humans.

Note: Examples of health care facilities include, but aren't limited to, hospitals, nursing homes, limited care facilities, supervisory care facilities, clinics, medical and dental offices, and ambulatory care facilities.

Patient Care Space. Any space in a health care facility where patients are intended to be examined or treated. ▶Figure 517–2

Note 1: The governing body of the facility designates patient care space in accordance with the type of patient care anticipated.

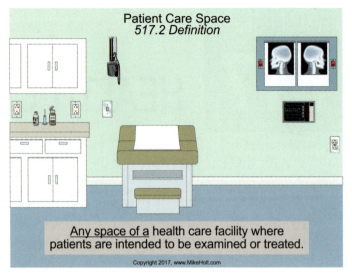

▶Figure 517–2

Note 2: Business offices, corridors, lounges, day rooms, dining rooms, or similar areas aren't classified as patient care space.

Basic Care (Category 3) Space. An area where failure of equipment or a system isn't likely to cause injury to the patients, staff, or visitors. ▶Figure 517–3

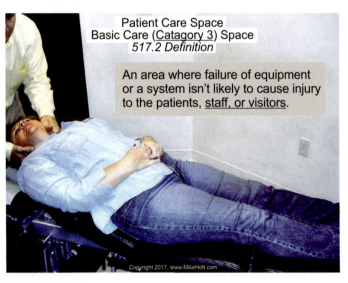

▶Figure 517–3

Note: Basic Care, Category 3 spaces, formerly known as basic care rooms (spaces) are typically where basic medical or dental care, treatment, or examinations are performed. Examples include, but aren't limited to, examination or treatment rooms in clinics, medical and dental offices, nursing homes, and limited care facilities.

Health Care Facilities | 517.13

General Care (Category 2) Space. An area where failure of equipment or a system is likely to cause minor injury to patients, staff, or visitors. ▶Figure 517–4

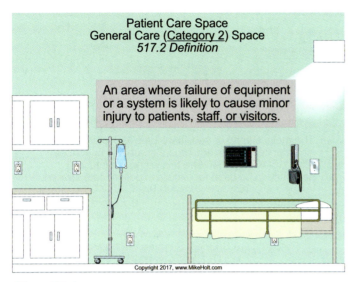

▶Figure 517–4

Note: General Care, Category 2 spaces, were formerly known as general care rooms (spaces). Examples include, but aren't limited to, patient bedrooms, in vitro fertilization rooms, procedural rooms, and similar rooms.

Critical Care (Category 1) Space. An area where failure of equipment or a system is likely to cause major injury or death to patients, staff, or visitors.

Note: Critical Care, Category 1 spaces, formerly known as critical care rooms (spaces), are typically where patients are intended to be subjected to invasive procedures and connected to line operated, patient care-related appliances. Examples include, but aren't limited to, special care patient rooms used for critical care, intensive care, and special care units such as angiography laboratories, cardiac catheterization laboratories, delivery rooms, operating rooms, post-anesthesia care units, trauma rooms, and other similar rooms.

Support (Category 4) Space. An area where failure of equipment or a system isn't likely to have a physical impact on patients, staff, or visitors.

Note: Support Category 4 spaces were formerly known as support rooms (spaces). Examples of these spaces include, but aren't limited to, anesthesia work rooms, sterile supply, laboratories, morgues, waiting rooms, utility rooms, and lounges.

Patient Care Vicinity. A space, within a location intended for the examination and treatment of patients, extending 6 ft beyond the normal location of the patient bed, chair, table, treadmill, or other device that supports the patient during examination and treatment and extending vertically to 7 ft 6 in. above the floor. ▶Figure 517–5

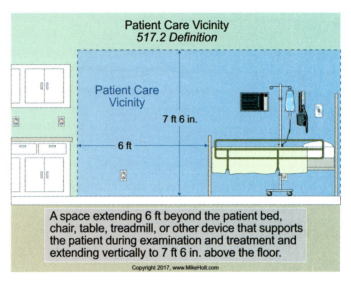

▶Figure 517–5

Part II. Wiring and Protection

517.12 Wiring Methods

Wiring methods must comply with the Chapter 1 through 4 provisions, except as modified in this article [90.3].

517.13 Grounding of Equipment in Patient Care Spaces

Wiring in patient care spaces must comply with (A) and (B):

> **Author's Comment:**
> - Patient care spaces include patient rooms as well as examining rooms, therapy areas, treatment rooms, and some patient corridors. They don't include business offices, corridors, lounges, day rooms, dining rooms, or similar areas not classified as patient care spaces [517.2].

(A) Wiring Methods. Branch circuit conductors serving patient care spaces must be contained in a metal raceway or cable having a metal sheath that qualifies as an equipment grounding conductor in accordance with 250.118. ▶Figure 517–6

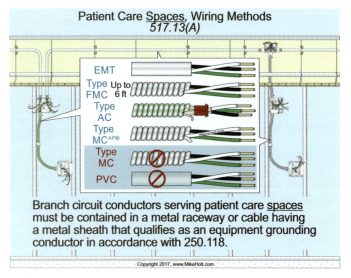

▶Figure 517–6

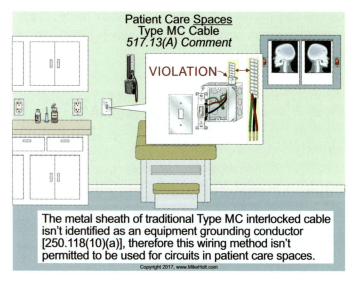

▶Figure 517–7

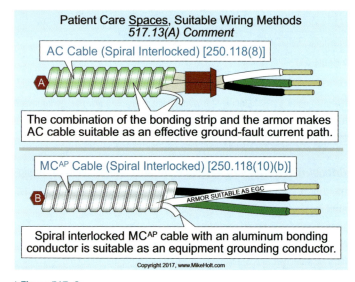

▶Figure 517–8

Author's Comment:

- The metal sheath of traditional Type MC interlocked cable isn't identified as an equipment grounding conductor [250.118(10)(a)], therefore this wiring method isn't permitted to be used for circuits in patient care spaces. ▶Figure 517–7

- The metal sheath of Type AC cable is identified as an equipment grounding conductor in 250.118(8) because it contains an internal bonding strip that's in direct contact with the metal sheath of the interlock cable. ▶Figure 517–8 Part A

- The metal sheath of Type MC^{AP} cable is identified as an equipment grounding conductor in 250.118(10)(a) because it contains an internal bonding strip that's in direct contact with the metal sheath of the interlock cable. See ▶Figure 517–8 Part B.

(B) Insulated Equipment Grounding Conductors and Insulated Bonding Jumpers.

(1) General. The following must be directly connected to an insulated copper equipment grounding conductor that has green insulation along its entire length and installed with the branch-circuit conductors in wiring methods as permitted in 517.13(A).

(1) The grounding contact of receptacles, other than isolated ground receptacles. ▶Figure 517–9

(2) Metal enclosures containing circuit conductors. ▶Figure 517–10

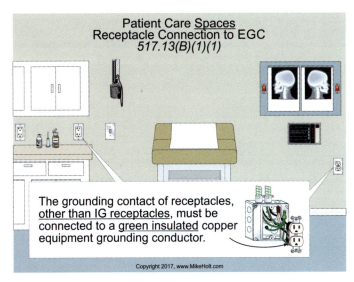

▶Figure 517–9

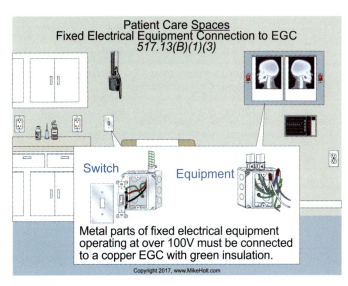

▶Figure 517–11

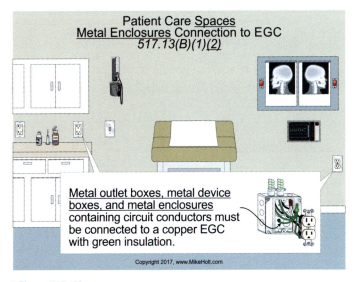

▶Figure 517–10

(3) Noncurrent-carrying conductive surfaces of fixed electrical equipment likely to become energized that are subject to personal contact, operating at over 100V. ▶Figure 517–11

Ex 1: *For other than isolated ground receptacles*, an insulated equipment bonding jumper that directly connects to the equipment grounding conductor can connect the metal box and receptacle(s) to the equipment grounding conductor. Isolated ground receptacles must comply with the requirements contained in 517.16.

Ex 2: Metal faceplates for switches and receptacles can be connected to the equipment grounding conductor by the metal mounting screws that secure the faceplate to a metal outlet box or metal mounting yoke of switches [404.9(B)] and receptacles [406.4(C)]. ▶Figure 517–12

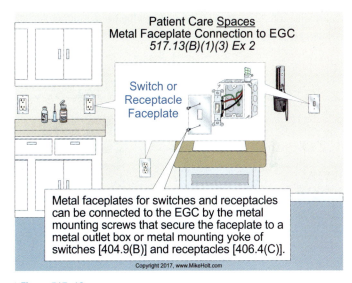

▶Figure 517–12

Ex 3: Luminaires located more than 7½ ft above the floor and switches located outside of the patient care vicinity are permitted to be connected to an equipment grounding return path complying with 517.13(A) or (B). ▶Figure 517–13

517.16 | Health Care Facilities

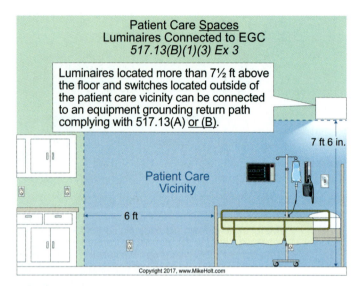

▶Figure 517–13

(2) Sizing. Where metal receptacle boxes are used, the connection between the receptacle grounding terminal and the metal box must be copper wire sized no smaller than 12 AWG. Where receptacles and fixed electrical equipment are provided with overcurrent protection rated over 20A, equipment and bonding jumpers must be sized in accordance with 250.122, based on the rating of the overcurrent protection device. ▶Figure 517–14

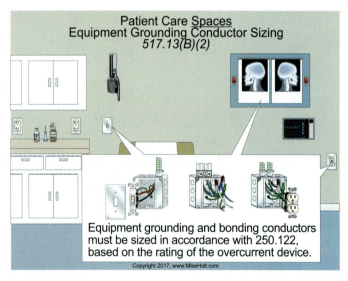

▶Figure 517–14

517.16 Isolated Ground Receptacles

(A) Inside Patient Care Vicinity. Isolated grounding receptacles are permitted within the patient care space, but not within the patient care vicinity. ▶Figure 517–15

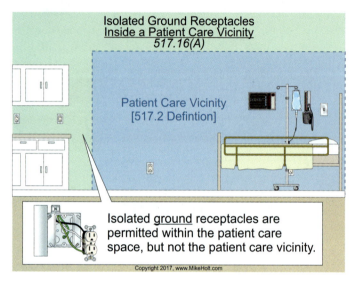

▶Figure 517–15

Author's Comment:

- The patient care vicinity is a space extending 6 ft beyond the normal location of the patient bed, chair, table, treadmill, or other device that supports the patient during examination and treatment and extends vertically to 7 ft 6 in. above the floor [517.2 Definition].

(B) Outside Patient Care Vicinity [as defined in 517.2]. Isolated ground receptacles within the patient care space [as defined in 517.2], but outside a patient care vicinity [as defined in 517.2] must comply with the following: ▶Figure 517–16

(1) The grounding terminal of isolated grounding receptacles in a patient care space must be connected to an insulated equipment grounding conductor in accordance with 250.146(D) in addition to the equipment grounding conductor paths required in 517.13(A). The equipment grounding conductor for the isolated grounding receptacle in the patient care space must have green insulation with one or more yellow stripes along its entire length.

Health Care Facilities | 517.16

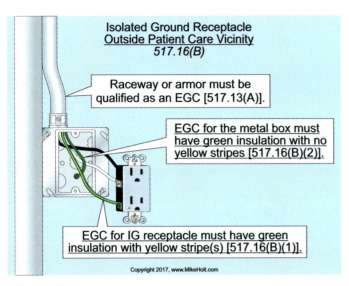

▶Figure 517–16

(2) The insulated equipment grounding conductor required in 517.13(B)(1) must have green insulation with no yellow stripes and it isn't permitted to be connected to the grounding terminal of the isolated ground receptacle; the insulated equipment grounding conductor required by 517.13(B)(1) must be connected to the metal enclosure containing the receptacle as required by 517.13(B)(1)(2) and to conductive surfaces of fixed electrical equipment as required by 517.13(B)(1)(3).

Note 1: This type of installation is typically used where a reduction of electrical noise (electromagnetic interference) is necessary, and parallel grounding paths are to be avoided.

Note 2: Care should be taken in specifying a system containing isolated ground receptacles, because the grounding impedance is controlled only by the grounding wires and doesn't benefit from any conduit or building structure in parallel with the grounding path.

Notes

ARTICLE 525 — CARNIVALS, CIRCUSES, FAIRS, AND SIMILAR EVENTS

Introduction to Article 525—Carnivals, Circuses, Fairs, and Similar Events

Article 525 covers the installation of portable wiring and equipment for carnivals, circuses, exhibitions, fairs, traveling attractions, and similar functions [525.1]. At first glance, a couple of questions arise, "Aren't these just like assembly occupancies?" and "Why do we need Article 525 if Article 518 covers the same thing?"

Yes, these locations are similar to assembly occupancies [Article 518], but they're not the same. In fact, there are two big differences:

- Article 525 applications are temporary, while Article 518 occupancies aren't.
- Article 518 doesn't cover amusement rides and attractions, while Article 525 does.

You may want to compare these two articles to see if you can spot other similarities and differences between them. Doing so will help you understand both articles better.

Part I. General Requirements

525.1 Scope

This article covers the installation of portable wiring and equipment for carnivals, circuses, exhibitions, fairs, traveling attractions, and similar functions. ▶Figure 525–1

Part IV. Grounding and Bonding

525.30 Equipment Bonding

The following equipment must be bonded to the electric power source in accordance with 525.31:

(1) Metal raceways and metal-sheathed cable

(2) Metal enclosures of electrical equipment

(3) Metal frames and metal parts of portable structures, trailers, trucks, or other equipment that contain or support electrical equipment

The circuit equipment grounding conductor of the circuit supplying the equipment in (1), (2), or (3) can serve as the bonding means.

▶Figure 525–1

525.31 Equipment Grounding

Equipment required to be grounded must be connected to an equipment grounding conductor of a type recognized by 250.118. The circuit equipment grounding conductor must be connected to the neutral conductor at the service equipment [250.24] or source of the separately derived system [250.30] in accordance with 250.142.

The neutral circuit conductor isn't permitted to be connected to the circuit equipment grounding conductor on the load side of the service disconnect or on the load side of a separately derived system disconnecting means.

525.32 Portable Equipment Grounding Conductor Continuity

The continuity of the circuit equipment grounding conductor for portable electrical equipment must be verified each time the equipment is connected.

Author's Comment:

- Verification of the circuit equipment grounding conductor is necessary to ensure electrical safety. This rule doesn't specify how it's verified, what circuits must be verified, how the verification is recorded, or who's required or qualified to perform the verification.

ARTICLE 547 AGRICULTURAL BUILDINGS

Introduction to Article 547—Agricultural Buildings

Two factors (dust and moisture) have a tremendous influence on the lifespan of agricultural equipment.

Dust gets into mechanisms and causes premature wear. But with electricity on the scene, dust adds two other dangers: fire and explosion. Dust from hay, grain, and fertilizer is highly flammable. Litter materials, such as straw, are also highly flammable. Excrement from farm animals may cause corrosive vapors that eat at mechanical equipment and wiring methods and can cause electrical equipment to fail. For these reasons, Article 547 includes requirements for dealing with dust and corrosion.

Another factor to consider in agricultural buildings is moisture, which causes corrosion. Water is present for many reasons, including wash down. Thus, this article has requirements for dealing with wet and damp environments, and also includes other rules. For example, you must install equipotential planes in all concrete floor confinement areas of livestock buildings containing metallic equipment accessible to animals and likely to become energized.

Livestock animals have a low tolerance to small voltage differences, which can cause loss of milk production and, at times, livestock fatality. As a result, the *NEC* contains specific requirements for an equipotential plane in buildings that house livestock.

547.1 Scope

Article 547 applies to agricultural buildings or to that part of a building or adjacent areas of similar nature as specified in (A) or (B). ▶Figure 547–1

(A) Excessive Dust and Dust with Water. Buildings or areas where excessive dust and/or dust with water may accumulate, such as areas of poultry, livestock, and fish confinement systems where litter or feed dust may accumulate.

(B) Corrosive Atmosphere. Buildings or areas where a corrosive atmosphere exists, and where the following conditions exist:

(1) Poultry and animal excrement.

(2) Corrosive particles that may combine with water.

(3) Areas made damp or wet by periodic washing.

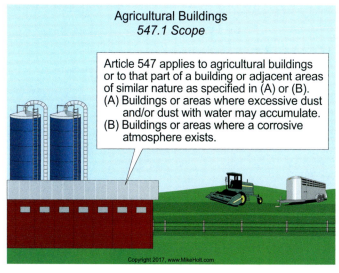

▶Figure 547–1

547.2 | Agricultural Buildings

547.2 Definitions

Equipotential Plane. An area where conductive elements are embedded in or placed under concrete, and bonded to the electrical system to minimize voltage differences within the plane. ▶Figure 547–2

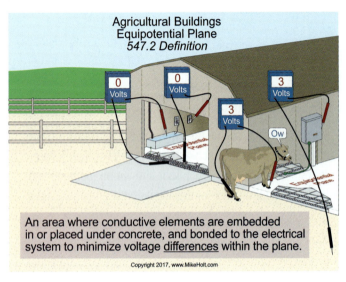

▶Figure 547–2

547.5 Wiring Methods

(F) Separate Equipment Grounding Conductor. An equipment grounding conductor for circuits in agricultural buildings must be insulated when installed underground. ▶Figure 547–3

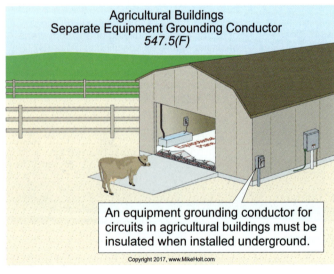

▶Figure 547–3

Note: Aluminum equipment grounding conductors aren't permitted to come in direct contact with masonry or terminate within 18 in. of the earth [250.120(B)].

(G) GFCI-Protected Receptacles. GFCI protection is required for 15A and 20A, 125V receptacles located in: ▶Figure 547–4

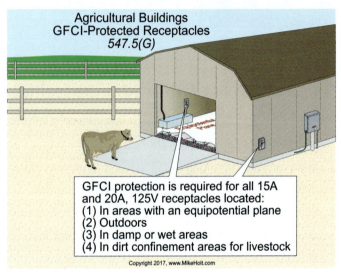

▶Figure 547–4

(1) Areas having an equipotential plane in accordance with 547.10(A)

(2) Outdoors

(3) Damp or wet locations

(4) Dirt confinement areas for livestock

547.10 Equipotential Planes

(A) Where Required.

(1) Indoors. An equipotential plane must be installed in indoor concrete floor confinement areas. ▶Figure 547–5

(2) Outdoors. An equipotential plane must be installed in outdoor confinement areas with concrete floors where livestock stand. ▶Figure 547–6

The equipotential plane must encompass the area around the equipment where the livestock stand.

(B) Bonding. The equipotential plane must be connected to the building electrical grounding system with a solid, insulated, covered, or bare copper bonding conductor, not smaller than 8 AWG. The bonding conductor must terminate at pressure connectors or clamps approved by the authority having jurisdiction [250.8]. ▶Figure 547–7

Agricultural Buildings | 547.10

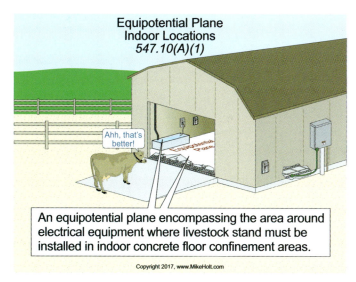

▶Figure 547–5

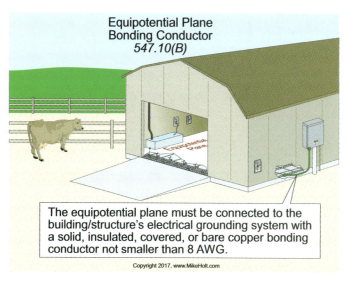

▶Figure 547–7

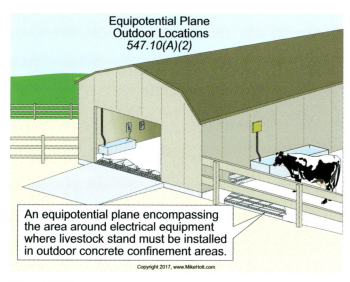

▶Figure 547–6

Note 1: Methods to establish equipotential planes are described in the American Society of Agricultural and Biological Engineers (ASABE) EP473.2, *Equipotential Planes in Animal Containment Areas*.

Author's Comment:

- The *Equipotential Planes in Animal Containment Areas* standard provides the recommendation of a voltage gradient ramp at the entrances of agricultural buildings. ▶Figure 547–8

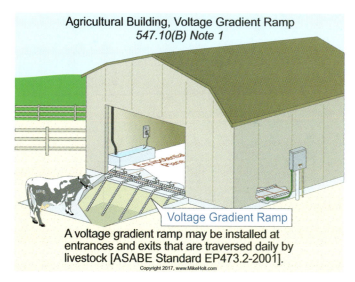

▶Figure 547–8

Note 2: See the American Society of Agricultural and Biological Engineers (ASABE) EP342.3, *Safety for Electrically Heated Livestock Waterers*.

Mike Holt Enterprises • www.MikeHolt.com • 888.NEC.CODE (632.2633)   237

547.10 | Agricultural Buildings

Author's Comment:

- The bonding requirements contained in Article 547 are unique because of the sensitivity of livestock to small voltage differences, especially in wet or damp concrete animal confinement areas.

- In most instances the voltage difference between metal parts and the earth will be too low to present a shock hazard to people. However, livestock might detect the voltage difference if they come in contact with the metal parts. Although voltage differences may not be life threatening to the livestock, it's been reported that as little as 0.50V RMS can adversely affect milk production.

- For more information, visit www.MikeHolt.com, "Technical" link, then "Stray Voltage."

ARTICLE 555 — MARINAS, BOATYARDS, AND COMMERCIAL AND NON-COMMERCIAL DOCKING FACILITIES

Introduction to Article 555—Marinas, Boatyards, and Commercial and Noncommercial Docking Facilities

Water levels aren't constant. Ocean tides rise and fall, while lakes and rivers vary in depth in response to rain. To provide power to a marina, boatyard, or docking facility, you must allow for these variations in water level between the point of use and the electric power source. Article 555 addresses this issue.

This article begins with the concept of the electrical datum plane. You might think of it as the border of a "demilitarized zone" for electrical equipment. Or, you can think of it as a line that marks the beginning of a "no man's land" where you simply don't place electrical equipment. Once you determine where this plane is, don't locate transformers, connections, or receptacles below that line.

555.1 Scope

Article 555 covers the installation of wiring and equipment for fixed or floating piers, wharfs, docks, and other areas in marinas, boatyards, boat basins, boathouses, and similar occupancies, including one-, two-, and multifamily dwellings, and residential condominiums. ▶Figure 555–1

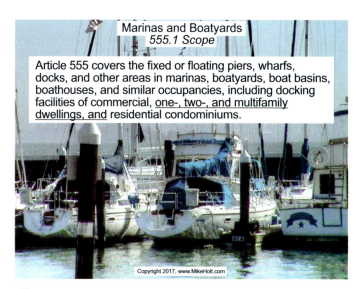

Marinas and Boatyards
555.1 Scope

Article 555 covers the fixed or floating piers, wharfs, docks, and other areas in marinas, boatyards, boat basins, boathouses, and similar occupancies, including docking facilities of commercial, one-, two-, and multifamily dwellings, and residential condominiums.

▶Figure 555–1

Author's Comment:

- GFCI protection is required for outdoor 15A and 20A, 125V receptacles [210.8].

555.15 Grounding

(B) Equipment Grounding Conductor. The equipment grounding conductor must be an insulated conductor, and conductors 6 AWG and smaller must have a continuous outer finish that's green or green with one or more yellow stripes. ▶Figure 555–2

Equipment grounding conductors 4 AWG and larger or multiconductor cables can be identified in accordance with 250.119.

(C) Size of Equipment Grounding Conductor. The insulated equipment grounding conductor must be sized in accordance with 250.122, based on the rating of the overcurrent protection device, but not smaller than 12 AWG.

555.15 | Marinas, Boatyards, and Commercial and Noncommercial Docking Facilities

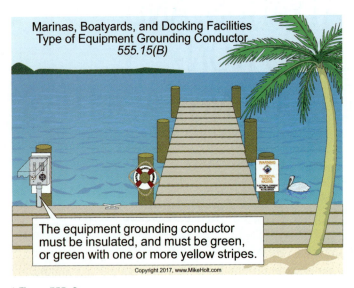

▶Figure 555–2

CHAPTER 5

PRACTICE QUESTIONS

Please use the 2017 *Code* book to answer the following questions.

Article 501. Class I Hazardous (Classified) Locations

1. In Class I locations, the locknut-bushing and double-locknut types of contacts shall not be depended on for bonding purposes.

    (a) True
    (b) False

2. When FMC or LFMC is used as permitted in Class I, Division 2 locations, it shall include an equipment bonding jumper of the wire type in compliance with 250.102.

    (a) True
    (b) False

Article 502. Class II Hazardous (Classified) Locations

3. In Class II locations, a permitted method of bonding is the use of bonding jumpers with proper fittings.

    (a) True
    (b) False

4. Where LFMC is used in a Class II, Division 1 location as permitted in 502.10, it shall _____.

    (a) not be unsupported
    (b) not exceed 6 ft in length
    (c) include an equipment bonding jumper of the wire type
    (d) be listed for use in Class I locations

Article 503. Class III Hazardous (Classified) Locations

5. Article 503 covers the requirements for electrical and electronic equipment and wiring in Class III locations where fire or explosion hazards may exist due to ignitible _____.

    (a) gases or vapors
    (b) fibers/flyings
    (c) dust
    (d) all of these

6. In Class III locations, locknut-bushing and double-locknut types of fittings may be depended on for bonding purposes.

    (a) True
    (b) False

7. Where LFMC is used in a Class III location as permitted in 503.10, it shall _____.

    (a) not be unsupported
    (b) not exceed 6 ft in length
    (c) include an equipment bonding jumper of the wire type in accordance with 250.102
    (d) be listed for use in a Class I hazardous (classified) location

Article 517. Health Care Facilities

8. Article 517 applies to electrical construction and installation criteria in health care facilities that provide services to _____.

   (a) human beings
   (b) animals
   (c) a and b
   (d) none of these

9. All branch circuits serving patient care spaces shall be provided with an effective ground-fault current path by installation in a metal raceway system, or a cable having a metallic armor or sheath assembly. The metal raceway system, metallic cable armor, or sheath assembly shall itself qualify as an equipment grounding conductor in accordance with 250.118.

   (a) True
   (b) False

10. In patient care spaces, an insulated equipment bonding jumper that directly connects to the equipment grounding conductor is permitted to connect the box and receptacle(s) to the equipment grounding conductor for other than _____ ground receptacles.

    (a) AFCI-protected
    (b) GFCI-protected
    (c) isolated
    (d) all of these

11. Metal faceplates for switches and receptacles can be connected to the equipment grounding conductor by means of a metal mounting screw(s) securing the faceplate to a grounded outlet box or grounded wiring device in patient care spaces.

    (a) True
    (b) False

12. In patient care spaces, luminaires more than _____ ft above the floor and switches located outside of the patient care vicinity shall be permitted to be connected to an equipment grounding return path complying with 517.13(A) or (B).

    (a) 7
    (b) 7½
    (c) 7¾
    (d) 8

13. In health care facilities, _____ ground receptacle(s) installed in patient care spaces outside of a patient care vicinity(s) shall comply with 517.16(B)(1) and (2).

    (a) AFCI-protected
    (b) GFCI-protected
    (c) isolated
    (d) all of these

14. In health care facilities, the grounding terminals of isolated ground receptacles installed in branch circuits for patient care _____ shall be connected to an insulated equipment grounding conductor in accordance with 250.146(D) in addition to the equipment grounding conductor path required in 517.13(A).

    (a) vicinities
    (b) spaces
    (c) a or b
    (d) none of these

15. In health care facilities, the equipment grounding conductor connected to the grounding terminals of isolated ground receptacles in patient care spaces shall be clearly _____ along the equipment grounding conductor's entire length by green insulation with one or more yellow stripes.

    (a) listed
    (b) labeled
    (c) identified
    (d) approved

16. In health care facilities, the insulated grounding conductor required in 517.13(B)(1) shall be clearly _____ along its entire length by green insulation, with no yellow stripes, and shall not be connected to the grounding terminals of isolated ground receptacles but shall be connected to the box or enclosure indicated in 517.13(B)(1)(2) and to noncurrent-carrying conductive surfaces of fixed electrical equipment indicated in 517.13(B)(1)(3).

    (a) listed
    (b) labeled
    (c) identified
    (d) approved

17. In health care facilities, care should be taken in specifying a system containing isolated ground receptacles, because the grounding impedance is controlled only by the _____ wires and does not benefit from any conduit or building structure in parallel with the grounding path.

    (a) grounding
    (b) grounded
    (c) bonding
    (d) bonded

Article 525. Carnivals, Circuses, Fairs, and Similar Events

18. Article _____ covers the installation of portable wiring and equipment for carnivals, circuses, fairs, and similar functions.

    (a) 518
    (b) 525
    (c) 590
    (d) all of these

19. The _____ conductor of the circuit supplying metal parts of portable structures at a carnival, circus, or fair can serve as the required bonding means.

    (a) grounded
    (b) equipment grounding
    (c) grounding electrode
    (d) ungrounded

20. The continuity of the equipment grounding conductors at carnivals, circuses, fairs, and similar events shall be verified each time that portable electrical equipment is connected.

    (a) True
    (b) False

Article 547. Agricultural Buildings

21. Agricultural buildings where excessive dust and dust with water may accumulate, including all areas of _____ confinement systems where litter dust or feed dust may accumulate shall comply with Article 547.

    (a) poultry
    (b) livestock
    (c) fish
    (d) all of these

22. An equipotential plane is an area where wire mesh or other conductive elements are embedded in or placed under concrete, and bonded to _____.

    (a) all metal structures
    (b) fixed nonelectrical equipment that may become energized
    (c) the electrical grounding system
    (d) all of these

23. Where an equipment grounding conductor is installed underground within an agricultural building, it shall be _____.

    (a) insulated
    (b) copper
    (c) bare
    (d) covered

24. Where livestock is housed, any portion of an underground equipment grounding conductor run to the building or structure shall be _____.

    (a) insulated
    (b) covered
    (c) a or b
    (d) none of these

25. All 15A and 20A, 125V, single-phase receptacles installed _____ of agricultural buildings shall be GFCI protected.

    (a) in areas having an equipotential plane
    (b) outdoors
    (c) in dirt confinement areas for livestock
    (d) any of these

26. An equipotential plane shall be installed in all concrete floor confinement areas of livestock buildings, and all outdoor confinement areas with a concrete slab that contains metallic equipment accessible to livestock and that may become energized.

    (a) True
    (b) False

27. The equipotential plane in an agricultural building shall be connected to the electrical grounding system with a solid copper, insulated, covered, or bare conductor and not smaller than _____ AWG.

    (a) 10
    (b) 8
    (c) 6
    (d) 4

Article 555. Marinas, Boatyards, and Commercial and Noncommercial Docking Facilities

28. The equipment grounding conductor at a marina is required to be an insulated copper conductor for all circuits.

    (a) True
    (b) False

CHAPTER 6 SPECIAL EQUIPMENT

Introduction to Chapter 6—Special Equipment

Chapter 6, which covers special equipment, is the second of four *NEC* chapters that deal with special topics. Chapters 5 and 7 focus on special occupancies, and special conditions respectively. Remember, the first four chapters of the *Code* are sequential and form a foundation for each of the subsequent four. Chapter 8 covers communications systems (twisted wire, antennas, and coaxial cable) and isn't subject to the requirements of Chapters 1 through 7 except where the requirements are specifically referenced in Chapter 8. What exactly is "Special Equipment"? It's equipment that, by the nature of its use, construction, or by its unique nature creates a need for additional measures to ensure the "safeguarding of people and property" mission of the *NEC*, as stated in Article 90. The *Code* groups the articles in this chapter logically, as you might expect. Here are the general groupings:

- Prefabricated items that are assembled in the field. Articles 600 through 605. These are signs, manufactured wiring systems, and office furnishings.
- Lifting equipment. Articles 610 and 620. Cranes, hoists, elevators, dumbwaiters, wheelchair lifts, and escalators are included.
- Electric vehicle charging systems. Article 625.
- Electric welders. Article 630.
- Equipment for creating or processing information. Article 645 covers computers (information technology) and Article 646 pertains to portable (modular) data centers.
- X-ray equipment. Article 660.
- Process and production equipment. Articles 665 through 675. Induction heaters, electrolytic cells, electroplating, and irrigation machines are included.
- Swimming Pools, Spas, Hot Tubs, Fountains, and Similar Installations. Article 680.
- "New Energy" Technologies. Article 690 covers solar PV systems, Article 692 addresses fuel cells, and Article 694 pertains to small wind systems.
- Fire pumps. Article 695.

Author's Comment:

- The NFPA also produces a fire pump standard. It's NFPA 20, *Standard for the Installation of Stationary Pumps for Fire Protection*.

Chapter 6 | Special Equipment

- **Article 600—Electric Signs and Outline Lighting.** This article covers the installation of conductors and equipment for electric signs and outline lighting as defined in Article 100. Electric signs and outline lighting include all products and installations that utilize neon tubing, such as signs, decorative elements, skeleton tubing, or art forms.

- **Article 640—Audio Signal Processing, Amplification, and Reproduction Equipment.** Article 640 covers equipment and wiring for audio signal generation, recording, processing, amplification and reproduction, distribution of sound, public address, speech input systems, temporary audio system installations, and electronic musical instruments such as electric organs, electric guitars, and electronic drums/percussion.

- **Article 645—Information Technology Equipment.** This article applies to equipment, power-supply wiring, equipment interconnecting wiring and grounding of information technology equipment and systems, including terminal units in an information technology equipment room.

- **Article 680—Swimming Pools, Spas, Hot Tubs, Fountains, and Similar Installations.** This article covers the installation of electric wiring and equipment that supplies swimming, wading, therapeutic and decorative pools, fountains, hot tubs, spas, and hydromassage bathtubs, whether permanently installed or storable.

- **Article 690—Solar Photovoltaic (PV) Systems.** Article 690 focuses on reducing the electrical hazards that may arise from installing and operating a solar PV system, to the point where it can be considered safe for property and people. The requirements of the *NEC* Chapters 1 through 4 apply to these installations, except as specifically modified by Article 690.

Author's Comment:

- The full extent of Article 690 Solar PV systems is beyond the scope of this textbook and is included in a separate book, *Understanding NEC Requirements for Solar Photovoltaic Systems*. As the solar market continues to grow, the rules governing installations continue to evolve. Whether you're a designer, service contractor, installer, inspector, or instructor, you need to understand the *Code* requirements for solar installations. Mike's textbook and DVDs will give you the edge. His writing style, combined with the hundreds of instructional graphics, will help you better understand the *NEC* safety requirements and how they should be applied. The DVDs feature Mike and a panel of world-renowned solar experts who break down the rules and clarify their intent. To get your copy, visit www.MikeHolt.com/17Solar, or call 888.632.2633.

ARTICLE 600 — ELECTRIC SIGNS AND OUTLINE LIGHTING

Introduction to Article 600—Electric Signs and Outline Lighting

One of the first things you'll notice when entering a strip mall is that there's a sign for every store. Every commercial occupancy needs a form of identification, and the standard method is the electric sign; thus, 600.5 requires a sign outlet for the entrance of each tenant location. Article 600 requires a disconnect within sight of a sign unless it can be locked in the open position.

Author's Comment:

- Article 100 defines an electric sign as any "fixed, stationary, or portable self-contained, electrically illuminated utilization equipment with words or symbols designed to convey information or attract attention."

Another requirement is height. Freestanding signs, such as those that might be erected in a parking lot, must be located at least 14 ft above vehicle areas unless they're protected from physical damage.

Neon art forms or decorative elements are subsets of electric signs and outline lighting. If installed and not attached to an enclosure or sign body, they're considered skeleton tubing for the purpose of applying the requirements of Article 600. However, if that neon tubing is attached to an enclosure or sign body, which may be a simple support frame, it's considered a sign or outline lighting subject to all of the provisions that apply to signs and outline lighting, such as 600.3, which requires the product to be listed.

600.1 Scope

Article 600 covers the installation of conductors, equipment, and field wiring for electric signs and outline lighting, retrofit kits including neon tubing for signs, decorative elements, skeleton tubing, or art forms. ▶Figure 600–1

Author's Comment:

- Outline lighting is an arrangement of incandescent lamps or electric-discharge lighting to outline or call attention to certain features, such as the shape of a building or the decoration of a window [Article 100]. ▶Figure 600–2

▶Figure 600–1

600.7 | Electric Signs and Outline Lighting

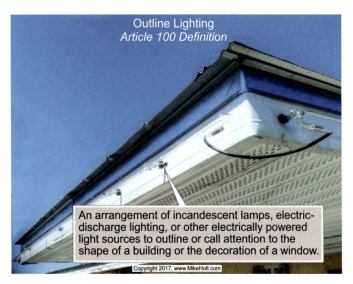

▶Figure 600–2

Note: Sign and outline lighting systems can include cold cathode neon tubing, high-intensity discharge lamps (HID), fluorescent or incandescent lamps, light-emitting diodes (LEDs), and electroluminescent and inductance lighting.

600.7 Grounding and Bonding

(A) Grounding.

(1) Equipment Grounding. Metal equipment of signs, outline lighting systems, and skeleton tubing must be connected to the circuit equipment grounding conductor of a type recognized in 250.118. ▶Figure 600–3

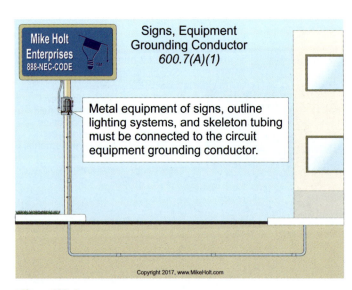

▶Figure 600–3

(2) Size of Equipment Grounding Conductor. The equipment grounding conductor must be sized in accordance with 250.122, based on the rating of the overcurrent protection device.

(3) Connections. Equipment grounding conductor connections must be made in accordance with 250.130, and in a method specified in 250.8.

> **Author's Comment:**
>
> - According to 250.8, equipment grounding conductors must terminate in any of the following methods:
>   (1) Listed pressure connectors
>   (2) Terminal bars
>   (3) Pressure connectors listed for grounding and bonding
>   (4) Exothermic welding
>   (5) Machine screws that engage at least two threads or are secured with a nut
>   (6) Self-tapping machine screws that engage at least two threads
>   (7) Connections that are part of a listed assembly
>   (8) Other listed means

(4) Auxiliary Grounding Electrode. Auxiliary grounding electrodes aren't required for signs, but if installed, they must comply with 250.54. ▶Figure 600–4

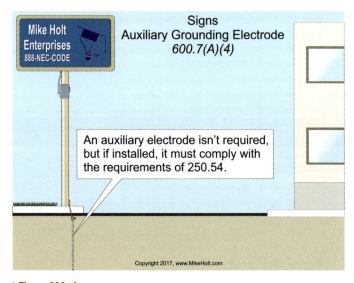

▶Figure 600–4

Author's Comment:

- According to 250.54, auxiliary electrodes need not be bonded to the building grounding electrode system, the grounding conductor to the electrode need not be sized in accordance with 250.66, and the contact resistance of the electrode to the earth isn't required to comply with the 25-ohm requirement of 250.53(A)(2) Ex.

- The earth must not be used as the effective ground-fault current path required by 250.4(A)(4) and 250.4(A)(5). This is because the contact resistance of a grounding electrode to the earth is high, and very little ground-fault current returns to the electrical supply source via the earth. The result is the circuit overcurrent protection device won't open and clear a ground fault; therefore, metal parts will remain energized with dangerous voltage.

(B) Bonding.

(1) Metal Parts. Metal parts of signs and outline lighting systems must be bonded to the transformer or power-supply equipment grounding conductor.

Ex: The metal parts of a section sign or outline lighting system supplied by a remote Class 2 power supply aren't required to be connected to an equipment grounding conductor.

(2) Bonding Connections. Bonding connections must be made in accordance with 250.8.

Author's Comment:

- According to 250.8, bonding conductors must terminate in any of the following methods:
    (1) Listed pressure connectors
    (2) Terminal bars
    (3) Pressure connectors listed for grounding and bonding
    (4) Exothermic welding
    (5) Machine screws that engage at least two threads or are secured with a nut
    (6) Self-tapping machine screws that engage at least two threads
    (7) Connections that are part of a listed assembly
    (8) Other listed means

(4) Flexible Metal Conduit Length. Listed flexible metal conduit or listed liquidtight flexible metal conduit for secondary circuit conductors for neon tubing can be used as a bonding means if the total cumulative length of the conduit doesn't exceed 100 ft.

(7) Bonding Conductors.

(1) Bonding conductors must be copper and not smaller than 14 AWG.

(2) Bonding conductors installed externally of a sign or raceway must be protected from physical damage.

Notes

ARTICLE 640 — AUDIO SIGNAL PROCESSING, AMPLIFICATION, AND REPRODUCTION EQUIPMENT

Introduction to Article 640—Audio Signal Processing, Amplification, and Reproduction Equipment

If you understand the three major goals of Article 640, you'll be able to better understand and apply the requirements. These three goals are to:

- Reduce the spread of fire and smoke.
- Comply with other articles.
- Prevent shock. This article includes several requirements, such as specifics in the mechanical execution of work, and requirements when audio equipment is located near bodies of water to reduce shock hazards peculiar to audio equipment installations.

In addition, Article 640 distinguishes between permanent and temporary audio installations. Part II provides requirements for permanent installations, and Part III provides requirements for portable and temporary installations.

Part I. General

640.1 Scope

(A) Covered. Article 640 covers equipment and wiring for permanent and temporary audio sound and public address system installations. ▶Figure 640–1

Note: Audio system locations include, but aren't limited to, restaurants, hotels, business offices, commercial and retail sales environments, churches, schools, auditoriums, theaters, stadiums, and outdoor events such as fairs, festivals, circuses, public events, and concerts.

(B) Not Covered. This article doesn't cover audio systems for fire and burglary alarms.

Article 640 covers equipment and wiring for permanent and temporary audio sound and public address system installations.

▶Figure 640–1

640.7 | Audio Signal Processing, Amplification, and Reproduction Equipment

640.7 Grounding and Bonding

(A) General. Wireways without power conductors must be connected to an equipment grounding conductor of a type recognized in 250.118, sized in accordance with 250.122, based on the rating of the overcurrent device.

(C) Isolated Ground Receptacles. Receptacles with insulated grounding terminals (isolated ground receptacles) must be connected to an insulated equipment grounding conductor in accordance with 250.146(D). ▶Figure 640–2

Note: Receptacles of the isolated grounding conductor type must be identified by an orange triangle marking on the face of the receptacle [406.3(D)].

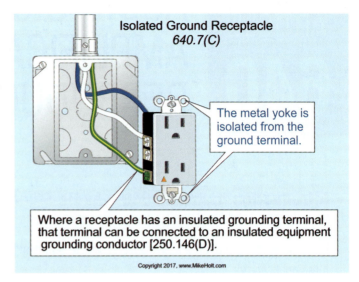

▶Figure 640–2

ARTICLE 645 — INFORMATION TECHNOLOGY EQUIPMENT

Introduction to Article 645—Information Technology Equipment

One of the unique things about Article 645 is the requirement for a shutoff switch readily accessible from the exit doors of information technology equipment rooms [645.10]. This requirement seems to be wrong on its face because it allows someone to shut power to the IT room off from a single point. So despite having a UPS and taking every precaution against a power outage, the IT system is still vulnerable to a shutdown from a readily accessible switch at the principal exit door(s).

What was the Code Making Panel thinking of when they added this requirement? They were thinking of fire and rescue teams. Having a means to shut down the power and disconnect the batteries before entering the IT room during a fire allows the rescue team to use fire hoses and other equipment without risking contact with energized equipment. Yes, there's loss of IT function during the shutdown, but if the room needs fire and rescue teams, that loss is the least of anyone's problems at that time. The shutdown allows the rescue of people and property. A breakaway lock can protect the IT room from inadvertent shutdown via this switch.

What about the rest of Article 645? The major goal is to reduce the spread of fire and smoke. The raised floors common in IT rooms pose additional challenges to achieving this goal, so this article devotes a fair percentage of its text to raised floor requirements. Fire-resistant walls, separate HVAC systems, and other requirements further help to achieve this goal.

645.1 Scope

Article 645 provides optional alternative wiring methods and materials to those methods and materials required in other chapters of this *Code* for information technology equipment and systems in an information technology equipment room. ▶Figure 645–1

Note: An information technology equipment room is an enclosed area specifically designed to comply with the construction and fire protection provisions of NFPA 75, *Standard for the Fire Protection of Information Technology Equipment.*

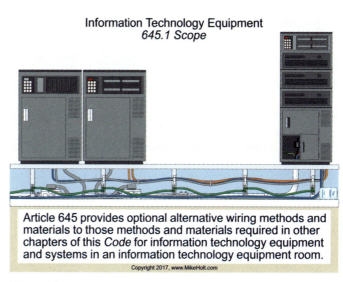
▶Figure 645–1

645.14 System Grounding and Bonding

Separately derived power systems used for information technology equipment (power distribution units) must be grounded and bonded in accordance with 250.30.

645.15 | Information Technology Equipment

645.15 Equipment Grounding and Bonding

Exposed metal parts of an information technology system must be connected to the circuit equipment grounding conductor. ▶Figure 645–2

Where signal reference structures are installed, they must be bonded to the circuit equipment grounding conductor provided for the information technology equipment. ▶Figure 645–3

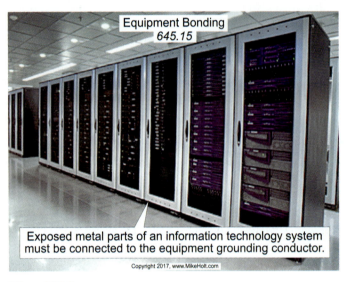

▶Figure 645–2

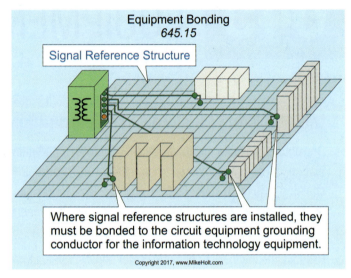

▶Figure 645–3

Note 2: If isolated ground receptacles are installed, they must be connected to an insulated equipment grounding conductor in accordance with 250.146(D) and 406.3(D).

ARTICLE 680 — SWIMMING POOLS, SPAS, HOT TUBS, FOUNTAINS, AND SIMILAR INSTALLATIONS

Introduction to Article 680—Swimming Pools, Spas, Hot Tubs, Fountains, and Similar Installations

The requirements contained in Article 680 apply to the installation of electrical wiring and equipment for swimming pools, spas, hot tubs, fountains, and hydromassage bathtubs. The overriding concern of this article is to keep people and electricity separated.

Article 680 is divided into seven parts. The various parts apply to certain types of installations, so be careful to determine which parts of this article apply to what and where. For instance, Part I and Part II apply to spas and hot tubs installed outdoors, except as modified in Part IV. In contrast, hydromassage bathtubs are only covered by Part VII. Read the details of this article carefully so you'll be able to provide a safe installation.

- **Part I. General.**
- **Part II. Permanently Installed Pools.** Installations at permanently installed pools must comply with both Parts I and II of this article.
- **Part IV. Spas and Hot Tubs.** Spas and hot tubs must comply with Parts I and IV of this article; outdoor spas and hot tubs must also comply with Part II in accordance with 680.42.
- **Part V. Fountains.** Parts I and II apply to permanently installed fountains. If they have water in common with a pool, Part II also applies. Self-contained, portable fountains are covered by Article 422, Parts II and III.
- **Part VII. Hydromassage Bathtubs.** Part VII applies to hydromassage bathtubs, but no other parts of Article 680 do.
- **Part VIII. Electrically Powered Pool Lifts.** Part VIII applies to electrically powered pool lifts, but no other parts of this article do.

680.1 | Swimming Pools, Spas, Hot Tubs, Fountains, and Similar Installations

Part I. General Requirements for Pools, Spas, Hot Tubs, and Fountains

Author's Comment:

- The requirements contained in Part I of Article 680 apply to permanently installed pools [680.20], storable pools [680.30], spas and hot tubs [680.42 and 680.43], and fountains [680.50].

680.1 Scope

The requirements contained in Article 680 apply to the installation of electric wiring and equipment for swimming pools, hot tubs, spas, fountains, and hydromassage bathtubs. ▶Figure 680–1

▶Figure 680–2

▶Figure 680–1

680.2 Definitions

Forming Shell. A structure mounted in the wall of permanently installed pools, storable pools, outdoor spas, outdoor hot tubs, or fountains designed to support a wet-niche luminaire. ▶Figure 680–2

Fountain. An ornamental pool, display pool, or reflection pool.

Hydromassage Bathtub. A permanently installed bathtub with a recirculating piping system designed to accept, circulate, and discharge water after each use. ▶Figure 680–3

Low-Voltage Contact Limit. A voltage not exceeding the following values: ▶Figure 680–4

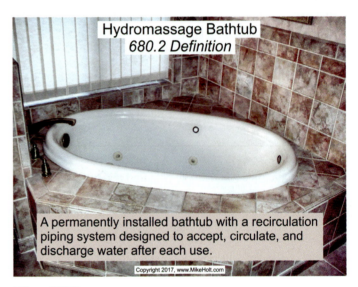

▶Figure 680–3

(1) 15V (RMS) for sinusoidal alternating current

(2) 21.20V peak for nonsinusoidal alternating current

(3) 30V for continuous direct current

(4) 12.40V peak for direct current that's interrupted at a rate of 10 to 200 Hz

Permanently Installed Swimming, Wading, Immersion, and Therapeutic Pools. Those constructed in the ground or partially in the ground, and all others capable of holding water in a depth greater than 42 in., and pools installed inside of a building, regardless of water depth, whether or not served by electrical circuits of any nature. ▶Figure 680–5

Swimming Pools, Spas, Hot Tubs, Fountains, and Similar Installations | 680.2

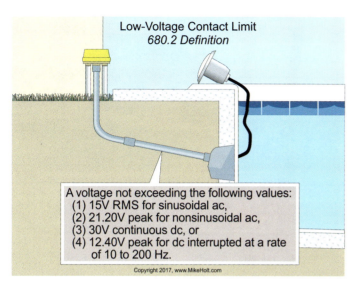

▶Figure 680–4

▶Figure 680–5

Pool. Manufactured or field-constructed equipment designed to contain water on a permanent or semipermanent basis and used for swimming, wading, immersion, or other purposes.

Author's Comment:

- The definition of a pool includes baptisteries (immersion pools), which must comply with the requirements of Article 680.

Spa or Hot Tub. A hydromassage pool or tub designed for recreational or therapeutic use, and not typically drained after each use. ▶Figure 680–6

▶Figure 680–6

Storable Swimming Pool, or Storable/Portable Spas and Hot Tubs. Swimming, wading, or immersion pools intended to be stored when not in use, constructed on or above the ground and are capable of holding water to a maximum depth of 42 in., or a pool, spa, or hot tub constructed on or above the ground, with nonmetallic, molded polymeric walls or inflatable fabric walls regardless of dimension. ▶Figure 680–7

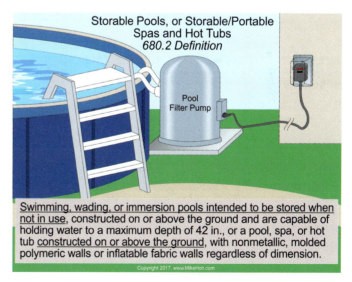

▶Figure 680–7

680.7 | Swimming Pools, Spas, Hot Tubs, Fountains, and Similar Installations

Author's Comment:

- Storable pools are sold as a complete package that consists of the pool walls, vinyl liner, plumbing kit, and pump/filter device. Underwriters Laboratories, Inc. (UL) requires the pump/filter units to have a minimum 25-ft cord to discourage the use of extension cords.

Wet-Niche Luminaire. A luminaire intended to be installed in a forming shell where the luminaire will be completely surrounded by water. ▶Figure 680–8

▶Figure 680–8

▶Figure 680–9

680.7 Grounding and Bonding Terminals

Grounding and bonding terminals must be identified for use in wet and corrosive environments and be listed for direct burial use. ▶Figure 680–9

680.8 Cord-and-Plug-Connected Equipment

Fixed or stationary equipment other than an underwater luminaire for permanently installed pools can be cord-and-plug-connected to facilitate removal or disconnection for maintenance or repair.

(A) Length. Except for storable pools, the flexible cord must not exceed 3 ft in length.

Author's Comment:

- The NEC doesn't specify a maximum flexible cord length for a storable pool pump motor.

(B) Equipment Grounding Conductor. The flexible cord must have a copper equipment grounding conductor not smaller than 12 AWG and the flexible cord must terminate at a grounding-type attachment plug.

Part II. Permanently Installed Pools, Outdoor Spas, and Outdoor Hot Tubs

680.20 General

The installation requirements contained in Part I and Part II apply to permanently installed pools [680.20], spas, and hot tubs [680.42 and 680.43].

680.21 Motors

(A) Wiring Methods. The wiring to a pool-associated motor must comply with (A)(1) unless modified by (A)(2), (A)(3), (A)(4), or (A)(5).

(1) General. Where branch-circuit wiring for pool-associated motors is subject to physical damage or exposed to damp, wet, or corrosive locations, rigid metal conduit, intermediate metal conduit, rigid polyvinyl chloride conduit, and reinforced thermosetting resin conduit, or Type MC cable listed for the location must be used. ▶Figure 680–10

Swimming Pools, Spas, Hot Tubs, Fountains, and Similar Installations | 680.23

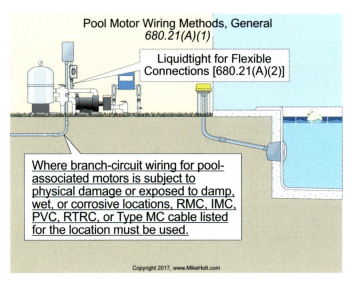

▶Figure 680–10

The wiring methods must contain an insulated copper equipment grounding conductor sized in accordance with 250.122, based on the rating of the circuit overcurrent protection device, but in no case can the equipment grounding conductor be sized smaller than 12 AWG. Wiring in dry and noncorrosive locations can be in any wiring method permitted in Chapter 3.

(2) Flexible Connections. Liquidtight flexible metal or liquidtight flexible nonmetallic conduit with listed fittings are permitted.

(3) Cord-and-Plug Connections. Cords for pool motors are permitted if the length doesn't exceed 3 ft and the cord contains a copper equipment grounding conductor, sized in accordance with 250.122, based on the rating of the overcurrent protection device, but not smaller than 12 AWG. ▶Figure 680–11

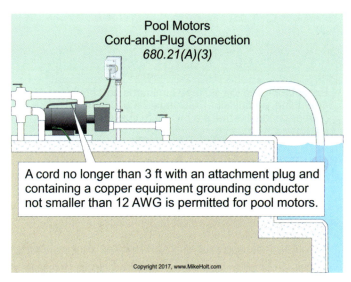

▶Figure 680–11

Author's Comment:

- For outdoor spas and hot tubs, the flexible cord must be GFCI protected and it can be up to 15 ft long [680.42(A)(2)].

680.23 Underwater Luminaires

(B) Wet-Niche Underwater Luminaires.

(1) Forming Shells. Forming shells for wet-niche underwater luminaires must be equipped with provisions for raceway entries. Forming shells used with PVC conduit systems must include provisions for terminating an 8 AWG copper conductor.

(2) Wiring to the Forming Shell. The raceway that extends directly to the underwater pool wet-niche forming shell must comply with (a) or (b).

(a) Metal Raceway. Brass or corrosion-resistant rigid metal conduit approved by the authority having jurisdiction.

(b) Nonmetallic Raceway. A nonmetallic raceway to the forming shell must contain an 8 AWG insulated (solid or stranded) copper bonding jumper that terminates to the forming shell and junction box. ▶Figure 680–12

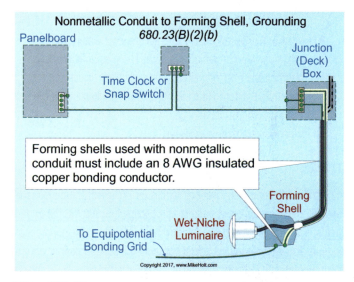

▶Figure 680–12

The termination of the 8 AWG bonding jumper in the forming shell must be covered with a listed potting compound to protect the connection from the possible deteriorating effects of pool water.

(6) Servicing. The forming shell location and length of flexible cord in the forming shell must allow for personnel to place the removed luminaire on the deck or other dry location for maintenance. The luminaire maintenance location must be accessible without entering or going in the pool water. ▶Figure 680–13

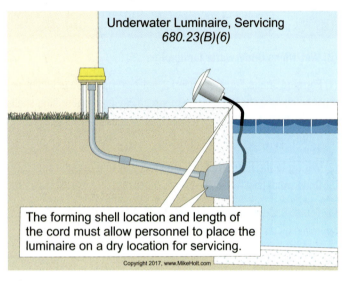

▶Figure 680–13

Author's Comment:

- While it may be necessary to enter the pool water, possibly with underwater breathing apparatus in some cases, the flexible cord must be long enough to allow the luminaire to be brought out and placed on a deck or other dry location where the relamping, maintenance, or inspection can take place without entering the pool water.

(F) Branch-Circuit Wiring.

(1) General. Where branch-circuit wiring for underwater luminaires is installed in corrosive environments as described in 680.14, the wiring methods must comply with 680.14(B) or be liquidtight flexible nonmetallic conduit. The wiring methods must contain an insulated copper equipment grounding conductor sized in accordance with 250.122, based on the rating of the overcurrent protection device, but in no case can it be smaller than 12 AWG. ▶Figure 680–14

In noncorrosive environments, any Chapter 3 wiring method is permitted.

Ex: If connecting to transformers or power supplies for pool lights, liquidtight flexible metal conduit is permitted in individual lengths not exceeding 6 ft.

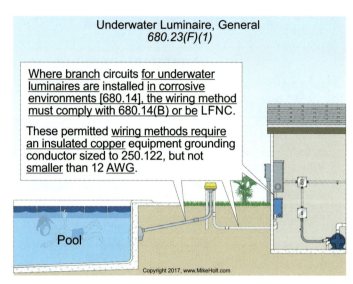

▶Figure 680–14

(2) Equipment Grounding Conductor. For other than listed low-voltage luminaires not requiring grounding, branch-circuit conductors for an underwater luminaire must contain an insulated copper equipment grounding conductor sized in accordance with Table 250.122, based on the rating of the overcurrent protection device, but not smaller than 12 AWG. ▶Figure 680–15

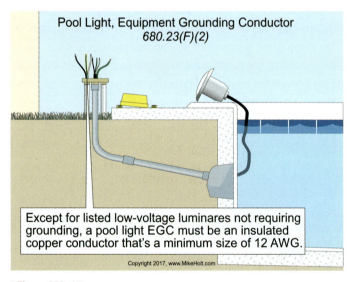

▶Figure 680–15

The circuit equipment grounding conductor for the underwater luminaire isn't permitted to be spliced, except as permitted in (a) or (b).

(a) If more than one underwater luminaire is supplied by the same branch circuit, the circuit equipment grounding conductor can terminate at a listed pool junction box that meets the requirements of 680.24(A).

Swimming Pools, Spas, Hot Tubs, Fountains, and Similar Installations | 680.25

(b) The circuit equipment grounding conductor can terminate at the grounding terminal of a listed pool transformer that meets the requirements of 680.23(A)(2).

(3) Conductors. The branch-circuit conductors on the load side of a GFCI or transformer that complies with 680.23(A)(8) for underwater luminaires must not occupy raceways or enclosures with other conductors unless one of the following conditions apply:

(1) The other conductors are GFCI protected.

(2) The conductor is an equipment grounding conductor as required by 680.23(B)(2)(b).

(3) The other conductors supply a feed-through type GFCI.

(4) The other conductors are GFCI protected within the panelboard.

680.24 Junction Box, Transformer, or GFCI Enclosure

(A) Junction Box. The junction box (deck box) that connects directly to an underwater permanently installed pool, outdoor spa, or outdoor hot tub luminaire forming shell must comply with the following:

(1) Construction. The junction box must be listed, labeled, and identified as a swimming pool junction box, and must be: ▶Figure 680–16

(1) Equipped with threaded entries or a nonmetallic hub,

(2) Constructed of copper, brass, or corrosion-resistant material approved by the authority having jurisdiction, and

(3) Provide electrical continuity between metal raceways and grounding terminals within the junction box.

Author's Comment:

- In addition, the junction box must be provided with at least one grounding terminal more than the number of raceway entries [680.24(D)], and the junction box must have a strain relief for the flexible cord [680.24(E)].

(F) Grounding. The metal parts of a junction box, transformer enclosure, or other enclosure in the supply circuit to a wet-niche luminaire must be connected to the equipment grounding terminal of the supplied circuit panelboard. ▶Figure 680–17

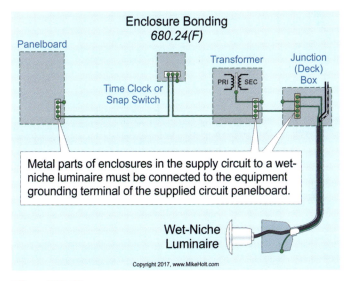

▶Figure 680–17

680.25 Feeders

(A) Wiring Methods. Where feeder wiring is installed in corrosive environments as described in 680.14, the wiring methods must comply with 680.14(B) or be liquidtight flexible nonmetallic conduit. The wiring methods must contain an insulated copper equipment grounding conductor sized in accordance with 250.122, based on the rating of the overcurrent protection device, but in no case can it be smaller than 12 AWG. ▶Figure 680–18

▶Figure 680–16

680.26 | Swimming Pools, Spas, Hot Tubs, Fountains, and Similar Installations

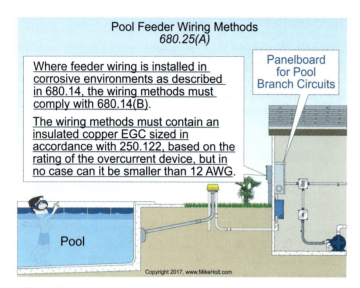

▶Figure 680–18

In noncorrosive environments, any Chapter 3 wiring method is permitted.

Author's Comment:

- The bonding requirements of this section don't apply to spas and hot tubs [680.42].

680.26 Equipotential Bonding

(A) Performance. The required equipotential bonding is intended to reduce voltage gradients in the area around a permanently installed pool. ▶Figure 680–19

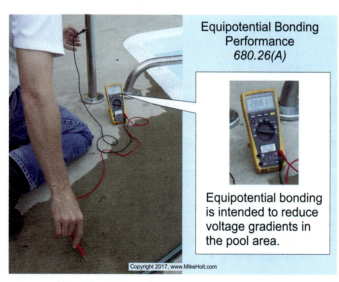

▶Figure 680–19

(B) Bonded Parts. The parts of a permanently installed pool listed in (B)(1) through (B)(7) must be bonded together with a solid copper conductor not smaller than 8 AWG with listed pressure connectors, terminal bars, exothermic welding, or other listed means in accordance with 250.8(A). ▶Figure 680–20

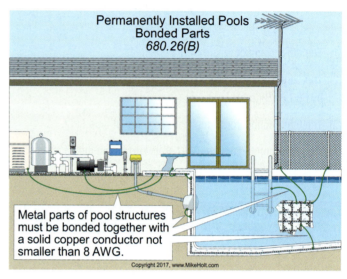

▶Figure 680–20

Equipotential bonding isn't required to extend to or be attached to any panelboard, service equipment, or grounding electrode.

(1) Concrete Pool Shells.

(a) Structural Reinforcing Steel. Unencapsulated (bare) structural reinforcing steel must be bonded together by steel tie wires or the equivalent. Where structural reinforcing steel is encapsulated in a nonconductive compound, a copper conductor grid must be installed in accordance with 680.26(B)(1)(b). ▶Figure 680–21

(b) Copper Conductor Grid. A copper conductor grid must comply with (b)(1) through (b)(4).

(1) Minimum 8 AWG bare solid copper conductors bonded to each other at all points of crossing in accordance with 250.8 or other approved means.

(2) Conform to the contour of the pool.

(3) Be arranged in a 12-in. by 12-in. network of conductors in a uniformly spaced perpendicular grid pattern with a tolerance of 4 in.

(4) Be secured within or under the pool no more than 6 in. from the outer contour of the pool shell.

Swimming Pools, Spas, Hot Tubs, Fountains, and Similar Installations | 680.26

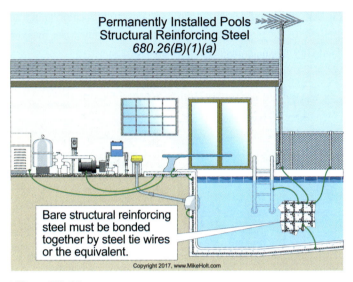
▶Figure 680–21

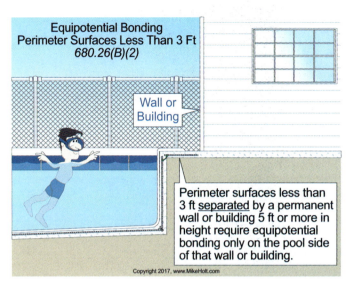
▶Figure 680–23

(2) Perimeter Surfaces. Equipotential bonding must extend a minimum of 3 ft horizontally beyond the inside walls of a pool, where not separated from the pool by a permanent wall or building of 5 ft in height. ▶Figure 680–22 and ▶Figure 680–23

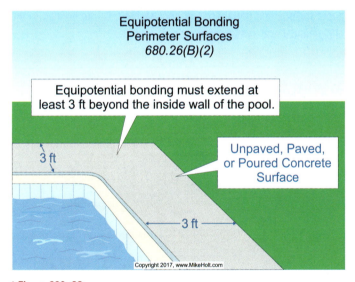
▶Figure 680–22

(a) Structural Reinforcing Steel. Structural reinforcing steel must be bonded together by steel tie wires or the equivalent in accordance with 680.26(B)(1)(a). ▶Figure 680–24

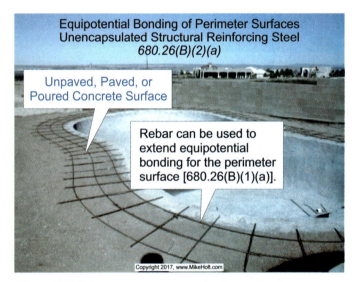
▶Figure 680–24

Author's Comment:

- The *NEC* doesn't provide any guidance on the installation requirements for structural reinforcing steel when used as a perimeter equipotential bonding method.

(b) Alternative Means. Where structural reinforcing steel isn't available (or is encapsulated in a nonconductive compound such as epoxy), equipotential bonding meeting all of the following requirements must be installed: ▶Figure 680–25

(1) The bonding conductor must be 8 AWG bare solid copper.

680.26 | Swimming Pools, Spas, Hot Tubs, Fountains, and Similar Installations

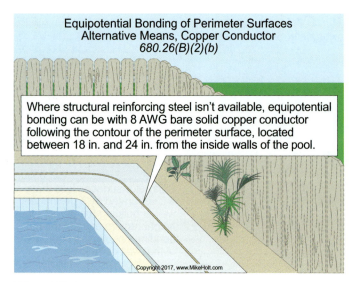

▶Figure 680–25

(2) The bonding conductor must follow the contour of the perimeter surface.

(3) Listed splicing devices must be used.

(4) The required conductor must be located between 18 in. and 24 in. from the inside walls of the pool.

(5) The bonding conductor must be secured in or under the deck or unpaved surface within 4 in. to 6 in. below the subgrade.

(3) Metallic Components. Metallic parts of the pool structure must be bonded to the equipotential grid.

(4) Underwater Metal Forming Shells. Metal forming shells must be bonded to the equipotential grid. ▶Figure 680–26

▶Figure 680–26

(5) Metal Fittings. Metal fittings 4 in. and larger located within or attached to the pool structure, such as ladders and handrails, must be bonded to the equipotential grid. ▶Figure 680–27

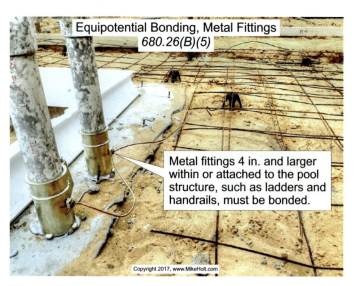

▶Figure 680–27

(6) Electrical Equipment. Metal parts of electrical equipment associated with the pool water circulating system, such as water heaters, pump motors, and metal parts of pool covers must be bonded to the equipotential grid. ▶Figure 680–28

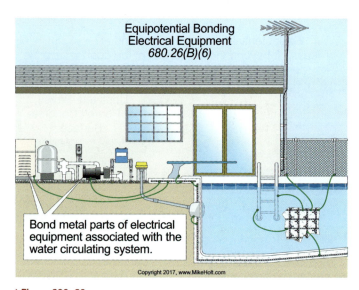

▶Figure 680–28

Ex: Metal parts of listed double-insulated equipment aren't required to be bonded.

(a) Double-Insulated Water-Pump Motors. If a double-insulated water-pump motor is installed, a solid 8 AWG copper bonding conductor must be provided for a replacement motor.

(7) Fixed Metal Parts. Fixed metal parts must be bonded to the equipotential grid, including but not limited to, metal-sheathed cables and raceways, metal piping, metal awnings, metal fences, and metal door and window frames. ▶Figure 680–29

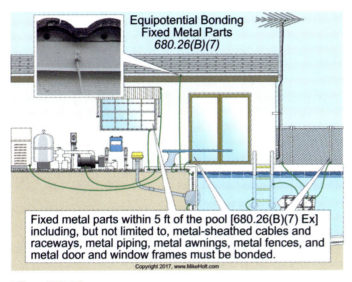

▶Figure 680–29

Ex 1: Those parts separated from the pool structure by a permanent barrier that prevents contact by a person aren't required to be bonded.

Ex 2: Those parts located more than 5 ft horizontally from the inside walls of the pool structure aren't required to be bonded. ▶Figure 680–30

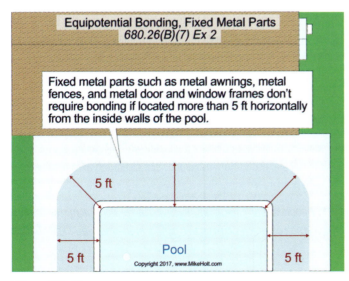

▶Figure 680–30

Ex 3: Those parts located more than 12 ft measured vertically above the maximum water level aren't required to be bonded.

(C) Pool Water. If the pool water doesn't have an electrical connection to one of the bonded parts described in 680.26(B), an approved corrosion-resistant conductive surface that's at least 9 sq in. must be in contact with the water. The corrosion-resistance conductive surface must be bonded in accordance with 680.26(B), and be located in an area where it won't be dislodged or damaged during normal pool usage. ▶Figure 680–31

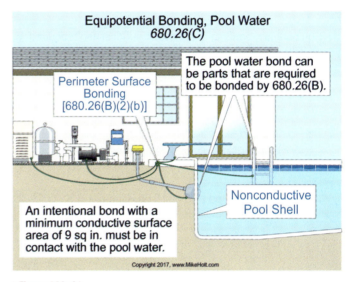

▶Figure 680–31

Part IV. Spas and Hot Tubs

680.40 General

Electrical installations for spas and hot tubs must comply with Part I as well.

680.42 Outdoor Installations

(B) Equipotential Bonding. Equipotential bonding of perimeter surfaces in accordance with 680.26(B)(2) isn't required for outdoor spas and hot tubs if:

(1) The spa or hot tub is listed, <u>labeled, and identified</u> as a self-contained spa or hot tub for aboveground use. ▶Figure 680–32

(2) The spa or hot tub isn't identified as suitable for indoor use.

(3) The spa or hot tub is located on or above grade.

680.43 | Swimming Pools, Spas, Hot Tubs, Fountains, and Similar Installations

▶Figure 680–32

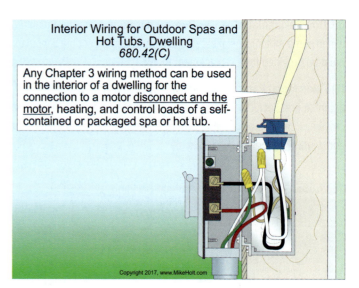

▶Figure 680–34

(4) The top rim of the spa or hot tub is at least 28 in. above a perimeter surface located within 30 in. from the spa or hot tub. ▶Figure 680–33

▶Figure 680–33

(C) Interior Dwelling Unit Wiring for Outdoor Spas or Hot Tubs. Any Chapter 3 wiring method is permitted in the interior of a dwelling unit for the connection to a motor disconnect and the motor, heating, and control loads that are part of a self-contained spa or hot tub or a packaged spa or hot tub equipment assembly. ▶Figure 680–34

680.43 Indoor Installations

Electrical installations for an indoor spa or hot tub must comply with Parts I and II of Article 680, except as modified by this section. Indoor installations of spas or hot tubs must be connected by any of the wiring methods contained in Chapter 3.

Ex 2: The equipotential bonding for perimeter surfaces contained in 680.26(B)(2) don't apply to a listed self-contained spa or hot tub installed above an indoor finished floor.

(D) Bonding. The following parts of an indoor spa or hot tub must be bonded together:

(1) Metal fittings within or attached to the indoor spa or hot tub structure.

(2) Metal parts of electrical equipment associated with the indoor spa or hot tub water circulating system unless part of a listed self-contained spa or hot tub.

(3) Metal raceways and metal piping within 5 ft of the inside walls of the indoor spa or hot tub, and not separated from the indoor spa or hot tub by a permanent barrier.

(4) Metal surfaces within 5 ft of the inside walls of an indoor spa or hot tub not separated from the indoor spa or hot tub area by a permanent barrier.

Ex 1: Nonelectrical equipment, such as towel bars or mirror frames, which aren't connected to metallic piping, aren't required to be bonded.

(E) Methods of Bonding. Metal parts associated with the spa or hot tub as described in 680.43(D) must be bonded by any of the following methods:

(1) Interconnection of threaded metal piping and fittings

(2) Metal-to-metal mounting to a common frame or base

(3) A solid copper bonding jumper; insulated, covered, or bare, not smaller than 8 AWG

Part V. Fountains

680.50 General

The general installation requirements contained in Part I apply to fountains. In addition, fountains that have water common to a permanently installed pool must comply with Part I and Part II of this article. This part doesn't cover self-contained, portable fountains. Portable fountains must comply with Parts II and III of Article 422.

Author's Comment:

- A "Fountain" is defined as an ornamental, display, or reflection pool [680.2].

680.53 Bonding

Metal-piping systems associated with a fountain must be bonded to the circuit equipment grounding conductor of the branch circuit that supplies the fountain equipment.

680.55 Methods of Equipment Grounding

(B) Supplied by a Flexible Cord. Fountain equipment supplied by a flexible cord must have all exposed metal parts connected to an insulated copper equipment grounding conductor that's an integral part of the cord. ▶Figure 680–35

Part VII. Hydromassage Bathtubs

680.70 General

A hydromassage bathtub is only required to comply with the requirements of Part VII; it's not required to comply with the other parts of this article.

▶Figure 680–35

Author's Comment:

- A "Hydromassage Bathtub" is defined as a permanently installed bathtub with a recirculating piping system designed to accept, circulate, and discharge water after each use [680.2].

680.74 Equipotential Bonding

(A) General. The following parts must be bonded together.

(1) Metal fittings within or attached to the hydromassage tub structure that are in contact with the circulating water.

(2) Metal parts of electrical equipment associated with the hydromassage tub water circulating system, including pump and blower motors.

(3) Metal-sheathed cables, metal raceways, and metal piping within 5 ft of the inside walls of the hydromassage tub and not separated from the tub area by a permanent barrier.

(4) Exposed metal surfaces within 5 ft of the inside walls of the hydromassage tub and not separated from the tub by a permanent barrier.

(5) Electrical devices not associated with the hydromassage tubs located within 5 ft from the hydromassage tub.

Ex 1: Small conductive surfaces not likely to become energized, such as air and water jets, supply valve assemblies, and drain fittings not connected to metallic piping, and towel bars, mirror frames, and similar nonelectrical equipment not connected to metal framing aren't required to be bonded.

Ex 2: Double-insulated motors and blowers aren't required to be bonded.

(B) Bonding Conductor. Metal parts required to be bonded by 680.74(A) must be bonded together using a solid copper conductor not smaller than 8 AWG. The bonding jumper isn't required to be extended or attached to any remote panelboard, service equipment, or any electrode. ▶Figure 680–36

A bonding jumper long enough to terminate on a replacement nondouble-insulated pump or blower motor must be provided and it must terminate to the equipment grounding conductor of the branch circuit of the motor when a double-insulated circulating pump or blower motor is used. ▶Figure 680–37

Part VIII. Electrically Powered Pool Lifts

680.80 General

Electrically powered pool lifts are only required to comply with the requirements of Part VIII; they're not required to comply with the other parts of this article.

680.83 Bonding

Electrically powered pool lifts must be bonded in accordance with 680.26(B)(5) and (B)(7).

▶Figure 680–36

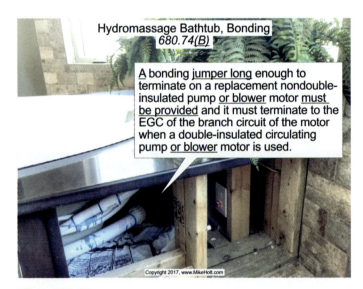

▶Figure 680–37

ARTICLE 690 SOLAR PHOTOVOLTAIC (PV) SYSTEMS

Introduction to Article 690—Solar Photovoltaic (PV) Systems

You've seen, or maybe own, devices powered by photovoltaic cells, such as night lights, car coolers, and toys. These generally consist of a small solar module powering a small device running on less than 10V dc and drawing only a fraction of an ampere. A solar PV system that powers a house or interconnects with an electric utility to offset a building's energy consumption operates on the same principles but on a much larger scale.

Solar PV systems that provide electrical power to an electrical system are large, heavy, and complex. There are mechanical and site selection issues that require expert knowledge as well as complex structural and architectural concerns that must be addressed. In this textbook we'll only address these installations as they pertain to Article 690 of the *NEC* and the installation of non-utility solar PV systems.

The purpose of the *NEC* is to safeguard persons and property from the hazards arising from the use of electricity. Article 690 keeps that theme by focusing on reducing the electrical hazards that may arise from installing and operating a PV system, to a point where it can be considered safe for property and people.

This article consists of eight Parts and the general requirements of Chapters 1 through 4 apply to these installations, except as specifically modified by Article 690.

Part I. General

690.1 Scope

Article 690 applies to solar PV systems, array circuit(s), inverter(s), and charge controller(s) for PV systems, not covered in Article 691. These solar PV systems may be interactive with other electrical power sources (electric utility power, wind, generator) or stand-alone, or both, and may not be connected to an energy storage system (batteries). ▶Figure 690–1

690.2 Definitions

Array. A mechanically and electrically integrated assembly of PV module(s) or panel(s) consisting of support structures, trackers, and other components to form a dc or ac power-producing unit. ▶Figure 690–2

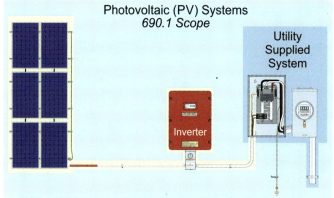

▶Figure 690–1

690.31 | Solar Photovoltaic (PV) Systems

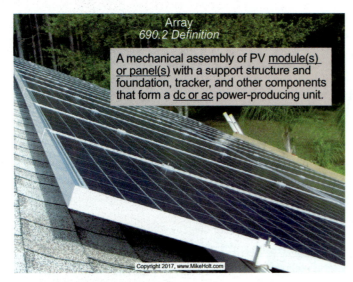

▶Figure 690–2

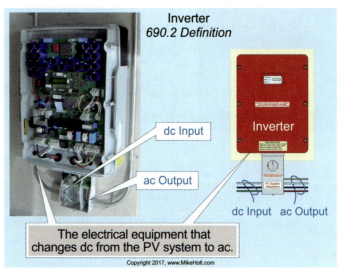

▶Figure 690–4

Functional Grounded PV System. A PV system that has an electrical reference to ground that isn't solidly grounded.

Note: A functional grounded PV system is grounded through a listed ground-fault protection system that's part of the inverter instead of being solidly grounded

Interactive System. A PV system that operates in parallel (interactive) with, and may deliver power to, an electric utility power source. ▶Figure 690–3

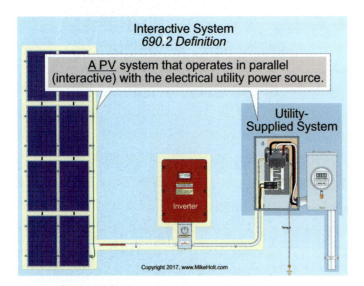

▶Figure 690–3

Inverter. Electrical equipment that changes dc power from the PV system to ac power. ▶Figure 690–4

Author's Comment:

- Inverters change direct current produced by the PV modules or batteries into alternating current. Grid-tied interactive inverters synchronize the ac output current with the utility's ac frequency, thus allowing the PV system to transfer current to the electric utility grid. Battery-based inverters for stand-alone systems often include a charge controller, which can charge a battery bank from a generator during cloudy weather.

- A listed interactive inverter automatically ceases exporting power upon loss of electric utility or other power source and automatically resumes exporting power once the electric or other utility power source has been restored [705.40 Ex.].

Panel. A collection of solar modules mechanically fastened together, wired, and designed to provide a field-installable unit.

Part IV. Wiring Methods

690.31 Wiring Methods

(I) Bipolar Photovoltaic Systems. Where the sum of the PV system voltages of two monopole subarrays exceeds the rating of the conductors and equipment, monopole subarrays must be physically separated and the electrical output circuits from each monopole subarray must be installed in separate raceways until connected to the bipolar inverter. ▶Figure 690–5

The disconnecting means and overcurrent protective devices for each monopole subarray output must be in separate enclosures.

Solar Photovoltaic (PV) Systems | 690.41

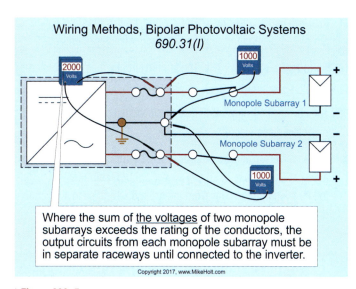

▶Figure 690–5

Solidly grounded bipolar PV systems must be clearly marked with a permanent, legible warning notice indicating that the disconnection of the grounded conductor(s) may result in overvoltage on the equipment.

Ex: Listed switchgear for bipolar systems rated for the maximum voltage between circuits with a physical barrier separating the disconnecting means for each monopole subarray can be used instead of disconnecting means in separate enclosures.

690.33 Connectors

Connectors, other than those covered in 690.32, must comply with the following requirements: ▶Figure 690–6

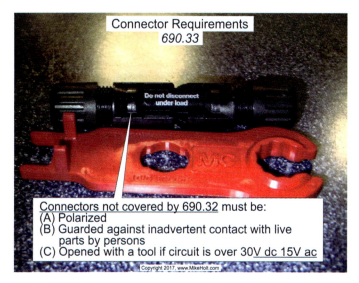

▶Figure 690–6

(A) Configuration. Connectors must be polarized.

(B) Guarding. Connectors must be constructed and installed so they guard against inadvertent contact with live parts by persons.

(C) Type. Connectors must be of the latching or locking type; where readily accessible and used in circuits operating at over 30V dc or 15V ac, the connector must require a tool for opening.

(D) Grounding Member. The grounding member must be the first to make and the last to break contact with the mating connector.

(E) Interruption of Circuit. Connectors must be one of the following:
▶Figure 690–7

▶Figure 690–7

(1) Rated to interrupt current without hazard to the operator, or

(2) Require a tool to open and be marked "Do Not Disconnect Under Load" or "Not for Current Interrupting."

Part V. Grounding and Bonding

690.41 System Grounding

(A) PV System Grounding Configurations. PV systems must be grounded via one or more of the following grounding configurations:

(1) 2-wire PV arrays with one functional grounded conductor ▶Figure 690–8

(2) Bipolar PV arrays according to 690.7(C) with a functional ground reference (center tap) ▶Figure 690–9

(3) PV arrays not isolated from the grounded inverter output circuit

690.42 | Solar Photovoltaic (PV) Systems

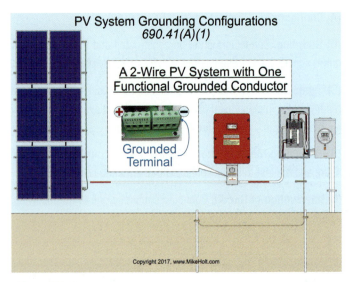

▶Figure 690–8

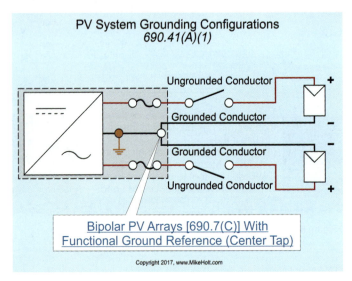

▶Figure 690–9

(4) Ungrounded PV arrays

(5) Solidly grounded PV arrays as permitted in 690.41(B) Ex

(6) PV systems that use other methods that accomplish equivalent system protection in accordance with 250.4(A) with equipment listed and identified for the use

(B) Ground-Fault Protection. To reduce fire hazards, direct-current PV arrays must be provided with dc ground-fault protection meeting the following requirements:

Ex: Ground-fault protection isn't required for solidly-grounded PV arrays containing two or fewer PV source circuits and not installed on or in a building.

(1) Ground-Fault Detection. The ground-fault protective device or system must be listed for providing PV ground-fault protection.

(2) Isolating Faulted Circuits. The faulted circuits must be isolated by one of the following methods:

(1) The current-carrying conductors of the faulted circuit must be automatically disconnected.

(2) The inverter or charge controller fed by the faulted circuit must automatically cease to supply power to output circuits and isolate the PV system dc circuits from the ground reference in a functional grounded system.

690.42 Point of Grounding Connection

Systems with ground-fault protection in accordance with 690.41(B) must have current-carrying conductor-to-ground connection made by the ground-fault protective device.

For solidly grounded PV systems, the dc circuit grounding connection must be made at any single point on the PV output circuit.

690.43 Equipment Grounding and Bonding

Exposed noncurrent-carrying metal parts of PV module frames, electrical equipment, and conductor enclosures must be grounded in accordance with 250.134 or 250.136(A).

Equipment grounding conductors and devices must comply with the following:

(A) Photovoltaic Module Mounting Systems and Devices. Devices and systems used for mounting and bonding PV module frames must be listed, labeled, and identified for bonding PV modules, and are permitted to bond adjacent PV modules. ▶Figure 690–10 and ▶Figure 690–11

(B) Equipment Secured to Grounded Metal Supports. Devices listed, labeled, and identified for bonding and grounding metal parts of PV systems can be used to bond the equipment to metal supports.

Metallic support structures for PV modules must have identified bonding jumpers installed between separate metallic sections, or the metal support structure must be identified for equipment bonding and be connected to the equipment grounding conductor. ▶Figure 690–12

Solar Photovoltaic (PV) Systems | 690.45

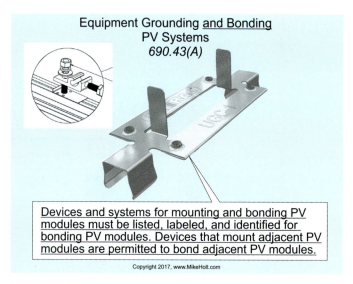
▶Figure 690–10

▶Figure 690–12

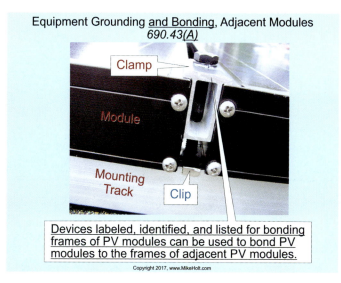
▶Figure 690–11

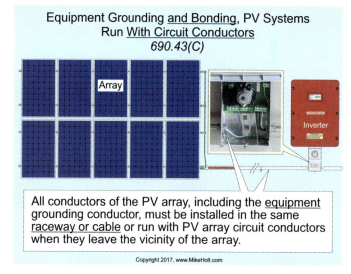
▶Figure 690–13

(C) With Circuit Conductors. Equipment grounding conductors for the PV array and support structure must be within the same raceway or cable when those circuit conductors leave the vicinity of the PV array. ▶Figure 690–13

690.45 Size of Equipment Grounding Conductors

Equipment grounding conductors for PV source and PV output circuits must be sized in accordance with 250.122 based on the rating of the circuit overcurrent protection device. Where no overcurrent protective device is provided for the PV source or PV output circuits, an assumed overcurrent protection device rated not less than 156 percent of the module-rated short-circuit current in accordance with 690.9(B) is to be used when applying Table 250.122. ▶Figure 690–14 and ▶Figure 690–15

690.46 | Solar Photovoltaic (PV) Systems

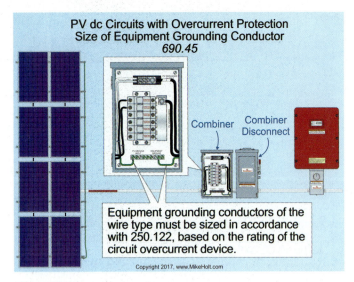
▶Figure 690–14

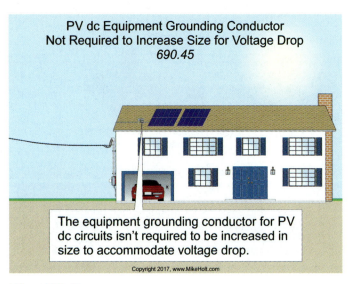
▶Figure 690–16

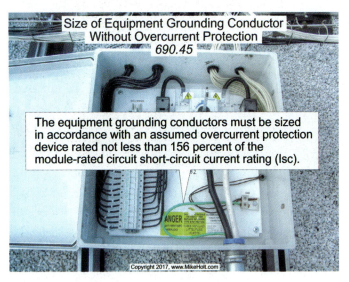
▶Figure 690–15

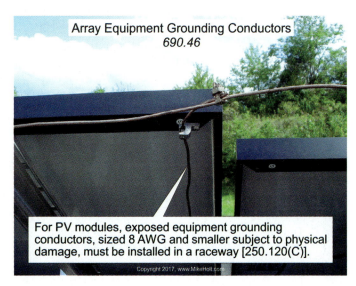
▶Figure 690–17

The equipment grounding conductor isn't required to be increased in size to address voltage-drop considerations. ▶Figure 690–16

690.46 Array Equipment Grounding Conductors

Exposed equipment grounding conductors, size 8 AWG and smaller that are subject to physical damage, must be installed within a raceway [250.120(C)]. ▶Figure 690–17

690.47 Grounding Electrode System

(A) Buildings or Structures Supporting a PV Array. A building or structure supporting a PV array must have a grounding electrode system installed at the building or structure that meets the requirements of Part III of Article 250. ▶Figure 690–18

PV array equipment grounding conductors must be connected to the grounding electrode system of the building or structure supporting the PV array in accordance with Part VII of Article 250. This connection is in addition to any other equipment grounding conductor requirements in 690.43(C).

Solar Photovoltaic (PV) Systems | 690.47

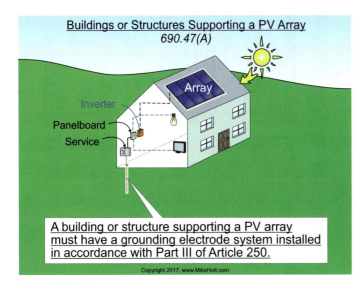

▶Figure 690–18

For PV systems that aren't solidly grounded, the equipment grounding conductor for the inverter output circuit of the PV system can serve as the connection to ground for ground-fault protection and equipment grounding of the PV array. ▶Figure 690–19

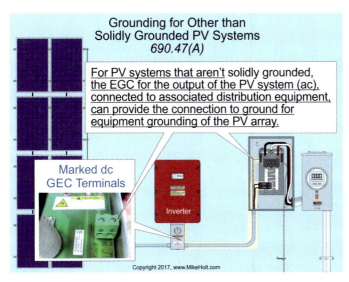

▶Figure 690–19

Note: Most PV systems are functional grounded systems, the ac equipment grounding conductor is the connection to ground for ground-fault protection and equipment grounding of the PV array.

(B) Auxiliary Electrode for Array Grounding. An auxiliary grounding electrode [250.54] is permitted to be connected to the array frame(s) or structure. The metal structure of a ground-mounted PV array can serve as a grounding electrode without qualifications [250.52(A)(8)]. Roof-mounted PV arrays can use the metal frame of a building or structure if the metal in-ground support structure is in direct contact with the earth vertically for 10 ft or more [250.52(A)(2)]. ▶Figure 690–20 and ▶Figure 690–21

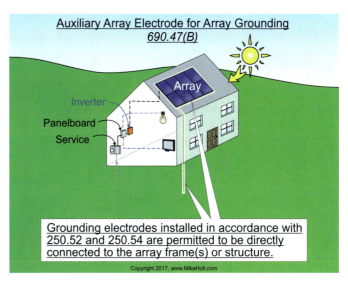

▶Figure 690–20

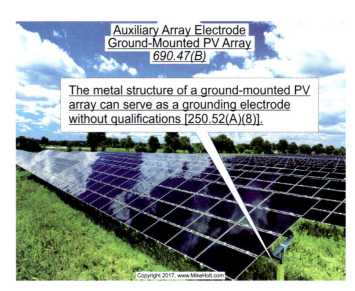

▶Figure 690–21

CHAPTER 6 PRACTICE QUESTIONS

Please use the 2017 *Code* book to answer the following questions.

Article 600. Electric Signs and Outline Lighting

1. Metal parts and equipment of signs and outline lighting systems shall be bonded together and to the transformer or power-supply equipment grounding conductor of the branch circuit or feeder supplying the sign or outline lighting system, with the exception that remote metal parts of a section sign or outline lighting system only supplied by a remote Class 2 power supply are not required to be connected to an equipment grounding conductor.

   (a) True
   (b) False

2. Listed flexible metal conduit or listed liquidtight flexible metal conduit for secondary circuit conductors for neon tubing can be used as a bonding means if the total accumulative length of the conduit in the secondary circuit does not exceed _____ ft.

   (a) 3
   (b) 10
   (c) 50
   (d) 100

Article 645. Information Technology Equipment

3. Exposed noncurrent-carrying metal parts of an information technology system shall be _____.

   (a) bonded to an equipment grounding conductor
   (b) double insulated
   (c) GFCI protected
   (d) a or b

Article 680. Swimming Pools, Spas, Hot Tubs, Fountains, and Similar Installations

4. Permanently installed swimming pools include those constructed in the ground or partially in the ground, and all others capable of holding water in a depth greater than _____ in.

   (a) 36
   (b) 42
   (c) 48
   (d) 54

5. A spa or hot tub is a hydromassage pool or tub and is generally not designed to have the contents drained or discharged after each use.

   (a) True
   (b) False

6. Storable swimming, wading, or immersion pools; or storable/portable spas and hot tubs are swimming, wading, or immersion pools that are intended to be stored when not in use, constructed on or above the ground and are capable of holding water to a maximum depth of _____ in., or a pool, spa, or hot tub constructed on or above the ground, with nonmetallic, molded polymeric walls or inflatable fabric walls regardless of dimension.

   (a) 12
   (b) 24
   (c) 42
   (d) 60

7. A wet-niche luminaire is intended to be installed in a _____.

   (a) transformer
   (b) forming shell
   (c) hydromassage bathtub
   (d) all of these

8. When installed for swimming pools, grounding and bonding terminals shall be _____ for direct burial use.

   (a) identified
   (b) labeled
   (c) listed
   (d) approved

9. Branch circuits installed in corrosive environments for pool-associated motors shall be installed in wiring methods including _____ conduit when installed in a corrosive environment. Any wiring method employed shall include an insulated copper equipment grounding conductor sized in accordance with Table 250.122, but not smaller than 12 AWG.

   (a) PVC
   (b) rigid metal
   (c) flexible metal
   (d) a or b

10. Wet-niche luminaires installed in swimming pools shall be removable from the water for inspection, relamping, or other maintenance. The luminaire maintenance location shall be accessible _____.

    (a) while the pool is drained
    (b) without entering the pool water
    (c) during construction
    (d) all of these

11. Wiring methods installed in corrosive environments as described in 680.14 shall contain an insulated copper equipment grounding conductor sized in accordance with Table 250.122, but not smaller than 12 AWG.

    (a) True
    (b) False

12. Where connecting to transformers or power supplies for pool lights in accordance with 680.23(F)(1), liquidtight flexible metal conduit shall be permitted but the length shall not exceed _____ ft for any one length or exceed _____ ft in total length used.

    (a) 3, 5
    (b) 4, 8
    (c) 6, 10
    (d) 8, 12

13. Wet-niche luminaires shall be connected to an equipment grounding conductor not smaller than _____ AWG.

    (a) 12
    (b) 10
    (c) 8
    (d) 6

14. A pool light junction box connected to a conduit that extends directly to a forming shell shall be _____ for this use.

    (a) listed
    (b) identified
    (c) labeled
    (d) all of these

15. The _____ conductor terminals of a junction box (pool deck box), transformer enclosure, or other enclosure in the supply circuit to a wet-niche luminaire shall be connected to the equipment grounding terminal of the panelboard.

    (a) equipment grounding
    (b) grounded
    (c) grounding electrode
    (d) ungrounded

16. The feeder to a swimming pool panelboard at a separate building or structure where installed in a corrosive environment can be supplied with any Chapter 3 wiring method provided the feeder has a separate insulated copper equipment grounding conductor.

    (a) True
    (b) False

17. An 8 AWG or larger solid copper equipotential bonding conductor shall be extended to service equipment to eliminate voltage gradients in the pool area.

    (a) True
    (b) False

Chapter 6 | Practice Questions

18. For equipotential bonding of pool and spa equipment, a solid 8 AWG copper conductor shall be run back to the service equipment. This conductor shall be unbroken.

    (a) True
    (b) False

19. For equipotential bonding, the perimeter surface to be bonded shall be considered to extend for _____ ft horizontally beyond the inside walls of the pool and shall include unpaved surfaces and other types of paving.

    (a) 3
    (b) 5
    (c) 10
    (d) 12

20. Perimeter surfaces separated from the pool by a permanent wall or building _____ ft in height or more shall require equipotential bonding only on the pool side of the permanent wall or building.

    (a) 3
    (b) 5
    (c) 10
    (d) 12

21. The swimming pool structure, including the structural reinforcing steel of the pool shell and deck, except reinforcing steel encapsulated with a nonconductive compound, shall be bonded.

    (a) True
    (b) False

22. Which of the following shall be bonded?

    (a) Metal parts of electrical equipment associated with the pool water circulating system.
    (b) Pool structural metal.
    (c) Metal fittings within or attached to the pool.
    (d) all of these

23. In the interior of a dwelling unit or in the interior of another building or structure associated with a dwelling unit, any of the wiring methods recognized or permitted in Chapter 3 of this *Code* shall be permitted to be used for the connection to the motor disconnecting means and the motor, heating, and control loads that are part of a self-contained _____ or a packaged spa or hot tub equipment assembly.

    (a) spa
    (b) hot tub
    (c) a or b
    (d) none of these

24. The equipotential bonding requirements for perimeter surfaces contained in 680.26(B)(2) don't apply to a listed self-contained spa or hot tub installed above a finished floor.

    (a) True
    (b) False

25. Metal parts of electric equipment associated with an indoor spa or hot tub water circulating system shall be bonded together unless they are a part of a listed, labeled, and identified self-contained spa or hot tub.

    (a) True
    (b) False

26. Metal raceways and metal piping within _____ ft of the inside walls of an indoor spa or hot tub, and not separated from the indoor spa or hot tub by a permanent barrier, shall be bonded together.

    (a) 4
    (b) 5
    (c) 7
    (d) 12

27. Metal piping systems associated with a fountain shall be bonded to the equipment grounding conductor of the _____.

    (a) branch circuit supplying the fountain
    (b) bonding grid
    (c) equipotential plane
    (d) grounding electrode system

28. Fountain equipment supplied by a flexible cord shall have all exposed noncurrent-carrying metal parts grounded by an insulated copper equipment grounding conductor that is an integral part of the cord.

    (a) True
    (b) False

29. Where installed for hydromassage bathtubs, _____ shall be bonded together.

    (a) all exposed metal surfaces that are within 5 ft of the inside walls of the tub and not separated from the tub area by a permanent barrier
    (b) electrical devices and controls that are not associated with the hydromassage tubs and that are located within 5 ft from such units
    (c) a and b
    (d) none of these

30. For hydromassage bathtubs, small conductive surfaces not likely to become energized, such as air and water jets, supply valve assemblies, and drain fittings not connected to metallic piping, and towel bars, mirror frames, and similar nonelectrical equipment not connected to _____ shall not be required to be bonded.

    (a) metal framing
    (b) nonmetallic framing
    (c) metal gas piping
    (d) any of these

31. The 8 AWG solid bonding jumper required for equipotential bonding in the area of hydromassage bathtubs shall not be required to be extended to any _____.

    (a) remote panelboard
    (b) service equipment
    (c) electrode
    (d) any of these

Article 690. Solar Photovoltaic (PV) Systems

32. The provisions of 690 apply to solar _____ systems, including inverter(s), array circuit(s), and controller(s) for such systems.

    (a) photoconductive
    (b) PV
    (c) photogenic
    (d) photosynthesis

33. A mechanically integrated assembly of PV modules or panels with a support structure and foundation, tracker, and other components, as required, to form a dc or ac power-producing unit, is known as a(n) "_____."

    (a) pulse width modulator
    (b) array
    (c) capacitive supply bank
    (d) alternating-current photovoltaic module

34. A solar PV system that operates in parallel with, and may deliver power to, an electrical production and distribution network is known as a(n) "_____ system."

    (a) hybrid
    (b) inverted
    (c) interactive
    (d) internal

35. For PV systems, a(n) _____ is a device that changes direct-current input to an alternating-current output.

    (a) diode
    (b) rectifier
    (c) transistor
    (d) inverter

36. A ground-fault protection device or system required for PV systems shall _____.

    (a) interrupt the flow of fault current
    (b) detect a ground-fault current
    (c) be listed for PV ground-fault protection
    (d) b and c

37. Faulted circuits required to have ground-fault protection in a photovoltaic system shall be isolated by automatically disconnecting the _____ conductors, or the inverter charge controller fed by the faulted circuits shall automatically stop supplying power to output circuits.

    (a) ungrounded
    (b) grounded
    (c) equipment grounding
    (d) all of these

38. A grounded _____-wire PV system has one functional grounded conductor.

    (a) 2
    (b) 3
    (c) 4
    (d) 5

39. The direct-current system grounding connection shall be made at any _____ point(s) on the PV output circuit.

    (a) single
    (b) two
    (c) three
    (d) four

40. For PV systems, metallic mounting structures used for grounding purposes shall be _____ as equipment grounding conductors or have _____ bonding jumpers or devices connected between the separate metallic sections and be bonded to the grounding system.

    (a) listed, labeled
    (b) labeled, listed
    (c) identified, identified
    (d) a and b

41. Devices and systems used for mounting PV modules that also provide grounding of the module frames shall be _____ for the purpose of grounding PV modules.

    (a) listed
    (b) labeled
    (c) identified
    (d) all of these

42. Devices _____ for bonding the metallic frames of PV modules shall be permitted to bond the exposed metallic frames of PV modules to the metallic frames of adjacent PV modules.

    (a) listed
    (b) labeled
    (c) identified
    (d) all of these

43. All conductors of a circuit, including the equipment grounding conductor, shall be installed in the same raceway or cable, or otherwise run with the PV array circuit conductors when they leave the vicinity of the PV array.

    (a) True
    (b) False

44. Where no overcurrent protection is provided for the PV circuit, an assumed overcurrent device rated in accordance with 690.9(B) shall be used to size the equipment grounding conductor in accordance with _____.

    (a) 250.122
    (b) 250.66
    (c) Table 250.122
    (d) Table 250.66

45. Where exposed and subject to physical damage, PV array equipment grounding conductors smaller than 4 AWG shall be protected by a raceway or cable armor.

    (a) True
    (b) False

CHAPTER 8
COMMUNICATIONS SYSTEMS

Introduction to Chapter 8—Communications Systems

Chapter 8 of the *National Electrical Code* covers the wiring requirements for communications systems such as telephones, radio and TV antennas, satellite dishes, closed-circuit television (CCTV), and coaxial cable systems. ▶Figure 1

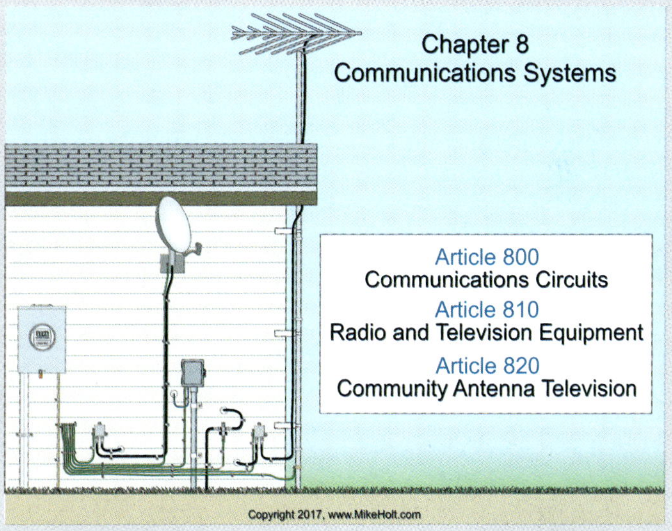

Communications systems aren't subject to the general requirements contained in Chapters 1 through 4 or the special requirements of Chapters 5 through 7, except where a Chapter 8 rule specifically refers to one of those chapters [90.3]. Also, installations of communications equipment under the exclusive control of communications utilities located outdoors, or in building spaces used exclusively for such installations, are exempt from the *NEC* [90.2(B)(4)].

▶Figure 1

- **Article 800—Communications Circuits.** Article 800 covers the installation requirements for telephone wiring and for other related telecommunications purposes such as computer local area networks (LANs), and outside wiring for fire and burglar alarm systems connected to central stations.

- **Article 810—Radio and Television Equipment.** This article covers antenna systems for radio and television receiving equipment, amateur radio transmitting and receiving equipment, and certain features of transmitter safety. It also includes antennas such as multi-element, vertical rod and dish, and the wiring and cabling that connects them to the equipment.

- **Article 820—Community Antenna Television (CATV) and Radio Distribution Systems (Coaxial Cable).** Article 820 covers the installation of coaxial cables to distribute limited-energy high-frequency signals for television, cable TV, and closed-circuit television (CCTV), which is often used for security purposes. It also covers the premises wiring of satellite TV systems where the dish antenna is outside and covered by Article 810.

Notes

ARTICLE 800 COMMUNICATIONS CIRCUITS

Introduction to Article 800—Communications Circuits

This article has its roots in telephone technology. Consequently, it addresses telephone and related systems that use twisted-pair wiring. Here are a few key points to remember about Article 800:

- Don't attach incoming communications cables to the service-entrance power mast.
- Keep the grounding electrode conductor for the primary protector as straight and as short as possible.
- If you locate communications cables above a suspended ceiling, route and support them to allow access via ceiling panel removal.
- Keep these cables separated from lightning protection circuits.
- If you install communications cables in a Chapter 3 raceway, you must do so in conformance with the *NEC* requirements for the raceway system.
- Special labeling and marking provisions apply—follow them carefully.

Part I. General

800.1 Scope

This article covers communications circuits and equipment that extend voice, audio, video, interactive services, and outside wiring for fire alarms and burglar alarms from the communications utility to the customer's communications equipment up to and including equipment such as a telephone, fax machine or answering machine, and communications equipment [800.2 Communications Circuit]. ▶Figure 800–1

Note: Communications circuits and equipment under the exclusive control of the communications utility are exempt from the *NEC* requirement, see 90.2(B)(4).

Author's Comment:

- The definition of "Communications Equipment" is contained in Article 100.

▶Figure 800–1

800.90 | Communications Circuits

Part III. Protection

800.90 Primary Protection

(A) Application. A listed primary protector is required for each communications circuit, and it must be installed in accordance with 110.3(B). ▶Figure 800–2

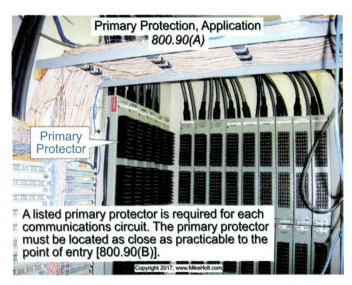
▶Figure 800–2

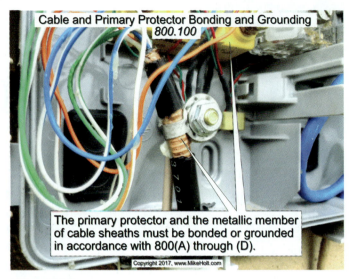
▶Figure 800–3

(2) Material. The conductor must be copper or other corrosion-resistant conductive material, stranded or solid.

(3) Size. The conductor isn't permitted to be smaller than 14 AWG with a current-carrying capacity of not less than the grounded metallic sheath member(s) or protected conductor(s) of the communications cable, but it's not required to be larger than 6 AWG.

(4) Length. The bonding conductor or grounding electrode conductor must be as short as practicable. For one- and two-family dwellings, the bonding conductor or grounding electrode conductor must not exceed 20 ft in length. ▶Figure 800–4

Author's Comment:

- Selecting a primary protector location to achieve the shortest practicable primary protector bonding conductor or grounding electrode conductor helps reduce differences in voltage between communications circuits and other metallic systems during lightning events.

Part IV. Grounding Methods

800.100 Cable and Primary Protector Bonding and Grounding

The primary protector and the metallic member of cable sheaths must be bonded or grounded in accordance with 800(A) through (D). ▶Figure 800–3

(A) Bonding Conductor or Grounding Electrode Conductor.

(1) Insulation. The conductor must be listed and can be insulated, covered, or bare.

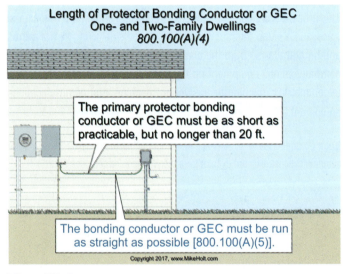
▶Figure 800–4

284 Mike Holt's Illustrated Guide to Understanding 2017 NEC Requirements for Bonding and Grounding

ARTICLE 810 — RADIO AND TELEVISION SATELLITE EQUIPMENT

Introduction to Article 810—Radio and Television Satellite Equipment

This article covers transmitter and receiver (antenna) equipment—and the wiring and cabling associated with that equipment. Here are a few key points to remember about Article 810:

- Avoid contact with conductors of other systems.
- Don't attach antennas or other equipment to the service-entrance power mast.
- Keep the bonding conductor or grounding electrode conductor as straight as practicable, and protect it from physical damage.
- If the mast isn't bonded properly, you risk flashovers and possible electrocution.
- Keep in mind that the purpose of bonding is to prevent a difference of voltage between metallic objects and other conductive items, such as swimming pools.
- Clearances are critical, and Article 810 contains detailed clearance requirements. For example, it provides separate clearance requirements for indoor and outdoor locations.

Part I. General

810.1 Scope

Article 810 contains the installation requirements for the wiring of television and radio receiving equipment, such as digital satellite receiving equipment for television signals and amateur/citizen band radio equipment antennas. ▶Figure 810–1

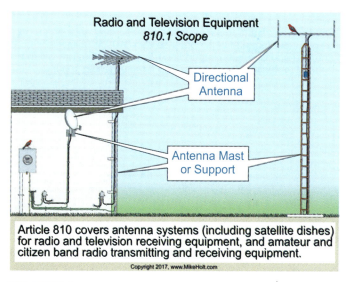

Article 810 covers antenna systems (including satellite dishes) for radio and television receiving equipment, and amateur and citizen band radio transmitting and receiving equipment.

▶Figure 810–1

Author's Comment:

■ Article 810 covers:
  ♦ Antennas that receive local television signals.
  ♦ Satellite antennas, which are often referred to as satellite dishes.
  ♦ Roof-mounted antennas for AM/FM/XM radio reception.
  ♦ Amateur radio transmitting and receiving equipment, including HAM radio equipment (a noncommercial [amateur] communications system).

810.7 | Radio and Television Satellite Equipment

810.7 Grounding Devices

Fittings used to connect bonding jumpers or grounding electrode conductors to equipment must be listed.

Part II. Receiving Equipment—Antenna Systems

810.15 Metal Antenna Supports—Grounding

Outdoor masts and metal structures that support antennas must be grounded in accordance with 810.21, unless the antenna and its related supporting mast or structure are within a zone of protection defined by a 150-ft radius rolling sphere. ▶Figure 810–2

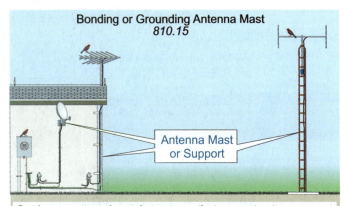

▶Figure 810–2

Note: See NFPA 780, *Standard for the Installation of Lightning Protection Systems*, 4.8.3.1 for the application of the term "rolling sphere."

810.20 Antenna Discharge Unit

(A) Where Required. Each lead-in conductor from an outdoor antenna must be provided with a listed antenna discharge unit. ▶Figure 810–3

(B) Location. The antenna discharge unit must be located outside or inside the building, nearest the point of entrance, but not near combustible material or in a hazardous (classified) location as defined in Article 500.

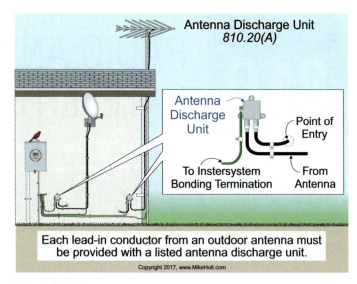

▶Figure 810–3

(C) Grounding. The antenna discharge unit must be bonded or grounded in accordance with 810.21.

810.21 Bonding Conductor and Grounding Electrode Conductors

The antenna mast [810.15] and antenna discharge unit [810.20(C)] must be bonded or grounded as follows.

(A) Material. The bonding conductor to the intersystem bonding termination or grounding electrode conductor to the grounding electrode [810.21(F)] must be copper or other corrosion-resistant conductive material. ▶Figure 810–4

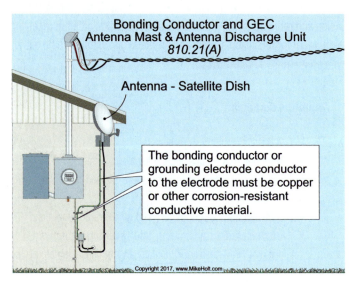

▶Figure 810–4

(B) Insulation. Insulation on bonding conductors or grounding electrode conductors isn't required.

(C) Supports. The bonding conductor or grounding electrode conductor must be securely fastened in place.

(D) Physical Protection. Bonding conductors or grounding electrode conductors must be mechanically protected where subject to physical damage; and where installed in a metal raceway, both ends of the raceway must be bonded to the bonding conductor or grounding electrode conductor. ▶Figure 810–5

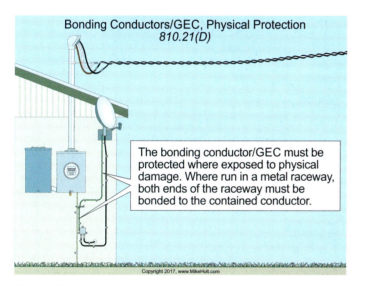

▶Figure 810–5

Author's Comment:

- Installing the bonding conductor or grounding electrode conductor in PVC conduit is a better practice.

(E) Run in Straight Line. The bonding conductor or grounding electrode conductor must be run in as straight a line as practicable.

Author's Comment:

- Lightning doesn't like to travel around corners or through loops, which is why the bonding conductor or grounding electrode conductor must be run as straight as practicable.

(F) Electrode. The bonding conductor or grounding electrode conductor must terminate in accordance with (1), (2), or (3).

(1) Buildings with an Intersystem Bonding Termination. The bonding conductor for the antenna mast and antenna discharge unit must terminate to the intersystem bonding termination as required by 250.94 [Article 100 and 250.94]. ▶Figure 810–6

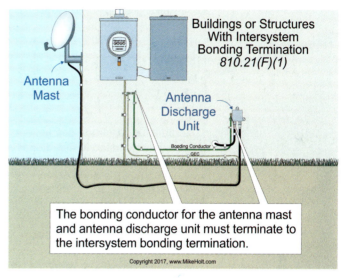

▶Figure 810–6

(2) In Buildings Without Intersystem Bonding Termination. The bonding conductor or grounding electrode conductor for the antenna mast and antenna discharge unit must terminate to the nearest accessible location on the following: ▶Figure 810–7

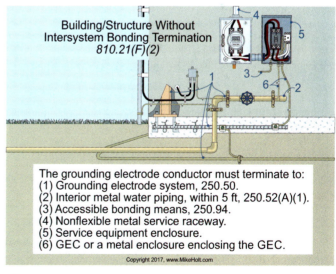

▶Figure 810–7

810.21 | Radio and Television Satellite Equipment

(1) The building grounding electrode system [250.50].

(2) The interior metal water piping system, within 5 ft from its point of entrance [250.52(A)(1)]. ▶Figure 810–8

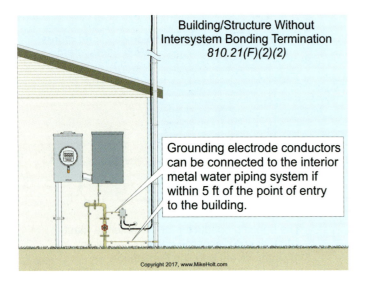
▶Figure 810–8

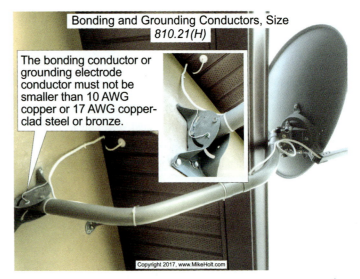
▶Figure 810–9

(3) The power service accessible means external to the building, as covered in 250.94, including the exception.

(4) The nonflexible metallic service raceway.

(5) The service equipment enclosure.

(6) The grounding electrode conductor or the grounding electrode conductor metal enclosure.

(3) In Buildings Without a Grounding Means. The grounding electrode conductor for the antenna mast and antenna discharge unit must be connected to a grounding electrode as described in 250.52.

(G) Inside or Outside Building. The bonding conductor or grounding electrode conductor can be installed either inside or outside the building.

(H) Size. The bonding conductor or grounding electrode conductor isn't permitted to be smaller than 10 AWG copper or 17 AWG copper-clad steel or bronze. ▶Figure 810–9

(J) Bonding of Electrodes. If a ground rod is installed to serve as the grounding electrode for the radio and television equipment, it must be bonded to the building's power grounding electrode system with a minimum 6 AWG conductor. ▶Figure 810–10

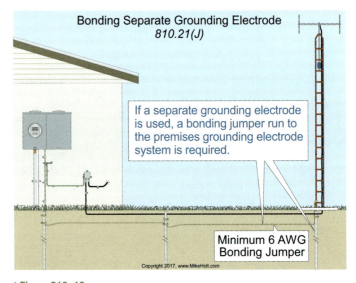
▶Figure 810–10

Author's Comment:

- Bonding of electrodes helps reduce induced voltage differences between the power and communications systems during lightning events. ▶Figure 810–11

(K) Electrode Connection. Termination of the bonding conductor or grounding electrode conductor must be by exothermic welding, listed lugs, listed pressure connectors, or listed clamps. Grounding fittings that are concrete-encased or buried in the earth must be listed for direct burial in accordance with 250.70.

Radio and Television Satellite Equipment | 810.58

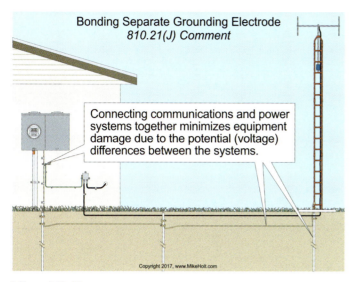

▶Figure 810–11

Author's Comment:

- Grounding the lead-in antenna cables and the mast helps prevent voltage surges caused by static discharge or nearby lightning strikes from reaching the center conductor of the lead-in coaxial cable. Because the satellite dish sits outdoors, wind creates a static charge on the antenna as well as on the cable to which it's attached. This charge can build up on both the antenna and the cable until it jumps across an air space, often passing through the electronics inside the low noise block down converter feedhorn (LNBF) or receiver. Connecting the coaxial cable and dish to the building's grounding electrode system (grounding) helps dissipate this static charge.

- Nothing can prevent damage from a direct lightning strike, but grounding with proper surge protection can help reduce damage to the satellite dish and other equipment from nearby lightning strikes.

Part III. Amateur and Citizen Band Transmitting and Receiving Antenna Systems

810.57 Antenna Discharge Units

Each lead-in conductor from an outdoor antenna must be provided with a listed antenna discharge unit or other suitable means that drains static charges from the antenna system.

Ex 1: If the lead-in is protected by a continuous metallic shield that's grounded in accordance with 810.58, an antenna discharge unit or other suitable means isn't required.

Ex 2: If the antenna is grounded in accordance with 810.58, an antenna discharge unit or other suitable means isn't required.

810.58 Bonding Conductor or Grounding Electrode Conductors

(A) Other Sections. The antenna mast [810.15] and antenna discharge unit [810.57] must be grounded as specified in 810.21.

(B) Size of Protective Bonding Conductor or Grounding Electrode Conductor. The bonding conductor or grounding electrode conductor must be the same size as the lead-in conductors, but not smaller than 10 AWG copper, bronze, or copper-clad steel.

(C) Size of Operating Bonding Conductor or Grounding Electrode Conductor. The operating bonding conductor or grounding electrode conductor for transmitting stations isn't permitted to be smaller than 14 AWG copper or its equivalent.

Notes

ARTICLE 820

COMMUNITY ANTENNA TELEVISION (CATV) AND RADIO DISTRIBUTION SYSTEMS (COAXIAL CABLE)

Introduction to Article 820—Community Antenna Television (CATV) and Radio Distribution Systems (Coaxial Cable)

This article focuses on the distribution of television and radio signals within a facility or on a property via cable, rather than their transmission or reception via antenna. These signals are limited energy, but they're high frequency.

- As with Article 800, you must determine the "point of entrance" for these circuits.
- Ground the incoming coaxial cable as close as practicable to the point of entrance.
- If coaxial cables are located above a suspended ceiling, route and support them to allow access via ceiling panel removal.
- Clearances are critical, and Article 820 contains detailed clearance requirements. For example, it requires at least 6 ft of clearance between coaxial cable and lightning conductors.
- If the building or structure has an intersystem bonding termination device, the bonding conductor must be connected to it.
- If you use a separate grounding electrode, you must run a bonding jumper to the power grounding system.

Author's Comment:

- For Articles 800, 810, and 820, the difference between a "bonding conductor" and a "grounding electrode conductor" is where they terminate. The bonding conductor terminates at the intersystem bonding termination; the grounding electrode conductor connects to the power grounding electrode system [250.50].

Part I. General

820.1 Scope

Article 820 covers the installation of coaxial cables for distributing high-frequency signals. ▶Figure 820–1

Note: The NEC installation requirements don't apply to communications utility equipment, such as coaxial cables located outdoors or in building spaces under the exclusive control of the communications utility [90.2(B)(4)]. ▶Figure 820–2

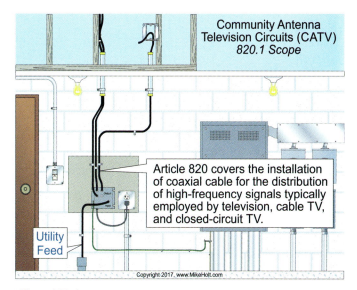

▶Figure 820–1

820.93 | Community Antenna Television (CATV) and Radio Distribution Systems (Coaxial Cable)

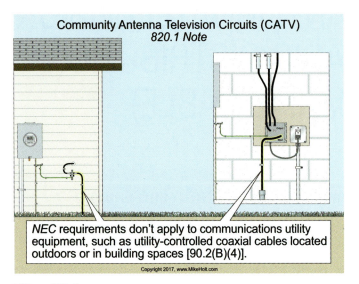

▶Figure 820–2

Author's Comment:

- Coaxial cables that connect antennas to television and radio receiving equipment [810.3] and community television systems [810.4] must be installed in accordance with this article. ▶Figure 820–3

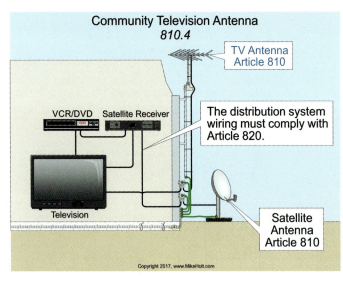

▶Figure 820–3

Part III. Protection

820.93 Grounding of the Outer Conductive Shield of Coaxial Cables

(A) Coaxial Cables Entering Building. Coaxial cables supplied to a building must have the metallic sheath members bonded and/or grounded as close as practicable to the point of entrance in accordance with 820.100. ▶Figure 820–4

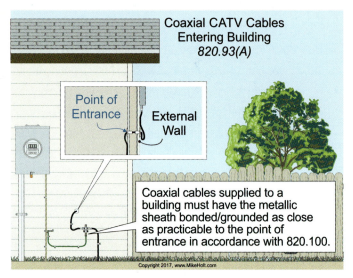

▶Figure 820–4

Part IV. Grounding Methods

820.100 Bonding and Grounding Methods

The outer conductive shield of a coaxial cable must be bonded or grounded in accordance with the following:

Ex: For systems using coaxial cable completely contained within the building (they don't exit the building) and isolated from outside cable systems, the shield can be grounded by a connection to an equipment grounding conductor as described in 250.118. This connection can be made through a grounded receptacle using a dedicated bonding jumper and a permanently connected listed device.

Use of a cord and plug for the connection to an equipment grounding conductor isn't permitted.

(A) Bonding Conductor or Grounding Electrode Conductor.

(1) Insulation. The bonding conductor or grounding electrode conductor must be listed and can be insulated, covered, or bare.

(2) Material. The bonding conductor or grounding electrode conductor must be copper or other corrosion-resistant conductive material, stranded or solid.

(3) Size. The bonding conductor or grounding electrode conductor isn't permitted to be smaller than 14 AWG with a current-carrying capacity of not less than the outer sheath of the coaxial cable, but not required to be larger than 6 AWG.

(4) Length. The bonding conductor or grounding electrode conductor must be as short as practicable. For one- and two-family dwellings, the bonding conductor or grounding electrode conductor must not exceed 20 ft. ▶Figure 820–5

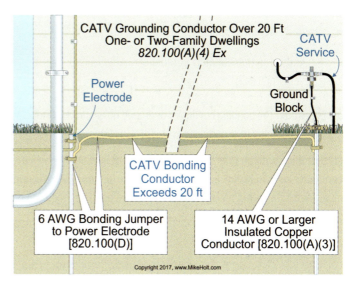
▶Figure 820–6

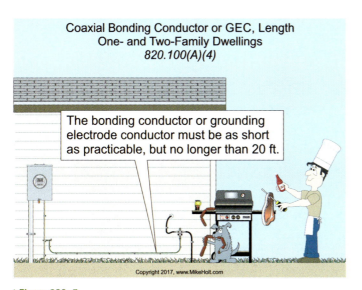
▶Figure 820–5

Note: Limiting the length of the bonding conductor or grounding electrode conductor at other than dwelling units will help to reduce voltage differences between the building's power and CATV systems during lightning events.

Ex: If it's not practicable to limit the coaxial bonding conductor or grounding electrode conductor to 20 ft in length for one- and two-family dwellings, a separate rod not less than 8 ft long [250.52(A)(5)], with fittings suitable for the application [250.70] must be installed. The additional rod must be bonded to the power grounding electrode system with a minimum 6 AWG conductor [820.100(D)]. ▶Figure 820–6

(5) Run in Straight Line. The bonding conductor or grounding electrode conductor to the electrode must be run in as straight a line as practicable.

Author's Comment:

- Lightning doesn't like to travel around corners or through loops, which is why the bonding conductor or grounding electrode conductor must be run as straight as practicable.

(6) Physical Protection. The bonding conductor or grounding electrode conductor must be mechanically protected where subject to physical damage, and where installed in a metal raceway both ends of the raceway must be bonded to the bonding conductor or grounding electrode conductor. ▶Figure 820–7

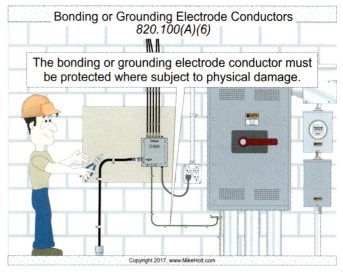
▶Figure 820–7

820.100 | Community Antenna Television (CATV) and Radio Distribution Systems (Coaxial Cable)

Author's Comment:

- Installing the bonding conductor in PVC conduit is a better practice.

(B) Electrode. The bonding conductor or grounding electrode conductor must be connected in accordance with (B)(1), (B)(2), or (B)(3).

(1) Buildings With an Intersystem Bonding Termination. The bonding conductor or grounding electrode conductor for the CATV system must terminate to the intersystem bonding termination as required by 250.94. ▶Figure 820–8

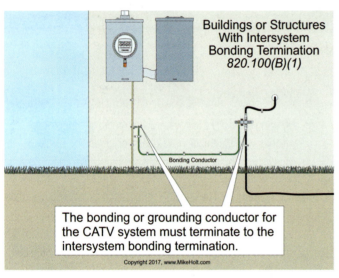

▶Figure 820–8

Author's Comment:

- According to the Article 100 definition, an "Intersystem Bonding Termination" is a device that provides a means to connect bonding conductors for communications systems to the grounding electrode system, in accordance with 250.94. ▶Figure 820–9

- Bonding all systems to the intersystem bonding termination helps reduce induced voltage differences between the power and the radio and television systems during lightning events.

(2) In Buildings With Grounding Means. If an intersystem bonding termination is established, 250.94(A) applies. If not, at existing structures, the bonding conductor or grounding electrode conductor must terminate to the nearest accessible: ▶Figure 820–10

(1) Building grounding electrode system [250.50].

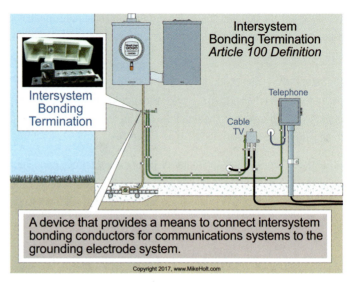

▶Figure 820–9

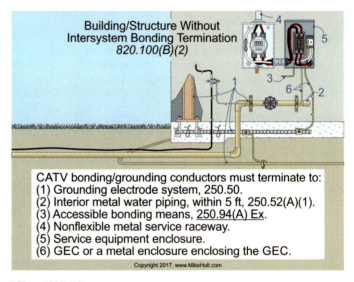

▶Figure 820–10

(2) Interior metal water piping system, within 5 ft from its point of entrance [250.52(A)(1)].

(3) Accessible means external to the building, using the options contained in 250.94(A) Ex.

(4) Nonflexible metallic service raceway of the power service.

(5) Service equipment enclosure.

(6) Grounding electrode conductor or the grounding electrode conductor metal enclosure.

(7) The grounding electrode conductor or the grounding electrode of a remote building disconnect [250.32].

The intersystem bonding termination must be mounted on the fixed part of an enclosure so it won't interfere with the opening of an enclosure door. A bonding device isn't permitted to be mounted on a door or cover even if the door or cover is nonremovable.

(3) In Buildings Without Intersystem Bonding Termination or Grounding Means. The bonding conductor or grounding electrode conductor must connect to:

(1) Any one of the individual grounding electrodes described in 250.52(A)(1), (A)(2), (A)(3), (A)(4), or

(2) Any individual grounding electrodes described in 250.52(A)(5), 250.52(A)(7), and (A)(8). ▶Figure 820–11

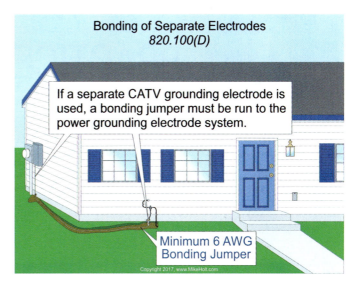

▶Figure 820–12

Note 2: Bonding all systems to the intersystem bonding termination device helps reduce induced voltage between the power and CATV system during lightning events. ▶Figure 820–13

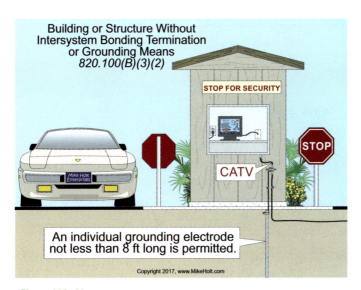

▶Figure 820–11

(C) Electrode Connection. Terminations to the grounding electrode must be by exothermic welding, listed lugs, listed pressure connectors, or clamps. Grounding fittings that are concrete-encased or buried in the earth must be listed for direct burial [250.70].

(D) Bonding of Electrodes. If a separate grounding electrode, such as a rod, is installed for the CATV system, it must be bonded to the building's power grounding electrode system with a minimum 6 AWG conductor. ▶Figure 820–12

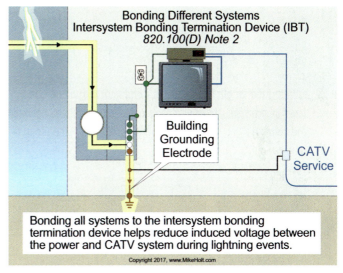

▶Figure 820–13

CHAPTER 8 PRACTICE QUESTIONS

Please use the 2017 *Code* book to answer the following questions.

Article 800. Communications Circuits

1. In one- and two-family dwellings, the primary protector bonding conductor or grounding electrode conductor for communications systems shall be as short as practicable, not to exceed _____ ft in length.

    (a) 5
    (b) 8
    (c) 10
    (d) 20

2. Limiting the length of the primary protector grounding conductors for communications circuits helps to reduce voltage between the building's _____ and communications systems during lightning events.

    (a) power
    (b) fire alarm
    (c) lighting
    (d) lightning protection

3. In one- and two-family dwellings where it is not practicable to achieve an overall maximum primary protector grounding electrode conductor length of 20 ft, a separate communications ground rod not less than _____ ft shall be driven and it shall be connected to the power grounding electrode system with a 6 AWG conductor.

    (a) 5
    (b) 8
    (c) 10
    (d) 20

4. For buildings with a grounding means but without an intersystem bonding termination, the grounding electrode conductor for communications circuits shall terminate to the power service accessible means external to enclosures using the options identified in 250.94(A) Ex.

    (a) True
    (b) False

5. Communications grounding electrodes shall be bonded to the power grounding electrode system at the building or structure served using a minimum _____ AWG copper bonding jumper.

    (a) 10
    (b) 8
    (c) 6
    (d) 4

Article 810. Radio and Television Equipment

6. Masts and metal structures supporting antennas shall be grounded in accordance with 810.21, unless the antenna and its related supporting mast or structure are within a zone of protection defined by a _____ radius rolling sphere.

    (a) 75-ft
    (b) 100-ft
    (c) 125-ft
    (d) 150-ft

7. NFPA 780-2014, *Standard for the Installation of Lightning Protection Systems*, provides information for the application of the term "rolling sphere" as used in 810.15.

    (a) True
    (b) False

8. Antenna discharge units shall be located outside the building only.

    (a) True
    (b) False

9. Radio and television receiving antenna systems shall have bonding or grounding electrode conductors that are _____.

    (a) copper or other corrosion-resistant conductive material
    (b) insulated, covered, or bare
    (c) securely fastened in place and protected where subject to physical damage
    (d) all of these

10. The grounding electrode conductor for an antenna mast shall be _____ where subject to physical damage.

    (a) electrically protected
    (b) protected
    (c) connected
    (d) disconnected

11. The bonding conductor or grounding electrode conductor for a radio/television antenna system shall be protected where subject to physical damage, and where installed in a metal raceway, both ends of the raceway shall be bonded to the _____ conductor.

    (a) contained
    (b) grounded
    (c) ungrounded
    (d) b or c

12. The bonding conductor or grounding electrode conductor for an antenna mast or antenna discharge unit shall be run to the grounding electrode in as straight a line as practicable.

    (a) True
    (b) False

13. If the building or structure served has an intersystem bonding termination, the bonding conductor for an antenna mast shall be connected to the intersystem bonding termination.

    (a) True
    (b) False

14. The grounding electrode conductor for an antenna mast or antenna discharge unit, if copper, shall not be smaller than 10 AWG.

    (a) True
    (b) False

15. If a separate grounding electrode is installed for the radio and television equipment, it shall be bonded to the building's electrical power grounding electrode system with a bonding jumper not smaller than _____ AWG.

    (a) 10
    (b) 8
    (c) 6
    (d) 1/0

Article 820. Community Antenna Television (CATV) and Ratio Distribution Systems

16. Article _____ covers the installation of coaxial cables for distributing radio frequency signals typically employed in community antenna television (CATV) systems.

    (a) 300
    (b) 430
    (c) 800
    (d) 820

17. The outer conductive shield of a CATV coaxial cable entering a building shall be grounded as close to the point of entrance as practicable.

    (a) True
    (b) False

18. For communications systems using coaxial cable completely contained within the building (that is, they do not exit the building) or the exterior zone of protection defined by a _____ radius rolling sphere and isolated from outside cable plant, the shield shall be permitted to be grounded by a connection to an equipment grounding conductor as described in 250.118.

    (a) 75-ft
    (b) 100-ft
    (c) 125-ft
    (d) 150-ft

19. The conductor used to ground the outer cover of a CATV coaxial cable shall be permitted to be _____.

    (a) insulated
    (b) 14 AWG minimum
    (c) bare
    (d) all of these

20. In one- and two-family dwellings, the grounding electrode conductor for CATV systems shall be as short as practicable, not to exceed _____ ft in length.

    (a) 5
    (b) 8
    (c) 10
    (d) 20

21. Limiting the length of the primary protector grounding conductors for community antenna television and radio systems reduces voltages that may develop between the building's _____ and communications systems during lightning events.

    (a) power
    (b) fire alarm
    (c) lighting
    (d) lightning protection

22. In one- and two-family dwellings where it is not practicable to achieve an overall maximum bonding conductor or equipment grounding conductor length of _____ ft for CATV, a separate grounding electrode as specified in 250.52(A)(5), (A)(6), or (A)(7) shall be used.

    (a) 5
    (b) 8
    (c) 10
    (d) 20

23. Bonding conductors and grounding electrode conductors shall be _____ where exposed to physical damage.

    (a) electrically continuous
    (b) arc-fault labeled
    (c) protected
    (d) none of these

24. For community antenna television and radio distribution systems, where the building or structure served has an intersystem bonding termination established, 250.94(a) shall apply.

    (a) True
    (b) False

25. For community antenna television and radio distribution systems, where the building or structure served has no intersystem bonding termination, the bonding conductor or grounding electrode conductor can be connected to the power service accessible means external to enclosures using the options identified in 250.94(A) Ex.

    (a) True
    (b) False

26. A bonding jumper not smaller than _____ AWG copper or equivalent shall be connected between the CATV system's grounding electrode and the power grounding electrode system at the building or structure served where separate electrodes are used.

    (a) 12
    (b) 8
    (c) 6
    (d) 4

FINAL EXAM A— STRAIGHT ORDER

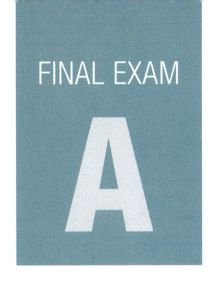

Please use the 2017 *Code* book to answer the following questions.

Article 90. Introduction to the *National Electrical Code*

1. The *NEC* is _____.

   (a) intended to be a design manual
   (b) meant to be used as an instruction guide for untrained persons
   (c) for the practical safeguarding of persons and property
   (d) published by the Bureau of Standards

2. Which of the following systems shall be installed and removed in accordance with the *NEC* requirements?

   (a) Signaling conductors, equipment, and raceways.
   (b) Communications conductors, equipment, and raceways.
   (c) Electrical conductors, equipment, and raceways.
   (d) all of these

3. Installations of communications equipment that are under the exclusive control of communications utilities, and located outdoors or in building spaces used exclusively for such installations _____ covered by the *NEC*.

   (a) are
   (b) are sometimes
   (c) are not
   (d) may be

4. Chapters 1 through 4 of the *NEC* apply _____.

   (a) generally to all electrical installations
   (b) only to special occupancies and conditions
   (c) only to special equipment and material
   (d) all of these

5. The _____ has the responsibility for deciding on the approval of equipment and materials.

   (a) manufacturer
   (b) authority having jurisdiction
   (c) testing agency
   (d) none of these

6. When the *Code* uses "_____," it means the identified actions are allowed but not required, and they may be options or alternative methods.

   (a) shall
   (b) shall not
   (c) shall be permitted
   (d) a or b

Article 100. Definitions

7. Capable of being removed or exposed without damaging the building structure or finish, or not permanently closed in by the structure or finish of the building is known as "_____."

   (a) accessible (as applied to equipment)
   (b) accessible (as applied to wiring methods)
   (c) accessible, readily
   (d) all of these

8. The connection between the grounded circuit conductor and the supply-side bonding jumper or equipment grounding conductor, or both, at a _____ is called a "system bonding jumper."

   (a) service disconnect
   (b) separately derived system
   (c) motor control center
   (d) separate building or structure disconnect

9. An effective ground-fault current path is an intentionally constructed, low-impedance electrically conductive path designed and intended to carry current during a ground-fault condition from the point of a ground fault on a wiring system to _____.

   (a) ground
   (b) earth
   (c) the electrical supply source
   (d) none of these

10. The *NEC* defines a "_____" as all circuit conductors between the service equipment, the source of a separately derived system, or other power supply source, and the final branch-circuit overcurrent device.

    (a) service
    (b) feeder
    (c) branch circuit
    (d) all of these

11. Connected to ground without the insertion of any resistor or impedance device is referred to as "_____."

    (a) grounded
    (b) solidly grounded
    (c) effectively grounded
    (d) grounding conductor

12. A conductor used to connect the system grounded conductor, or the equipment to a grounding electrode or to a point on the grounding electrode system, is called the "_____ conductor."

    (a) main grounding
    (b) common main
    (c) equipment grounding
    (d) grounding electrode

13. A handhole enclosure is an enclosure for use in underground systems, provided with an open or closed bottom, and sized to allow personnel to _____.

    (a) enter and exit freely
    (b) reach into but not enter
    (c) have full working space
    (d) visually examine the interior

14. Equipment or materials included in a list published by a testing laboratory acceptable to the authority having jurisdiction are said to be "_____."

    (a) booked
    (b) a digest
    (c) a manifest
    (d) listed

15. A panel, including buses and automatic overcurrent devices, designed to be placed in a cabinet or cutout box and accessible only from the front is known as a "_____."

    (a) switchboard
    (b) disconnect
    (c) panelboard
    (d) switch

16. A raceway is an enclosed channel designed expressly for the holding of wires, cables, or busbars, with additional functions as permitted in the *Code*.

    (a) True
    (b) False

17. Service conductors originate at the service point and terminate at the service disconnecting means.

    (a) True
    (b) False

18. A "structure" is that which is built or constructed, other than equipment.

    (a) True
    (b) False

Final Exam A—Straight Order

Article 110. Requirements for Electrical Installations

19. Conductor sizes are expressed in American Wire Gage (AWG) or in _____.

    (a) inches
    (b) circular mils
    (c) square inches
    (d) cubic inches

20. Connection of conductors to terminal parts shall ensure a thoroughly good connection without damaging the conductors and shall be made by means of _____.

    (a) solder lugs
    (b) pressure connectors
    (c) splices to flexible leads
    (d) any of these

21. Soldered splices shall first be spliced or joined so as to be mechanically and electrically secure without solder and then be soldered.

    (a) True
    (b) False

Article 250. Grounding and Bonding

22. A conductor installed on the supply side of a service or within a service equipment enclosure, or for a separately derived system, to ensure the required electrical conductivity between metal parts required to be electrically connected is known as the "_____."

    (a) supply-side bonding jumper
    (b) ungrounded conductor
    (c) electrical supply source
    (d) grounding electrode conductor

23. For grounded systems, normally noncurrent-carrying conductive materials enclosing electrical conductors or equipment, or forming part of such equipment, shall be connected together and to the _____ to establish an effective ground-fault current path.

    (a) ground
    (b) earth
    (c) electrical supply source
    (d) none of these

24. For grounded systems, the earth is considered an effective ground-fault current path.

    (a) True
    (b) False

25. In ungrounded systems, electrical equipment, wiring, and other electrically conductive material likely to become energized shall be installed in a manner that creates a low-impedance circuit from any point on the wiring system to the electrical supply source to facilitate the operation of overcurrent devices should a(n) _____ fault from a different phase occur on the wiring system.

    (a) isolated ground
    (b) second ground
    (c) arc
    (d) high impedance

26. Equipment grounding conductors, grounding electrode conductors, and bonding jumpers shall be connected by _____.

    (a) listed pressure connectors
    (b) terminal bars
    (c) exothermic welding
    (d) any of these

27. Alternating-current circuits of less than 50V shall be grounded if supplied by a transformer whose supply system exceeds 150 volts-to-ground.

    (a) True
    (b) False

28. Ungrounded alternating-current systems from 50V to less than 1,000V shall be legibly marked "Caution: Ungrounded System—Operating _____ Volts Between Conductors" at _____ of the system, with sufficient durability to withstand the environment involved.

    (a) the source
    (b) the first disconnecting means
    (c) every junction box
    (d) a or b

Final Exam A—Straight Order

29. The grounded conductor of an alternating-current system operating at 1,000V or less shall be routed with the ungrounded conductors and connected to each disconnecting means grounded conductor terminal or bus, which is then connected to the service disconnecting means enclosure via a(n) _____ that is installed between the service neutral conductor and the service disconnecting means enclosure.

    (a) equipment bonding conductor
    (b) main bonding jumper
    (c) grounding electrode
    (d) intersystem bonding terminal

30. Where a main bonding jumper is a screw only, the screw shall be identified with a(n) _____ that shall be visible with the screw installed.

    (a) silver or white finish
    (b) etched ground symbol
    (c) hexagonal head
    (d) green finish

31. The connection of the system bonding jumper for a separately derived system shall be made _____ on the separately derived system from the source to the first system disconnecting means or overcurrent device.

    (a) in at least two locations
    (b) in every location that the grounded conductor is present
    (c) at any single point
    (d) none of these

32. The grounding electrode conductor for a single separately derived system is used to connect the grounded conductor of the derived system to the grounding electrode.

    (a) True
    (b) False

33. Each tap conductor to a common grounding electrode conductor for multiple separately derived systems shall be sized in accordance with _____, based on the derived ungrounded conductors of the separately derived system it serves.

    (a) 250.66
    (b) 250.118
    (c) 250.122
    (d) 310.15

34. A grounding electrode at a separate building or structure shall be required where one multiwire branch circuit serves the building or structure.

    (a) True
    (b) False

35. The size of the grounding electrode conductor for a building or structure supplied by a feeder shall not be smaller than that identified in _____, based on the largest ungrounded supply conductor.

    (a) 250.66
    (b) 250.122
    (c) Table 310.15(B)(16)
    (d) none of these

36. High-impedance grounded neutral systems shall be permitted for three-phase ac systems of 480V to 1,000V where _____.

    (a) the conditions of maintenance and supervision ensure that only qualified persons service the installation
    (b) ground detectors are installed on the system
    (c) line-to-neutral loads are not served
    (d) all of these

37. Metal in-ground support structures permitted as grounding electrodes include, but are not limited to, pilings, casings, and other structural metal.

    (a) True
    (b) False

38. A ground ring encircling the building or structure can be used as a grounding electrode when the _____.

    (a) ring is in direct contact with the earth
    (b) ring consists of at least 20 ft of bare copper conductor
    (c) bare copper conductor is not smaller than 2 AWG
    (d) all of these

39. _____ shall not be used as grounding electrodes.

    (a) Metal underground gas piping systems
    (b) Aluminum
    (c) Metal well casings
    (d) a and b

40. Where a metal underground water pipe is used as a grounding electrode, the continuity of the grounding path or the bonding connection to interior piping shall not rely on _____ and similar equipment.

    (a) bonding jumpers
    (b) water meters or filtering devices
    (c) grounding clamps
    (d) all of these

41. The upper end of a ground rod electrode shall be _____ ground level unless the aboveground end and the grounding electrode conductor attachment are protected against physical damage.

    (a) above
    (b) flush with
    (c) below
    (d) b or c

42. Grounding electrode conductors of the wire type shall be _____.

    (a) solid
    (b) stranded
    (c) insulated or bare
    (d) any of these

43. A(n) _____ AWG or larger copper or aluminum grounding electrode conductor exposed to physical damage shall be protected in rigid metal conduit, IMC, PVC conduit, reinforced thermosetting resin conduit Type XW (RTRC-XW), EMT, or cable armor.

    (a) 10
    (b) 8
    (c) 6
    (d) 4

44. Where service equipment consists of more than one enclosure, grounding electrode conductor connections shall be permitted to be _____.

    (a) multiple individual grounding electrode conductors
    (b) one grounding electrode conductor at a common location
    (c) a common grounding electrode conductor and taps
    (d) any of these

45. A service consisting of 12 AWG service-entrance conductors requires a grounding electrode conductor sized no less than _____ AWG.

    (a) 10
    (b) 8
    (c) 6
    (d) 4

46. Mechanical elements used to terminate a grounding electrode conductor to a grounding electrode shall be accessible.

    (a) True
    (b) False

47. Interior metal water piping that is electrically continuous with a metal underground water pipe electrode and is located not more than _____ ft from the point of entrance to the building shall be permitted to extend the connection to an electrode(s).

    (a) 2
    (b) 4
    (c) 5
    (d) 6

48. A rebar-type concrete-encased electrode installed in accordance with 250.52(A)(3) with an additional rebar section extended from its location within the concrete to an accessible location that is not subject to _____ shall be permitted for connection of grounding electrode conductors and bonding jumpers.

    (a) physical damage
    (b) moisture
    (c) corrosion
    (d) any of these

49. Metal enclosures and raceways for other than service conductors shall be connected to the neutral conductor.

    (a) True
    (b) False

50. The normally noncurrent-carrying metal parts of service equipment, such as service _____, shall be bonded together.

    (a) raceways or service cable armor
    (b) equipment enclosures containing service conductors, including meter fittings, boxes, or the like, interposed in the service raceway or armor
    (c) cable trays
    (d) all of these

51. A means external to enclosures for connecting intersystem _____ conductors shall be provided at the service equipment or metering equipment enclosure and disconnecting means of buildings or structures supplied by a feeder.

    (a) bonding
    (b) ungrounded
    (c) secondary
    (d) a and b

Final Exam A—Straight Order

52. Means for connecting intersystem bonding conductors are not required where communications systems are not likely to be used.

    (a) True
    (b) False

53. Equipment bonding jumpers on the supply side of the service shall be no smaller than the sizes specified in _____.

    (a) Table 250.102(C)(1)
    (b) Table 250.122
    (c) Table 310.15(B)(16)
    (d) Table 310.15(B)(6)

54. What is the minimum size copper equipment bonding jumper for a 40A rated circuit?

    (a) 14 AWG
    (b) 12 AWG
    (c) 10 AWG
    (d) 8 AWG

55. Where isolated metal water piping systems are installed in a multiple-occupancy building, the water pipes can be bonded with bonding jumpers sized in accordance with Table 250.122, based on the size of the _____.

    (a) service-entrance conductors
    (b) feeder conductors
    (c) rating of the service equipment overcurrent device
    (d) rating of the largest overcurrent device supplying the occupancy

56. Exposed structural metal interconnected to form a metal building frame that is not intentionally grounded or bonded and is likely to become energized, shall be bonded to the _____.

    (a) service equipment enclosure or building disconnecting means
    (b) grounded conductor at the service
    (c) grounding electrode conductor where of sufficient size
    (d) any of these

57. If exposed structural metal that is interconnected to form the building frame exists in the area served by the separately derived system, it shall be bonded to the grounded conductor of each separately derived system and each bonding jumper shall be sized in accordance with Table 250.102(C)(1) based on the largest ungrounded conductor of the service.

    (a) True
    (b) False

58. Listed FMC can be used as the equipment grounding conductor if the conduit does not exceed trade size _____.

    (a) 1¼
    (b) 1½
    (c) 2
    (d) 2¼

59. The armor of Type AC cable is recognized by the NEC as an equipment grounding conductor.

    (a) True
    (b) False

60. Equipment grounding conductors of the wire type shall not be required to be larger than the circuit conductors.

    (a) True
    (b) False

61. Where circuit conductors are installed in parallel in multiple raceways or cables and include an EGC of the wire type, the equipment grounding conductor shall be installed in parallel in each raceway or cable, sized in compliance with 250.122 based on the overcurrent protective device for the feeder or branch circuit.

    (a) True
    (b) False

62. A(n) _____ shall be used to connect the grounding terminal of a grounding-type receptacle to a grounded box.

    (a) equipment bonding jumper
    (b) grounded conductor jumper
    (c) a or b
    (d) a and b

63. The arrangement of grounding connections shall be such that the disconnection or the removal of a receptacle, luminaire, or other device fed from the box does not interrupt the grounding continuity.

    (a) True
    (b) False

Article 300. General Requirements for Wiring Methods and Materials

64. Conductors installed in nonmetallic raceways run underground shall be permitted to be arranged as _____ installations. The raceways shall be installed in close proximity, and the conductors shall comply with the provisions of 300.20(B).

    (a) neutral
    (b) grounded conductor
    (c) isolated phase
    (d) all of these

Article 314. Outlet, Device, Pull, and Junction Boxes; Conduit Bodies; Fittings; and Handhole Enclosures

65. Metal boxes shall be _____ in accordance with Article 250.

    (a) grounded
    (b) bonded
    (c) a and b
    (d) none of these

66. Handhole enclosure covers shall require the use of tools to open, or they shall weigh over _____ lb.

    (a) 45
    (b) 70
    (c) 100
    (d) 200

Article 350. Liquidtight Flexible Metal Conduit (Type LFMC)

67. When LFMC is used to connect equipment where flexibility is necessary to minimize the transmission of vibration from equipment or for equipment requiring movement after installation, a(n) _____ conductor shall be installed.

    (a) main bonding
    (b) grounded
    (c) equipment grounding
    (d) none of these

Article 362. Electrical Nonmetallic Tubing (Type ENT)

68. ENT is composed of a material resistant to moisture and chemical atmospheres, and is _____.

    (a) flexible
    (b) flame retardant
    (c) fireproof
    (d) flammable

Article 386. Surface Metal Raceways

69. Surface metal raceway enclosures providing a transition from other wiring methods shall have a means for connecting a(n) _____ conductor.

    (a) grounded
    (b) ungrounded
    (c) equipment grounding
    (d) all of these

Article 404. Switches

70. A snap switch that does not have means for connection to an equipment grounding conductor shall be permitted for replacement purposes only where the wiring method does not include an equipment grounding conductor and the switch is _____.

    (a) provided with a faceplate of nonconducting, noncombustible material with nonmetallic screws
    (b) GFCI protected
    (c) a or b
    (d) none of these

71. Nonmetallic boxes for switches shall be installed with a wiring method that provides or includes a(n) _____.

    (a) grounded conductor
    (b) equipment grounding conductor
    (c) inductive balance
    (d) none of these

Article 406. Receptacles, Cord Connectors, and Attachment Plugs (Caps)

72. When replacing a non-grounding-type receptacle where attachment to an equipment grounding conductor does not exist in the receptacle enclosure, a _____ can be used as the replacement.

    (a) non-grounding-type receptacle
    (b) grounding receptacle
    (c) GFCI-type receptacle
    (d) a or c

73. Where attachment to an equipment grounding conductor does not exist in the receptacle enclosure, a non-grounding-type receptacle(s) shall be permitted to be replaced with a GFCI-type receptacle(s) where supplied through a ground-fault circuit interrupter and _____ shall be marked "GFCI Protected" and "No Equipment Ground," visible after installation.

    (a) the receptacle(s)
    (b) their cover plates
    (c) a or b
    (d) none of these

74. Where attachment to an equipment grounding conductor does not exist in the receptacle enclosure, a non-grounding-type receptacle(s) shall be permitted to be replaced with a GFCI-type receptacle(s) where supplied through a ground-fault circuit interrupter; however, some cord-and-plug-connected equipment or appliances require an equipment grounding conductor and are listed in 250.114.

    (a) True
    (b) False

Article 410. Luminaires, Lampholders, and Lamps

75. Metal raceways shall be bonded to the metal pole with a(n) _____.

    (a) grounding electrode
    (b) grounded conductor
    (c) equipment grounding conductor
    (d) any of these

76. Luminaires made of insulating material that are directly wired or attached to outlets supplied by a wiring method that does not provide a ready means for grounding attachment to an equipment grounding conductor shall be made of insulating material and shall have no exposed conductive parts.

    (a) True
    (b) False

Article 503. Class III Hazardous (Classified) Locations

77. Article 503 covers the requirements for electrical and electronic equipment and wiring in Class III locations where fire or explosion hazards may exist due to ignitible _____.

    (a) gases or vapors
    (b) fibers/flyings
    (c) dust
    (d) all of these

Article 517. Health Care Facilities

78. Article 517 applies to electrical construction and installation criteria in health care facilities that provide services to _____.

    (a) human beings
    (b) animals
    (c) a and b
    (d) none of these

79. In health care facilities, isolated grounding receptacles shall be installed in a patient care vicinity.

    (a) True
    (b) False

80. In health care facilities, isolated ground receptacles are typically installed where a reduction of electrical noise (electromagnetic interference) is necessary, and _____ grounding paths are to be avoided.

    (a) series
    (b) parallel
    (c) series-parallel
    (d) none of these

Article 525. Carnivals, Circuses, Fairs, and Similar Events

81. At circuses and carnivals, all equipment to be grounded shall be connected to a(n) _____ conductor of a type recognized by 250.118.

    (a) equipment grounding
    (b) grounded
    (c) grounding electrode
    (d) ungrounded

Article 547. Agricultural Buildings

82. The purpose of the equipotential plane in agricultural buildings or adjacent areas is to minimize voltage differences within the plane, as well as between planes, grounded equipment, and the earth.

    (a) True
    (b) False

83. Equipotential planes shall be installed in outdoor concrete slabs where metallic equipment is located that may become energized and is accessible to livestock, other than poultry.

    (a) True
    (b) False

Article 680. Swimming Pools, Spas, Hot Tubs, Fountains, and Similar Installations

84. For pools, fountains, and similar installations, the "low-voltage contact limit" is a voltage not exceeding _____.

    (a) 15V (RMS) for sinusoidal ac or 21.20V peak for nonsinusoidal ac
    (b) 30V for continuous dc
    (c) 12.40V peak for dc that is interrupted at a rate of 10 to 200 Hz
    (d) all of these

85. When installed for swimming pools, grounding and bonding terminals shall be _____ for use in wet and corrosive environments.

    (a) identified
    (b) labeled
    (c) inspected
    (d) approved

86. Where branch-circuit wiring on the supply side of enclosures and junction boxes connected to conduits run to underwater luminaires are installed in corrosive environments as described in 680.14, the wiring method of that portion of the branch circuit shall be _____.

    (a) RMC or IMC
    (b) LFNC and PVC conduit
    (c) any wiring method
    (d) a or b

87. The feeder to a swimming pool panelboard at a separate building or structure where installed in a corrosive environment can be supplied with any Chapter 3 wiring method provided the feeder has a separate insulated copper equipment grounding conductor.

    (a) True
    (b) False

88. An 8 AWG or larger solid copper equipotential bonding conductor shall be extended to service equipment to eliminate voltage gradients in the pool area.

    (a) True
    (b) False

89. The _____ pool bonding conductor shall be connected to the equipotential bonding grid either by exothermic welding or by pressure connectors in accordance with 250.8.

    (a) 8 AWG
    (b) insulated or bare
    (c) copper
    (d) all of these

90. Metal conduit and metal piping within _____ ft horizontally of the inside walls of the pool shall be bonded unless separated by a permanent barrier.

    (a) 4
    (b) 5
    (c) 8
    (d) 10

91. Metal parts associated with an indoor spa or hot tub shall be bonded by _____.

    (a) the interconnection of threaded metal piping and fittings
    (b) metal-to-metal mounting on a common frame or base
    (c) a solid copper bonding jumper not smaller than 8 AWG
    (d) any of these

Final Exam A—Straight Order

92. Where installed for hydromassage bathtubs, double-insulated _____ shall not be bonded.
    (a) motors
    (b) blowers
    (c) a and b
    (d) none of these

Article 690 Solar Photovoltaic (PV) Systems

93. The provisions of Article 690 apply to solar _____ systems, including inverter(s), array circuit(s), and controller(s) for such systems.
    (a) photoconductive
    (b) PV
    (c) photogenic
    (d) photosynthesis

94. A mechanically integrated assembly of PV modules or panels with a support structure and foundation, tracker, and other components, as required, to form a dc or ac power-producing unit, is known as a(n) "_____."
    (a) pulse width modulator
    (b) array
    (c) capacitive supply bank
    (d) alternating-current photovoltaic module

95. Grounded dc PV arrays shall be provided with direct-current _____ meeting the requirements of 690.41(B)(1)(2) to reduce fire hazards.
    (a) arc-fault protection
    (b) rectifier protection
    (c) ground-fault monitors
    (d) ground-fault protection

96. Devices _____ for grounding the metallic frames of PV modules and other equipment can be used to bond the exposed metal surfaces of the modules and equipment to the mounting structures.
    (a) identified
    (b) approved
    (c) listed
    (d) a and c

97. Equipment grounding conductors for PV circuits having overcurrent protection shall be sized in accordance with _____.
    (a) 250.122
    (b) 250.66
    (c) Table 250.122
    (d) Table 250.66

Article 800. Communications Circuits

98. Limiting the length of the primary protector grounding conductors for communications circuits helps to reduce voltage between the building's _____ and communications systems during lightning events.
    (a) power
    (b) fire alarm
    (c) lighting
    (d) lightning protection

99. For buildings with grounding means but without an intersystem bonding termination, the grounding electrode conductor for communications circuits shall terminate to the nearest _____.
    (a) building or structure grounding electrode system
    (b) interior metal water piping system, within 5 ft from its point of entrance
    (c) service equipment enclosure
    (d) any of these

Article 810. Radio and Television Equipment

100. Article _____ contains the installation requirements for the wiring of television and radio receiving equipment, such as digital satellite receiving equipment for television signals and amateur/citizen band radio equipment antennas.
    (a) 680
    (b) 700
    (c) 810
    (d) 840

FINAL EXAM B—RANDOM ORDER

Please use the 2017 *Code* book to answer the following questions.

1. If a building or structure is supplied by a feeder from an outdoor separately derived system, a system bonding jumper at both the source and the first disconnecting means shall be permitted if doing so does not establish a ____ path for the grounded conductor.

    (a) series
    (b) parallel
    (c) series-parallel
    (d) none of these

2. Where attachment to an equipment grounding conductor does not exist in the receptacle enclosure, a non-grounding-type receptacle(s) shall be permitted to be replaced with a GFCI-type receptacle(s) where supplied through a ground-fault circuit interrupter; however, some cord-and-plug-connected equipment or appliances require an equipment grounding conductor and are listed in 250.114.

    (a) True
    (b) False

3. Type ____ cable is a factory assembly of insulated circuit conductors within an armor of interlocking metal tape, or a smooth or corrugated metallic sheath.

    (a) AC
    (b) MC
    (c) NM
    (d) b and c

4. In an area served by a separately derived system, the ____ shall be connected to the grounded conductor of the separately derived system.

    (a) structural steel
    (b) metal piping
    (c) metal building skin
    (d) a and b

5. Where attachment to an equipment grounding conductor does not exist in the receptacle enclosure, a non-grounding-type receptacle(s) shall be permitted to be replaced with a GFCI-type receptacle(s) where supplied through a ground-fault circuit interrupter and ____ shall be marked "GFCI Protected" and "No Equipment Ground," visible after installation.

    (a) the receptacle(s)
    (b) their cover plates
    (c) a or b
    (d) none of these

6. When bonding enclosures, metal raceways, frames, and fittings, any nonconductive paint, enamel, or similar coating shall be removed at ____.

    (a) contact surfaces
    (b) threads
    (c) contact points
    (d) all of these

7. A grounding electrode conductor, sized in accordance with 250.66, shall be used to connect the equipment grounding conductors, the service-equipment enclosures, and, where the system is grounded, the grounded service conductor to the grounding electrode(s).

    (a) True
    (b) False

Final Exam B—Random Order

8. For community antenna television and radio distribution systems, where the building or structure served has no intersystem bonding termination, the bonding conductor or grounding electrode conductor can be connected to the power service accessible means external to enclosures using the options identified in 250.94(A), Ex.

   (a) True
   (b) False

9. Isolated ground receptacles installed in nonmetallic boxes shall be covered with a nonmetallic faceplate, unless the box contains a feature or accessory that permits the effective grounding of the faceplate.

   (a) True
   (b) False

10. The equipotential plane in an agricultural building shall be connected to the electrical grounding system with a solid copper, insulated, covered, or bare conductor and not smaller than _____ AWG.

    (a) 10
    (b) 8
    (c) 6
    (d) 4

11. Receptacles incorporating an isolated grounding conductor connection intended for the reduction of electrical noise shall be identified by _____ on the face of the receptacle.

    (a) an orange triangle
    (b) a green triangle
    (c) the color orange
    (d) the engraved word "ISOLATED"

12. The grounded conductor of each separately derived system shall be bonded to the nearest available point of the metal water piping system(s) in the area served by each separately derived system and each bonding jumper shall be sized in accordance with Table 250.102(C)(1) based on the largest ungrounded conductor of the separately derived system.

    (a) True
    (b) False

13. Metal water piping system(s) shall be bonded to the _____, or to one or more grounding electrodes used, if the grounding electrode conductor or bonding jumper to the grounding electrode is of sufficient size.

    (a) grounded conductor at the service
    (b) service equipment enclosure
    (c) grounding electrode conductor if of sufficient size
    (d) any of these

14. The grounding electrode conductor for an antenna mast shall be _____ where subject to physical damage.

    (a) electrically protected
    (b) protected
    (c) connected
    (d) disconnected

15. All branch circuits serving patient care spaces shall be provided with an effective ground-fault current path by installation in a metal raceway system, or a cable having a metallic armor or sheath assembly. The metal raceway system, metallic cable armor, or sheath assembly shall itself qualify as an equipment grounding conductor in accordance with 250.118.

    (a) True
    (b) False

16. In Class II locations, a permitted method of bonding is the use of bonding jumpers with proper fittings.

    (a) True
    (b) False

17. Service raceways threaded into metal service equipment such as bosses (hubs) are considered to be effectively _____ to the service metal enclosure.

    (a) attached
    (b) bonded
    (c) grounded
    (d) none of these

18. _____ is a raceway of circular cross section having an outer liquid-tight, nonmetallic, sunlight-resistant jacket over an inner flexible metal core.

    (a) FMC
    (b) LFNMC
    (c) LFMC
    (d) none of these

19. Outlets supplying pool pump motors connected to single-phase, 120V through 240V branch circuits, whether by receptacle or by direct connection, shall be provided with _____ protection for personnel.

    (a) AFCI
    (b) GFCI
    (c) a or b
    (d) a and b

20. A _____ is the total components and subsystem that, in combination, convert solar energy into electric energy for connection to a utilization load.

    (a) photovoltaic system
    (b) solar array
    (c) a and b
    (d) none of these

21. The *NEC* requires that electrical equipment be _____.

    (a) installed in a neat and workmanlike manner
    (b) installed under the supervision of a licensed person
    (c) completed before being inspected
    (d) all of these

22. The metal structural frame of a building shall be permitted to be used as a conductor to interconnect electrodes that are part of the grounding electrode system, or as a grounding electrode conductor. Hold-down bolts securing the structural steel column that are connected to a concrete-encased electrode that complies with 250.52(A)(3) and is located in the support footing or foundation shall be permitted to connect the metal structural frame of a building or structure to the concrete-encased grounding electrode.

    (a) True
    (b) False

23. In Class III locations, locknut-bushing and double-locknut types of fittings may be depended on for bonding purposes.

    (a) True
    (b) False

24. Lightning protection system ground terminals _____ be bonded to the building or structure grounding electrode system.

    (a) shall
    (b) shall not
    (c) shall be permitted to
    (d) none of these

25. The grounding electrode used for grounding strike termination devices of a lightning protection system can be used as a grounding electrode system for the buildings or structures.

    (a) True
    (b) False

26. Currents that introduce noise or data errors in electronic equipment are considered objectionable currents in the context of 250.6(D) of the *NEC*.

    (a) True
    (b) False

27. Where an equipment grounding conductor is installed underground within an agricultural building, it shall be _____.

    (a) insulated
    (b) copper
    (c) bare
    (d) covered

28. A conducting object through which a direct connection to earth is established is a "_____."

    (a) bonding conductor
    (b) grounding conductor
    (c) grounding electrode
    (d) grounded conductor

29. Premises wiring includes _____ wiring from the service point or power source to the outlets.

    (a) interior
    (b) exterior
    (c) underground
    (d) a and b

30. Explanatory material, such as references to other standards, references to related sections of the *NEC*, or information related to a *Code* rule, are included in the form of Informational Notes.

    (a) True
    (b) False

Final Exam B—Random Order

31. Metal enclosures and raceways containing service conductors shall be connected to the grounded system conductor if the electrical system is grounded.

    (a) True
    (b) False

32. The bonding jumper used to bond the metal water piping system shall be installed in accordance with 250.64(A), 250.64(B), and 250.64(E) and the points of attachment of the bonding jumper(s) shall be _____.

    (a) readily accessible
    (b) accessible
    (c) a or b
    (d) none of these

33. Electrical equipment permanently mounted on skids, and the skids themselves, shall be connected to the equipment grounding conductor sized as required by _____.

    (a) 250.50
    (b) 250.66
    (c) 250.122
    (d) 310.15

34. Which of the following appliances installed in residential occupancies need not be connected to an equipment grounding conductor?

    (a) A toaster.
    (b) An aquarium.
    (c) A dishwasher.
    (d) A refrigerator.

35. Radio and television receiving antenna systems shall have bonding or grounding electrode conductors that are _____.

    (a) copper or other corrosion-resistant conductive material
    (b) insulated, covered, or bare
    (c) securely fastened in place and protected where subject to physical damage
    (d) all of these

36. When a ground ring is used as a grounding electrode, it shall be installed at a depth below the earth's surface of not less than _____.

    (a) 18 in.
    (b) 24 in.
    (c) 30 in.
    (d) 8 ft

37. Article 503 covers the requirements for electrical and electronic equipment and wiring in Class III locations where fire or explosion hazards may exist due to ignitible _____.

    (a) gases or vapors
    (b) fibers/flyings
    (c) dust
    (d) all of these

38. In the NEC, the word(s) "_____" indicate a mandatory requirement.

    (a) shall
    (b) shall not
    (c) shall be permitted
    (d) a or b

39. A pool light junction box connected to a conduit that extends directly to a forming shell shall be _____ for this use.

    (a) listed
    (b) identified
    (c) labeled
    (d) all of these

40. Metal parts of electric equipment associated with an indoor spa or hot tub water circulating system shall be bonded together unless they are a part of a listed, labeled, and identified self-contained spa or hot tub.

    (a) True
    (b) False

41. In judging equipment for approval, considerations such as _____ shall be evaluated.

    (a) mechanical strength
    (b) wire-bending space
    (c) arcing effects
    (d) all of these

42. Electrical continuity at service equipment, service raceways, and service conductor enclosures shall be ensured by _____.

    (a) bonding equipment to the grounded service conductor
    (b) connections utilizing threaded couplings on enclosures, if made up wrenchtight
    (c) other listed bonding devices, such as bonding-type locknuts, bushings, or bushings with bonding jumpers
    (d) any of these

43. For hydromassage bathtubs, small conductive surfaces not likely to become energized, such as air and water jets, supply valve assemblies, and drain fittings not connected to metallic piping, and towel bars, mirror frames, and similar nonelectrical equipment not connected to _____ shall not be required to be bonded.

    (a) metal framing
    (b) nonmetallic framing
    (c) metal gas piping
    (d) any of these

44. Installations shall comply with the material located in the NEC Annexes because they are part of the requirements of the Code.

    (a) True
    (b) False

45. Exposed noncurrent-carrying metal parts of an information technology system shall be _____.

    (a) bonded to an equipment grounding conductor
    (b) double insulated
    (c) GFCI protected
    (d) a or b

46. The connection between the grounded circuit conductor and the equipment grounding conductor at the service is accomplished by installing a(n) _____ bonding jumper.

    (a) main
    (b) system
    (c) equipment
    (d) circuit

47. An equipotential plane is an area where wire mesh or other conductive elements are embedded in or placed under concrete, and bonded to _____.

    (a) all metal structures
    (b) fixed nonelectrical equipment that may become energized
    (c) the electrical grounding system
    (d) all of these

48. Faulted circuits required to have ground-fault protection in a photovoltaic system shall be isolated by automatically disconnecting the _____ conductors, or the inverter charge controller fed by the faulted circuits shall automatically stop supplying power to output circuits.

    (a) ungrounded
    (b) grounded
    (c) equipment grounding
    (d) all of these

49. Where multimotor and combination-load equipment for air-conditioning and refrigeration is installed outdoors on a roof, a(n) _____ conductor of the wire type shall be installed in outdoor portions of metallic raceway systems that use non-threaded fittings.

    (a) equipment grounding
    (b) grounding
    (c) equipment bonding
    (d) bonding

50. Ground clamps and fittings that are exposed to physical damage shall be enclosed in _____ or equivalent protective covering.

    (a) metal
    (b) wood
    (c) concrete
    (d) a or b

51. Where more than one concrete-encased electrode is present at a building or structure, it shall be permitted to bond only one into the grounding electrode system.

    (a) True
    (b) False

52. In one- and two-family dwellings, the grounding electrode conductor for CATV systems shall be as short as practicable, not to exceed _____ ft in length.

    (a) 5
    (b) 8
    (c) 10
    (d) 20

53. The continuity of the equipment grounding conductors at carnivals, circuses, fairs, and similar events shall be verified each time that portable electrical equipment is connected.

    (a) True
    (b) False

54. A conductor used to connect the system grounded conductor or the equipment to a grounding electrode or to a point on the grounding electrode system is called the "_____ conductor."

    (a) main grounding
    (b) common main
    (c) equipment grounding
    (d) grounding electrode

55. For grounded systems, electrical equipment and other electrically conductive material likely to become energized shall be installed in a manner that creates a _____ from any point on the wiring system where a ground fault may occur to the electrical supply source.

    (a) circuit facilitating the operation of the overcurrent device
    (b) low-impedance circuit
    (c) circuit capable of safely carrying the ground-fault current likely to be imposed on it
    (d) all of these

56. Where LFMC is used in a Class III location as permitted in 503.10, it shall _____.

    (a) not be unsupported
    (b) not exceed 6 ft in length
    (c) include an equipment bonding jumper of the wire type in accordance with 250.102
    (d) be listed for use in a Class I hazardous (classified) location

57. Permanently installed swimming pools include those constructed in the ground or partially in the ground, and all others capable of holding water in a depth greater than _____ in.

    (a) 36
    (b) 42
    (c) 48
    (d) 54

58. Masts and metal structures supporting antennas shall be grounded in accordance with 810.21, unless the antenna and its related supporting mast or structure are within a zone of protection defined by a _____ radius rolling sphere.

    (a) 75-ft
    (b) 100-ft
    (c) 125-ft
    (d) 150-ft

59. Type _____ cable is a factory assembly that encloses two or more insulated conductors within a nonmetallic jacket.

    (a) AC
    (b) MC
    (c) NM
    (d) b and c

60. Where the supply conductors are larger than 1,100 kcmil copper or 1,750 kcmil aluminum, the main bonding jumper shall have an area that is _____ the area of the largest phase conductor when of the same material.

    (a) at least equal to
    (b) at least 50 percent of
    (c) not less than 12½ percent of
    (d) not more than 12½ percent of

61. A system intended to provide protection of equipment from damaging line-to-ground fault currents by causing a disconnecting means to open all ungrounded conductors of the faulted circuit at current levels less than the supply circuit overcurrent device defines "_____."

    (a) ground-fault protection of equipment
    (b) guarded
    (c) personal protection
    (d) automatic protection

62. For PV systems, a(n) _____ is a device that changes direct-current input to an alternating-current output.

    (a) diode
    (b) rectifier
    (c) transistor
    (d) inverter

63. The 8 AWG solid bonding jumper required for equipotential bonding in the area of hydromassage bathtubs shall not be required to be extended to any _____.

    (a) remote panelboard
    (b) service equipment
    (c) electrode
    (d) any of these

64. All conductors of a circuit, including the equipment grounding conductor, shall be installed in the same raceway or cable, or otherwise run with the PV array circuit conductors when they leave the vicinity of the PV array.

    (a) True
    (b) False

65. Where installed to reduce electrical noise for electronic equipment on the grounding circuit, a metal raceway can terminate to a(n) _____ nonmetallic fitting(s) or spacer on the electronic equipment. The metal raceway shall be supplemented by an internal insulated equipment grounding conductor.

    (a) listed
    (b) labeled
    (c) identified
    (d) marked

66. Metal parts of cord-and-plug-connected equipment, if grounded, shall be connected to an equipment grounding conductor that terminates to a grounding-type attachment plug.

    (a) True
    (b) False

67. Grounding electrode conductors _____ AWG and larger that are not exposed to physical damage can be run along the surface of the building construction without metal covering or protection.

    (a) 10
    (b) 8
    (c) 6
    (d) 4

68. As used in the *NEC*, equipment includes _____.

    (a) fittings
    (b) appliances
    (c) machinery
    (d) all of these

69. A snap switch with an integral nonmetallic enclosure complying with 300.15(E) is required to be connected to an equipment grounding conductor.

    (a) True
    (b) False

70. Luminaires and equipment shall be mechanically connected to an equipment grounding conductor as specified in 250.118 and shall be sized in accordance with _____.

    (a) Table 250.66
    (b) Table 250.122
    (c) Table 310.16
    (d) a and c

71. _____ is a raceway of circular cross section made of a helically wound, formed, interlocked metal strip.

    (a) Type MC cable
    (b) Type AC cable
    (c) LFMC
    (d) FMC

72. Where conditions of maintenance and supervision ensure only qualified persons service the installation in _____ buildings, the entire length of the metal water piping system can be used for grounding purposes, provided the entire length, other than short sections passing through walls, floors, or ceilings, is exposed.

    (a) industrial
    (b) institutional
    (c) commercial
    (d) all of these

73. Equipment grounding conductors for motor branch circuits shall be sized in accordance with Table 250.122, based on the rating of the _____ device.

    (a) motor overload
    (b) motor over-temperature
    (c) branch-circuit short-circuit and ground-fault protective
    (d) feeder overcurrent protection

74. Grounding and bonding connection devices that depend solely on _____ shall not be used.

    (a) pressure connections
    (b) solder
    (c) lugs
    (d) approved clamps

75. Listed or labeled equipment shall be installed and used in accordance with any instructions included in the listing or labeling.

    (a) True
    (b) False

76. When FMC or LFMC is used as permitted in Class I, Division 2 locations, it shall include an equipment bonding jumper of the wire type in compliance with 250.102.

    (a) True
    (b) False

77. In Class I locations, the locknut-bushing and double-locknut types of contacts shall not be depended on for bonding purposes.

    (a) True
    (b) False

78. Where the main bonding jumper is installed from the grounded conductor terminal bar to the equipment grounding terminal bar in service equipment, the _____ conductor is permitted to be connected to the equipment grounding terminal bar.

    (a) grounding
    (b) grounded
    (c) grounding electrode
    (d) none of these

79. If the grounding electrode conductor or bonding jumper connected to a single or multiple rod, pipe, or plate electrode(s), or any combination thereof, as described in 250.52(A)(5) or (A)(7), does not extend on to other types of electrodes that require a larger size conductor, the grounding electrode conductor shall not be required to be larger than _____ AWG copper wire.

    (a) 10
    (b) 8
    (c) 6
    (d) 4

80. For communications systems using coaxial cable completely contained within the building (that is, they do not exit the building) or the exterior zone of protection defined by a _____ radius rolling sphere and isolated from outside cable plant, the shield shall be permitted to be grounded by a connection to an equipment grounding conductor as described in 250.118.

    (a) 75-ft
    (b) 100-ft
    (c) 125-ft
    (d) 150-ft

81. Connectors and terminals for conductors more finely stranded than Class B and Class C, as shown in Table 10 of Chapter 9, shall be _____ for the specific conductor class or classes.

    (a) listed
    (b) approved
    (c) identified
    (d) all of these

82. Nonmandatory Informative Annexes contained in the back of the *Code* book are _____.

    (a) for information only
    (b) not enforceable as a requirement of the *Code*
    (c) enforceable as a requirement of the *Code*
    (d) a and b

83. Bonding jumper(s) from grounding electrode(s) shall be permitted to be connected to an aluminum or copper busbar not less than _____ and of sufficient length to accommodate the number of terminations necessary for the installation in accordance with 250.64(F).

    (a) 1/8 in. thick × 1 in. wide
    (b) 1/8 in. thick × 2 in. wide
    (c) 1/4 in. thick × 1 in. wide
    (d) 1/4 in. thick × 2 in. wide

84. In one- and two-family dwellings, the primary protector bonding conductor or grounding electrode conductor for communications systems shall be as short as practicable, not to exceed _____ ft in length.

    (a) 5
    (b) 8
    (c) 10
    (d) 20

85. An interactive inverter is an inverter intended for use in parallel with a(n) _____ to supply common loads that may deliver power to the utility.

    (a) electric utility
    (b) photovoltaic (PV) system
    (c) battery
    (d) none of these

86. If a separate grounding electrode is installed for the radio and television equipment, it shall be bonded to the building's electrical power grounding electrode system with a bonding jumper not smaller than _____ AWG.

    (a) 10
    (b) 8
    (c) 6
    (d) 1/0

87. The largest size grounding electrode conductor required is _____ copper.

    (a) 6 AWG
    (b) 1/0 AWG
    (c) 3/0 AWG
    (d) 250 kcmil

88. A grounded _____-wire PV system has one functional grounded conductor.

    (a) 2
    (b) 3
    (c) 4
    (d) 5

89. Equipment or materials to which a label, symbol, or other identifying mark of a product evaluation organization that is acceptable to the authority having jurisdiction has been attached is known as "_____."

    (a) listed
    (b) labeled
    (c) approved
    (d) identified

90. An important consideration for limiting imposed voltage on electrical systems is to remember that bonding and grounding electrode conductors should not be any longer than necessary and unnecessary bends and loops should be avoided.

    (a) True
    (b) False

91. The grounding conductor connection to the grounding electrode shall be made by _____.

    (a) listed lugs
    (b) exothermic welding
    (c) listed pressure connectors
    (d) any of these

92. In an ac system, if the size of the grounding electrode conductor or bonding jumper connected to a concrete-encased electrode does not extend on to other types of electrodes that require a larger size of conductor, the grounding electrode conductor shall not be required to be larger than _____ AWG copper.

    (a) 10
    (b) 8
    (c) 6
    (d) 4

93. If a common grounding electrode conductor is installed for multiple separately derived systems as permitted by 250.30(A)(6), and exposed structural metal that is interconnected to form the building frame or interior metal piping exists in the area served by the separately derived system, the metal piping and the structural metal member shall be bonded to the common grounding electrode conductor in the area served by the separately derived system.

    (a) True
    (b) False

94. Metal components shall not be required to be connected to the equipment grounding conductor or supply-side bonding jumper where the metal components are _____.

    (a) installed in a run of nonmetallic raceway(s) and isolated from possible contact by a minimum cover of 18 in. to any part of the metal components
    (b) part of an installation of nonmetallic raceway(s) and are isolated from possible contact to any part of the metal components by being encased in not less than 2 in. of concrete
    (c) a or b
    (d) none of these

95. A grounded conductor shall not be connected to normally noncurrent-carrying metal parts of equipment on the _____ side of the system bonding jumper of a separately derived system except as otherwise permitted in Article 250.

    (a) supply
    (b) grounded
    (c) high-voltage
    (d) load

96. The building or structure grounding electrode system shall be used as the _____ electrode for the separately derived system.

    (a) grounding
    (b) bonding
    (c) grounded
    (d) bonded

97. Steel or aluminum cable tray systems shall be permitted to be used as an equipment grounding conductor, provided the cable tray sections and fittings are identified as _____, among other requirements.

    (a) an equipment grounding conductor
    (b) special
    (c) industrial
    (d) all of these

98. Where the resistance-to-ground of 25 ohms or less is not achieved for a single rod electrode, _____.

    (a) other means besides electrodes shall be used in order to provide grounding
    (b) the single rod electrode shall be supplemented by one additional electrode
    (c) no additional electrodes are required
    (d) none of these

99. The swimming pool structure, including the structural reinforcing steel of the pool shell and deck, except reinforcing steel encapsulated with a nonconductive compound shall be bonded.

    (a) True
    (b) False

100. When a permanently installed generator _____, the requirements of 250.30 shall apply.

    (a) is a separately derived system
    (b) is not a separately derived system
    (c) supplies only cord-and-plug-connected loads
    (d) none of these

APPENDIX A

ANALYSIS OF 2017 *NEC* CHANGES RELATING TO BONDING AND GROUNDING

This appendix contains the summaries and analyses of of the changes to the 2017 *NEC* relating to bonding and grounding, extracted from *Mike Holt's Illustrated Guide to Changes to the National Electrical Code, Based on the 2017 NEC*. These rules are identified throughout the textbook with the icon [2017 CC] next to the *Code* rule.

ARTICLE 90—INTRODUCTION TO THE *NATIONAL ELECTRICAL CODE*

90.2 Scope of the *NEC*

Changes to this section include a new requirement for the removal of conductors, equipment, and raceways and clarification that utility energy storage equipment isn't covered by the *NEC*.

Analysis

NEW

Removal of Equipment. Although the *Code* is an installation standard, there are a few requirements that deal with the removal of electrical equipment, mainly limited-energy cables. Sections 640.6(B), 645.5(G), 725.25, 770.25, 800.25, and 820.25 require abandoned cables to be removed and 590.3(D) requires temporary wiring installations to be removed immediately upon the completion of the purpose for which they were installed. The scope of the previous edition of the *NEC* only discussed installation of the cables, not their removal. The 2017 edition of the *Code* corrected this oversight.

CLARIFIED

Utility Energy Storage Systems. The *NEC* now provides an exemption for utility energy storage systems that allow the utility to produce electricity at load demand, store it, and then provide it to customers when the demand is high. These energy storage systems are every bit as involved as the utility equipment that's already exempt from the *Code* (generation, transmission, distribution, and so forth) and therefore deserve exemption as well.

90.3 *Code* Arrangement

Editorial revisions to the arrangement of the *Code* clarify how the different chapters in the *NEC* apply, supplement, or modify each other.

Analysis

CLARIFIED

Many people skip over Article 90 because they want to dive into the meat and potatoes of the *Code* book. Most don't even realize this is a mistake until quite late in their career. Article 90 is the

•••

baseline of the *NEC* and tells you how the *Code* is laid out and how it works within itself.

Skipping this article is very much like doing electrical work without understanding theory—sure, you can run raceways and pull wire, but you don't really understand why you're doing what you're doing.

When you wire a doctor's office [Article 517], for example, you had better understand that everything in Chapters 1 through 4 apply to what you're doing, unless Article 517 specifically changes it, which it does. If you fail to read 517.13, which requires a special type of wiring method for patient care areas, you may find yourself ripping out all of the work you just did.

How about temporary installations? Temporary installations are covered in Chapter 5, specifically, Article 590. Do you think the rules for temporary installations are less restrictive or more restrictive than they are for a "normal" installation? They're more restrictive! That's because all of the rules in Chapters 1 through 4 apply, except as modified in Article 590. It doesn't modify much, but when it does, more rules are usually provided; not fewer.

When you install 12V landscape lighting near a pool, how far away from the nearest edge of the water must it be? The answer is 10 ft [411.5(B)] and this rule also applies to swimming pools, spas, and fountains. This is another example how Chapters 1 through 4 apply to your electrical installations unless modified by Chapters 5 through 7. In this case Article 680 doesn't supplement or modify Article 411 so those requirements apply.

Here's a very strange example of how 90.3 works: What's the working space required in front of a power-limited fire alarm control panel that operates at 24V? Most *Code* experts agree this is equipment that's likely to require examination, adjustment, servicing, or maintenance while energized, and therefore 110.26 applies, which mandates 3 ft in front of the equipment. Because fire alarms are covered in Article 760 (Chapter 7), there could be a modification to this requirement within that article. Since there isn't, 110.26 applies. You need 3 ft of working space in front of the equipment.

Now consider a telephone board, which operates at about 50V to 60V, and goes up to around 90V when the telephone is ringing. One would think you'd need at least the same amount of working space here, since it runs at a higher voltage, but that isn't the case. Telephone equipment is covered in Article 800, which is in Chapter 8.

Remember that 90.3 tells us Chapter 8 is almost its own little *Code* book. Nothing in Chapters 1 through 7 applies to a Chapter 8 installation unless it says it does. So…what's the clearance? If there were a clearance requirement it would have to be located in Chapter 8, but there is none.

The change in the 2017 edition of the *NEC* is very subtle, but it clarifies that the rules in Chapters 5 through 7 sometimes modify each other. This should come in handy if you ever find yourself wiring a fire pump [Article 695] in a hospital [Article 517].

90.7 Examination of Equipment for Product Safety

Edits were made to clarify that the listing of a product doesn't necessarily make it suitable for use.

Analysis

CLARIFIED

In some cases a listed product may not be suitable for use because it doesn't meet the *NEC* requirements. Examples include "cheater plugs" and screw-shell receptacles, as well as LED lamps used in a retrofit application. While the lamp itself may be listed, 410.6 requires the lamp to be part of a UL 1598C listed retrofit conversion kit if it's used for a fixture conversion. This change clarifies that having a listing doesn't make a product suitable for an application unless the product's listing is compatible with the requirements of the *Code*.

CHAPTER 1— GENERAL RULES

ARTICLE 100—DEFINITIONS

Article 100—Definitions

Some definitions were relocated to Article 100, and the Code Making Panel responsible for each definition is now identified.

Analysis

This revision of the *Code* saw some definitions moved from specific articles to Article 100 to reduce confusion as they're used in other sections of the *NEC*. Few things are more frustrating than trying to find the definition of a term that isn't located in Article 100. In general, only those terms used in two or more articles are defined in here. Some terms, such as "Dust-Ignitionproof," Dusttight," "Hermetically Sealed [as applied to Hazardous (Classified) Locations]," "Information Technology Equipment (ITE)," and "Oil Immersion [as applied to Hazardous (Classified) Locations]" were relocated to Article 100 from other articles.

In order to identify the CMP (Code Making Panel) responsible for each definition, a short identifier was added. One example is the definition for "Bathroom" followed by (CMP-2) to identify Code Making Panel 2 as the one responsible for this definition.

> *Bathroom.* An area including a basin with one or more of the following: a toilet, a urinal, a tub, a shower, a bidet, or similar plumbing fixtures. (CMP-2)

Building

Changes to this definition ensure that building codes, not the *NEC*, are the appropriate place to define a "building."

Analysis

The term "building" may not seem like something that needs to be defined in the *Code*, but it's actually an important concept. The most common application of this definition is as it relates to the number of services (or feeders) a building may have.

CLARIFIED

Building. One of the fundamental concepts of building codes is determining how large a building can be. This is determined by three main factors: What the building is used for (is it a dynamite factory or an office building), what it's built of (is it wood or concrete and steel), and how far away it is from property lines (if it's on fire, is it going to take the entire city down with it).

If a building larger than what the building code allows is needed, a "fire wall" through it can be built. There are now two buildings, each of which is within the size parameters allowed by the building code. This ensures that if a fire occurs, it will be confined to only one of them.

Be careful though because not all fire-resistance rated walls are really fire walls. There are also fire barriers, fire partitions, and other walls that aren't fire walls. This is something you need to discuss with the architect or, better still, the building official before you attempt to change a single structure into multiple buildings.

The change to this edition of the *Code* removes the language about fire doors as opening protective devices. Obviously the *NEC* isn't the right document to determine this, and even if it's accurate, changes may occur in the building codes that would render the *Code* inaccurate and therefore a potential source of conflict.

Electric Sign

The definition of "electric sign" clarifies that the sign doesn't have to be Illuminated.

Analysis

CLARIFIED It's hard to even contemplate our world without electric signage. In fact, electrical signs are so popular that the *Code* requires a circuit for them in every commercial building, and every commercial occupancy that's accessible to pedestrians [600.5(A)]. Electric signs are covered in Article 600, and include LED signs, neon tubing, section signs, and skeleton tubing.

The words "operated and/or" that were added should clarify that a sign doesn't need to be for illumination purposes only. Although most people think of a sign as something that says "open" or perhaps tells us the price of gas at a gas station, there are other signs that are quite subtle. For example, some signs aren't illuminated at all but are electrically operated. An example of this could be an unilluminated sign with a motor that moves parts on it to convey a message. According the UL standard, that's also an electric sign, and needs to be installed in accordance with Article 600. The added language to this definition now conveys that information.

Interactive Inverter

This term used to be "Utility Interactive Inverter."

Analysis

CLARIFIED An inverter changes direct-current power into alternating-current power. An interactive inverter allows the ac power from the inverter output to be in parallel with another ac power system. Of interest is to know that an interactive inverter will only provide ac power output when it's connected to another power system. If the other power system shuts down, then the interactive inverter stops providing ac power. This means that a dc system without an energy storage device (battery) can't be used for backup power.

An interactive inverter is permitted to be connected to a source of ac power other than the utility, although it would be unusual. By removing the word "utility" from the definition, we remove any argument about it.

Photovoltaic (PV) System

A change to this definition removes any arguments about whether or not the energy created is "suitable" for connecting to a load.

Analysis

CLARIFIED A PV system is made up of all of the equipment necessary to convert solar energy into electrical energy. The PV system includes the PV modules that capture and change solar energy into electrical energy, source circuits, output circuits, inverters, string combiners, batteries, charge controllers, and several other pieces of equipment; all of which are components of a PV system.

The electrical energy created by a PV system will be, hopefully, "suitable" for connecting to utilization loads. Who determines what's suitable and what isn't? Who cares...it's not part of the definition anymore.

Raceway

The definition of "raceway" no longer contains construction specifications, such as "metallic" or "nonmetallic."

Analysis

CLARIFIED Raceways include conduit, tubing, wireways, communications raceways, and obscure types like strut-type channel and cellular floor raceways. All of these raceways have the same purpose—to install conductors and cables and provide the ability to remove them.

All conduits are raceways, but not all raceways are conduits. For example, electrical metallic tubing (EMT) is a raceway, but it's not a conduit, it's a tubing (which is a raceway). A wireway isn't a conduit or a tubing, but it's still a raceway, and that's what's important. All of the raceways in the *Code* are discussed in their own article in Chapter 3. Be careful though, a common misconception is that cable tray systems are considered raceways; they aren't, they're a support system for cables and raceways [392.2].

In the 2014 *NEC*, the definition of a "raceway" specified they could be metallic or nonmetallic. That didn't exactly clear things up, did it? Because those words offered no real value, they're no longer in the *Code*. It may be a small change, but definitions work best when they're short and simple, so if we can remove some words, why not do so?

Receptacle

A small change was made in order to comply with the *NEC* style manual, and new text regarding a new type of receptacle was added.

Analysis

NEW

The receptacle is probably the most important component of an installation as it relates to convenience and usability, and due to that, everyone pretty much knows what one is. A duplex receptacle is constructed of two receptacles, a triplex receptacle is constructed of three receptacles, and a single pin and sleeve type of connection on a generator is also a single receptacle.

Another piece of equipment that you wouldn't think of as a receptacle is new device that allows for luminaires and paddle fans to be quickly installed, removed, or replaced. As can happen when a new rule is added in one part of the *NEC*, it might have a negative impact on other rules in the *Code*. For example, do all of the general receptacle rules in the *NEC* apply to this new type of "receptacle?" If it's installed in a residential garage, is it required to be GFCI protected in accordance with 210.8? One thing is sure, this is going to be an argument for many until the 2020 *Code* clears it up.

Structure

A change to this definition clarifies that stand-alone equipment is no longer considered a structure.

Analysis

CLARIFIED

The previous definition stated that a structure was "That which is built or constructed." This was a source of many, many debates in the electrical industry. Certainly buildings are structures, but the general statement that anything that's constructed was considered a structure was crazy! New to this edition of the *Code* is a clarification that "equipment" isn't considered a structure; so a free-standing switchboard, light pole, traffic signal, disconnect on a structure, or electric billboard sign isn't a structure.

ARTICLE 110—REQUIREMENTS FOR ELECTRICAL INSTALLATIONS

110.3 Examination, Identification, Installation, Use, and Listing of Equipment

Changes to this section of the *Code* include addressing reconditioned, refurbished, or remanufactured equipment and providing rules for who may list electrical equipment.

Analysis

NEW

Remanufactured Equipment. In a perfect world all electrical equipment would be shiny and new; but that isn't reality. Sometimes older electrical equipment must continue to be used for many reasons, the most common is availability and cost. It would be nice if we could change all of the existing equipment in the world into new, but since we can't we have to make do. This often includes installing electrical equipment that isn't new, but is

•••

reconditioned, refurbished, or remanufactured instead. This is commonly done with circuit breakers for obscure panels that haven't been manufactured in decades. A new Informational Note points out that the inspector shouldn't reject equipment based solely on the fact that it's remanufactured.

Listing. A new subsection (C), covering listing, was added. Although the definition of "listed" in Article 100 states that a testing laboratory that tests and lists products must be acceptable to the AHJ, it does little else in terms of regulating the listing agency. This makes sense, because definitions aren't supposed to contain rules.

So, who does the testing and listing, and what do they use as their basis of acceptance? Can I open my own company, test a product in my backyard shop by plugging it in, put a sticker on it, and call it listed? With the revisions in the 2017 *NEC*, I can't. Testing laboratories must be recognized as being qualified and one source of finding out which ones are is OSHA, which lists Nationally Recognized Testing Laboratories (NRTLs).

110.5 Conductors

A change to this rule clarifies that conductors are to be copper or aluminum unless otherwise restricted by the *NEC*.

Analysis

CLARIFIED This section used to stipulate that, where conductor material wasn't specified in the *Code* rule, copper conductors were to be used. This made for some strange interpretations of the *NEC*, none of which made sense or could be justified as necessary.

Aluminum conductors have the same negative stigma (for some) that they've had for decades, despite being made from different and far superior alloys than their predecessors. With the change to this section, there's no argument about the allowed conductor types. Aluminum can be used unless there's a specific requirement by the equipment listing or *Code* rule, such as 517.13(B)(1).

110.14 Conductor Termination and Splicing

A properly calibrated tool must be used when torquing terminal connections.

Analysis

NEW When electrical fires or failures occur, they usually do so at terminations, not in the middle of a cable or conductor. With that said, the rules in 110.14 are some of the most important in the entire *Code*.

Studies have found that approximately 75 to 80 percent of conductor terminations aren't installed correctly unless a torque measuring device, such as a torque wrench or screwdriver, is used. Approximately 60 percent of conductor terminations aren't tight enough and 20 percent are too tight, leaving about only 20 percent meeting the manufacturer's torquing requirements.

This new rule requires the installer to use a properly calibrated tool for conductor terminations when a tightening torque is specified by the manufacturer for the terminal.

Enforcement of this new rule will prove challenging. Does the electrical inspector need to be on site when the terminations are made so he or she can verify the tool being used? How will he or she know the tool is calibrated correctly? Has the tool been dropped since being calibrated and is now therefore inaccurate? Should the inspectors carry their own tools?

As with any new *Code* rule, this one might create growing pains, but we can all certainly agree on one thing; this rule is intended to increase safety by ensuring proper terminations. Let's not lose sight of the big picture—electrical safety.

CHAPTER 2— WIRING AND PROTECTION

ARTICLE 250—GROUNDING AND BONDING

250.4 Performance Requirements for Grounding and Bonding

New Informational Notes were added to inform *Code* users of NFPA 780, *Standard for the Installation of Lightning Protection Systems*.

Analysis

NEW

The reason we earth ground systems to the earth is to reduce overvoltage, from lightning induced energy, and other events, on the conductors and electrical components (such as transformer and motor windings) of the installation.

Adding an Informational Note referencing NFPA 780 *Standard for the Installation of Lightning Protection Systems* makes no sense, since a lightning protection system won't assist in reducing overvoltage on systems addressed by 250.4. But the Code Making Panel apparently thinks it does…

250.6 Objectionable Current

This section was clarified to allow the use of multiple means to avoid objectionable current.

Analysis

CLARIFIED

The literal language of this article in the 2014 edition of the *Code* only allowed a single method to be used to eliminate objectionable current. In actuality, multiple means may be employed and the new language clarifies the intent.

250.24 Service Equipment— Grounding and Bonding

Clarification that the sizing requirements for service neutral conductors apply to cable-type wiring methods was made.

Analysis

CLARIFIED

I've always liked to visualize the utility neutral conductor as a white wire with green stripes on it. That's really what it is; the service neutral wire carries the unbalanced return (white) and it's the fault-clearing conductor on the supply side of the service (green stripe).

Because the service neutral conductor serves the role of carrying unbalanced current and is intended to provide a low-impedance fault return path to the utility secondary winding, it must be sized to carry the neutral load and the fault current back to the source in the event of a ground fault.

Think about it, if we have a 400A three-phase service supplying only three-phase motors and one 20A line-to-neutral lighting circuit, what size neutral wire do we need?

A 12 AWG conductor will certainly carry the lighting circuit neutral load, but what about the fault current? Have you ever seen a 500 kcmil phase conductor collide with a 12AWG equipment grounding conductor? I haven't either, but I can guess that there wouldn't be anything left of the 12AWG conductor, other than copper vapor floating around in the air, should it happen.

To ensure a safe installation, the *Code* requires the service neutral conductor to be sized in accordance with Table 250.102(C)(1). In our 400 kcmil example, this would be a 1/0 AWG copper neutral. That kind of mass can carry the fault current without any problem.

Since none of this is actually new to the *NEC*, what changed? The 2014 *Code* was clear when it came to sizing the neutral conductor in a raceway, but it was dead silent when it came to sizing the neutral conductor in a cable assembly. It's now clear that the service neutral conductor must be sized in accordance with 250.61 and 250.102(C)(1), whether the installation is a raceway or a cable.

250.30 Separately Derived Systems—Grounding and Bonding

The requirement to use either structural metal or water piping as the preferred grounding electrodes was removed. Metal water piping can now be used for multiple separately derived systems, and the dimensions of the busbar used to splice grounding electrode conductors was clarified.

Analysis

The past few *Code* cycles have seen many revisions to 250.30 and 250.68 to clarify what items can and can't be called a grounding electrode. These revisions have had varying amounts of success. This cycle includes a change that definitely makes things easier.

Grounding Electrode. When grounding a separately derived system, we need to connect the neutral point to the building's grounding electrode system. Previous editions of the *NEC* stipulated that the separately derived system needed to be connected to the structural metal or water pipe, and if those weren't present we could then seek other types of electrodes. Now in 2017, the *Code* simply requires us to connect the separately derived system to the building's grounding electrode system.

Multiple Separately Derived Systems. When grounding multiple separately derived systems, we've had the option of terminating grounding electrode taps to a common 3/0 AWG copper grounding electrode conductor or to structural metal. Why shouldn't we be allowed to terminate to interior metal water piping? Now we can.

Busbar Terminations. Lastly, the dimensions of the busbar that can be used to splice the common grounding electrode conductor and the taps have been clarified. The busbar must be ¼ in. thick by 2 in. wide, and whatever length is necessary to accommodate the terminations.

250.52 Grounding Electrode Types

Changes to this section clarified that structural metal is allowed to be an electrode and added a requirement prohibiting the use of swimming pool steel as an electrode.

Analysis

Structural Metal Electrode. Over the last several *Code* cycles changes have been made attempting to try to clearly indicate when the structural metal of a building is considered a grounding electrode. For years the *NEC* didn't really say anything at all, and it was just assumed by most that the structural metal was a grounding electrode.

The *Code* then clarified that the structural metal of a building can be used as a conductor, but it wasn't necessarily a grounding electrode, unless it's in the earth, or if we connected a wire to it from an object that is in the earth (like a water pipe or a concrete-encased electrode). This makes sense, since grounding electrodes are supposed to be in the earth, after all.

We've now come a full 180 degrees from where we started. The structural metal is now called "metal in-ground support structure(s)." The metal of a building isn't a grounding electrode unless it's actually in the earth for ten vertical feet, hence the name "metal in-ground support structure(s)."

Structural metal that isn't an electrode (because it isn't in the earth for ten feet) can still be used to interconnect electrodes [250.68(C)(2)], so when you get right down to it, this change is really a change to the language.

Swimming Pool Steel as Electrode. I have no idea why a person would use the rebar in a swimming pool as a grounding electrode, but if you were doing that, then you need to stop. It isn't allowed anymore!

250.53 Grounding Electrode Installation Requirements

The installation requirements for ground ring electrodes were revised for consistency with other rules.

Analysis

EDITED
Instead of "burying" a ground ring, we now "install" a ground ring.

250.60 Lightning Protection Electrode

The Informational Notes regarding lightning protection electrodes were both revised.

Analysis

CLARIFIED
Although lightning protection systems aren't within the scope of the *NEC*, when they are installed it's a good practice to do so in accordance with NFPA 780, the *Standard for the Installation of Lightning Protection Systems*. NFPA 70E includes requirements such as bonding and separation of lighting protection components from premises wiring equipment.

Note 1 revisions clarify that there could be rules for all sorts of lightning protection equipment, and not just strike termination devices (formerly known as "air terminals" or "lightning rods").

Note 2 was revised to clarify that the potential difference discussed in Note 2 relates to voltage. Perhaps by calling them "potential differences," as was done in previous *Code* versions, people were thinking that the differences were differences of opinion and not voltage. I'm really not sure…

250.64 Grounding Electrode Conductor Installation

This section was revised into a list format to make it easier to use.

Analysis

CLARIFIED
This *Code* cycle the Code Making Panels have made an effort, throughout all of *NEC*, to improve its ease of usage, and this section is no exception. The requirements were reorganized into a list so they're easier to read and understand.

250.66 Sizing Grounding Electrode Conductor

The text of "sole connection" for rods, pipes, rings, and concrete-encased electrodes was clarified.

Analysis

CLARIFIED
Although many people don't read the rules in 250.66, they allow for smaller grounding electrode conductors for driven rods, concrete-encased electrodes, and ground rings than those in Table 250.66.

These smaller grounding electrode conductors, as compared to Table 250.66, can only be used when the grounding electrode conductor is the "sole connection" to these electrodes.

What exactly does "sole connection" mean? In this edition of the *Code* we won't be asking this question any longer because that language was replaced. We can use the smaller grounding electrode conductors if they don't also connect to an electrode requiring a larger grounding electrode conductor.

This was the intent all along, and you could easily argue that the *NEC* was already clear on this, but now it's even more so, and that's always worth the effort.

250.68 Termination to the Grounding Electrode

Requirements were clarified for a grounding electrode conductor connection to a metal underground water pipe, building steel that's a grounding electrode conductor, and rebar electrodes that extend vertically through a slab.

Analysis

Underground Metal Water Pipe. The 2017 *Code* has cleared up what we all thought was a requirement in the 2014 *NEC*. For quite some time now we've had to connect to the underground metal piping system for grounding the electrical equipment. Because of the very real concern of interior metal piping being replaced with nonmetallic varieties, the *Code* has required that we make the grounding electrode connection within 5 ft of where the metal underground water pipe enters the building. This makes a lot of sense and has merit, as we're seeing less and less copper, and more and more plastics.

Search through the previous editions of the *NEC* and you'll have a hard time finding this rule; it was accidentally changed to permissive language during some of the (rather extensive) editing of this section in the past. The issue is resolved now by making it mandatory text once again.

Building Steel. As was discussed in 250.52(A)(2), the structural metal of a building isn't always a grounding electrode. In fact, it seldom is. We can use it as a conductor, however, and it makes a great one with all of the cross-sectional area that it has.

If we connect the structural metal to a concrete-encased electrode it doesn't magically become an electrode (it still doesn't have 10 ft of steel vertically in the earth), but it can now be used to connect, say, the underground water pipe to the concrete-encased electrode. How do we connect the concrete-encased electrode to the metal? We do so by connecting the bolts for the metal that are in the footings to the rebar (concrete-encased electrode) in the footings. On the other hand, we could just run a piece of wire and call it done, but that might prove too easy!

Rebar Electrode. The practice of continuing a piece of rebar vertically through the top of a foundation wall and connecting a grounding electrode conductor to it isn't new. It's been done for decades, and proven effective. In the 2014 *Code* it was made clear that this practice is acceptable. In 2017, it's also being made clear that this is only permitted if the exposed rebar isn't subject to corrosion and if it doesn't make contact with the earth, as that would cause corrosion.

250.80 Service Raceways and Enclosures

The items that aren't required to be bonded in underground service raceways have been expanded.

Analysis

Connecting isolated metal electrical components is one of the most important safety requirements in the entire *Code* book. Section 250.4(A)(3) and perhaps even 300.10 say it best; you need to able to read continuity between any two metal objects in which there are conductors. This is a simple statement, but it's critically important.

You should be able to read continuity between the metal parts of any luminaire to the grounding terminal of any receptacle in a building, or any metal part of the electrical system. By doing so, you're satisfying the real goal; ensuring a low-impedance path of continuity between all metal electrical parts to the power supply—typically the utility neutral.

There are some exceptions; Ex 1 to 300.10 says that a short sleeve of metal raceway that's just protecting a cable like Type NM from physical damage doesn't need to be bonded to the electrical system. This makes sense, as the likelihood of a raceway that short becoming energized is quite small.

Another object that doesn't require connection to the electrical system is a metal elbow buried 18 in. deep in an underground installation of a nonmetallic raceway containing service conductors. If that elbow was to become energized due to a ground fault (which is highly unlikely to begin with), there would be very little risk of electrical shock due to its burial depth, and there would be no risk of fire.

Changes in the 2017 *NEC* now address other underground components that have 18 in. of cover. This might include a rigid coupling, for example, as the risk is no greater with a coupling than it is with a metal elbow.

250.86 Other Enclosures

The items that aren't required to be bonded in underground raceways containing branch circuits and feeders have been expanded beyond just metal elbows.

Analysis

EXPANDED

It seems there was a question about which small metal parts installed as part of a nonmetallic raceway system needed to be bonded. Metal elbows were previously an exception to this requirement as long as they were isolated from possible contact by a minimum cover of 18 in. The exception has been expanded to any small metal components that are isolated from possible contact—not just elbows.

250.94 Bonding for Communications Systems

The title of this section was revised, options for bonding communications systems to the electrical system were clarified, an exception for buildings or structures unlikely to need communications systems, and a note addressing "electrical noise" were added.

Analysis

CLARIFIED

Communications systems need to be electrically connected together and to the premises wiring system. For twisted pair circuits see 800.100, antennas see 810.21, and coaxial cables see 820.100.

Oftentimes it's the satellite or cable TV installer who makes this bonding connection, and we obviously can't expect them to open and work on an energized panel to connect the metal parts of their system to premises wiring.

Several *Code* cycles ago this rule only required an exposed, nonflexible metallic service conductor raceway for bonding purposes. The communications contractors bonded their systems to the electrical system by installing a bonding conductor to a bonding strap, which is listed for indoor locations only, onto the service raceway. Since metal service raceways for underground services are becoming extinct, the 2008 *NEC* required terminals for this application and called them an "intersystem bonding termination."

In some commercial installations, a busbar is commonly used to bond communications and premises systems together. Since there's no safety reason not to allow a busbar for bonding purposes, it's recognized as a permitted option in the 2017 *NEC*.

NEW

A new exception to the communications bonding rule addresses buildings or structures supplied with electricity that are unlikely to need any communications systems. A chicken coop or a detached storage building come to mind immediately, although stand-alone equipment like a temporary power pedestal is less obvious but equally deserving of this allowance.

NEW

A new Informational Note alerts the *Code* user that "electrical noise" can be reduced on communications systems by bonding all communications systems to the premises system via an intersystem bonding termination. The term "electrical noise" isn't defined, and there are plenty of people who would argue that using an intersystem bonding termination actually adds "noise," so it's still a bit unclear about how valuable this note will prove to be.

250.102 Grounded Conductor, Bonding Conductors, and Jumpers

The title was revised for accuracy, the allowance of aluminum as a bonding conductor was clarified, and the titles of 250.102 250.102(C)(2) were revised.

Analysis

EDITED

Because this section is referenced by numerous requirements in the *Code*, its title was edited to clearly include the "grounded" or neutral conductors.

For example, a 400A service that only feeds three-phase motors and one lighting circuit might only need a 12 AWG neutral conductor for the unbalanced load [220.61]; but 250.24(C) refers us to Table 250.102(C)(1) to size the grounded/neutral conductor to carry the fault current.

CLARIFIED

Aluminum Bonding Conductor. Section 250.102(A) tells us that the types of materials permitted for an equipment bonding jumper are copper or other corrosion-resistant material. Contrary to popular belief, aluminum is corrosion resistant, so mentioning just copper here might make you think aluminum can't be used. This isn't the case, and the intent of this rule has been clarified.

NEW

Cable in Raceway. Sizing a bonding jumper on the supply side of a service must be done when a metal raceway is used for service conductors [250.92]. Previous editions of the *NEC* had requirements for single and parallel conductors installed in metal service raceways. Although it's not common, cables might also be installed in a metal service raceway rather than insulated conductors. If this is done, we would probably size the bonding jumper exactly the same way, but the *Code* didn't mention this. It was an oversight, probably caught by very few, that's now been addressed.

250.104 Bonding of Piping Systems and Exposed Structural Metal

The requirements for bonding piping systems and structural metal have been editorially revised.

Analysis

REORGANIZED

At first glance, it looks like the text in this section of the *NEC* was drastically revised. Further examination, however, shows that most of the work done here was reorganization and some minor editorial changes to the language were made. As discussed in 250.52, over the past *Code* cycles, there was a concerted effort to address structural metal as it relates to grounding and bonding. The changes in this rule are simply a continuation of that effort.

You still have to bond the structural metal of a building if it's exposed and likely to become energized. The conductor used to do this is still sized the same as before, and it must still comply with the same installation requirements.

Although nothing really changed in this section, it's written more accurately. More accurate language usually results in fewer interpretations and arguments, so changes like this are still worthwhile.

250.118 Types of Equipment Grounding Conductors

The permitted uses of flexible metal conduit as an equipment grounding conductor were clarified.

Analysis

CLARIFIED

Generally speaking, all metal electrical equipment must be connected to an equipment grounding conductor. Section 250.118 gives us a list of all of the items that can be used as an equipment grounding conductor, including EMT, RMC, IMC, flexible metal conduit, and several others.

The use of flexible metal conduit as the equipment grounding conductor has restrictions because it's inherently limited in how much fault current it can carry due to its higher resistance/impedance as compared to nonflexible metallic raceways. Flexible metal conduit can be used as an equipment grounding conductor in lengths not exceeding 6 ft, containing 15A and/or 20A branch circuits, where flexibility after the installation isn't required, and now for the 2017 *NEC*, only in sizes up to and including trade size 1¼.

Compliance with this change will probably be automatic, given that it's pretty rare to see a raceway that large used for 15A or 20A circuits.

250.122 Sizing Equipment Grounding Conductor

The requirements for sizing EGCs for voltage drop and for feeder circuits have been expanded.

Analysis

EXPANDED

Sizing the EGC for parallel raceway or cable installations has been a controversial issue for decades, and now the 2017 *NEC* revisions have solved this problem! The EGC is now required to be sized based on the size of the overcurrent protection device.

250.148 Continuity and Attachment of Equipment Grounding Conductors to Boxes

This section was edited to require all equipment grounding conductors in the same enclosure to be connected together.

Analysis

EDITED

It's very common to have multiple circuit conductors spliced or terminated on equipment within a box. For safety reasons, it's imperative that the equipment grounding conductors for these circuits be spliced together and to the metal box. The revision changes the word "any" to "all," clarifying that all of the equipment grounds in a given enclosure must be spliced together and not be in separate groups.

CHAPTER 3— WIRING METHODS AND MATERIALS

ARTICLE 300—GENERAL REQUIREMENTS FOR WIRING METHODS AND MATERIALS

300.3 Conductors

The exception allowing for parallel isolated phase installations was clarified.

Analysis

CLARIFIED

Section 300.3 contains some of the most fundamental, yet important rules in the entire *NEC*. Section 300.3(A), for example, requires that conductors be installed in a *Code*-compliant wiring method, meaning that a person can't just install individual conductors through the walls and ceilings of a building.

Section 300.3(B) requires all conductors of a circuit (ungrounded, neutral, and equipment grounding conductors) to be installed in the same raceway, cable tray, or trench. This is a principle that's been in the *Code* for about 80 years to address "inductive heating," which occurs any time individual conductors are installed in ferrous (steel) raceways. The exception permits individual raceways to contain a single phase conductor or neutral for underground installations containing nonmetallic raceways in accordance with 300.20. This approach is sometimes used in large occupancies with multiple parallel sets to make it easier to terminate the conductors and still comply with 310.10(H)(2). The change to 300.3(B)(1) Ex clarifies that the "neutral" conductor can be installed isolated, not just the phase conductors. Although 300.5(I) Ex 2 says the same thing, this clarification clears up what was construed as a conflict by some.

CHAPTER 4

ARTICLE 404—SWITCHES

404.9 Switch Faceplates

A new requirement for metal faceplates to be "grounded" was added.

Analysis

Isn't this already in the *Code*? Yes, and no! Switch plates were already required to be connected to the equipment grounding conductor to clear a fault, but now it appears they want us to connect them to the earth as well. Using the term "grounded" here adds confusion to what we're really trying to accomplish. It appears the intent of this change was to make metal switch plates safer in the case of contact with an energized conductor. Connecting metal parts to the earth won't do that, but bonding it to the EGC will. I suspect we'll see this changed in a future edition of the *NEC*.

ARTICLE 406—RECEPTACLES, CORD CONNECTORS, AND ATTACHMENT PLUGS (CAPS)

406.4 General Installation Requirements

Two Informational Notes about replacing nongrounding type receptacles have been added, and a new exception addresses the required AFCI protection of replacement receptacles.

Analysis

Nongrounding Receptacles (GFCI Required). When replacing nongrounding (two-wire) receptacles we have a few options. We can replace the receptacle with another nongrounding-type receptacle, install an equipment grounding conductor to a grounding-type receptacle, or install a grounding-type receptacle that's GFCI protected. Because of the difficulty in adding an equipment grounding conductor in most existing buildings, the option of providing GFCI protection is far and away the most common practice.

The instructions for equipment that must be plugged into a receptacle might require an equipment grounding conductor. If the product is listed, then 110.3(B) requires us to follow those listing instructions. In addition, 250.114 contains a list of equipment required to be connected to an equipment grounding conductor if supplied by a receptacle. These include washing machines, refrigerators, kitchen waste disposals, and others. Under these conditions, you can't replace a nongrounding-type receptacle with another nongrounding-type receptacle; the receptacle must be of the grounding type that's either connected to an equipment grounding conductor or GFCI protected.

Nongrounding Receptacles (AFCI Required). When replacing nongrounding (two-wire) receptacles with a grounding type we have to be aware that in addition to required GCFI protection, AFCI protection may also be required by 210.12. In most cases replacing the circuit breaker with an AFCI device will satisfy this requirement and still allow you to replace the 2-wire receptacle with a GFCI-type receptacle. If the panel is older and an AFCI breaker isn't an option, a dual rated AFCI/GFCI receptacle is permitted. An exception was added exempting dormitory receptacles from this requirement.

ARTICLE 440—AIR-CONDITIONING AND REFRIGERATION EQUIPMENT

440.9 Grounding and Bonding

A wire-type equipment grounding conductor is now required for some air-conditioning installations.

Analysis

NEW

Electrical metallic tubing is permitted to be used as an equipment grounding conductor [250.118(4)]; research done by the Georgia Institute of Technology proves this wiring method serves this purpose.

The concern is that the installation must have all fittings installed and tightened properly [110.3(B) and 250.4(A)(3)], and the raceway must not be subject to severe physical damage [358.12(1)]. Experience has shown that when EMT is installed on rooftops workers often step on it thinking that it's impervious to damage. It isn't.

If EMT is used as the required circuit equipment grounding conductor, and it comes apart due to being stepped on, we have a recipe for disaster. If the raceway becomes energized due to a ground fault it remains energized. This rule also applies to any other metal raceway types that are installed using non-threaded fittings. Such a disaster has happened before, resulting in death, and it will (unfortunately) probably happen again. With this new rule in effect, it's hoped that we can reduce this hazard for future generations.

CHAPTER 5— SPECIAL OCCUPANCIES

ARTICLE 517—HEALTH CARE FACILITIES

517.2 Definitions

New definitions for "Governing Body" and "Medical Office (Dental Office)" have been added, and existing definitions for "Health Care Facility" and "Patient Care Space" have been clarified.

Analysis

CLARIFIED

Health Care Facility. Most health care facilities are easily recognizable as such. When you drive by a hospital, there isn't much doubt as to what you're looking at. Mobile health care facilities are something you see every day although you may not realize it.

On large commercial construction sites where critical care is needed regularly, you can find mobile emergency care facilities (which are basically a trailer with medical facilities inside) on site to deal with the very real dangers of heat exhaustion, dehydration, heat stroke, and other medical concerns. Some other examples of mobile healthcare facilities covered by this rule are blood bank trailers, mobile radiology trailers, and mobile trauma trailers. What are the rules for the wiring in these mobile facilities? They're the same as in any other patient care space.

CLARIFIED

Patient Care Space. The 2014 *Code* changed "patient care area" to "patient care space" in most locations in Article 517. Changes to this edition finish that job by using the terms correctly throughout the article, and changes in the definitions have been made for clarification. Most of the changes are in the form of Informational Notes which will help the governing body of the facility to determine the correct type of patient care space. The changes that aren't in the Notes simply clarify that caregivers aren't the only people who are considered. Other members of medical staff may not be caregivers, but could be injured due to a failure of equipment or system.

517.13 Grounding of Equipment in Patient Care Spaces

The title of this section was changed to match the rest of the article, some requirements for equipment grounding conductors (EGCs) in patient care spaces have been expanded while others are now reduced. Exception 2 of 517.13(B) was clarified and isolated ground receptacles are no longer a black hole in this rule.

Analysis

Metal Enclosures. In patient care spaces we need two equipment grounding conductors: one must be metal cable armor or a raceway type complying with 517.13(A); the other must be of the wire type installed inside the permitted wiring method in accordance with 517.13(B).

The rules for the wire-type equipment grounding conductor in 517.13(B) have been changed to add clarity. For example, in the previous version of the *NEC*, 517.13(B)(1)(2) required metal receptacle boxes to be connected to a wire-type equipment grounding conductor, but was silent on other metal enclosures! Now any metal enclosure housing electrical equipment must be connected to the equipment grounding conductor.

Luminaires. Exception 2 to 517.13(B) is one of the most misunderstood and misapplied allowances in the *Code*. In previous editions, luminaires above 7 ft 6 in., as well as switches outside the patient vicinity, only needed to comply with 517.13(A) and didn't need to satisfy 517.13(B). While that sounds great at first glance, it didn't do what most people thought it did.

In the 2014 *NEC*, after applying the exception, if you used a cable wiring method, you couldn't use traditional Type MC cable. Inspectors across the country regularly find themselves in situations where they must require thousands of feet of Type MC cable above the ceiling of a patient care space to be removed. Each time it's due to a misunderstanding of the exceptions in this section of the *Code*. The change to 517.13(B) Ex 2 will permit compliance by meeting the requirements of either 517.13(A) or (B). This means that typical MC cable can be used 7 ft 6 in. above a patient care space.

Isolated Ground Receptacles. Isolated ground (IG) receptacles have long been a problem in this section. How does a person satisfy these rules when using an IG receptacle? Up until now it was easy…you couldn't use an IG receptacle and still satisfy the letter of this section. Changes to the 2017 edition now remedy this problem by giving specific provisions for IG receptacles, but remember that their use is still quite limited by the requirements in 517.16.

517.16 Isolated Ground Receptacles

The allowances for isolated ground receptacles in health care facilities now make sense.

Analysis

In the 2011 *NEC*, a change was made that prohibited isolated ground (IG) receptacles in patient care spaces. This change seemed warranted, as it's impossible to comply with the expanded equipment grounding requirements in 517.13 while using an IG receptacle. In fact, using an IG receptacle completely defeats the extra safety provided for in that section.

In the 2014 *Code*, IG receptacles were once again allowed in patient care spaces, but not in patient care vicinities. This change ensured that the patient reaped the safety benefits of 517.13, and allowed equipment such as computers (that aren't near the patient) to use an IG receptacle. The problem is that the language in 2014 said that the IG receptacle installation couldn't circumvent the safety afforded by 517.13…which is impossible.

A compromise has been achieved, IG receptacles can be used where they won't injure the patient, and they can be installed legally due to the removal of the preposterous language added in 2014.

ARTICLE 547—AGRICULTURAL BUILDINGS

547.2 Definitions

The definition of equipotential plane was revised for accuracy.

Analysis

CLARIFIED

In previous editions of the *Code*, the definition of this term included a statement that the equipotential plane minimized voltages. Not only is that untrue, it's not possible. Installing rebar in concrete and connecting a conductor to it can't magically make neutral to earth (NEV) voltage go away. But it does reduce voltage differences between points in the equipotential plane and electrical equipment that's reachable from that plane. The rephrasing of this definition will help eliminate one of many misconceptions about grounding by removing it from the *NEC*.

ARTICLE 555—MARINAS, BOATYARDS, AND COMMERCIAL AND NONCOMMERCIAL DOCKING FACILITIES

555.1 Scope

The title of this article, its scope, and many of its provisions were changed to include residential installations.

Analysis

EXPANDED

It's not an exaggeration to say that marinas and boatyards are becoming a major problem in the electrical industry. People are swimming in these locations and they're being electrocuted or drowning due to electric shock and the subsequent inability to swim. This phenomenon is known as Electric Shock Drowning (ESD). A quick search on the Internet will find dozens of such stories.

Over the past few *Code* cycles we've seen added safety requirements for these locations as the risk of electrical hazards has become more and more apparent. While these changes certainly help, they were always inherently limited by the scope of this article, because single-family dwelling installations were entirely exempt. One could even argue that townhouses and two-family dwellings, as well as apartment facilities weren't covered. This is no longer the case, as the scope has been expanded to include dwellings and end any argument whatsoever about the applicability to residential installations.

CHAPTER 6— SPECIAL EQUIPMENT

ARTICLE 600—ELECTRIC SIGNS AND OUTLINE LIGHTING

600.1 Scope

Retrofit kits for signs are now covered by this article.

Analysis

CLARIFIED

A retrofit kit is typically used to convert an incandescent or fluorescent luminaire into an LED luminaire. These retrofit kits have been discussed in Article 410 and even in Article 600, although the scope of 600 was silent on the issue. By including them in the scope of Article 600, it's clear that retrofit kits are covered in this article.

It's important to note that we're talking about retrofit kits. You can't just buy an LED driver, some wires, and an LED module to create your own LED light or electric sign. You need to use a listed retrofit kit, not just listed components [600.3].

ARTICLE 680—SWIMMING POOLS, SPAS, HOT TUBS, FOUNTAINS, AND SIMILAR INSTALLATIONS

680.2 Definitions

A new definition for "electrically powered pool lift" was added, and the definition for storable pools (and other storable features) was revised.

Analysis

CLARIFIED

Storable Pools. This definition was revised to clarify that storable pools are for aboveground use only. The previous *Code* edition stated that storable pools are constructed aboveground, but now it's clear they're only used aboveground.

680.7 Grounding and Bonding Terminals

Grounding and bonding terminals now have specific location-driven requirements.

Analysis

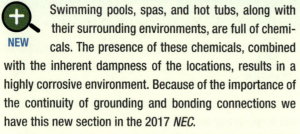
NEW

Swimming pools, spas, and hot tubs, along with their surrounding environments, are full of chemicals. The presence of these chemicals, combined with the inherent dampness of the locations, results in a highly corrosive environment. Because of the importance of the continuity of grounding and bonding connections we have this new section in the 2017 *NEC*.

This new rule has two independent requirements. First, all grounding and bonding terminals must be identified (see Article 100) for use in wet and corrosive environments; this applies to terminals installed in the field and by the manufacturer. These grounding and bonding terminals aren't required to be specifically listed for this application because such a product doesn't exist.

Terminals that are field-installed must be copper, copper alloy, or stainless steel and be listed for direct burial. It's worth noting that terminals, such as those commonly used on rebar, that are listed for direct burial are also listed for concrete encasement.

680.21 Motors

The allowable methods for wiring a pool motor have been greatly simplified.

Analysis

CLARIFIED

The rules for how to wire a swimming pool motor in previous editions of the *NEC* were difficult to follow both for installers and inspectors. In this *Code* cycle numerous revisions were made that make it easier to understand and follow the rules for this section. The *NEC* now allows any wiring method contained in Chapter 3, such as RMC, IMC, PVC, and RTRC conduits, unless it's installed in a corrosive atmosphere and then the 680.14(B) requirements must be followed.

680.23 Underwater Luminaires

Some unenforceable language about GFCI protection has been removed, and the allowable wiring methods for underwater luminaires have been simplified.

Analysis

CLARIFIED

GFCI protection. The *Code* previously required GFCI protection for underwater luminaires to be installed in a manner that prevents shock hazard during relamping. It also required the physical location of the GFCI device (the test and reset buttons) to be such that there's "no shock hazard...," but this is impossible. A GFCI will still allow you to get shocked, but in most cases it will keep the shock from being a fatal one. If you're

INDEX

Description	Rule Page
A	
Agricultural Buildings	235
Air-Conditioning and Refrigeration Equipment	209
Armored Cable (Type AC)	169
Audio Signal Equipment	251
B	
Bonding	55
Bonding	**106**
General Requirements	55
System Grounding and Bonding	67
Boxes	165
C	
Cable Trays	189
Carnivals, Circuses, Fairs, and Similar Events	233
CATV	295
Class I Hazardous (Classified) Locations	219
Class II Hazardous (Classified) Locations	221
Class III Hazardous (Classified) Locations	223
Communications Circuits	283
D	
Definitions	21
E	
Electric Signs and Outline Lighting	247
Electrical Metallic Tubing (Type EMT)	183
Electrical Nonmetallic Tubing (Type ENT)	185
F	
Flexible Metal Conduit (Type FMC)	175
G	
Grounding	**55**
Equipment Grounding and Equipment Grounding Conductors	120
General Requirements	55
Grounding Electrode System and Grounding Electrode Conductor	86
Grounding Enclosure, Raceway, and Service Cable Connections	106
Methods of Equipment Grounding	131
System Grounding and Bonding	67
H	
Health Care Facilities	225
I	
Information Technology Equipment	253
L	
Liquidtight Flexible Metal Conduit (Type LFMC)	177
Liquidtight Flexible Nonmetallic Conduit (Type LFNC)	181
Luminaires, Lampholders, and Lamps	205

Index

Description	Page

M

Marinas, Boatyards, and Commercial and Noncommercial Docking Facilities	239
Metal-Clad Cable (Type MC)	171

N

Nonmetallic-Sheathed Cable (Types NM and NMC)	173

R

Radio and Television Satellite Equipment	289
Receptacles, Cord Connectors, and Attachment Plugs (Caps)	199
Requirements for Electrical Installations	39
Rigid Polyvinyl Chloride Conduit (Type PVC)	179

S

Solar Photovoltaic (PV) Systems	269
Surface Metal Raceways	187
Swimming Pools, Spas, Hot Tubs, Fountains, and Similar Installations	**255**
Electrically Powered Pool Lifts	268
Fountains	267
General Requirements	256
Hydromassage Bathtubs	267
Permanently Installed Pools, Outdoor Spas, and Outdoor Hot Tubs	258
Spas and Hot Tubs	265
Switchboards, Switchgear, and Panelboards	203
Switches	197

T

Transformers	211

W

Wiring Methods and Materials	161

ABOUT THE AUTHOR

Mike Holt—Author

Founder and President
Mike Holt Enterprises
Groveland, FL

Mike Holt's electrical career has spanned all aspects of the trade from being an apprentice to becoming a contractor and inspector. His teaching career began in 1974 when he became an exam preparation instructor at a local community school. He was so successful that his students encouraged him to open his own training school dedicated to helping the electrical industry. In 1975, Mike opened his school while also running a full-service electrical contracting firm. His school became so successful that by 1980 he stopped electrical contracting to completely devote his time to electrical training at a national level. Today, Mike Holt Enterprises is a leading training and publishing company for the industry, specializing in helping electrical professionals take their careers to the next level.

A part of Mike's story that impacts the way he designs training programs is his own educational journey. As a young man he was unable to complete the requirements for his high school diploma due to life circumstances. Realizing that success depends on one's education, Mike immediately attained his GED. Then ten years later he attended the University of Miami's Graduate School for a Master's degree in Business Administration. Because of this experience, he understands the needs of his students, and strongly encourages and motivates them to continue their own education. He's never lost sight of how hard it can be for students who are intimidated by the complexity of the *NEC*, by school, or by their own feelings about learning. His ultimate goal has always been about increasing electrical safety and improving lives—his commitment and vision continue to guide him to this day.

Mike has written hundreds of books, and created DVDs, online programs, MP3s, and other training materials that have made a huge impact on the industry. He's mastered the art of explaining complicated concepts in a simple but direct style. His ability to simplify technical concepts and his one-of-a-kind presentation style explain his unique position as one of the premier speakers and *Code* experts in the United States. In addition to Mike's extensive list of companies around the world for whom he's provided training, and materials he's produced, Mike has written articles that have been seen in numerous industry magazines including, *Electrical Construction & Maintenance* (EC&M), *CEE News, Electrical Design and Installation* (EDI), *Electrical Contractor* (EC), *International Association of Electrical Inspectors* (IAEI News), *The Electrical Distributor* (TED), *Power Quality* (PQ) *Magazine*, and *Solar Pro Magazine*.

Mike resides in Central Florida, is the father of seven children, has five grandchildren, and enjoys many outside interests and activities. His commitment to pushing boundaries and setting high standards has also extended into his personal life. He's an 8-time National Barefoot Waterskiing Champion, has set many world records in that sport, and has competed in three World Barefoot Waterskiing Tournaments. In 2015, he started a new career in competitive mountain bike racing and continues to find ways to motivate himself mentally and physically.

What distinguishes Mike is his commitment to living a balanced lifestyle; placing God first, family, career, and self.

Special Acknowledgments

My Family. First, I want to thank God for my godly wife who's always by my side and my children, Belynda, Melissa, Autumn, Steven, Michael, Meghan, and Brittney.

My Staff. A personal thank you goes to my team at Mike Holt Enterprises for all the work they do to help me with my mission of changing people's lives through education. In particular my daughter Belynda, who works tirelessly to ensure that in addition to our products meeting and exceeding the educational needs of our customers, we stay committed to building life-long relationships with them throughout their electrical careers.

The National Fire Protection Association. A special thank you must be given to the staff at the National Fire Protection Association (NFPA), publishers of the *NEC*—in particular, Jeff Sargent for his assistance in answering my many *Code* questions over the years. Jeff, you're a "first class" guy, and I admire your dedication and commitment to helping others understand the *NEC*. Other former NFPA staff members I would like to thank include John Caloggero, Joe Ross, and Dick Murray for their help in the past.

ABOUT THE ILLUSTRATOR

Mike Culbreath—Illustrator

Mike Culbreath
Graphic Illustrator
Alden, MI
www.MikeHolt.com

Mike Culbreath devoted his career to the electrical industry and worked his way up from apprentice to master electrician. He started in the electrical field doing residential and light commercial construction, and later did service work and custom electrical installations. While working as a journeyman electrician, he suffered a serious on-the-job knee injury. As part of his rehabilitation, Mike completed courses at Mike Holt Enterprises, and then passed the exam to receive his Master Electrician's license. In 1986, with a keen interest in continuing education for electricians, he joined the staff to update material and began illustrating Mike Holt's textbooks and magazine articles.

Mike started with simple hand-drawn diagrams and cut-and-paste graphics. When frustrated by the limitations of that style of illustrating, he took a company computer home to learn how to operate some basic computer graphic software. Upon realizing that computer graphics offered increased flexibility for creating illustrations, Mike took every computer graphics class and seminar he could to help develop his computer graphic skills. He's now worked as an illustrator and editor with the company for over 30 years and, as Mike Holt has proudly acknowledged, has helped to transform his words and visions into lifelike graphics.

Originally from south Florida, Mike now lives in northern lower Michigan where he enjoys hiking, kayaking, photography, gardening, and cooking; but his real passion is his horses. Mike loves spending time with his children (Dawn and Mac) and his grandchildren Jonah, Kieley, and Scarlet.

Special Acknowledgments—I would like to thank Eric Stromberg, an electrical engineer and super geek (and I mean that in the most complimentary manner because I think this guy is brilliant), for helping me keep our graphics as technically correct as possible. I would also like to thank all of our students for the wonderful feedback they provide that helps us improve our graphics.

I also want to give a special thank you to Cathleen Kwas for making me look good with her outstanding layout design and typesetting skills; to Toni Culbreath who proofreads all of my material; and to Dawn Babbitt who assists me in the production and editing of our graphics. I would also like to acknowledge Belynda Holt Pinto, our Director of Operations, Brian House for his input (another really brilliant guy), and the rest of the outstanding staff at Mike Holt Enterprises, for all the hard work they do to help produce and distribute these outstanding products.

And last but not least, I need to give a special thank you to Mike Holt for not firing me over 30 years ago when I "borrowed" one of his computers and took it home to begin the process of learning how to do computer illustrations. He gave me the opportunity and time needed to develop my computer graphic skills. He's been an amazing friend and mentor ever since I met him as a student many years ago. Thanks for believing in me and allowing me to be part of the Mike Holt Enterprises family.

Save 25% On These Best-Selling Libraries

Understanding the NEC® Complete Training Library

This library makes it easy to learn the Code. Your library includes the following best-selling textbooks and DVDs:

Understanding the National Electrical Code® Volume 1 Textbook
Understanding the National Electrical Code® Volume 2 Textbook
NEC® Exam Practice Questions Workbook
General Requirements DVD
Wiring and Protection DVD
Bonding and Grounding DVDs (3)
Wiring Methods and Materials DVDs (2)
Equipment for General Use DVD
Special Occupancies and Special Equipment DVDs (3)
Limited Energy & Communications Systems DVD

Product Code: 17DECODVD   List Price: $599.00   Now only $449.25*

Electrical Theory DVD Training Program

Understanding electrical theory is critical for everyone who works with electricity. The topics in this textbook will help you understand what electricity is, how it's produced, and how it's used. You'll learn everything from a brief study of matter, to how to perform basic electrical calculations critical for everyday use.

Package includes:

Electrical Theory Textbook
Electrical Fundamentals and Basic Electricity DVD
Electrical Circuits, Systems, and Protection DVD
Alternating Current, Motors, Generators, and Transformers DVD

Product Code: ETLIBD   List Price: $299.00   Now only $224.25*

Solar PV Systems DVD Training Program

Everyone in the solar industry needs to understand the NEC® rules governing Solar PV Systems. This content must be mastered by the designer, contractor, installer, inspector, and instructor. As the market continues to grow, the rules governing solar installations continue to evolve. But don't be intimidated; Mike's textbook & DVDs will give you an edge because of the extra effort put forth to make the rules clear and explain how they should be applied.

Package includes:

Solar Photovoltaic Systems Textbook
Solar Photovoltaic Systems DVDs (3)

Product Code: 17SOLDVD   List Price: $299.00   Now Only $224.25*

*Prices subject to change. Discount applies to price at time of order.

Call Now 888.NEC.CODE (632.2633)

& mention discount code: B17NCT225

Mike Holt Enterprises

Save 25% On These Best-Selling Libraries

Understanding the NEC® Complete Training Library

This library makes it easy to learn the Code. Your library includes the following best-selling textbooks and DVDs:

Understanding the National Electrical Code® Volume 1 Textbook
Understanding the National Electrical Code® Volume 2 Textbook
NEC® Exam Practice Questions Workbook
General Requirements DVD
Wiring and Protection DVD
Bonding and Grounding DVDs (3)
Wiring Methods and Materials DVDs (2)
Equipment for General Use DVD
Special Occupancies and Special Equipment DVDs (3)
Limited Energy & Communications Systems DVD

Product Code: 17DECODVD   List Price: ~~$599.00~~   Now only $449.25*

Electrical Theory DVD Training Program

Understanding electrical theory is critical for everyone who works with electricity. The topics in this textbook will help you understand what electricity is, how it's produced, and how it's used. You'll learn everything from a brief study of matter, to how to perform basic electrical calculations critical for everyday use.

Package includes:

Electrical Theory Textbook
Electrical Fundamentals and Basic Electricity DVD
Electrical Circuits, Systems, and Protection DVD
Alternating Current, Motors, Generators, and Transformers DVD

Product Code: ETLIBD   List Price: ~~$299.00~~   Now only $224.25*

Solar PV Systems DVD Training Program

Everyone in the solar industry needs to understand the NEC® rules governing Solar PV Systems. This content must be mastered by the designer, contractor, installer, inspector, and instructor. As the market continues to grow, the rules governing solar installations continue to evolve. But don't be intimidated; Mike's textbook & DVDs will give you an edge because of the extra effort put forth to make the rules clear and explain how they should be applied.

Package includes:
Solar Photovoltaic Systems Textbook
Solar Photovoltaic Systems DVDs (3)

Product Code: 17SOLDVD   List Price: ~~$299.00~~   Now Only $224.25*

---

* Prices subject to change. Discount applies to price at time of order.

Call Now 888.NEC.CODE (632.2633)

& mention discount code: B17NCT225

Mike Holt Enterprises